JUNIOR BRAVES OF THE APOCALYPSE

BOOK 1: **A BRAVE IS BRAVE**

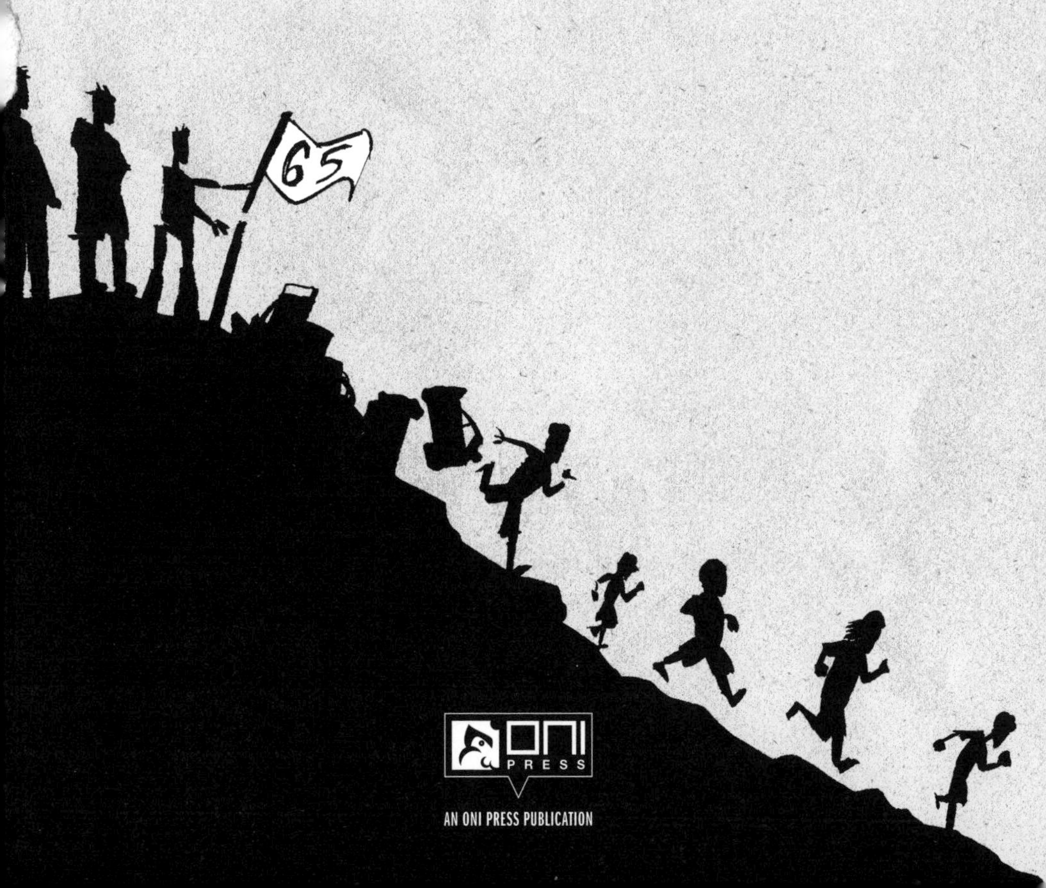

65

ONI PRESS

AN ONI PRESS PUBLICATION

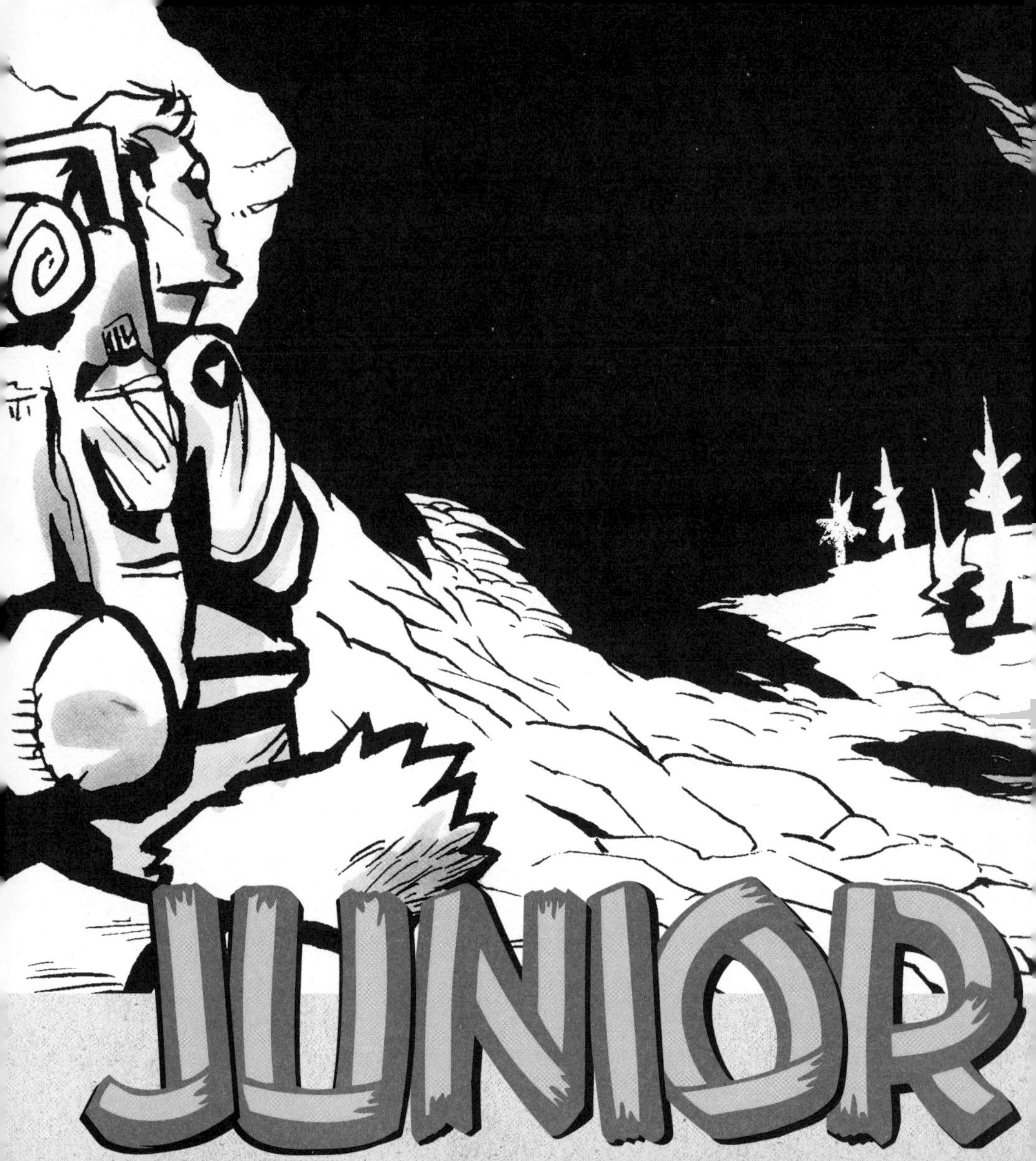

JUNIOR OF THE APOCALYPSE

BOOK 1: **A BRAVE IS BRAVE**

WRITTEN BY
Greg Smith &
Michael Tanner

ILLUSTRATED BY
Zach Lehner

BRAVES

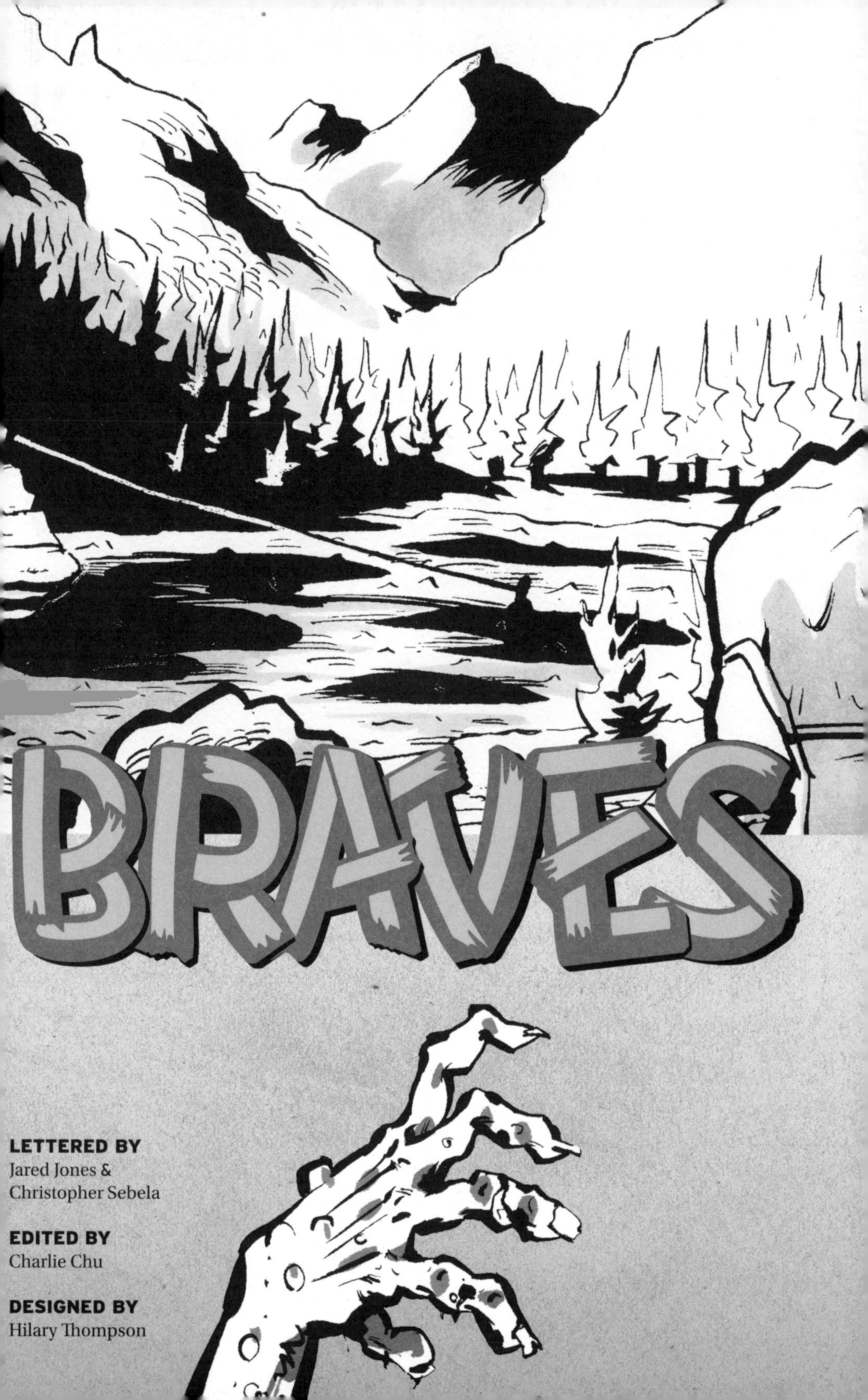

LETTERED BY
Jared Jones &
Christopher Sebela

EDITED BY
Charlie Chu

DESIGNED BY
Hilary Thompson

PUBLISHED BY ONI PRESS, INC.

JOE NOZEMACK • PUBLISHER

JAMES LUCAS JONES • EDITOR IN CHIEF

TIM WIESCH • V.P. OF BUSINESS DEVELOPMENT

CHEYENNE ALLOTT • DIRECTOR OF SALES

FRED RECKLING • DIRECTOR OF PUBLICITY

TROY LOOK • PRODUCTION MANAGER

HILARY THOMPSON • GRAPHIC DESIGNER

JARED JONES • PRODUCTION ASSISTANT

CHARLIE CHU • SENIOR EDITOR

ROBIN HERRERA • EDITOR

ARI YARWOOD • ASSOCIATE EDITOR

BRAD ROOKS • INVENTORY COORDINATOR

JUNG LEE • OFFICE ASSISTANT

ONI PRESS, INC
1305 SE MARTIN LUTHER KING, JR. BLVD
SUITE A
PORTLAND, OR 97214

ONIPRESS.COM
FACEBOOK.COM/ONIPRESS
TWITTER.COM/ONIPRESS
ONIPRESS.TUMBLR.COM
INSTAGRAM.COM/ONIPRESS

THATAMAZINGTWIT.TUMBLR.COM / @THATAMAZINGTWIT
DINERWOOD.BLOGSPOT.COM / @MIKEISERNIE
@2AMAZINGWRITERS
ZLEHNER.COM / @ZLEHNER

First edition: July 2015
ISBN 978-1-62010-144-5
eISBN 978-1-62010-145-2

Library of Congress Control Number: 2015900806

10 8 6 4 2 1 3 5 7 9

Printed in China

This book is dedicated to the memory of Frank Smith.

Thank you for marking the path.

✕

JUNIOR BRAVES

· A BRAVE IS BRAVE ·

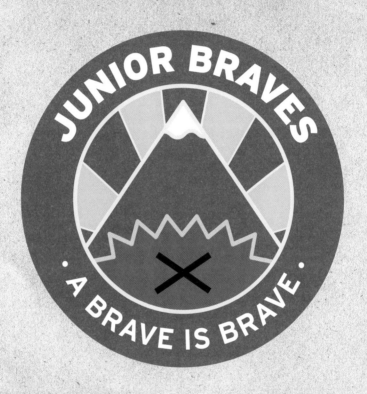

A
BRAVE
IS
BRAVE.

CHAPTER ONE

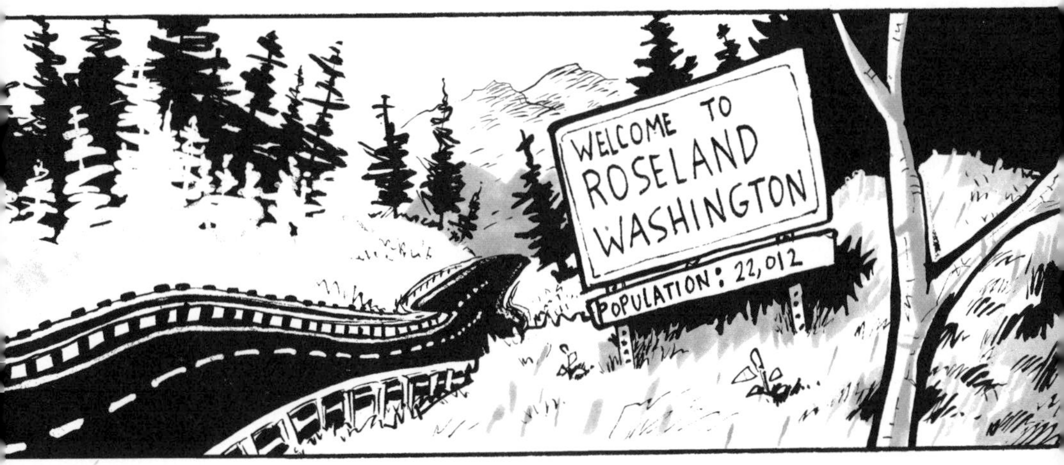
WELCOME TO
ROSELAND
WASHINGTON
POPULATION: 22,012

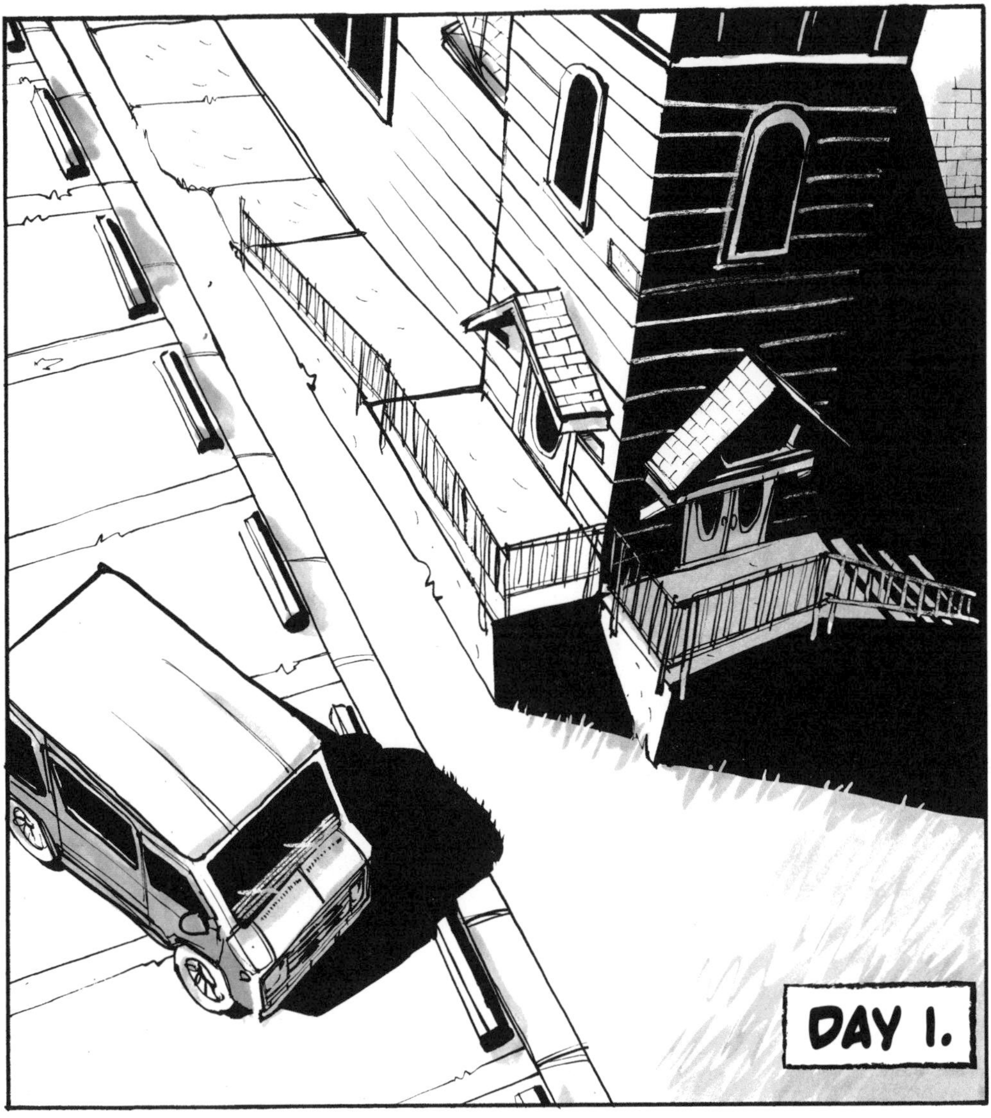
DAY 1.

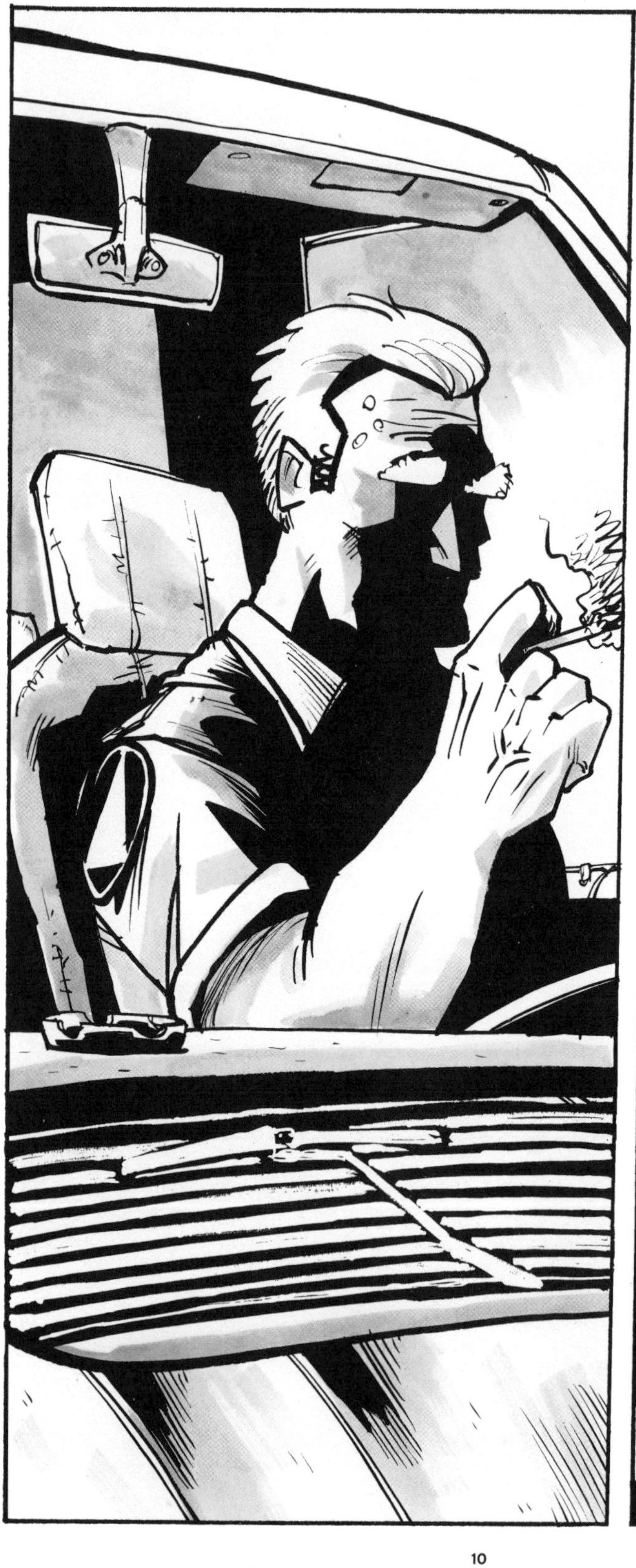
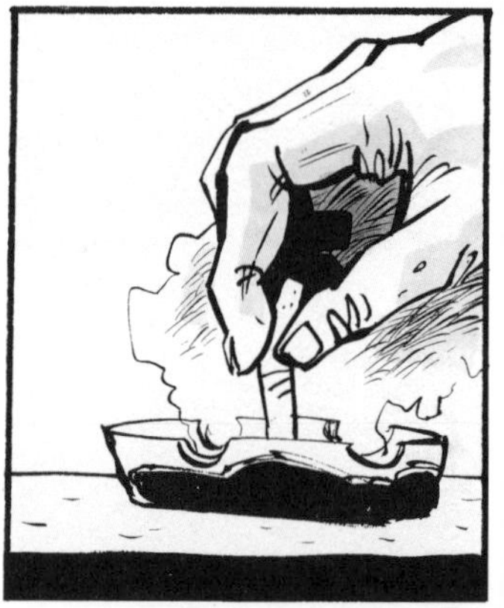
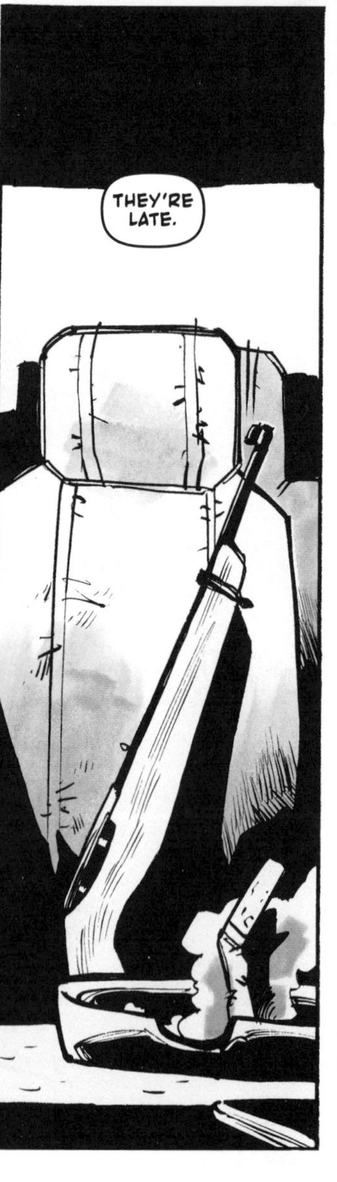
THEY'RE LATE.

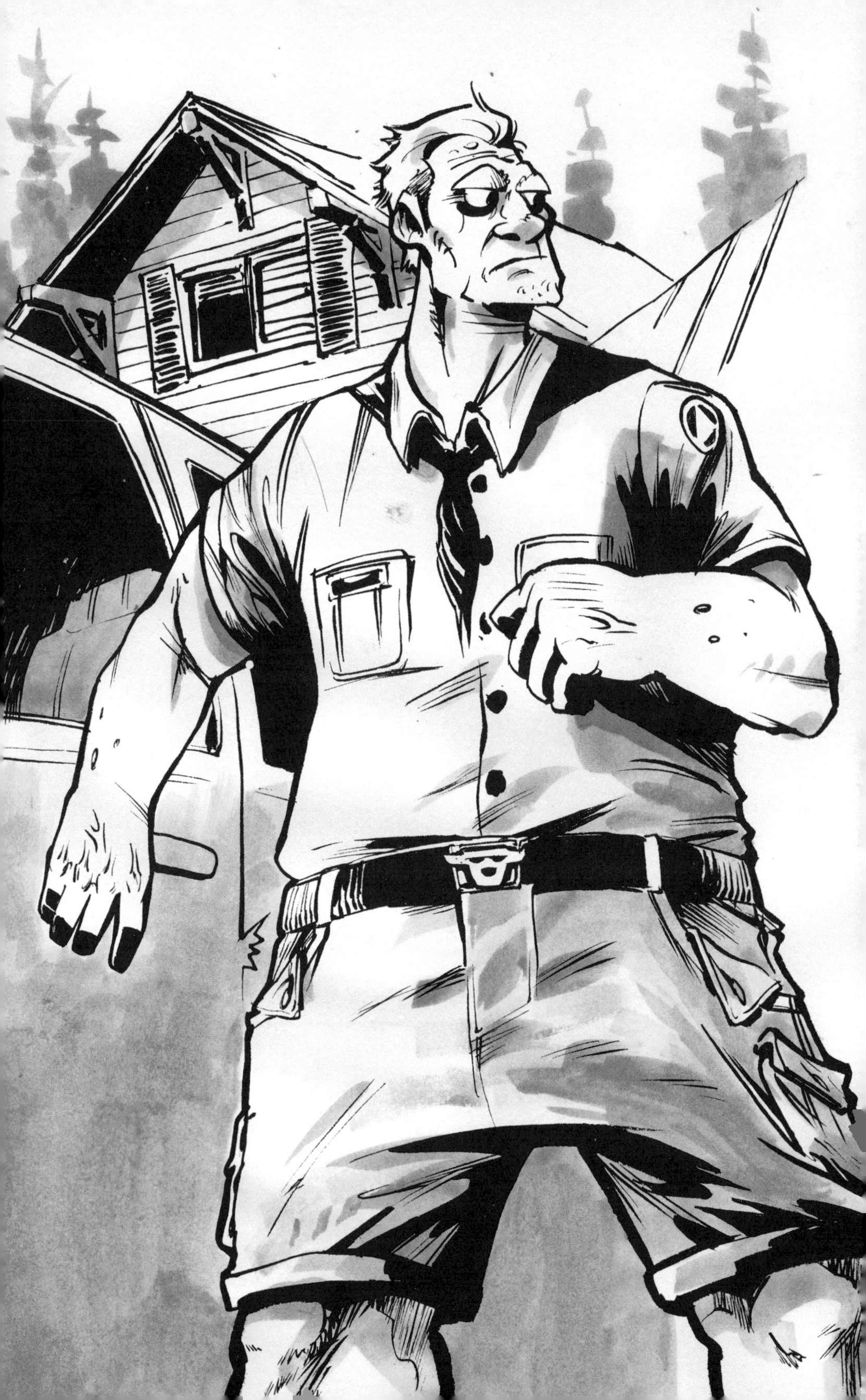

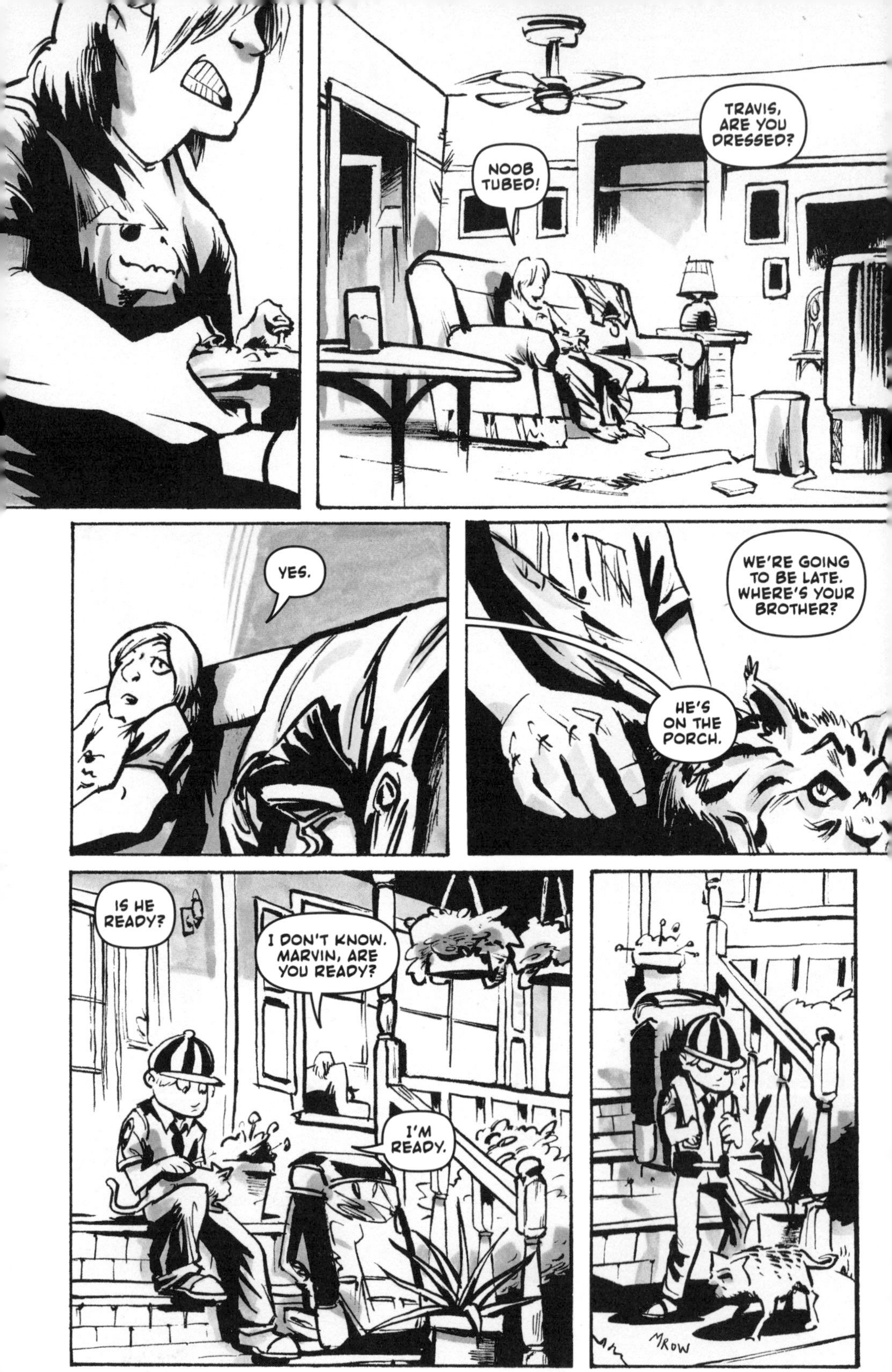
NOOB TUBED!
TRAVIS, ARE YOU DRESSED?
YES.
WE'RE GOING TO BE LATE. WHERE'S YOUR BROTHER?
HE'S ON THE PORCH.
IS HE READY?
I DON'T KNOW. MARVIN, ARE YOU READY?
I'M READY.
MROW

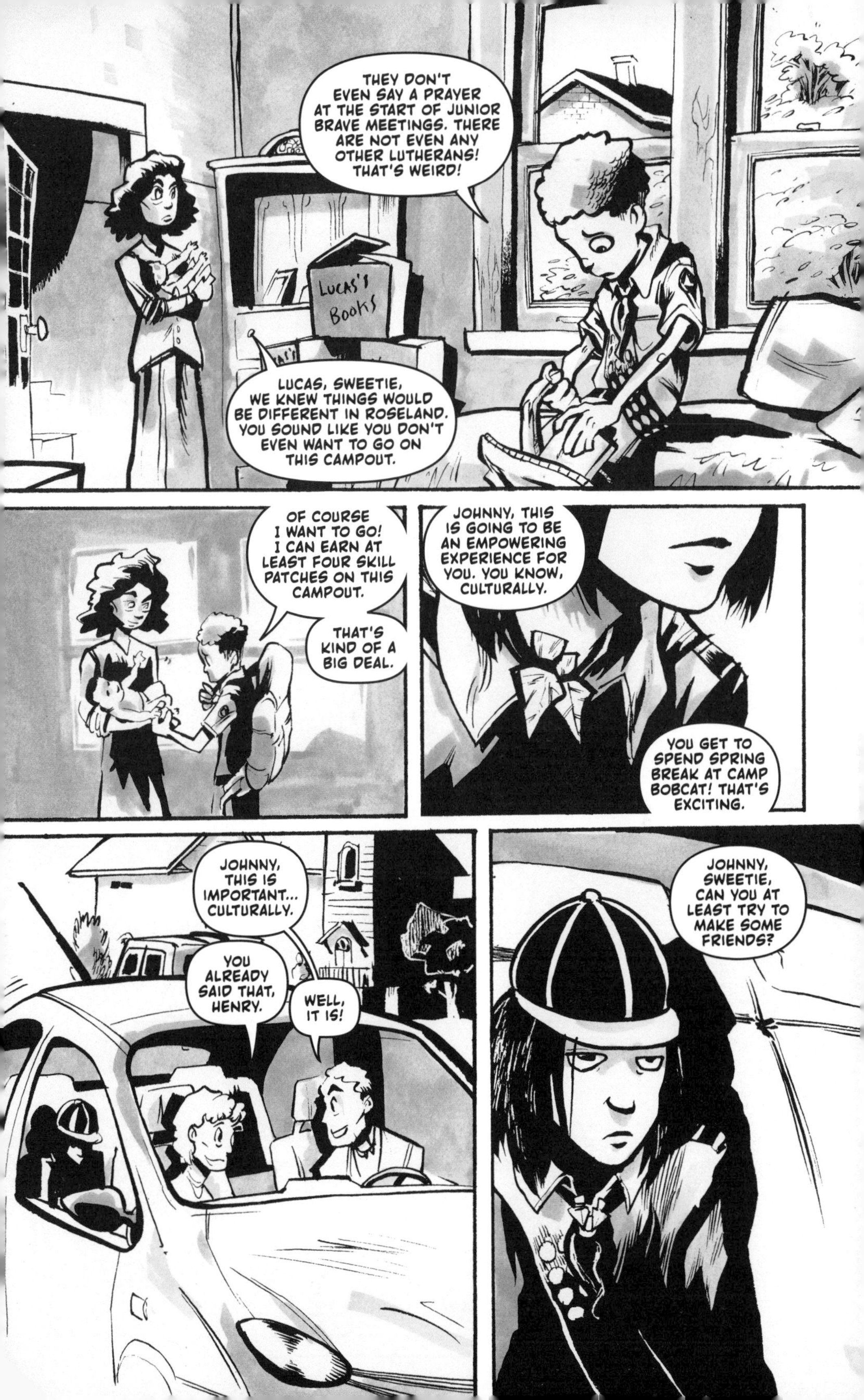
THEY DON'T EVEN SAY A PRAYER AT THE START OF JUNIOR BRAVE MEETINGS. THERE ARE NOT EVEN ANY OTHER LUTHERANS! THAT'S WEIRD!
LUCAS'S BOOKS
LUCAS, SWEETIE, WE KNEW THINGS WOULD BE DIFFERENT IN ROSELAND. YOU SOUND LIKE YOU DON'T EVEN WANT TO GO ON THIS CAMPOUT.
OF COURSE I WANT TO GO! I CAN EARN AT LEAST FOUR SKILL PATCHES ON THIS CAMPOUT.
THAT'S KIND OF A BIG DEAL.
JOHNNY, THIS IS GOING TO BE AN EMPOWERING EXPERIENCE FOR YOU. YOU KNOW, CULTURALLY.
YOU GET TO SPEND SPRING BREAK AT CAMP BOBCAT! THAT'S EXCITING.
JOHNNY, THIS IS IMPORTANT... CULTURALLY.
YOU ALREADY SAID THAT, HENRY.
WELL, IT IS!
JOHNNY, SWEETIE, CAN YOU AT LEAST TRY TO MAKE SOME FRIENDS?

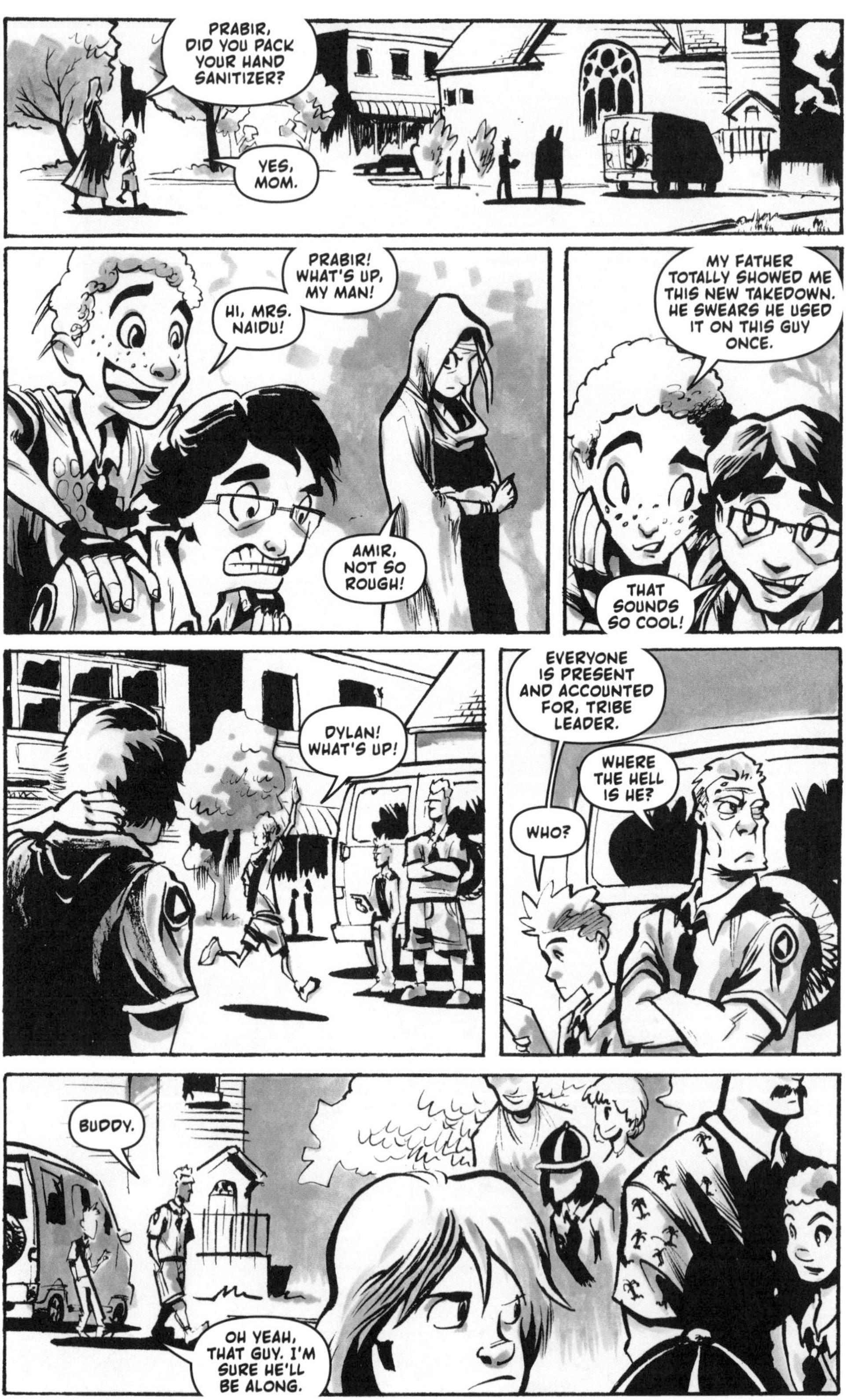
PRABIR, DID YOU PACK YOUR HAND SANITIZER?
YES, MOM.
HI, MRS. NAIDU!
PRABIR! WHAT'S UP, MY MAN!
AMIR, NOT SO ROUGH!
MY FATHER TOTALLY SHOWED ME THIS NEW TAKEDOWN. HE SWEARS HE USED IT ON THIS GUY ONCE.
THAT SOUNDS SO COOL!
DYLAN! WHAT'S UP!
EVERYONE IS PRESENT AND ACCOUNTED FOR, TRIBE LEADER.
WHERE THE HELL IS HE?
WHO?
BUDDY.
OH YEAH, THAT GUY. I'M SURE HE'LL BE ALONG.

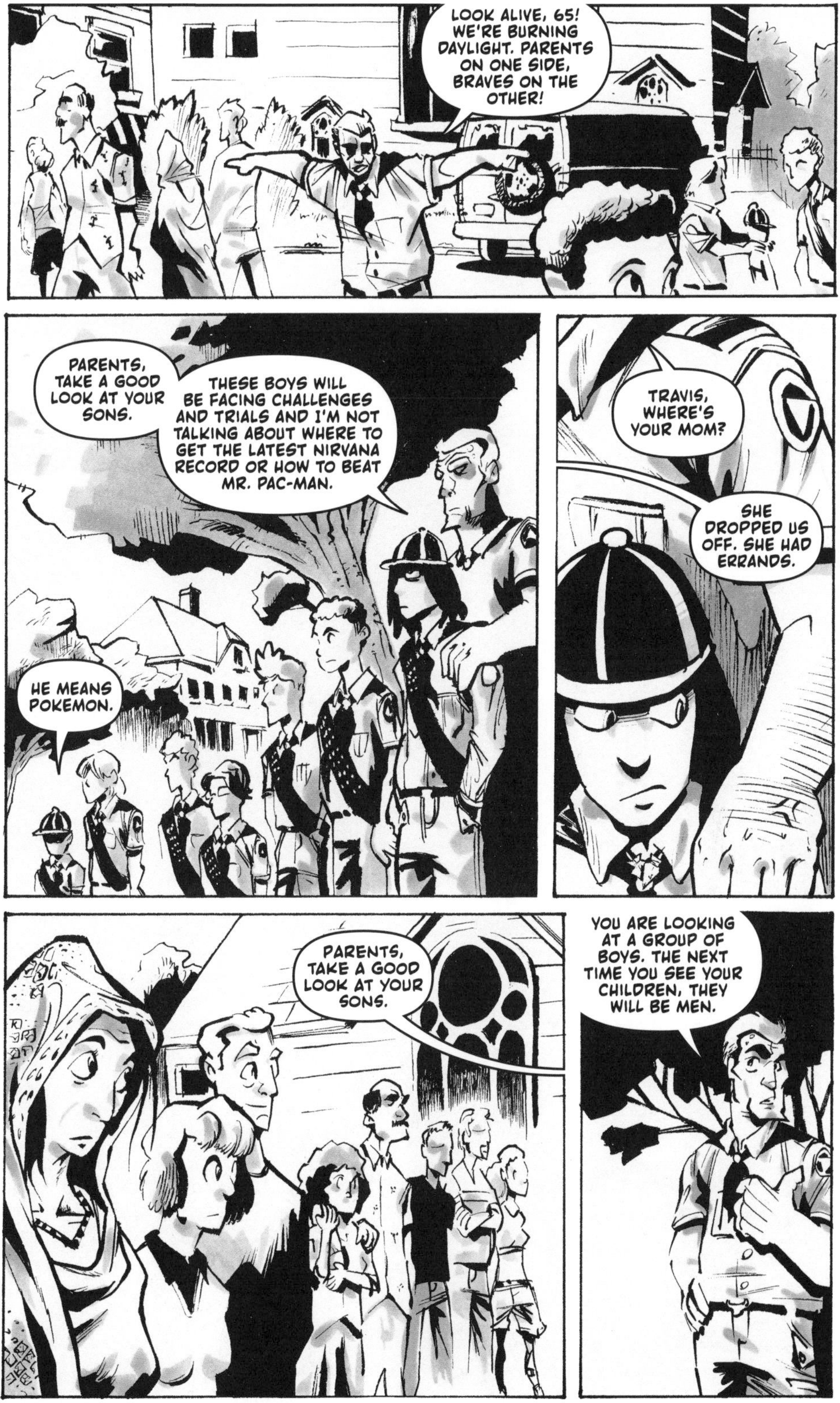
LOOK ALIVE, 65! WE'RE BURNING DAYLIGHT. PARENTS ON ONE SIDE, BRAVES ON THE OTHER!
PARENTS, TAKE A GOOD LOOK AT YOUR SONS.
THESE BOYS WILL BE FACING CHALLENGES AND TRIALS AND I'M NOT TALKING ABOUT WHERE TO GET THE LATEST NIRVANA RECORD OR HOW TO BEAT MR. PAC-MAN.
HE MEANS POKEMON.
TRAVIS, WHERE'S YOUR MOM?
SHE DROPPED US OFF. SHE HAD ERRANDS.
PARENTS, TAKE A GOOD LOOK AT YOUR SONS.
YOU ARE LOOKING AT A GROUP OF BOYS. THE NEXT TIME YOU SEE YOUR CHILDREN, THEY WILL BE MEN.

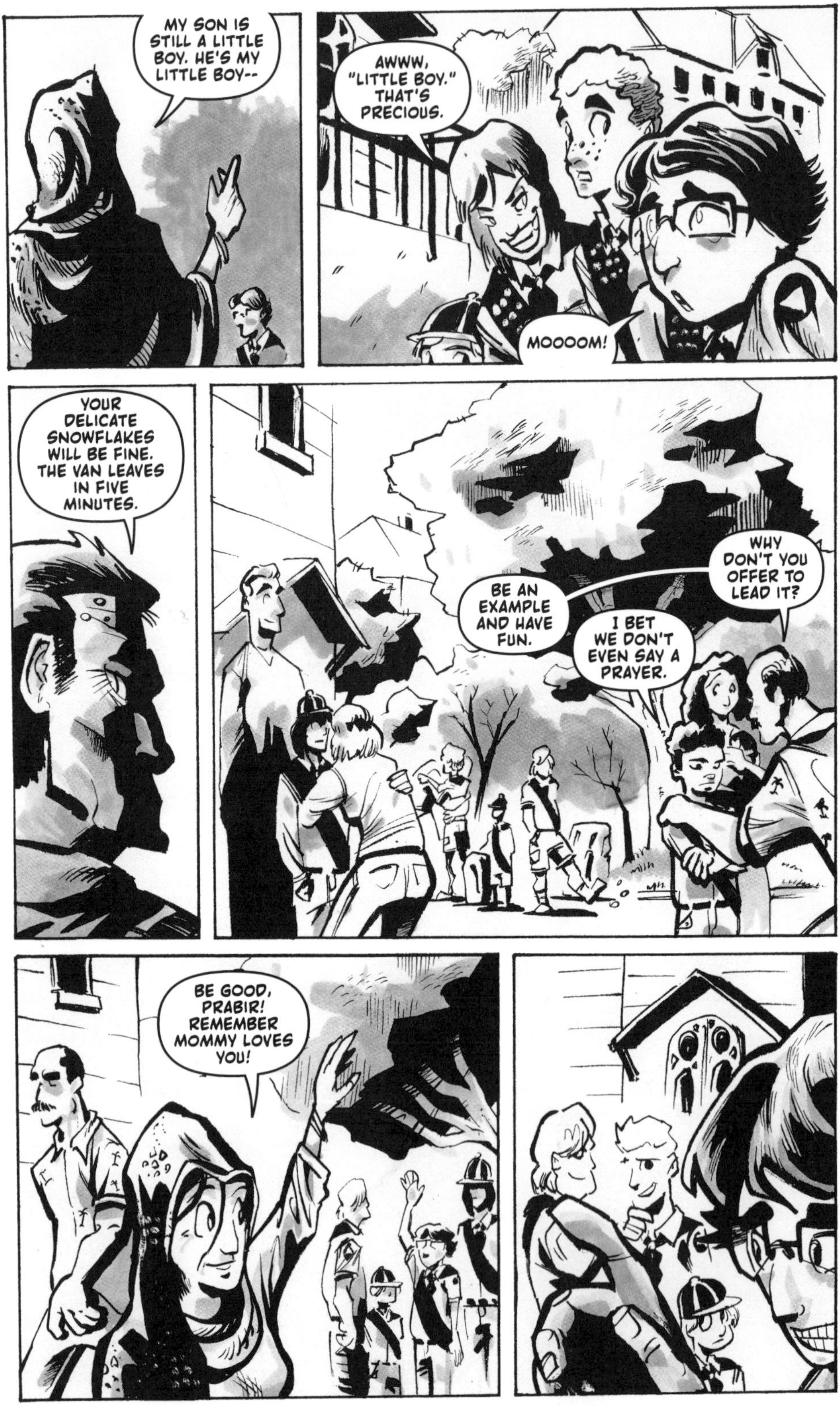
MY SON IS STILL A LITTLE BOY. HE'S MY LITTLE BOY--
AWWW, "LITTLE BOY." THAT'S PRECIOUS.
MOOOOM!
YOUR DELICATE SNOWFLAKES WILL BE FINE. THE VAN LEAVES IN FIVE MINUTES.
BE AN EXAMPLE AND HAVE FUN.
WHY DON'T YOU OFFER TO LEAD IT?
I BET WE DON'T EVEN SAY A PRAYER.
BE GOOD, PRABIR! REMEMBER MOMMY LOVES YOU!

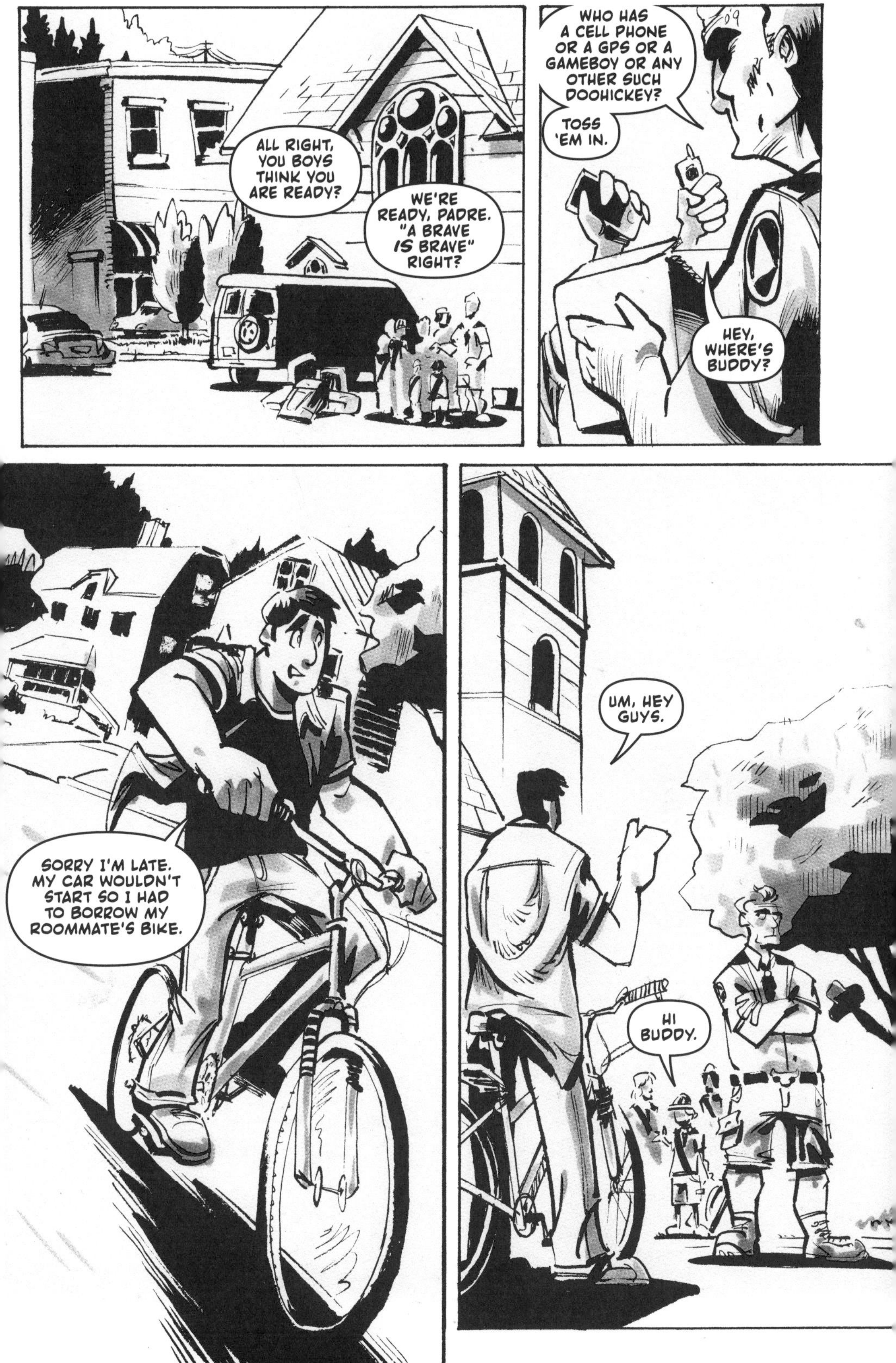
ALL RIGHT, YOU BOYS THINK YOU ARE READY?
WE'RE READY, PADRE. "A BRAVE IS BRAVE" RIGHT?
WHO HAS A CELL PHONE OR A GPS OR A GAMEBOY OR ANY OTHER SUCH DOOHICKEY?
TOSS 'EM IN.
HEY, WHERE'S BUDDY?
SORRY I'M LATE. MY CAR WOULDN'T START SO I HAD TO BORROW MY ROOMMATE'S BIKE.
UM, HEY GUYS.
HI BUDDY.

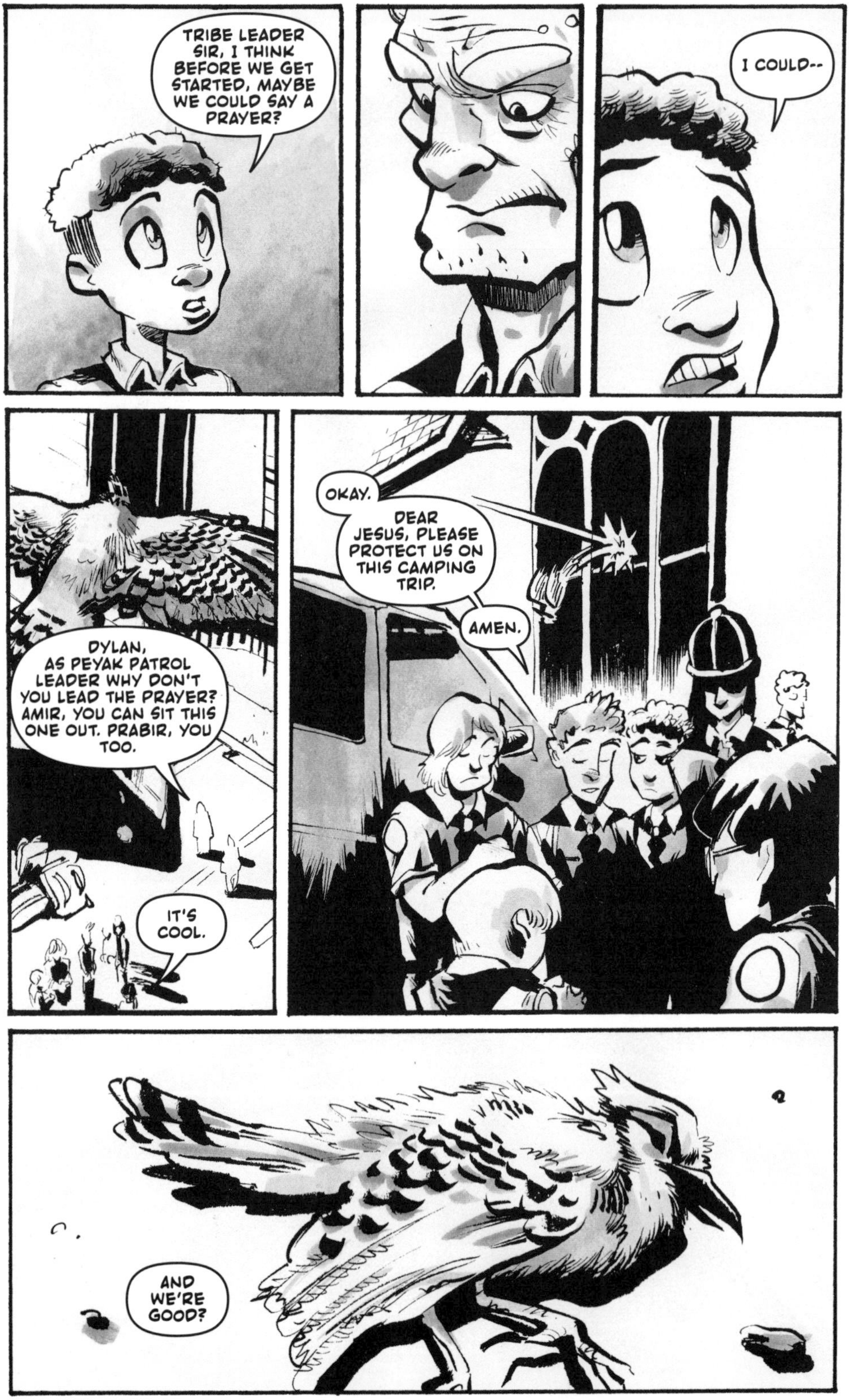
TRIBE LEADER SIR, I THINK BEFORE WE GET STARTED, MAYBE WE COULD SAY A PRAYER?
I COULD--
DYLAN, AS PEYAK PATROL LEADER WHY DON'T YOU LEAD THE PRAYER? AMIR, YOU CAN SIT THIS ONE OUT. PRABIR, YOU TOO.
IT'S COOL.
OKAY.
DEAR JESUS, PLEASE PROTECT US ON THIS CAMPING TRIP.
AMEN.
AND WE'RE GOOD?

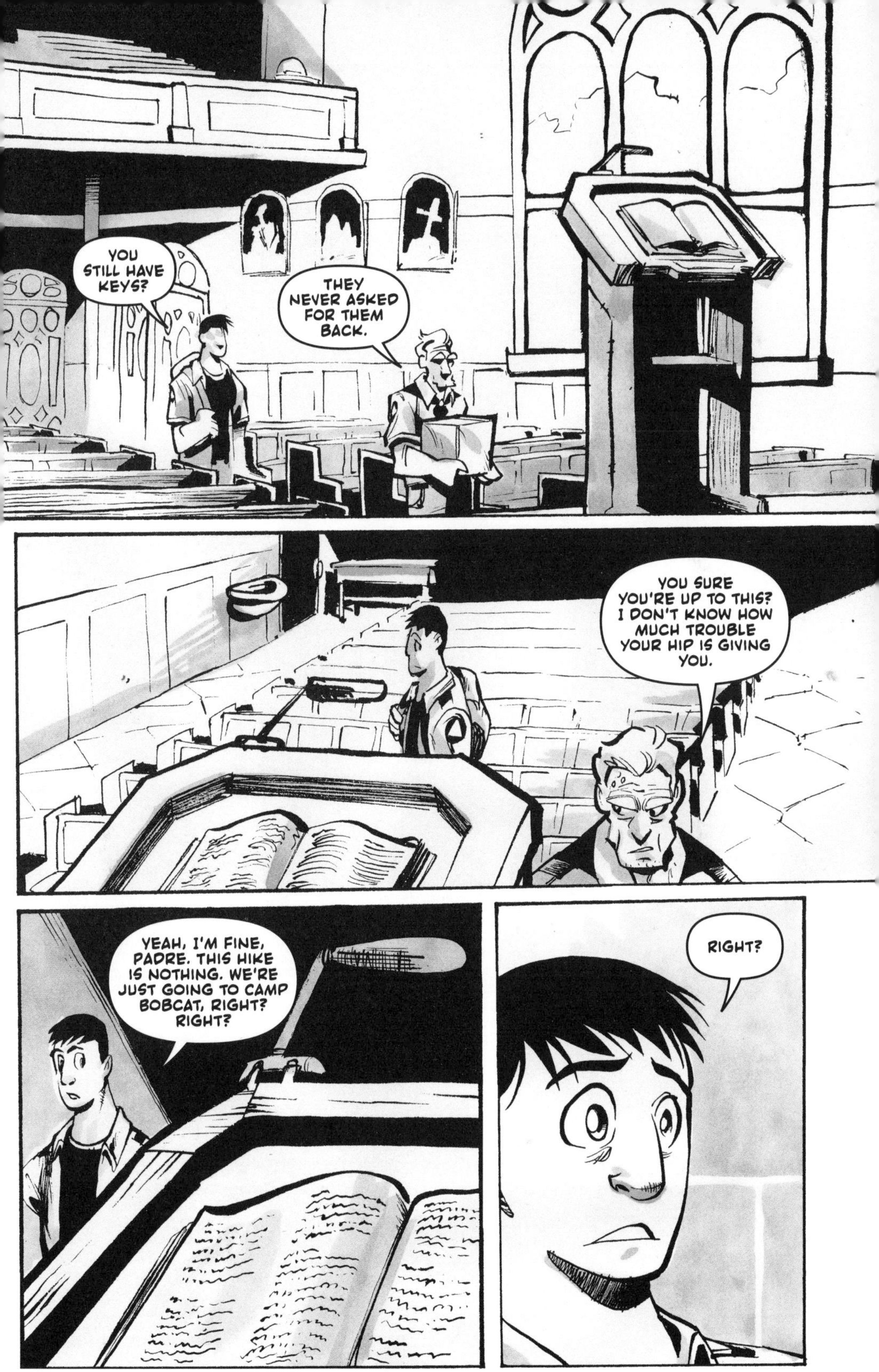
YOU STILL HAVE KEYS?
THEY NEVER ASKED FOR THEM BACK.
YOU SURE YOU'RE UP TO THIS? I DON'T KNOW HOW MUCH TROUBLE YOUR HIP IS GIVING YOU.
YEAH, I'M FINE, PADRE. THIS HIKE IS NOTHING. WE'RE JUST GOING TO CAMP BOBCAT, RIGHT? RIGHT?
RIGHT?

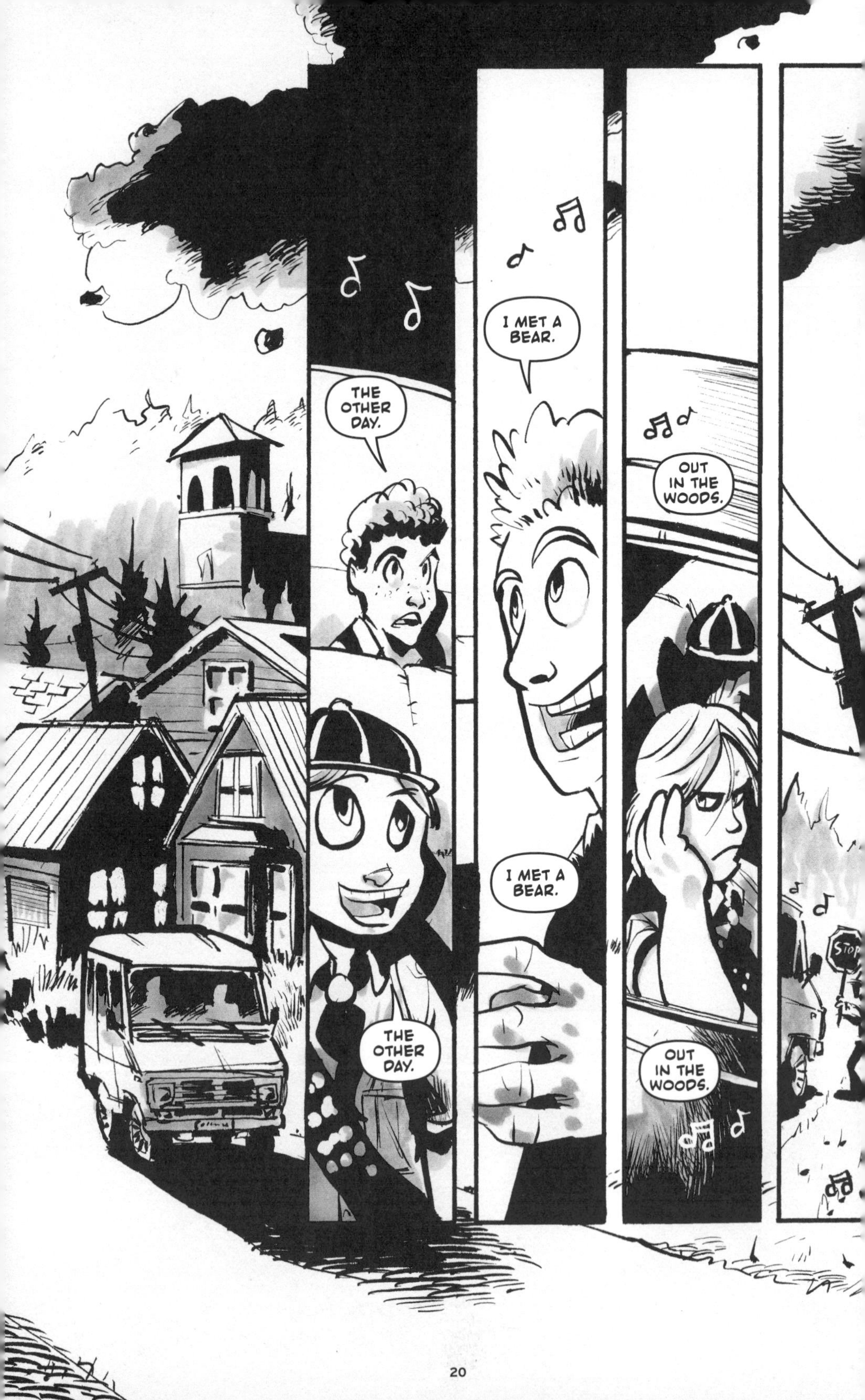
THE OTHER DAY.
I MET A BEAR.
OUT IN THE WOODS.
THE OTHER DAY.
I MET A BEAR.
OUT IN THE WOODS.
STOP

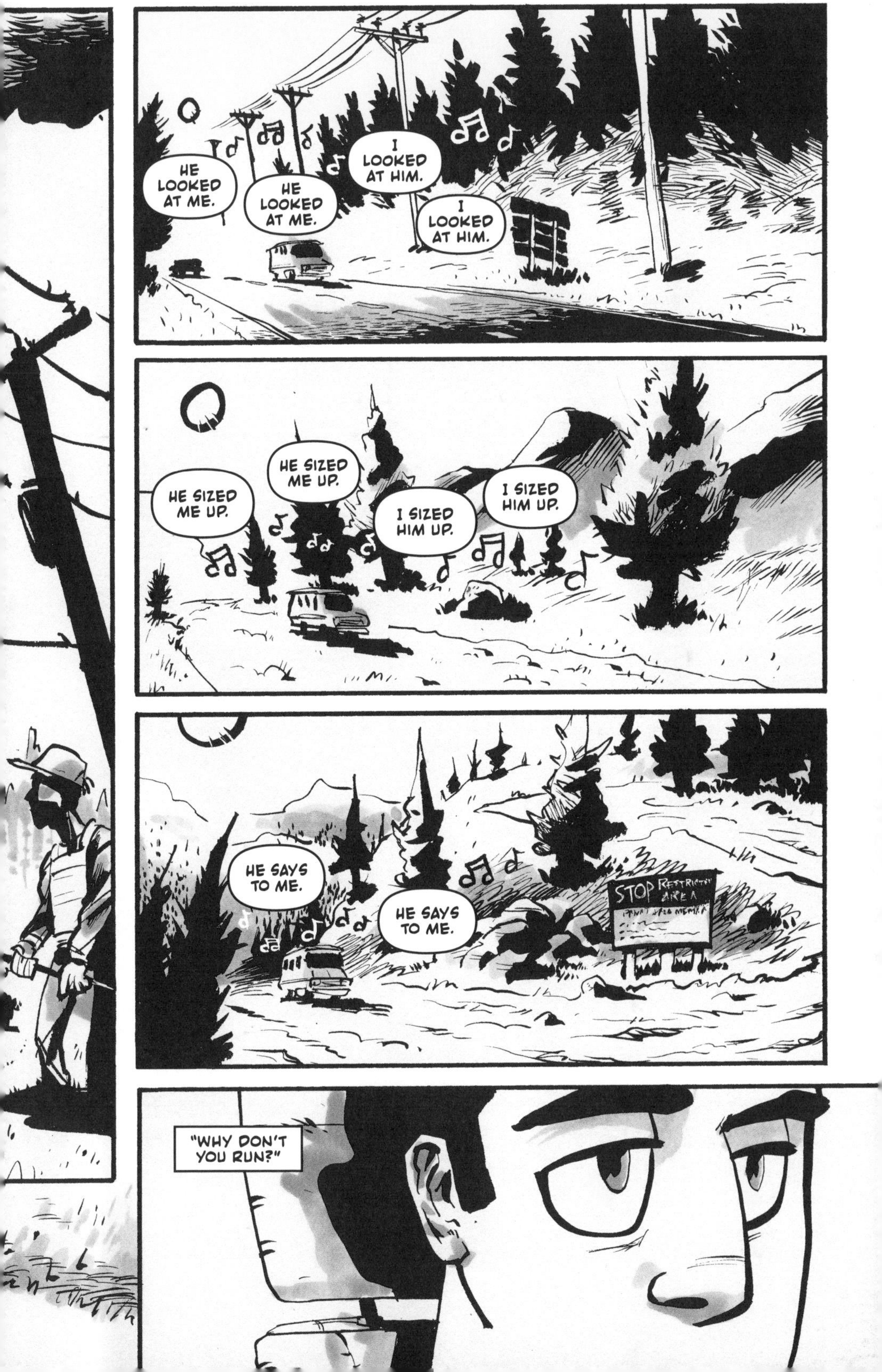
HE LOOKED AT ME.
HE LOOKED AT ME.
I LOOKED AT HIM.
I LOOKED AT HIM.
HE SIZED ME UP.
HE SIZED ME UP.
I SIZED HIM UP.
I SIZED HIM UP.
HE SAYS TO ME.
HE SAYS TO ME.
STOP
"WHY DON'T YOU RUN?"

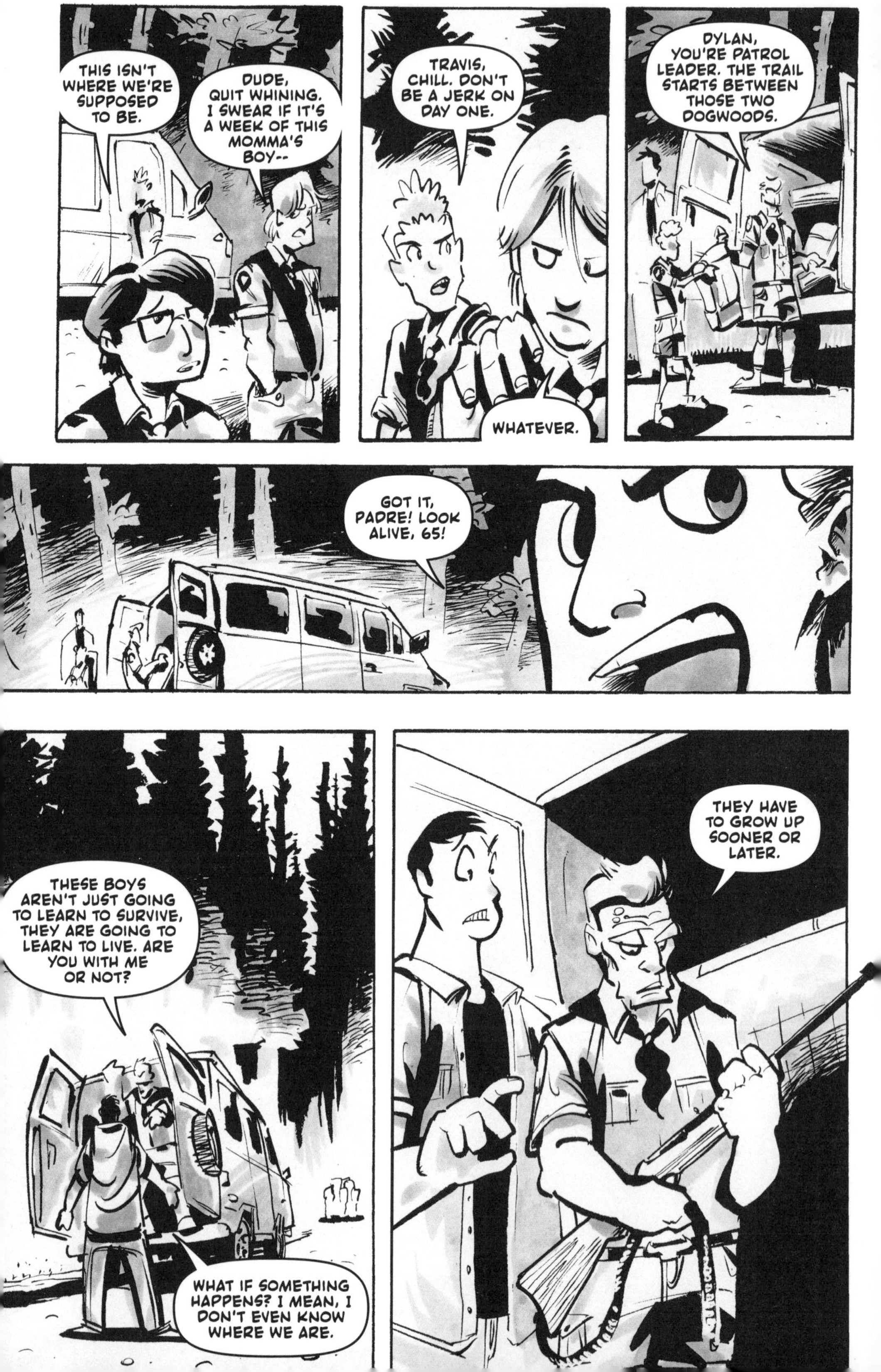
THIS ISN'T WHERE WE'RE SUPPOSED TO BE.
DUDE, QUIT WHINING. I SWEAR IF IT'S A WEEK OF THIS MOMMA'S BOY--
TRAVIS, CHILL. DON'T BE A JERK ON DAY ONE.
WHATEVER.
DYLAN, YOU'RE PATROL LEADER. THE TRAIL STARTS BETWEEN THOSE TWO DOGWOODS.
GOT IT, PADRE! LOOK ALIVE, 65!
THESE BOYS AREN'T JUST GOING TO LEARN TO SURVIVE, THEY ARE GOING TO LEARN TO LIVE. ARE YOU WITH ME OR NOT?
WHAT IF SOMETHING HAPPENS? I MEAN, I DON'T EVEN KNOW WHERE WE ARE.
THEY HAVE TO GROW UP SOONER OR LATER.

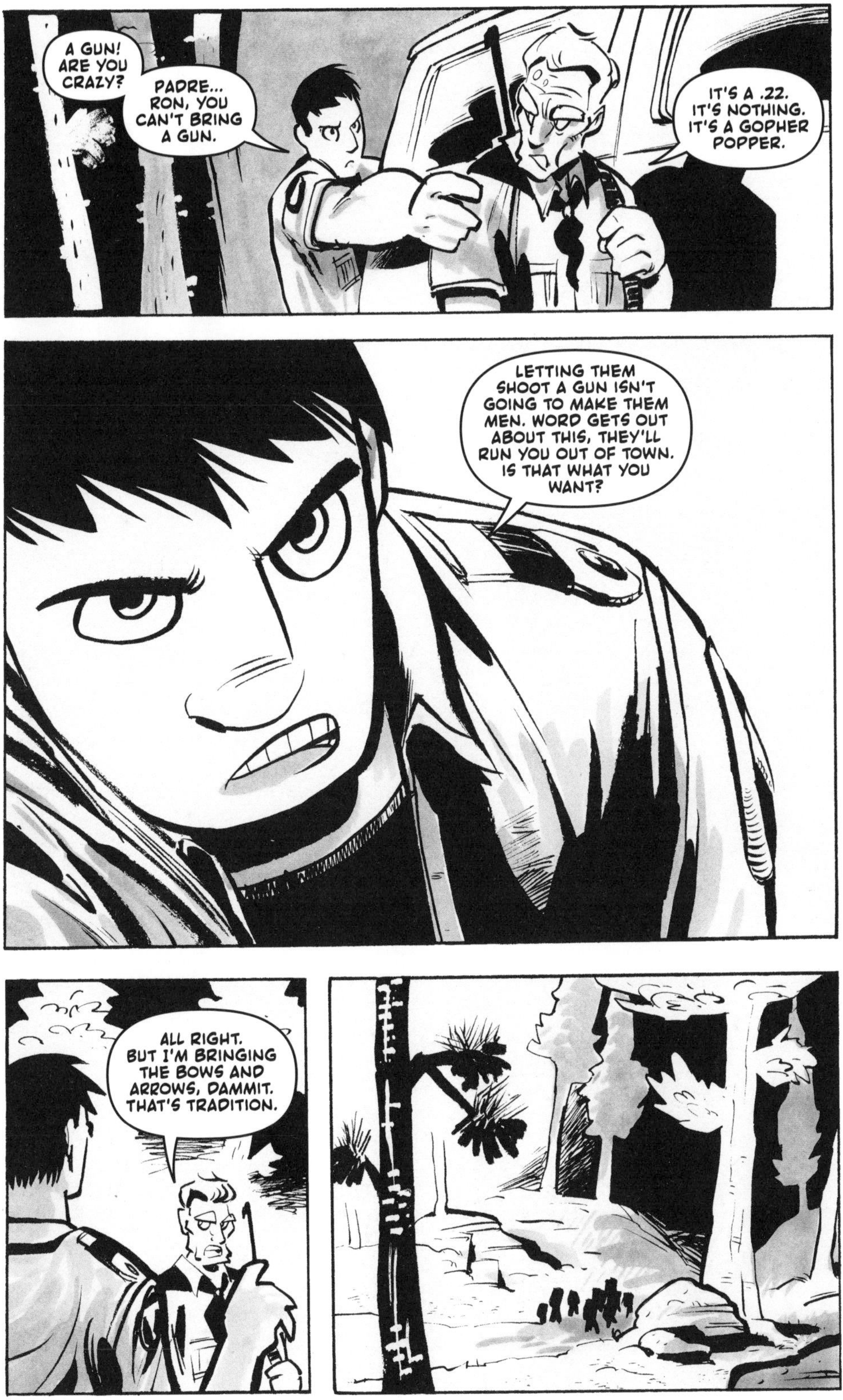
A GUN! ARE YOU CRAZY?
PADRE... RON, YOU CAN'T BRING A GUN.
IT'S A .22. IT'S NOTHING. IT'S A GOPHER POPPER.
LETTING THEM SHOOT A GUN ISN'T GOING TO MAKE THEM MEN. WORD GETS OUT ABOUT THIS, THEY'LL RUN YOU OUT OF TOWN. IS THAT WHAT YOU WANT?
ALL RIGHT. BUT I'M BRINGING THE BOWS AND ARROWS, DAMMIT. THAT'S TRADITION.

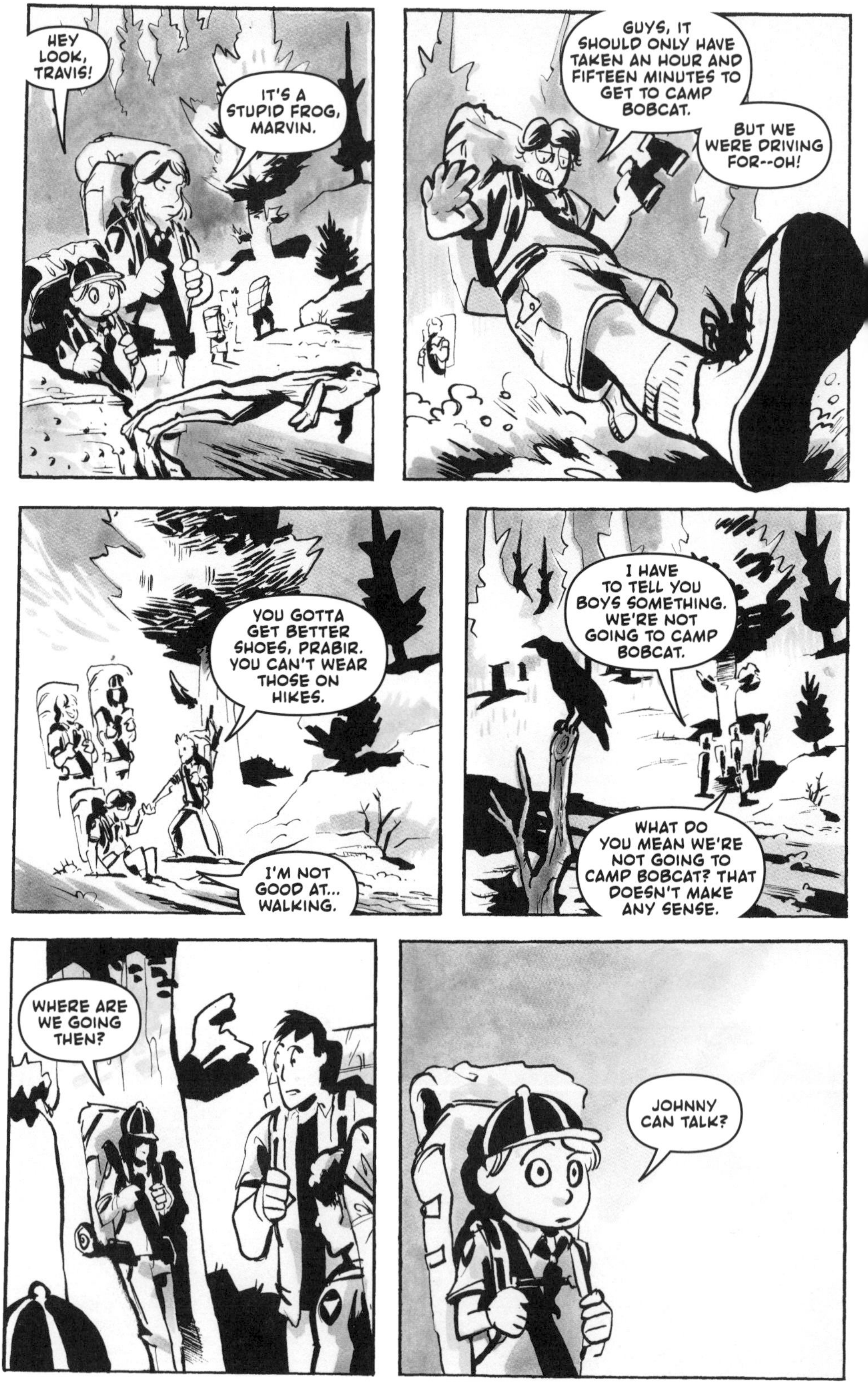
HEY LOOK, TRAVIS!
IT'S A STUPID FROG, MARVIN.
GUYS, IT SHOULD ONLY HAVE TAKEN AN HOUR AND FIFTEEN MINUTES TO GET TO CAMP BOBCAT.
BUT WE WERE DRIVING FOR--OH!
YOU GOTTA GET BETTER SHOES, PRABIR. YOU CAN'T WEAR THOSE ON HIKES.
I'M NOT GOOD AT... WALKING.
I HAVE TO TELL YOU BOYS SOMETHING. WE'RE NOT GOING TO CAMP BOBCAT.
WHAT DO YOU MEAN WE'RE NOT GOING TO CAMP BOBCAT? THAT DOESN'T MAKE ANY SENSE.
WHERE ARE WE GOING THEN?
JOHNNY CAN TALK?

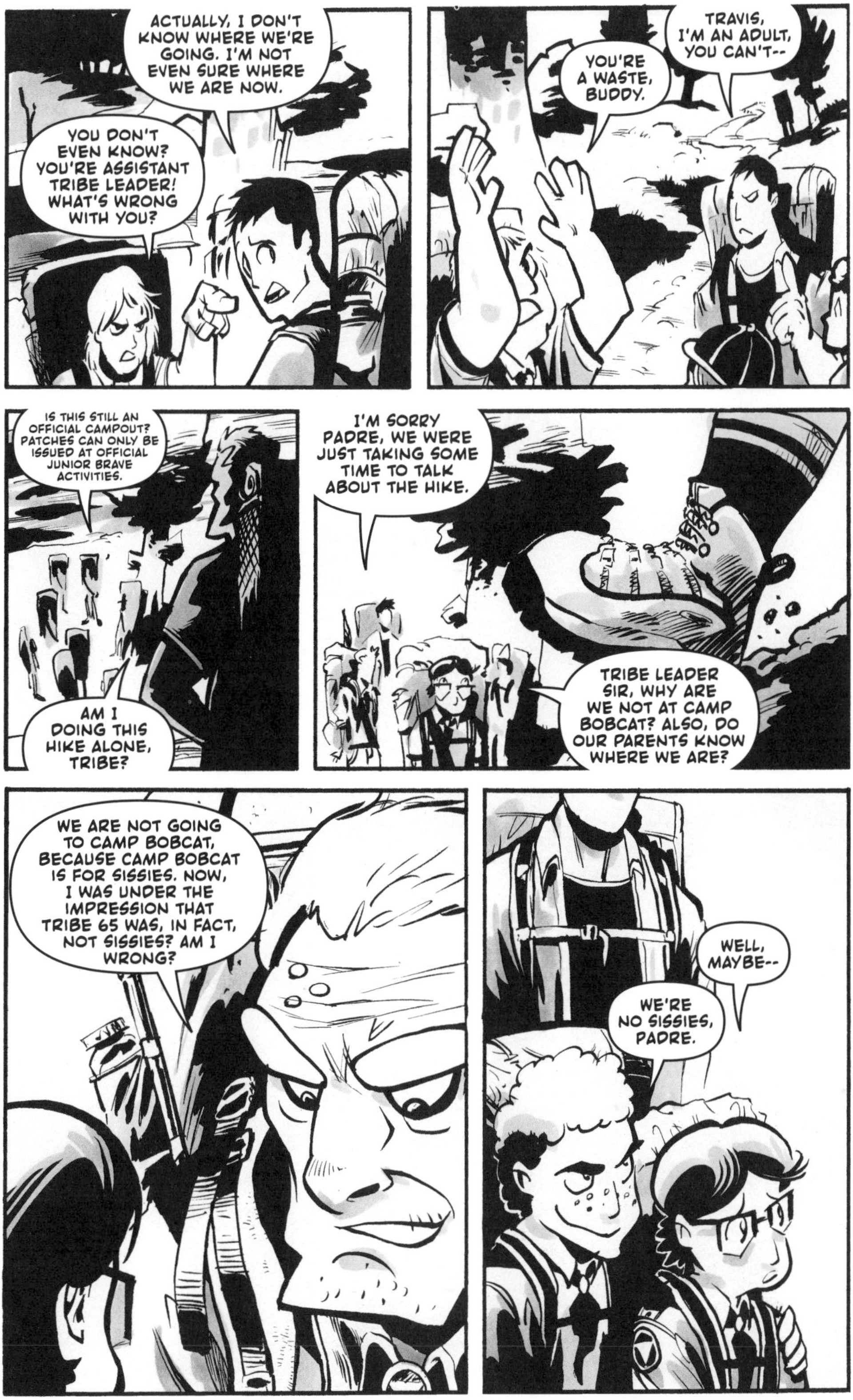
ACTUALLY, I DON'T KNOW WHERE WE'RE GOING. I'M NOT EVEN SURE WHERE WE ARE NOW.
YOU DON'T EVEN KNOW? YOU'RE ASSISTANT TRIBE LEADER! WHAT'S WRONG WITH YOU?
TRAVIS, I'M AN ADULT, YOU CAN'T--
YOU'RE A WASTE, BUDDY.
IS THIS STILL AN OFFICIAL CAMPOUT? PATCHES CAN ONLY BE ISSUED AT OFFICIAL JUNIOR BRAVE ACTIVITIES.
AM I DOING THIS HIKE ALONE, TRIBE?
I'M SORRY PADRE, WE WERE JUST TAKING SOME TIME TO TALK ABOUT THE HIKE.
TRIBE LEADER SIR, WHY ARE WE NOT AT CAMP BOBCAT? ALSO, DO OUR PARENTS KNOW WHERE WE ARE?
WE ARE NOT GOING TO CAMP BOBCAT, BECAUSE CAMP BOBCAT IS FOR SISSIES. NOW, I WAS UNDER THE IMPRESSION THAT TRIBE 65 WAS, IN FACT, NOT SISSIES? AM I WRONG?
WELL, MAYBE--
WE'RE NO SISSIES, PADRE.

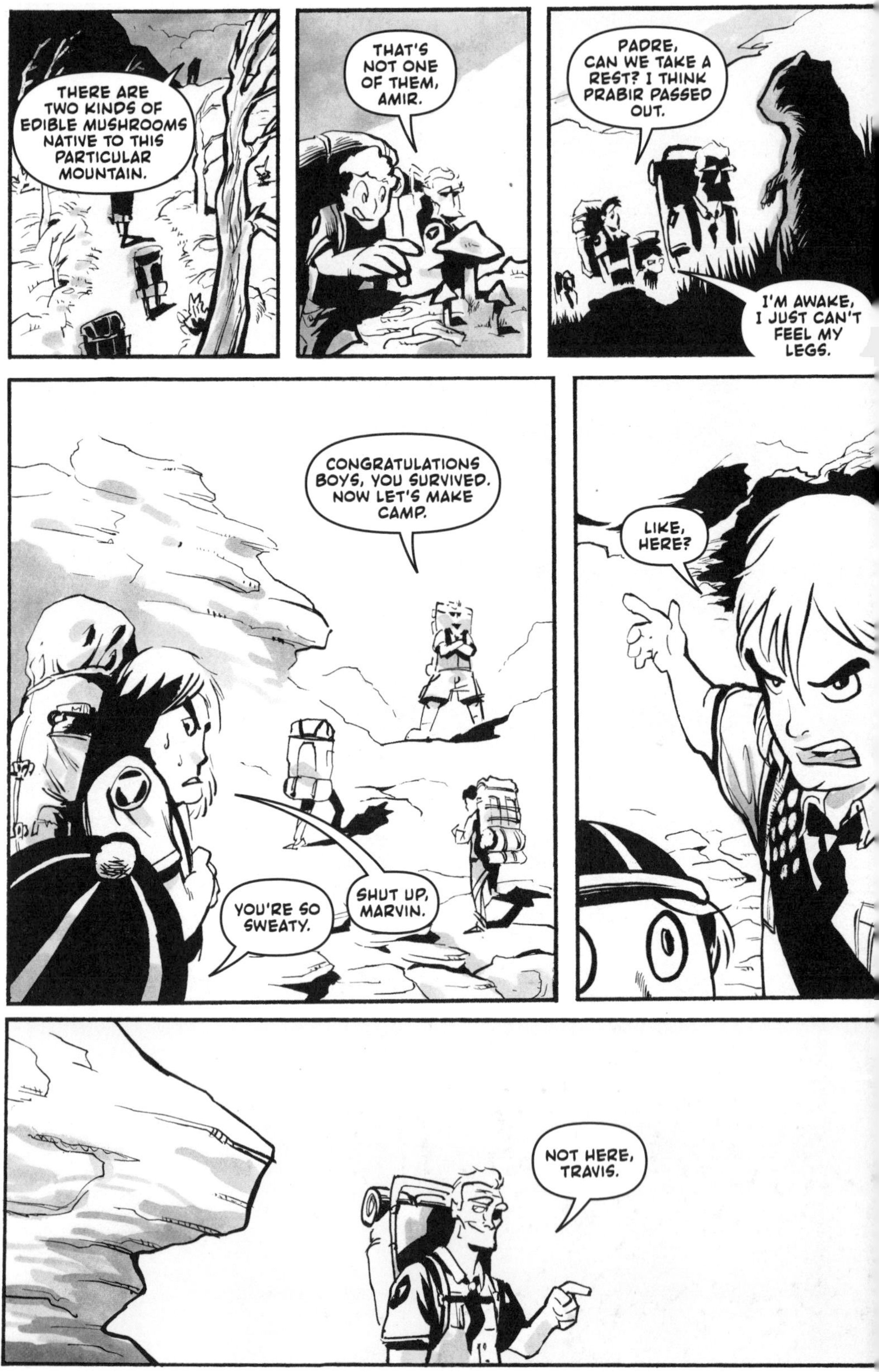
THERE ARE TWO KINDS OF EDIBLE MUSHROOMS NATIVE TO THIS PARTICULAR MOUNTAIN.
THAT'S NOT ONE OF THEM, AMIR.
PADRE, CAN WE TAKE A REST? I THINK PRABIR PASSED OUT.
I'M AWAKE, I JUST CAN'T FEEL MY LEGS.
CONGRATULATIONS BOYS, YOU SURVIVED. NOW LET'S MAKE CAMP.
YOU'RE SO SWEATY.
SHUT UP, MARVIN.
LIKE, HERE?
NOT HERE, TRAVIS.

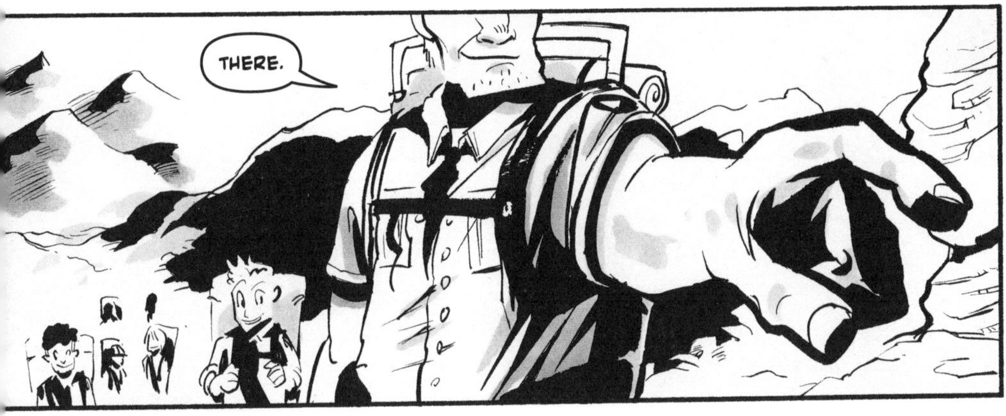
THERE.

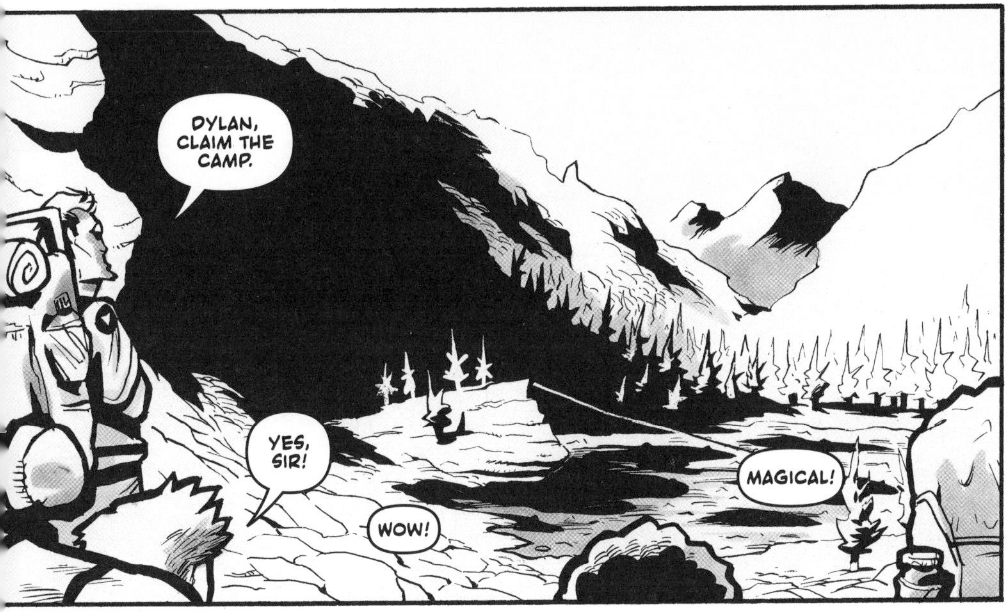
DYLAN, CLAIM THE CAMP.
YES, SIR!
WOW!
MAGICAL!

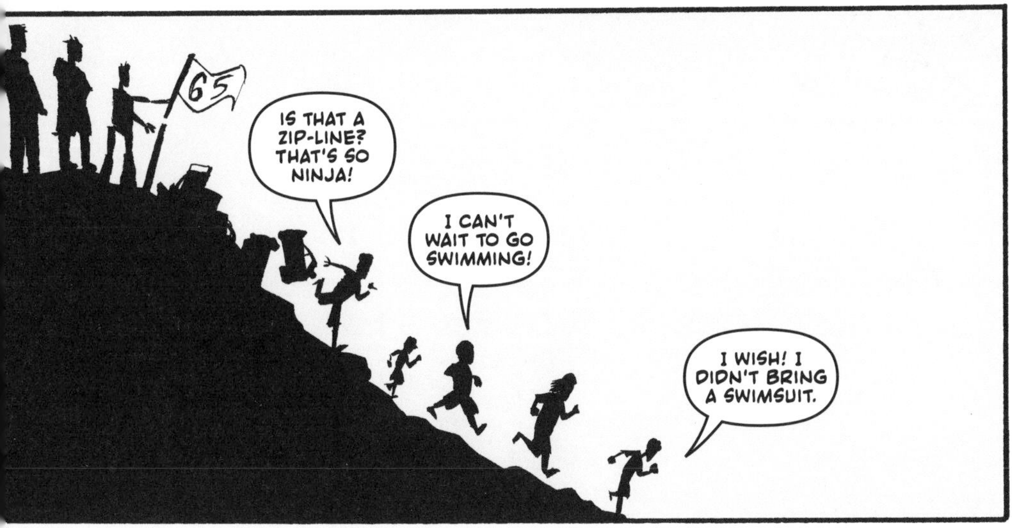
65
IS THAT A ZIP-LINE? THAT'S SO NINJA!
I CAN'T WAIT TO GO SWIMMING!
I WISH! I DIDN'T BRING A SWIMSUIT.

JUST DO WHAT WE DID WHEN I WAS YOUR AGE--STRIP DOWN AND HOP IN NAKED.

IT'S VERY FREEING.

THAT'S CREEPY.

WHAT? WHAT'D I SAY?

IT'S A GENERATIONAL THING.

IF YOU DON'T HAVE TRUNKS, JUST JUMP IN IN YOUR UNDERWEAR OR SHORTS. YOUR CLOTHES WILL DRY.

BOMBS AWAY!

SPLOOSH

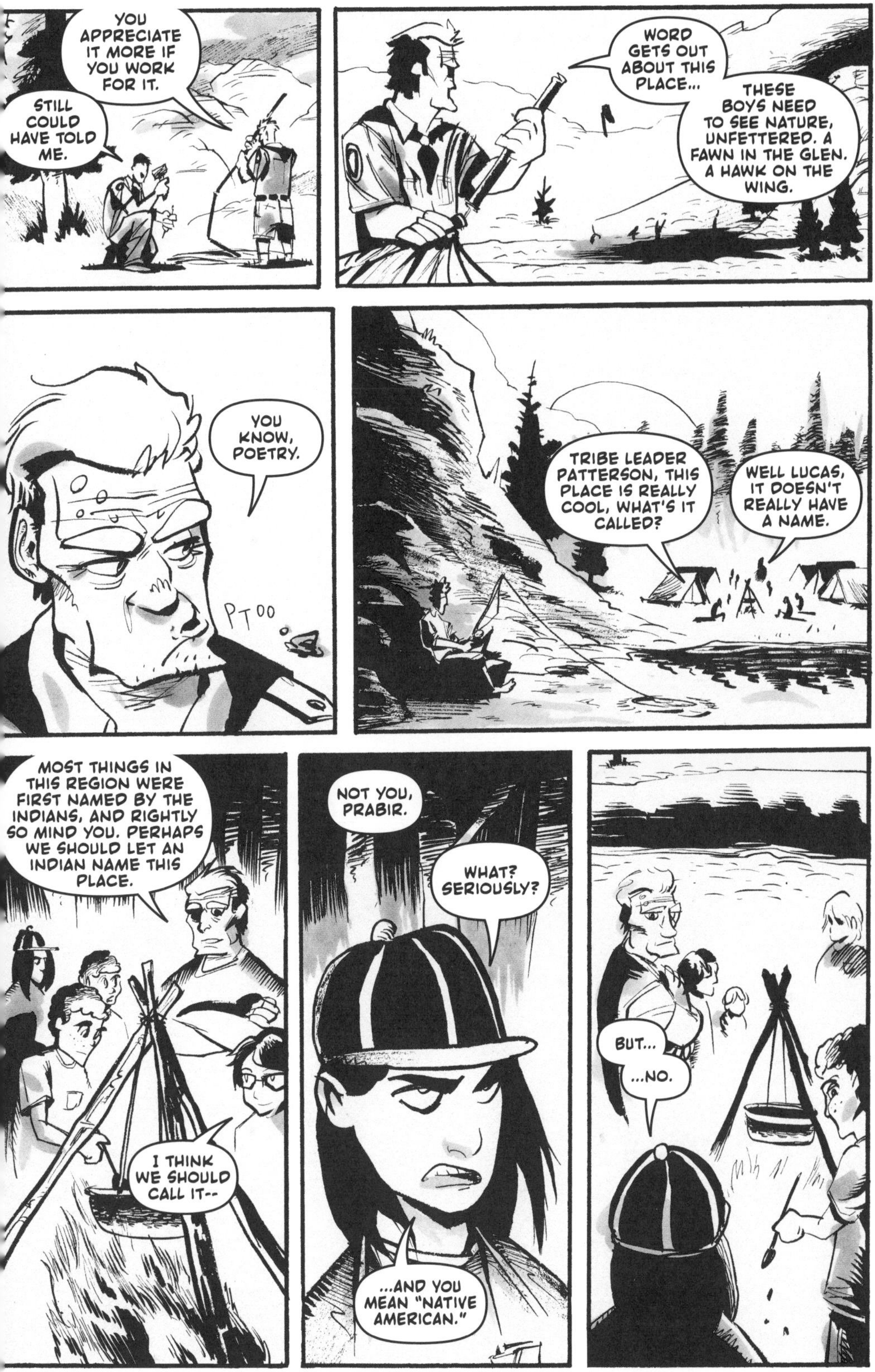
YOU APPRECIATE IT MORE IF YOU WORK FOR IT.
STILL COULD HAVE TOLD ME.
WORD GETS OUT ABOUT THIS PLACE...
THESE BOYS NEED TO SEE NATURE, UNFETTERED. A FAWN IN THE GLEN. A HAWK ON THE WING.
YOU KNOW, POETRY.
PTOO
TRIBE LEADER PATTERSON, THIS PLACE IS REALLY COOL, WHAT'S IT CALLED?
WELL LUCAS, IT DOESN'T REALLY HAVE A NAME.
MOST THINGS IN THIS REGION WERE FIRST NAMED BY THE INDIANS, AND RIGHTLY SO MIND YOU. PERHAPS WE SHOULD LET AN INDIAN NAME THIS PLACE.
I THINK WE SHOULD CALL IT--
NOT YOU, PRABIR.
WHAT? SERIOUSLY?
...AND YOU MEAN "NATIVE AMERICAN."
BUT...
...NO.

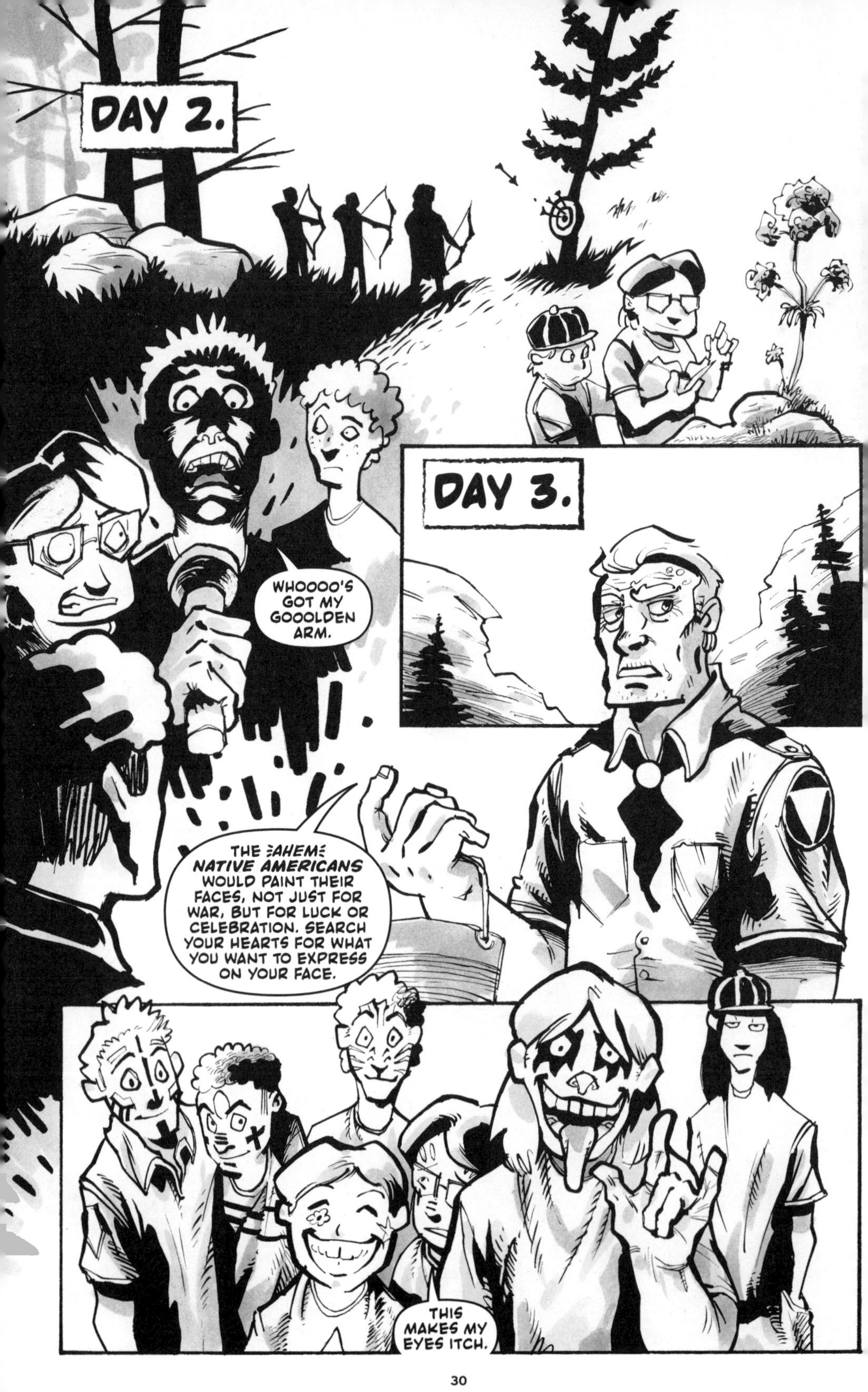
DAY 2.
WHOOOO'S GOT MY GOOOLDEN ARM.
DAY 3.
THE *AHEM* NATIVE AMERICANS WOULD PAINT THEIR FACES, NOT JUST FOR WAR, BUT FOR LUCK OR CELEBRATION. SEARCH YOUR HEARTS FOR WHAT YOU WANT TO EXPRESS ON YOUR FACE.
THIS MAKES MY EYES ITCH.

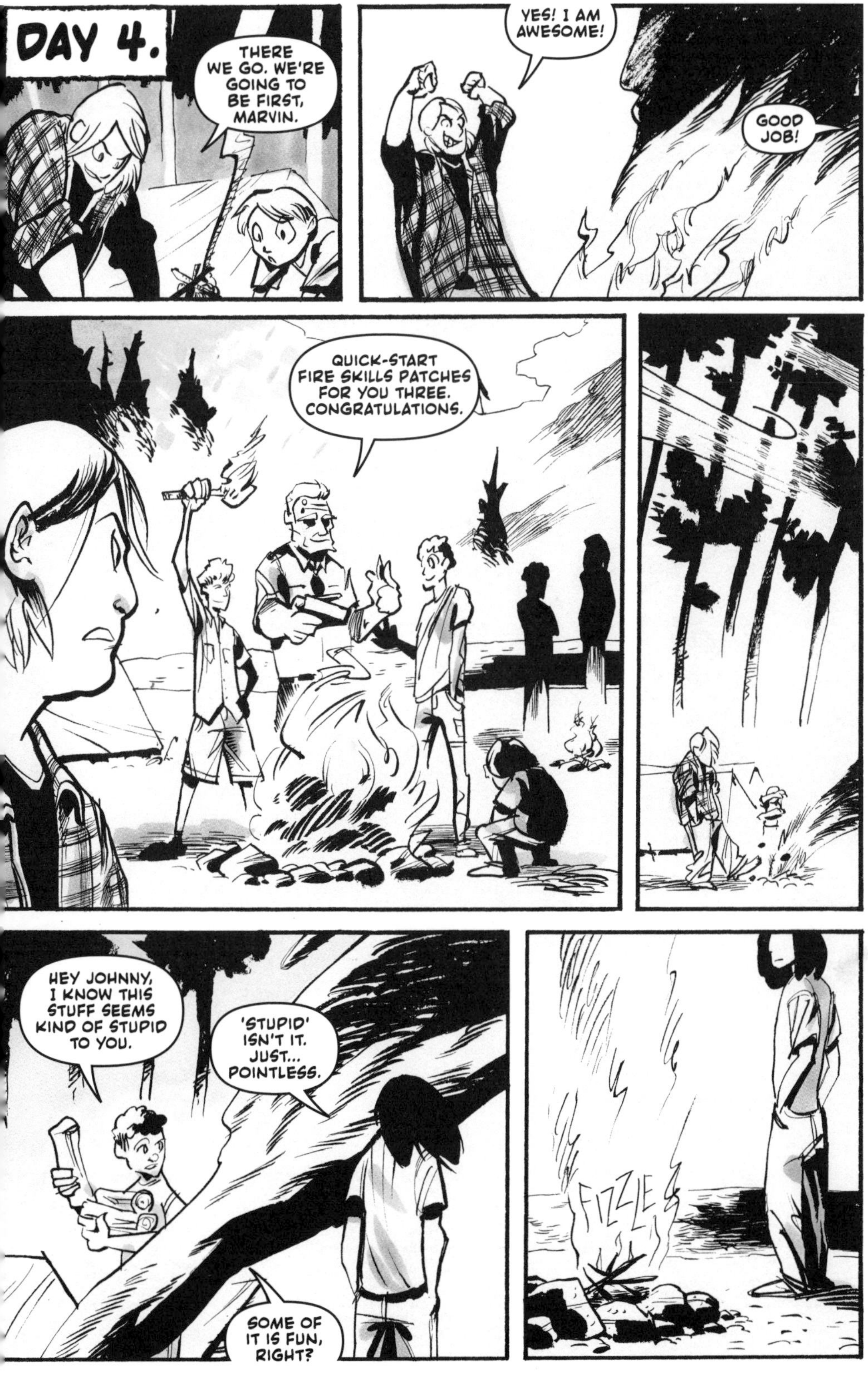

DAY 4.
THERE WE GO. WE'RE GOING TO BE FIRST, MARVIN.
YES! I AM AWESOME!
GOOD JOB!
QUICK-START FIRE SKILLS PATCHES FOR YOU THREE. CONGRATULATIONS.
HEY JOHNNY, I KNOW THIS STUFF SEEMS KIND OF STUPID TO YOU.
'STUPID' ISN'T IT. JUST... POINTLESS.
SOME OF IT IS FUN, RIGHT?
FIZZLE

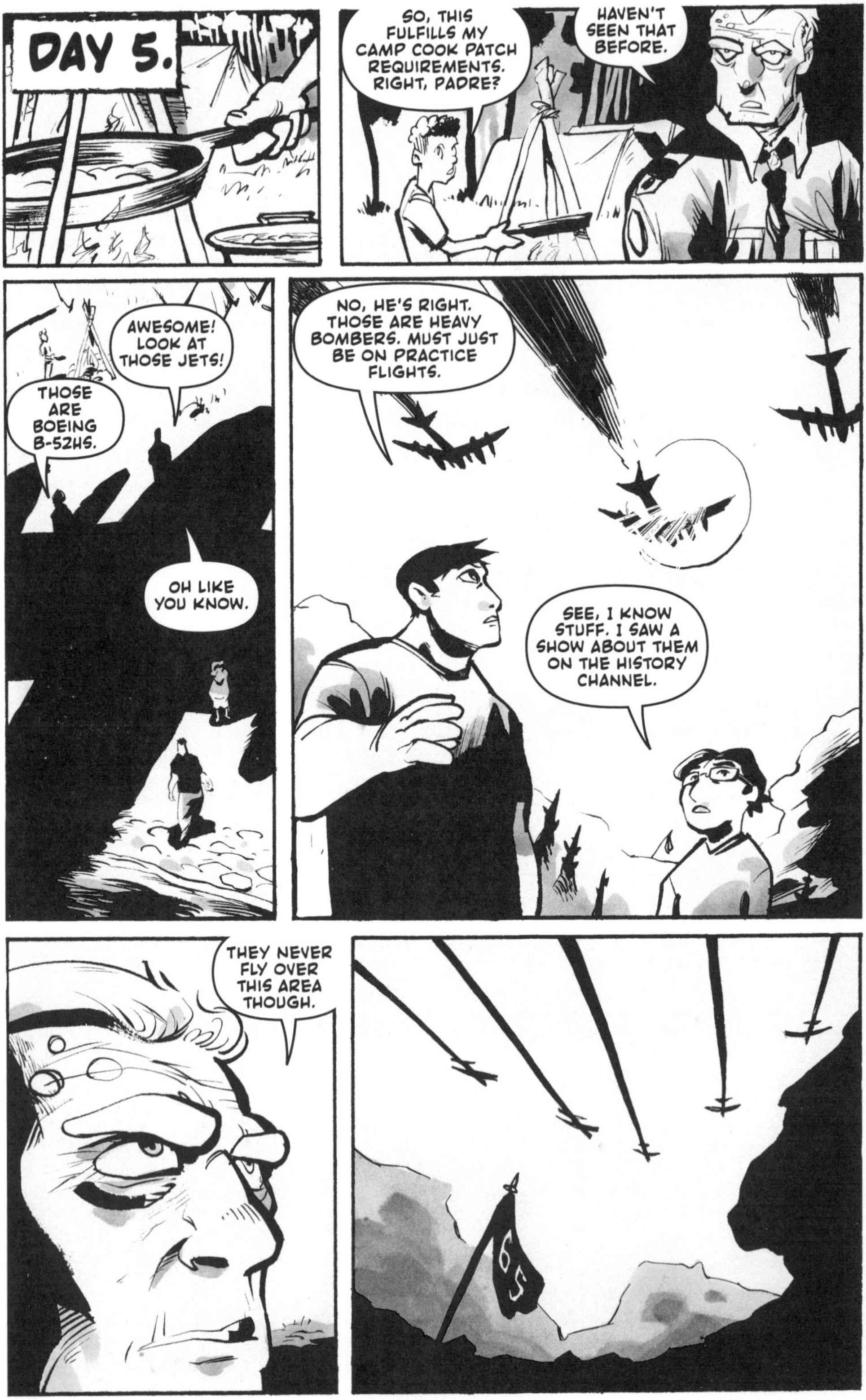
DAY 5.
SO, THIS FULFILLS MY CAMP COOK PATCH REQUIREMENTS. RIGHT, PADRE?
HAVEN'T SEEN THAT BEFORE.
AWESOME! LOOK AT THOSE JETS!
THOSE ARE BOEING B-52HS.
OH LIKE YOU KNOW.
NO, HE'S RIGHT. THOSE ARE HEAVY BOMBERS. MUST JUST BE ON PRACTICE FLIGHTS.
SEE, I KNOW STUFF. I SAW A SHOW ABOUT THEM ON THE HISTORY CHANNEL.
THEY NEVER FLY OVER THIS AREA THOUGH.
65

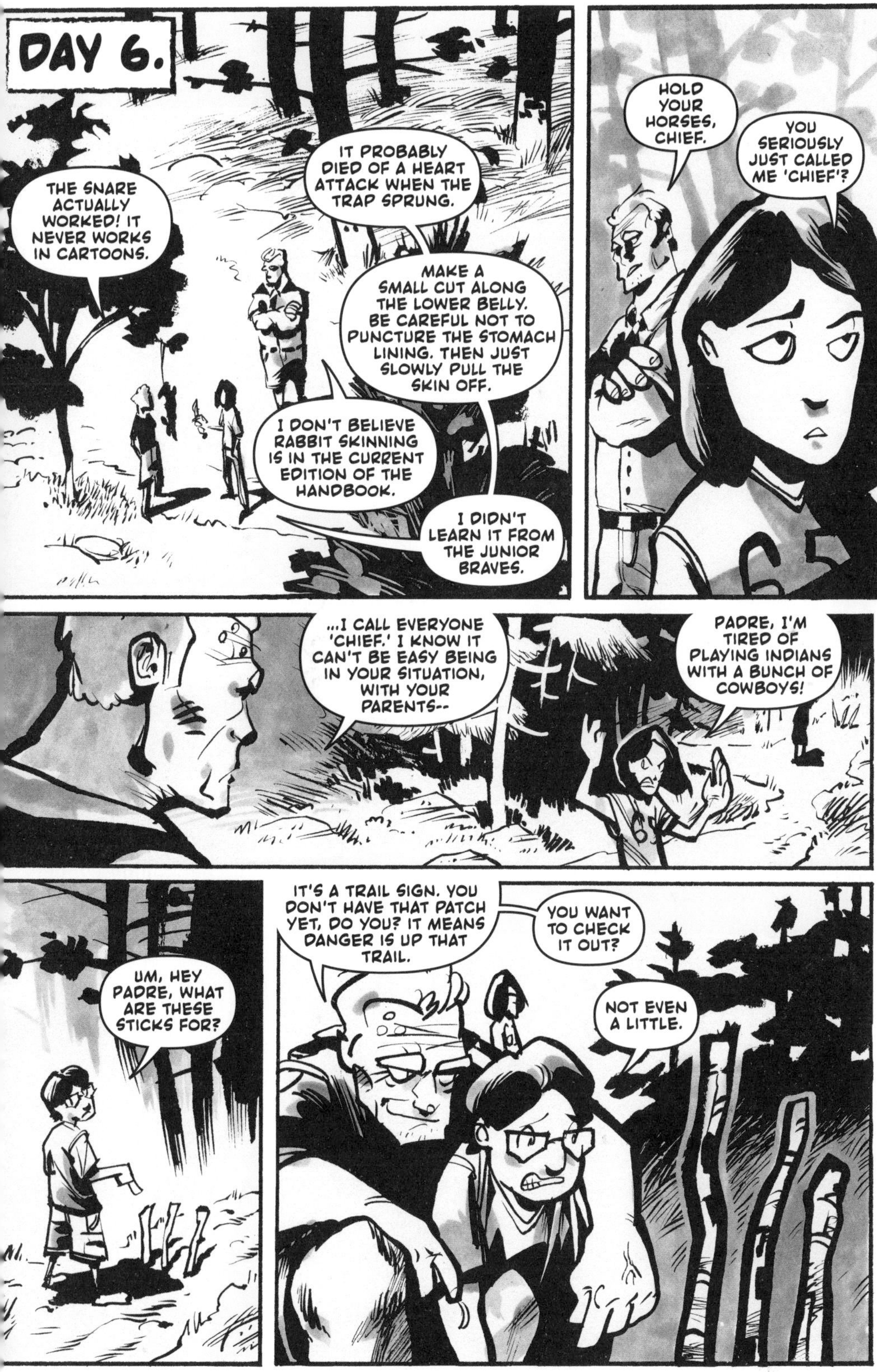
DAY 6.
THE SNARE ACTUALLY WORKED! IT NEVER WORKS IN CARTOONS.
IT PROBABLY DIED OF A HEART ATTACK WHEN THE TRAP SPRUNG.
MAKE A SMALL CUT ALONG THE LOWER BELLY. BE CAREFUL NOT TO PUNCTURE THE STOMACH LINING. THEN JUST SLOWLY PULL THE SKIN OFF.
I DON'T BELIEVE RABBIT SKINNING IS IN THE CURRENT EDITION OF THE HANDBOOK.
I DIDN'T LEARN IT FROM THE JUNIOR BRAVES.
HOLD YOUR HORSES, CHIEF.
YOU SERIOUSLY JUST CALLED ME 'CHIEF'?
...I CALL EVERYONE 'CHIEF.' I KNOW IT CAN'T BE EASY BEING IN YOUR SITUATION, WITH YOUR PARENTS--
PADRE, I'M TIRED OF PLAYING INDIANS WITH A BUNCH OF COWBOYS!
UM, HEY PADRE, WHAT ARE THESE STICKS FOR?
IT'S A TRAIL SIGN. YOU DON'T HAVE THAT PATCH YET, DO YOU? IT MEANS DANGER IS UP THAT TRAIL.
YOU WANT TO CHECK IT OUT?
NOT EVEN A LITTLE.

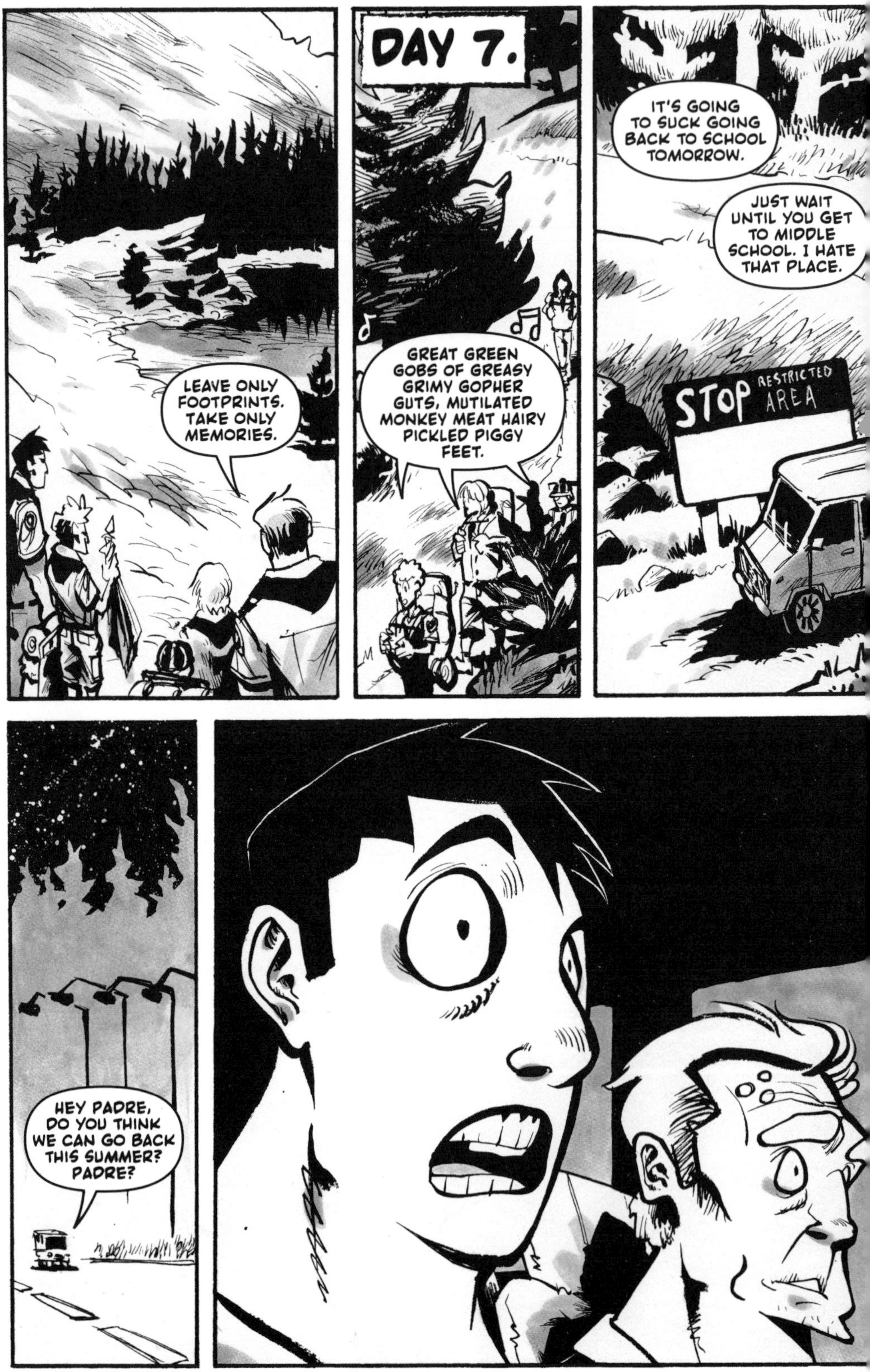
LEAVE ONLY FOOTPRINTS. TAKE ONLY MEMORIES.
DAY 7.
GREAT GREEN GOBS OF GREASY GRIMY GOPHER GUTS, MUTILATED MONKEY MEAT HAIRY PICKLED PIGGY FEET.
IT'S GOING TO SUCK GOING BACK TO SCHOOL TOMORROW.
JUST WAIT UNTIL YOU GET TO MIDDLE SCHOOL. I HATE THAT PLACE.
STOP RESTRICTED AREA
HEY PADRE, DO YOU THINK WE CAN GO BACK THIS SUMMER? PADRE?

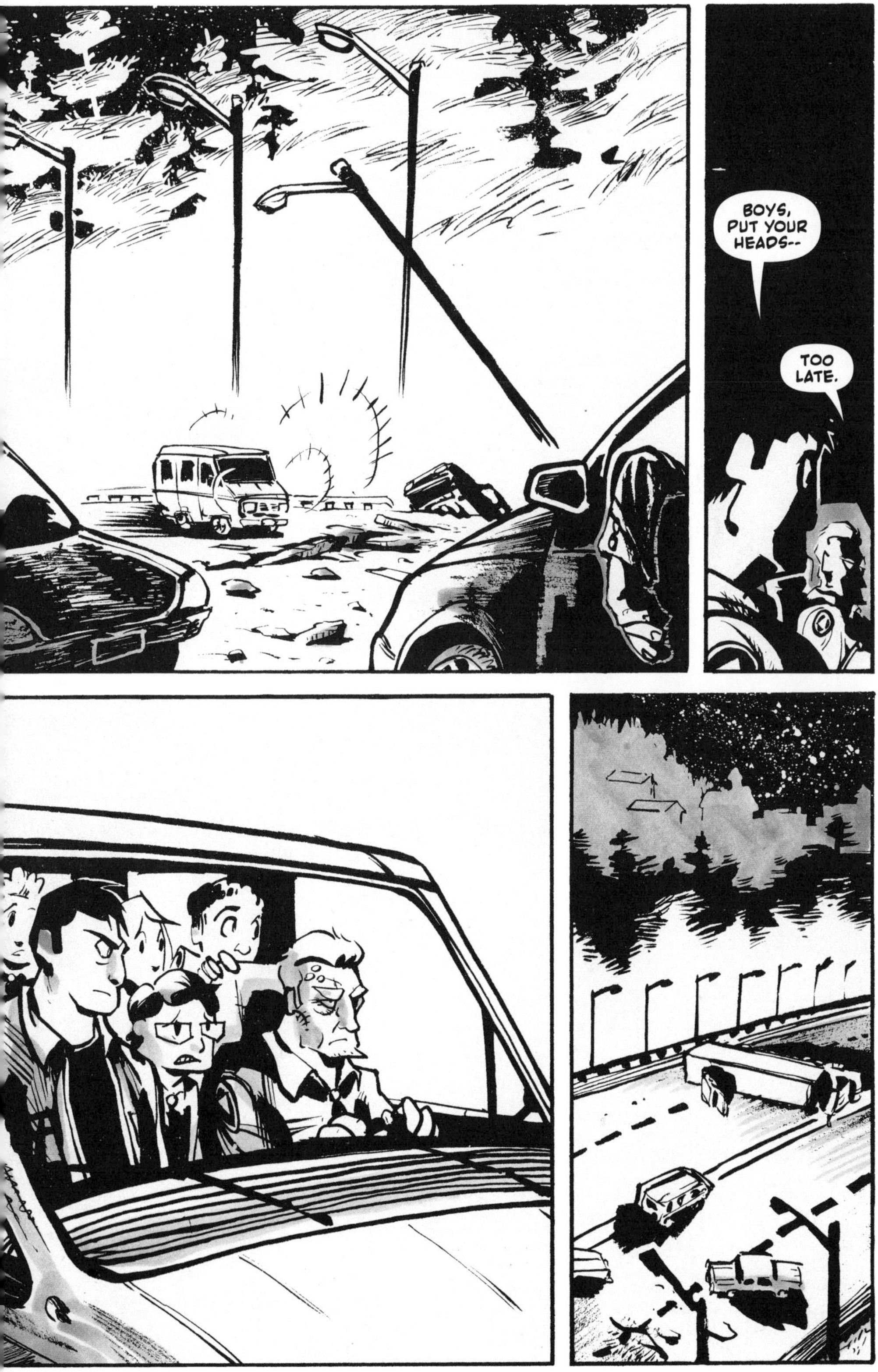
BOYS, PUT YOUR HEADS--
TOO LATE.

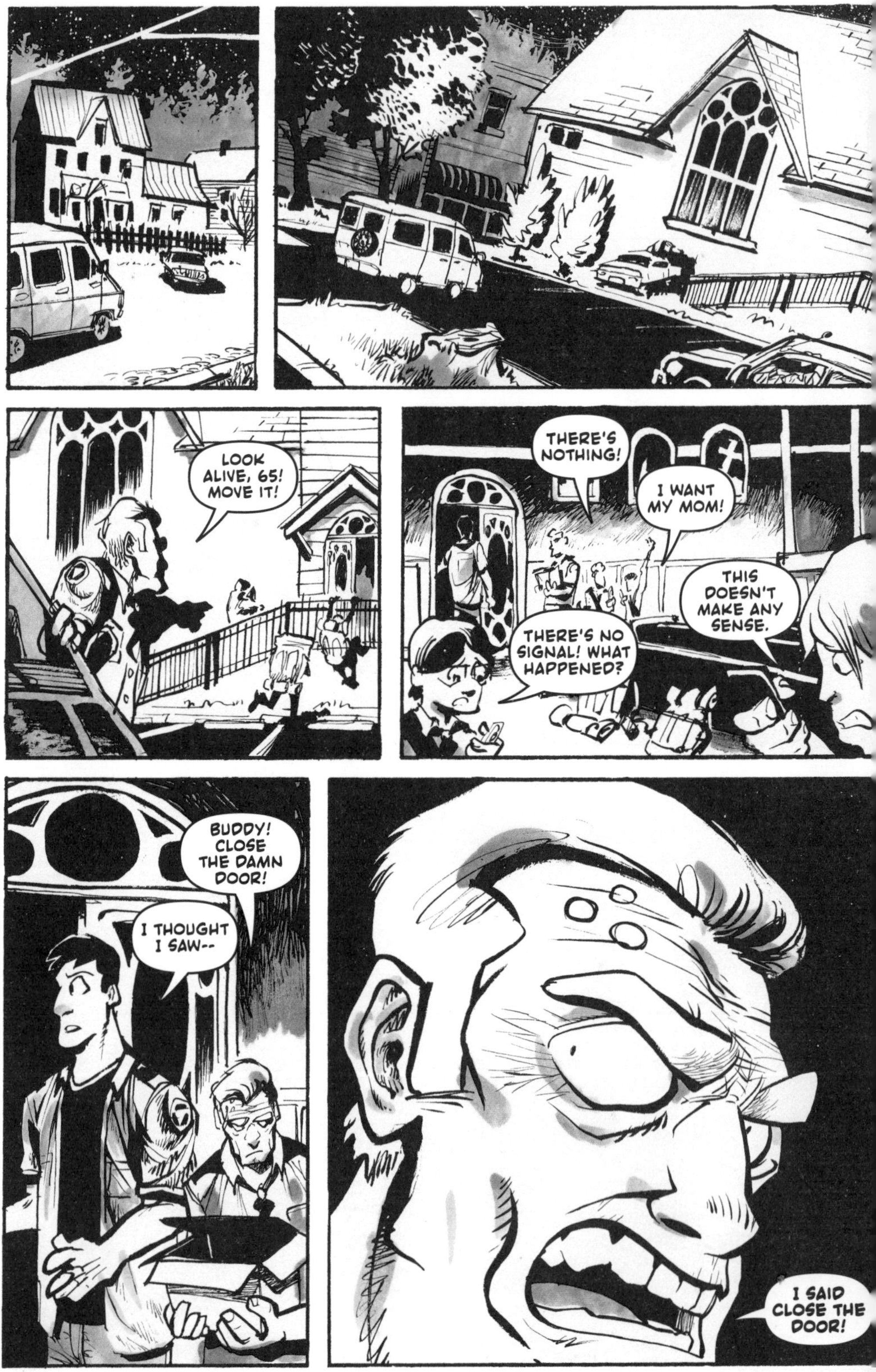
LOOK ALIVE, 65! MOVE IT!
THERE'S NOTHING!
I WANT MY MOM!
THIS DOESN'T MAKE ANY SENSE.
THERE'S NO SIGNAL! WHAT HAPPENED?
BUDDY! CLOSE THE DAMN DOOR!
I THOUGHT I SAW--
I SAID CLOSE THE DOOR!

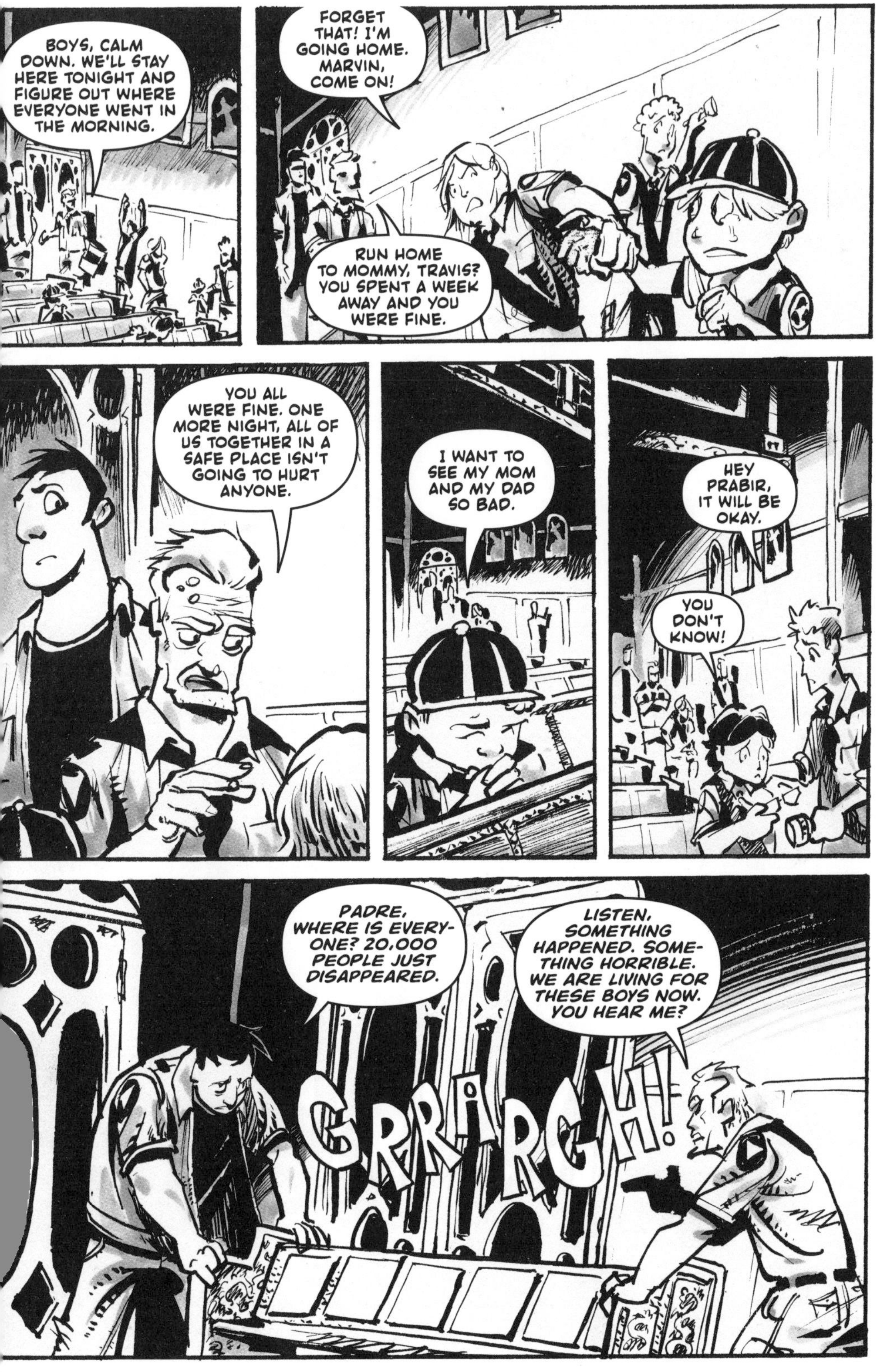
BOYS, CALM DOWN. WE'LL STAY HERE TONIGHT AND FIGURE OUT WHERE EVERYONE WENT IN THE MORNING.
FORGET THAT! I'M GOING HOME. MARVIN, COME ON!
RUN HOME TO MOMMY, TRAVIS? YOU SPENT A WEEK AWAY AND YOU WERE FINE.
YOU ALL WERE FINE. ONE MORE NIGHT, ALL OF US TOGETHER IN A SAFE PLACE ISN'T GOING TO HURT ANYONE.
I WANT TO SEE MY MOM AND MY DAD SO BAD.
HEY PRABIR, IT WILL BE OKAY.
YOU DON'T KNOW!
PADRE, WHERE IS EVERY-ONE? 20,000 PEOPLE JUST DISAPPEARED.
LISTEN. SOMETHING HAPPENED. SOME-THING HORRIBLE. WE ARE LIVING FOR THESE BOYS NOW. YOU HEAR ME?
GRRRRGH!

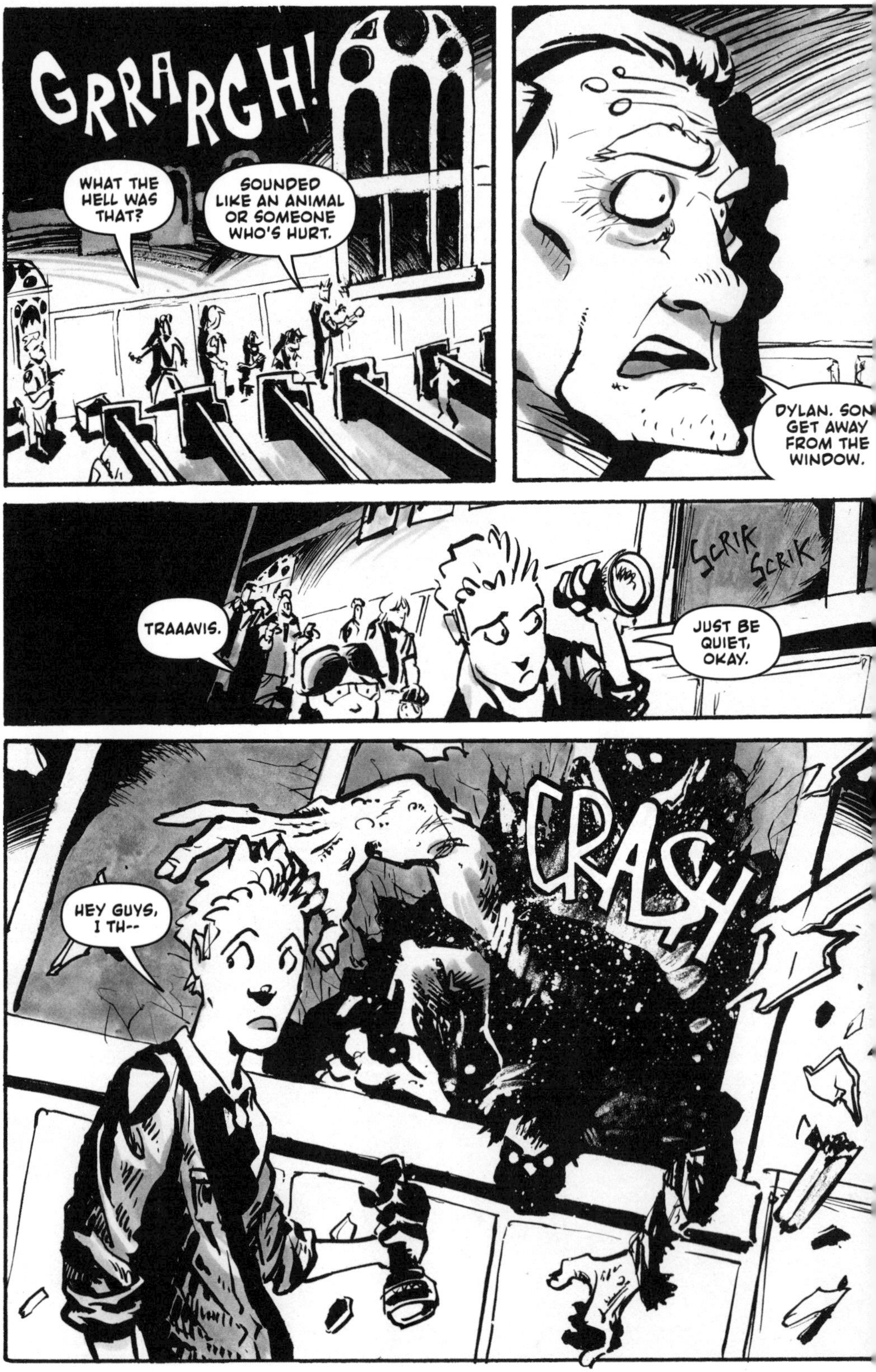
GRRARGH!
WHAT THE HELL WAS THAT?
SOUNDED LIKE AN ANIMAL OR SOMEONE WHO'S HURT.
DYLAN. SON GET AWAY FROM THE WINDOW.
SCRIK SCRIK
TRAAAVIS.
JUST BE QUIET, OKAY.
CRASH
HEY GUYS, I TH--

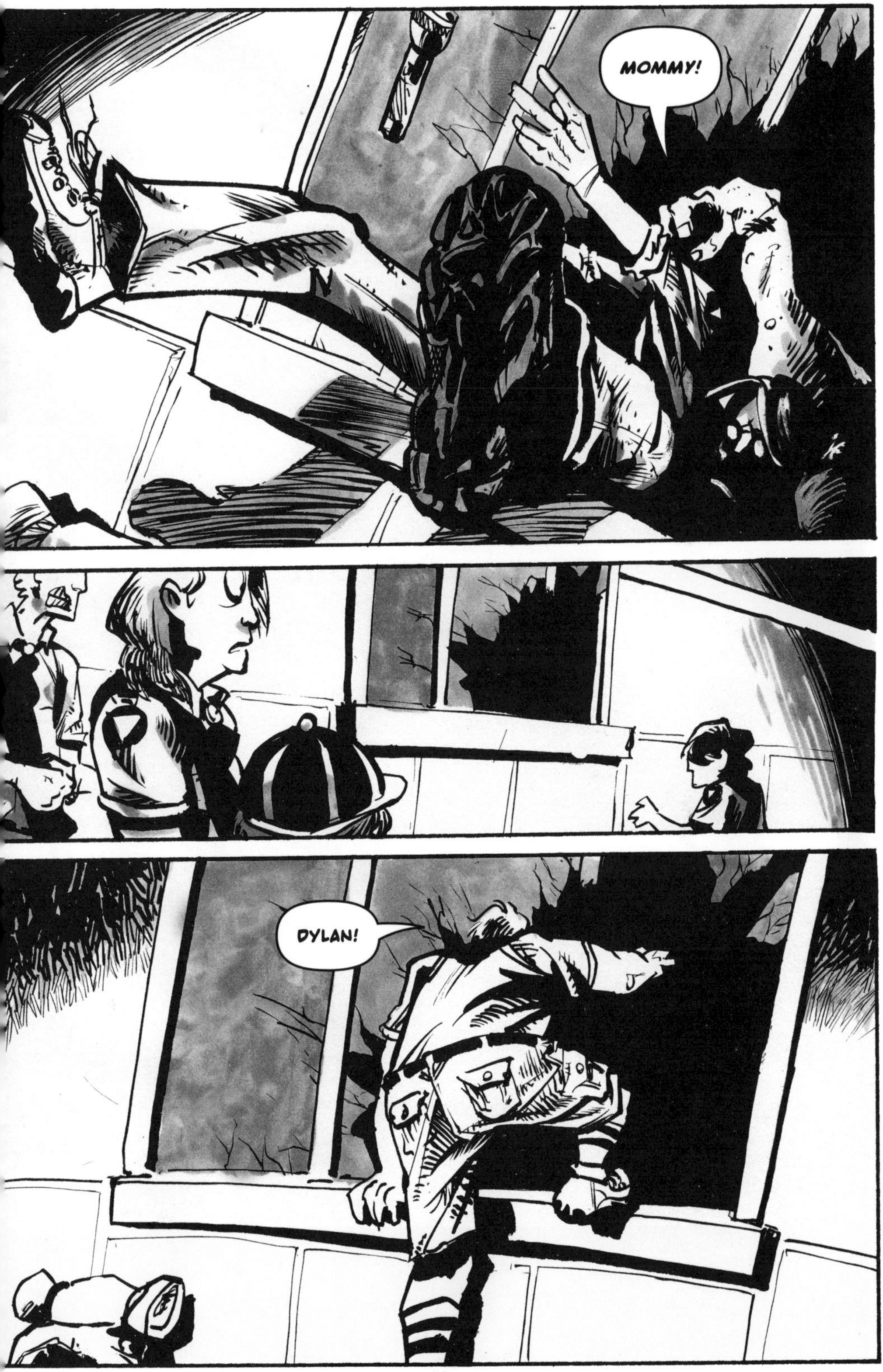
MOMMY!
DYLAN!

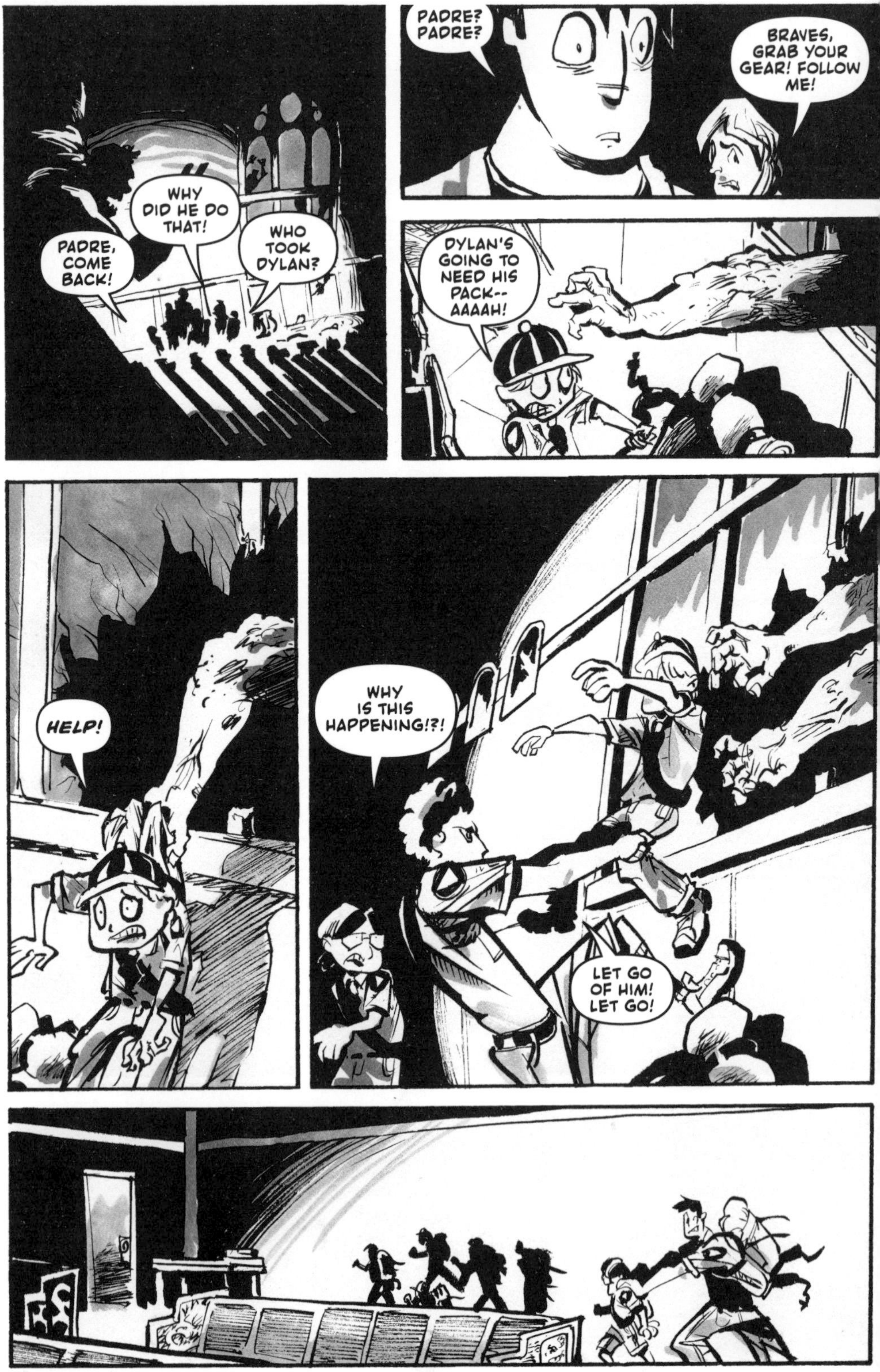
PADRE, COME BACK!
WHY DID HE DO THAT!
WHO TOOK DYLAN?
PADRE? PADRE?
BRAVES, GRAB YOUR GEAR! FOLLOW ME!
DYLAN'S GOING TO NEED HIS PACK-- AAAAH!
HELP!
WHY IS THIS HAPPENING!?!
LET GO OF HIM! LET GO!

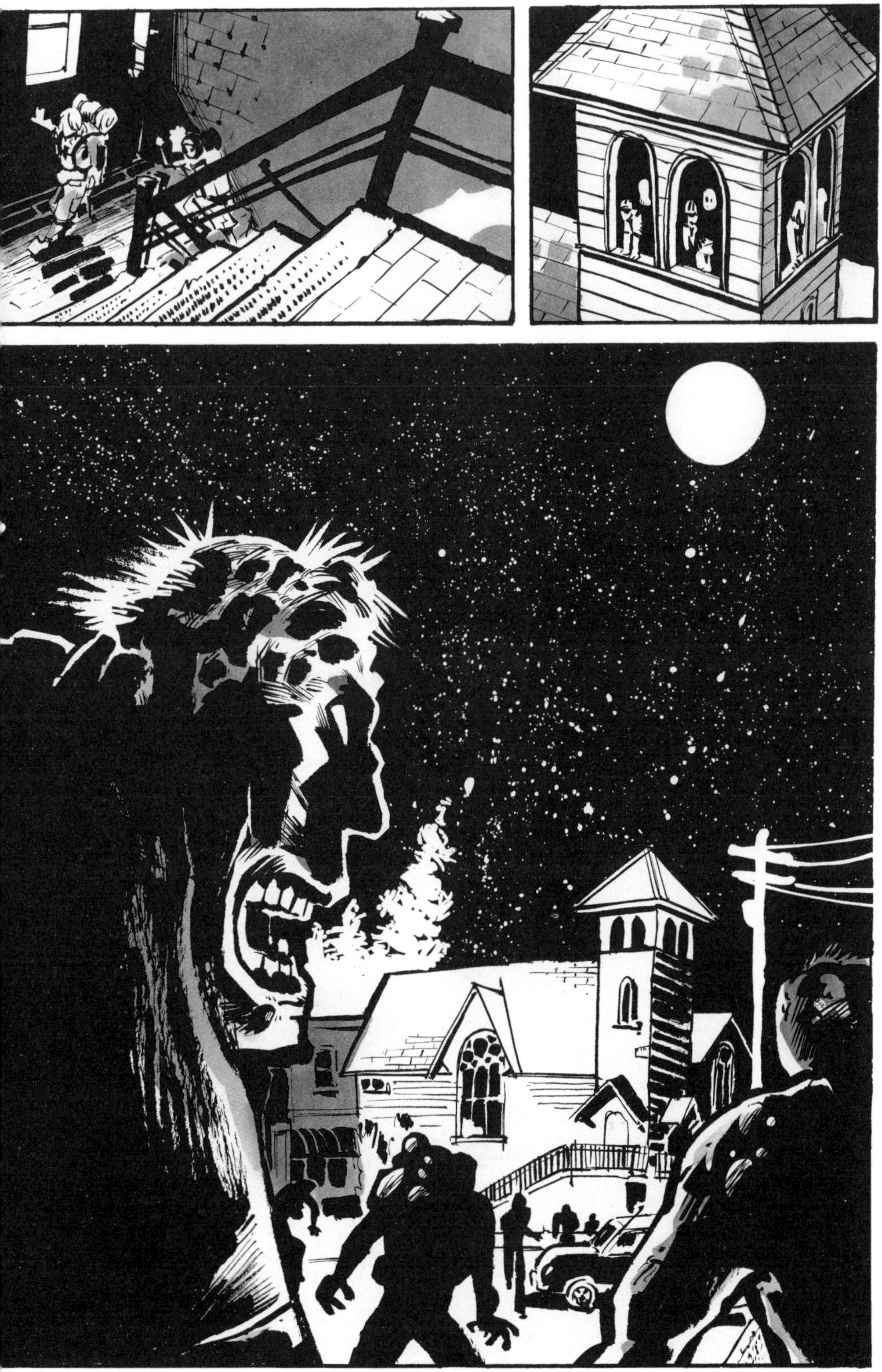

TRAIL MARKERS

A Junior Brave may find himself confronted with a strange path ahead. How will he know which way to proceed? If he's smart, he'll be observant for signs of those that came before him.

For centuries humans have used trail markers as a way to communicate to their fellow traveler. Some American Indians even shaped the very trees themselves into ancient "highway signs" pointing the path to villages or river crossings. Trail "blazes" are also a common form of marking. Although you may think "blaze" in this context refers to "fire," it actually means to cut a marker into the tree itself. Another method is the use of cairns, or pillars of rock, which can be used in areas without trees or plant growth. A favored form of trail marking by the Junior Braves is "posting," the planting of posts—or even simple sticks—in the ground to convey meaning.

On these pages you will find the most common symbols used in marking trails.

×

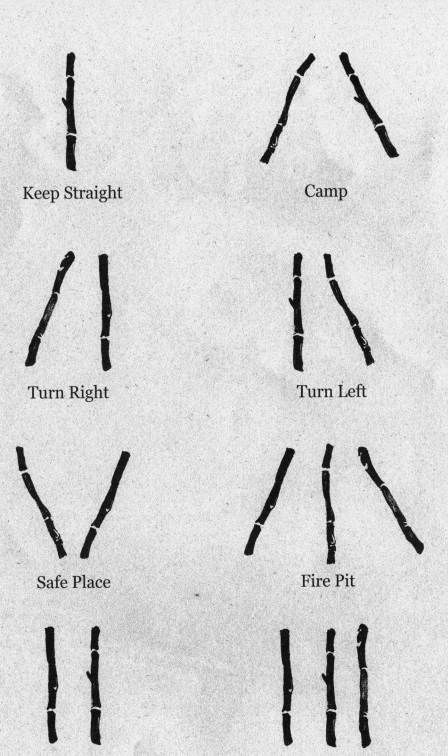

Keep Straight

Camp

Turn Right

Turn Left

Safe Place

Fire Pit

Be Careful

Danger

CHAPTER TWO

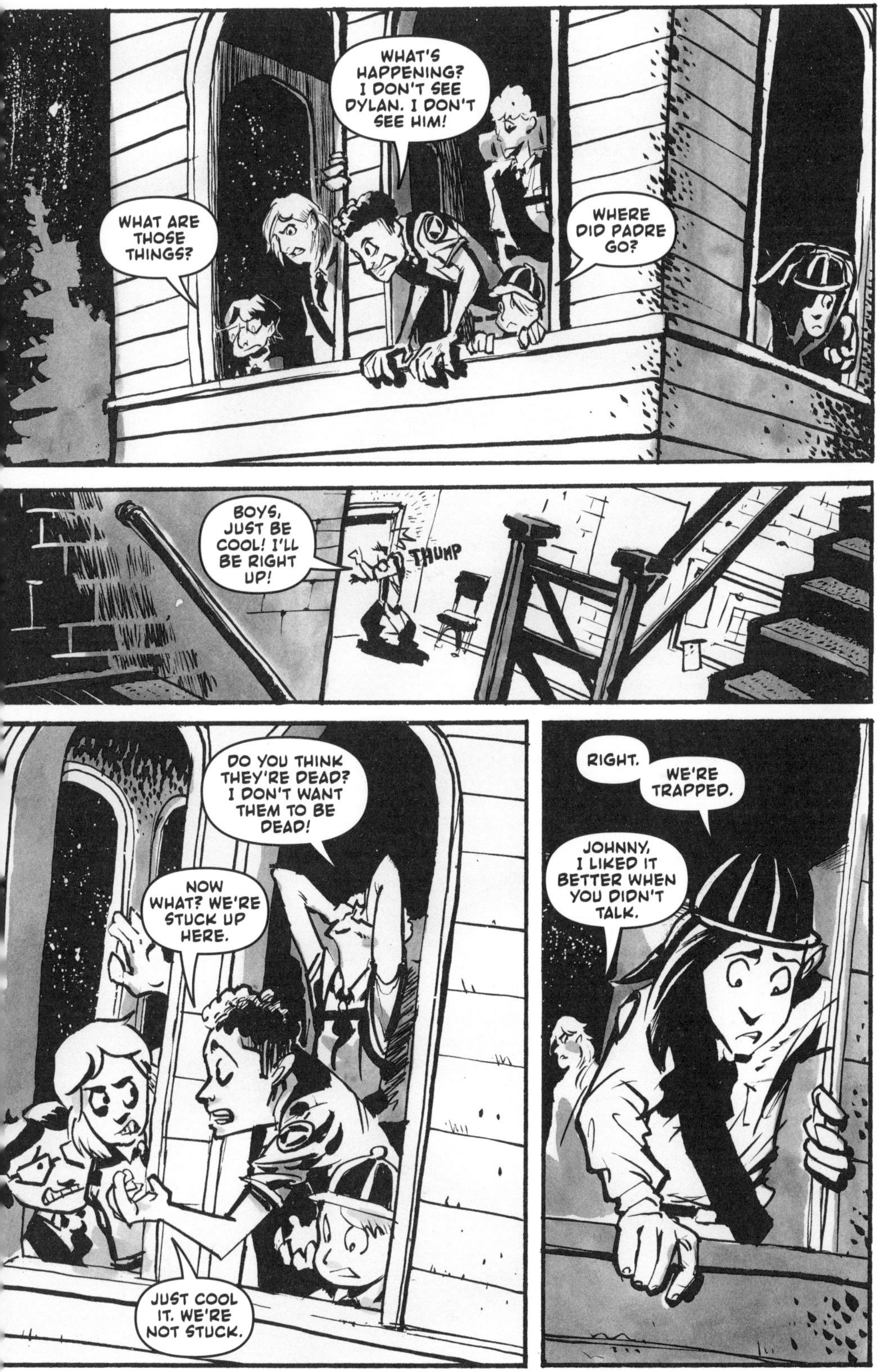
WHAT'S HAPPENING? I DON'T SEE DYLAN. I DON'T SEE HIM!
WHAT ARE THOSE THINGS?
WHERE DID PADRE GO?
BOYS, JUST BE COOL! I'LL BE RIGHT UP!
THUMP
DO YOU THINK THEY'RE DEAD? I DON'T WANT THEM TO BE DEAD!
NOW WHAT? WE'RE STUCK UP HERE.
JUST COOL IT. WE'RE NOT STUCK.
RIGHT.
WE'RE TRAPPED.
JOHNNY, I LIKED IT BETTER WHEN YOU DIDN'T TALK.

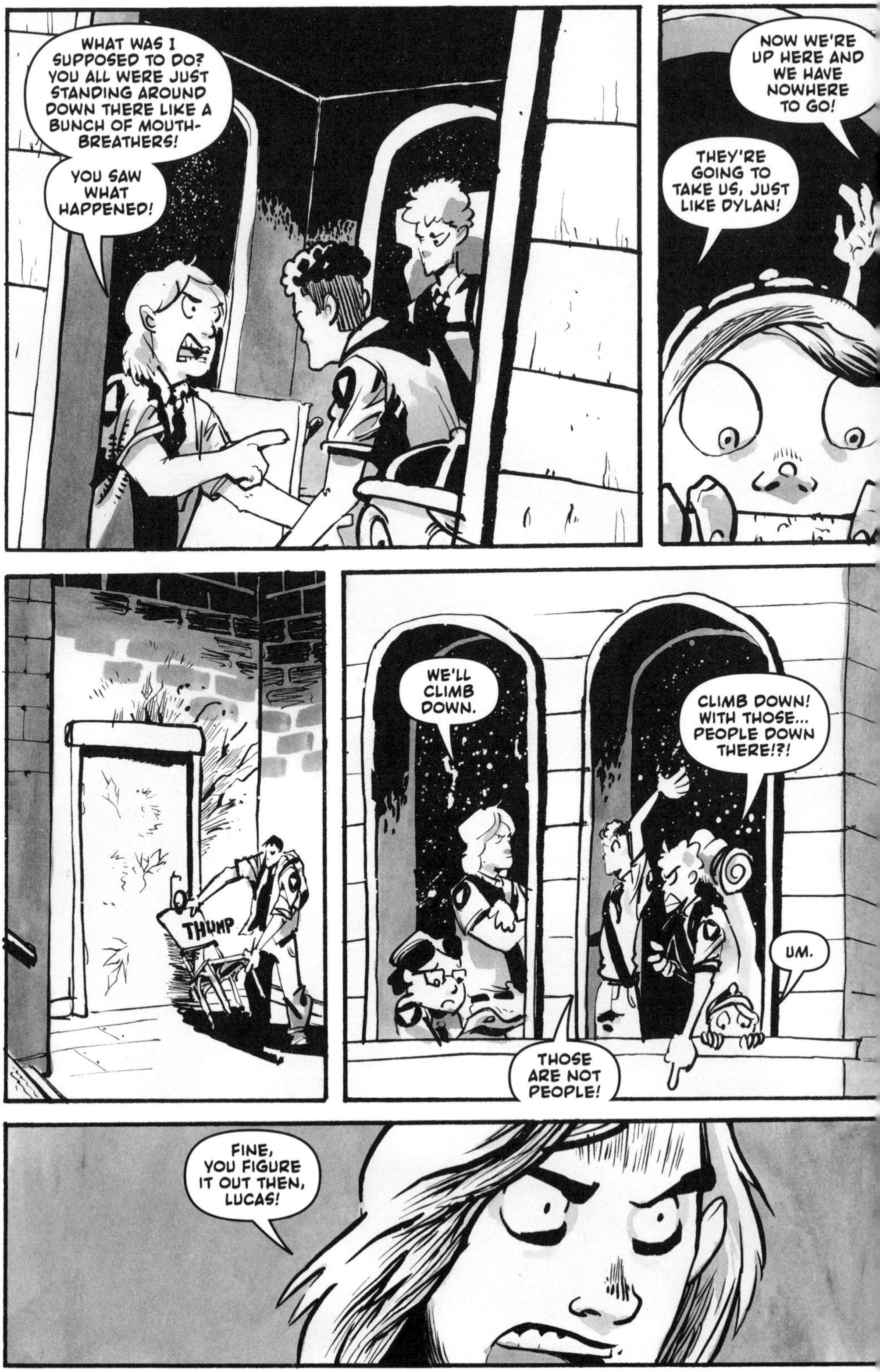
WHAT WAS I SUPPOSED TO DO? YOU ALL WERE JUST STANDING AROUND DOWN THERE LIKE A BUNCH OF MOUTH-BREATHERS!
YOU SAW WHAT HAPPENED!
NOW WE'RE UP HERE AND WE HAVE NOWHERE TO GO!
THEY'RE GOING TO TAKE US, JUST LIKE DYLAN!
THUMP
WE'LL CLIMB DOWN.
CLIMB DOWN! WITH THOSE... PEOPLE DOWN THERE!?!
UM.
THOSE ARE NOT PEOPLE!
FINE, YOU FIGURE IT OUT THEN, LUCAS!

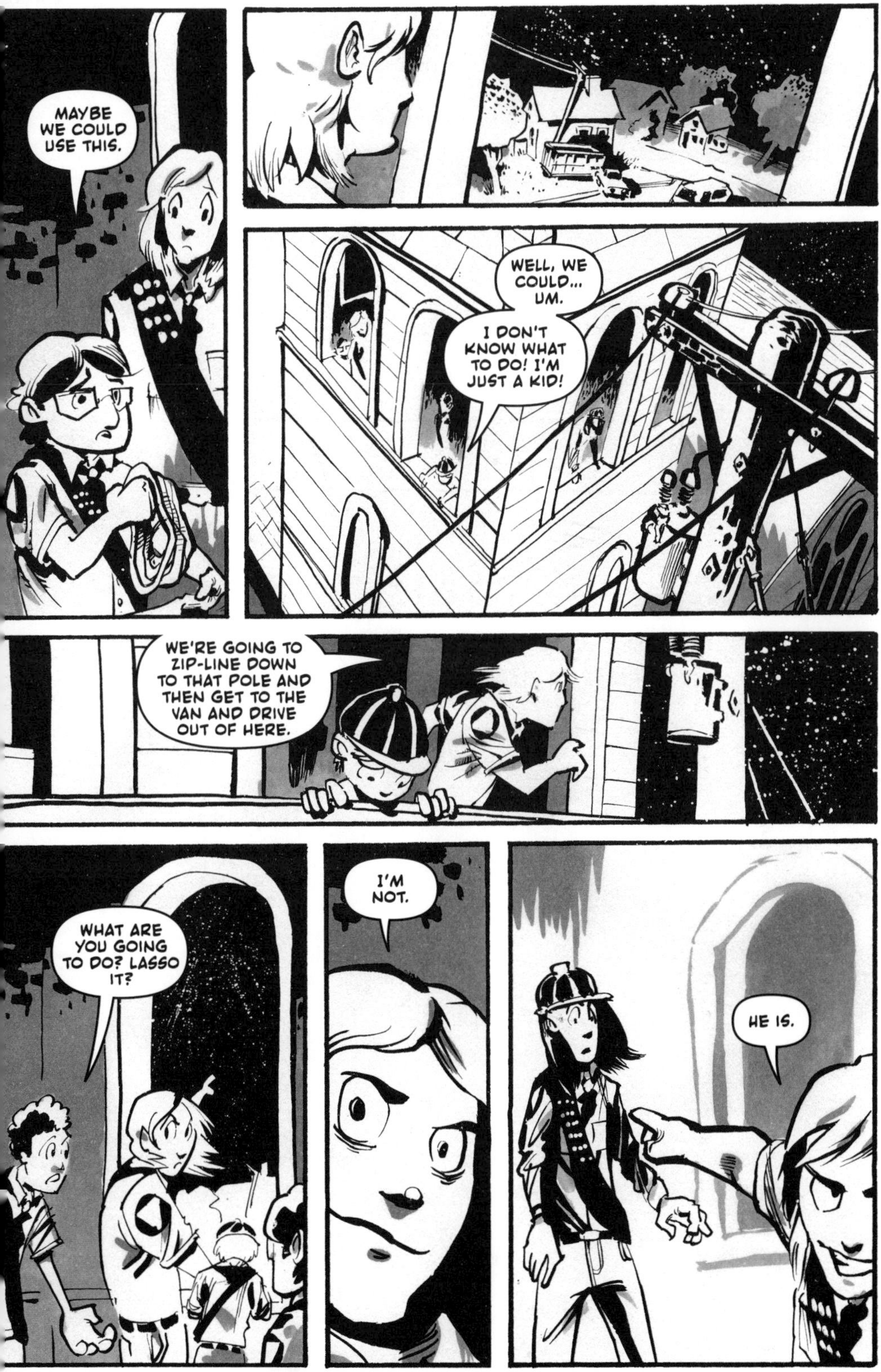
MAYBE WE COULD USE THIS.
WELL, WE COULD... UM.
I DON'T KNOW WHAT TO DO! I'M JUST A KID!
WE'RE GOING TO ZIP-LINE DOWN TO THAT POLE AND THEN GET TO THE VAN AND DRIVE OUT OF HERE.
WHAT ARE YOU GOING TO DO? LASSO IT?
I'M NOT.
HE IS.

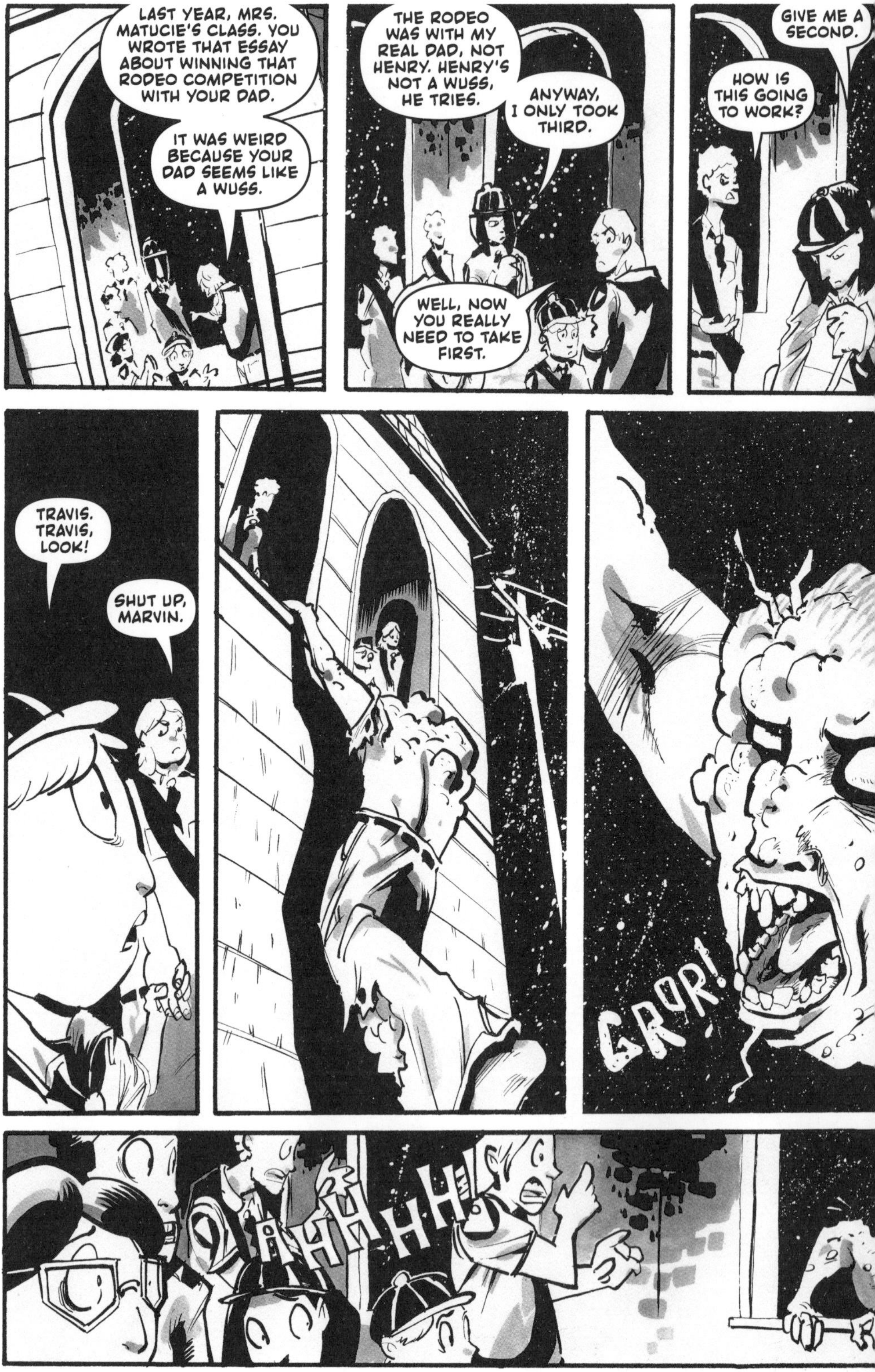
LAST YEAR, MRS. MATUCIE'S CLASS. YOU WROTE THAT ESSAY ABOUT WINNING THAT RODEO COMPETITION WITH YOUR DAD.
IT WAS WEIRD BECAUSE YOUR DAD SEEMS LIKE A WUSS.
THE RODEO WAS WITH MY REAL DAD, NOT HENRY. HENRY'S NOT A WUSS, HE TRIES.
ANYWAY, I ONLY TOOK THIRD.
WELL, NOW YOU REALLY NEED TO TAKE FIRST.
GIVE ME A SECOND.
HOW IS THIS GOING TO WORK?
TRAVIS. TRAVIS, LOOK!
SHUT UP, MARVIN.
GRoR!
AHHHHHH!

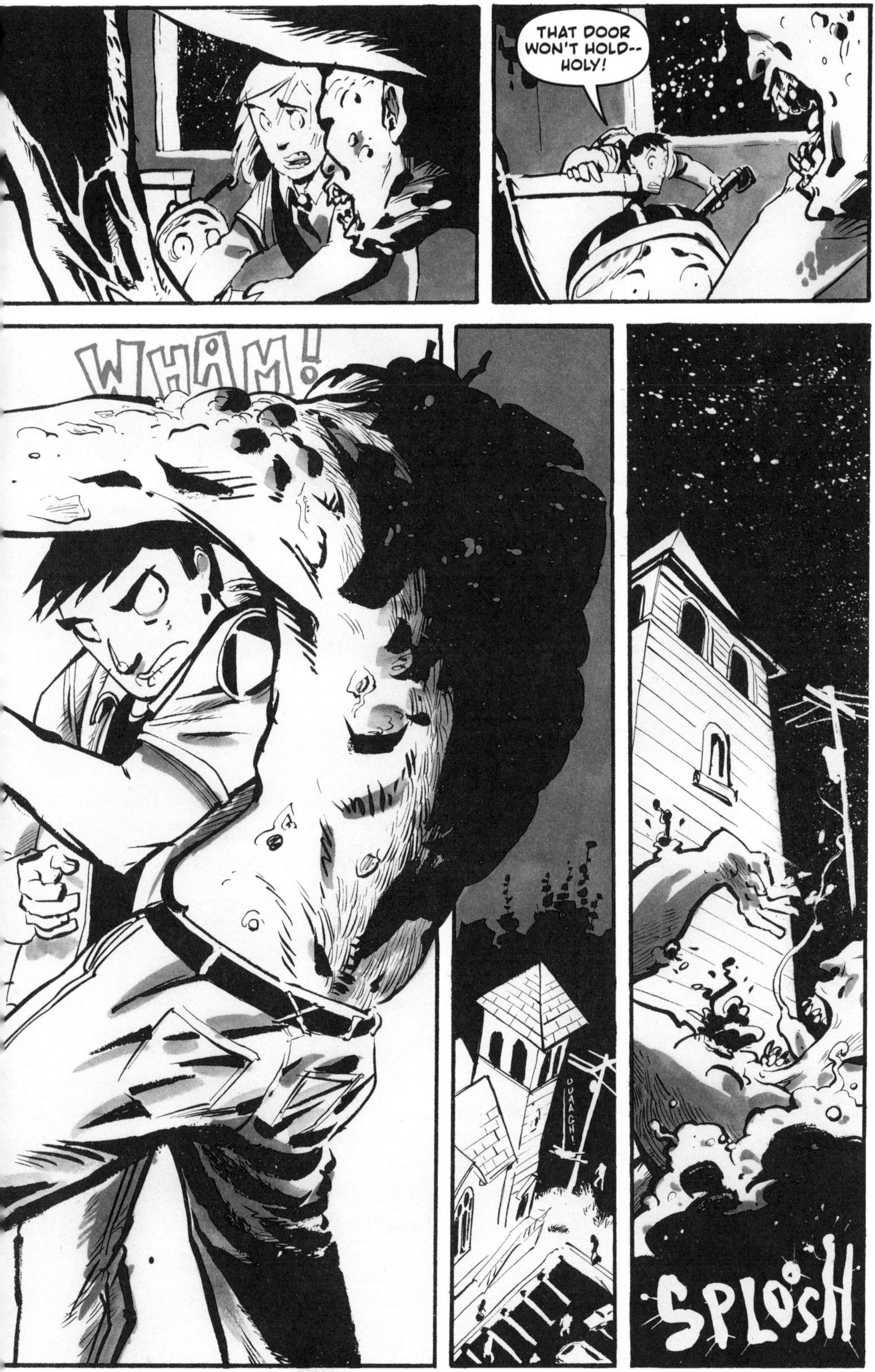
THAT DOOR WON'T HOLD-- HOLY!
WHAM!
UUAAGH!
SPLOSH

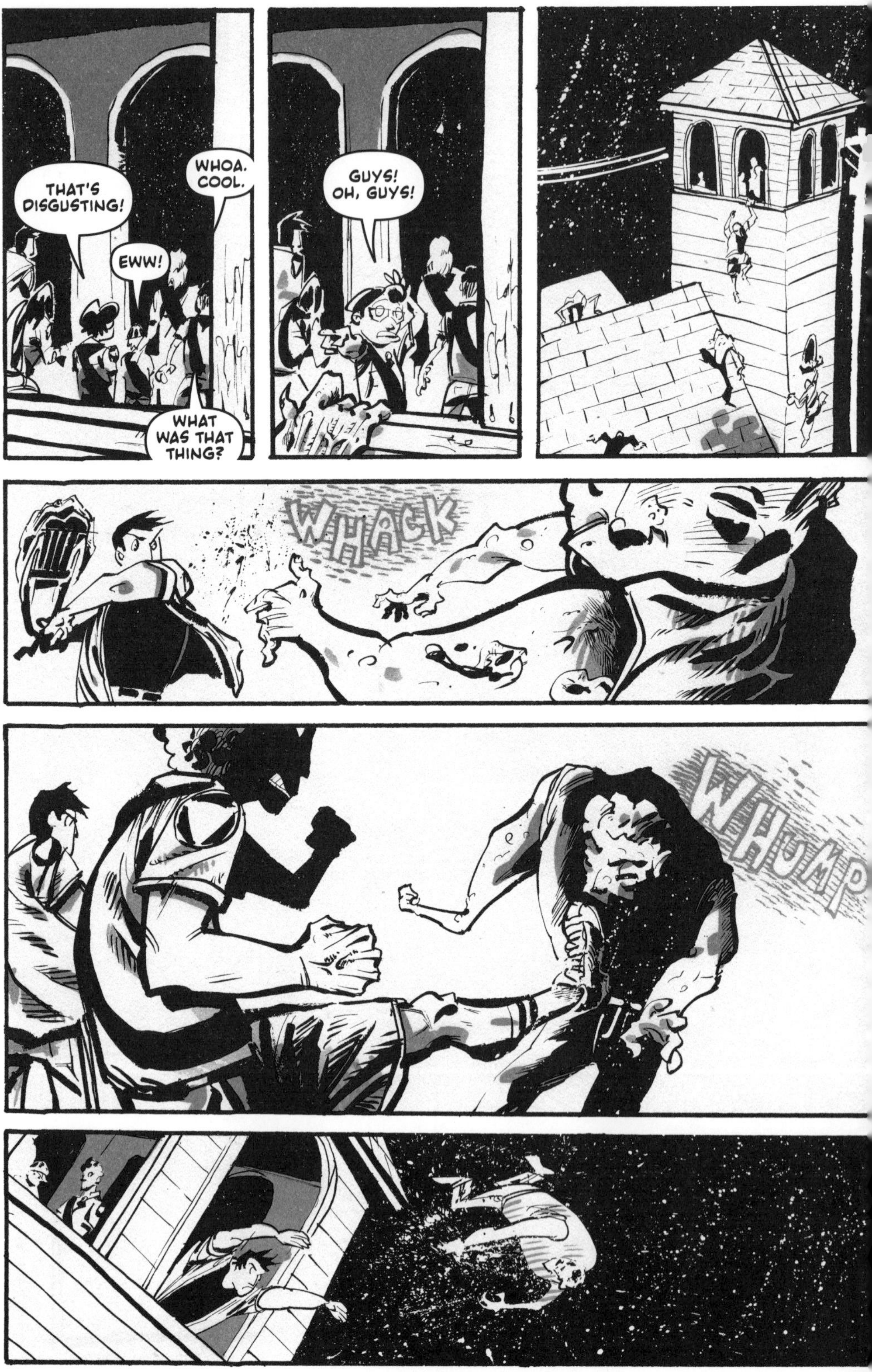
THAT'S DISGUSTING!
EWW!
WHOA. COOL.
WHAT WAS THAT THING?
GUYS! OH, GUYS!
WHACK
WHUMP

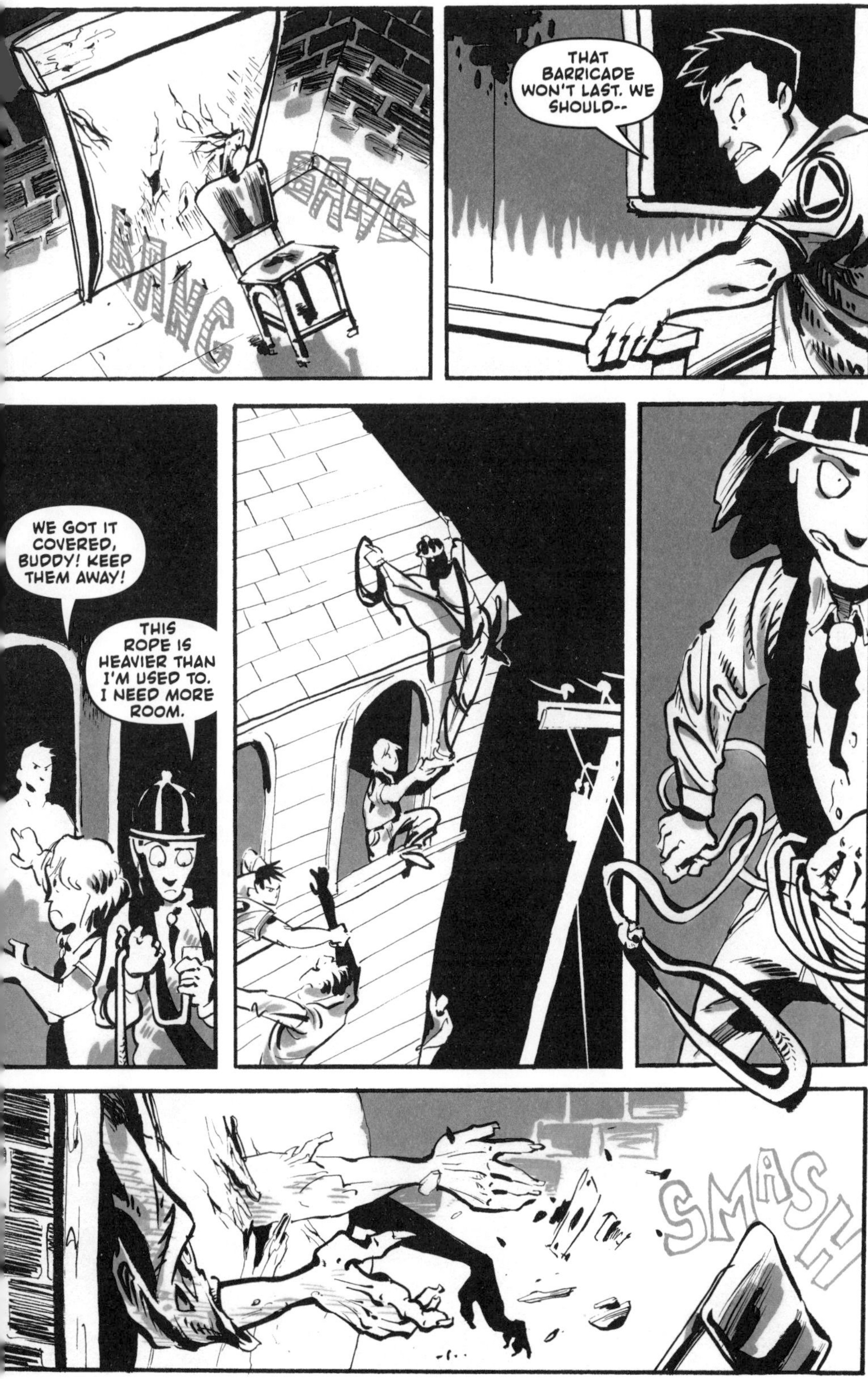
BANG
BANG
THAT BARRICADE WON'T LAST. WE SHOULD--
WE GOT IT COVERED, BUDDY! KEEP THEM AWAY!
THIS ROPE IS HEAVIER THAN I'M USED TO. I NEED MORE ROOM.
SMASH

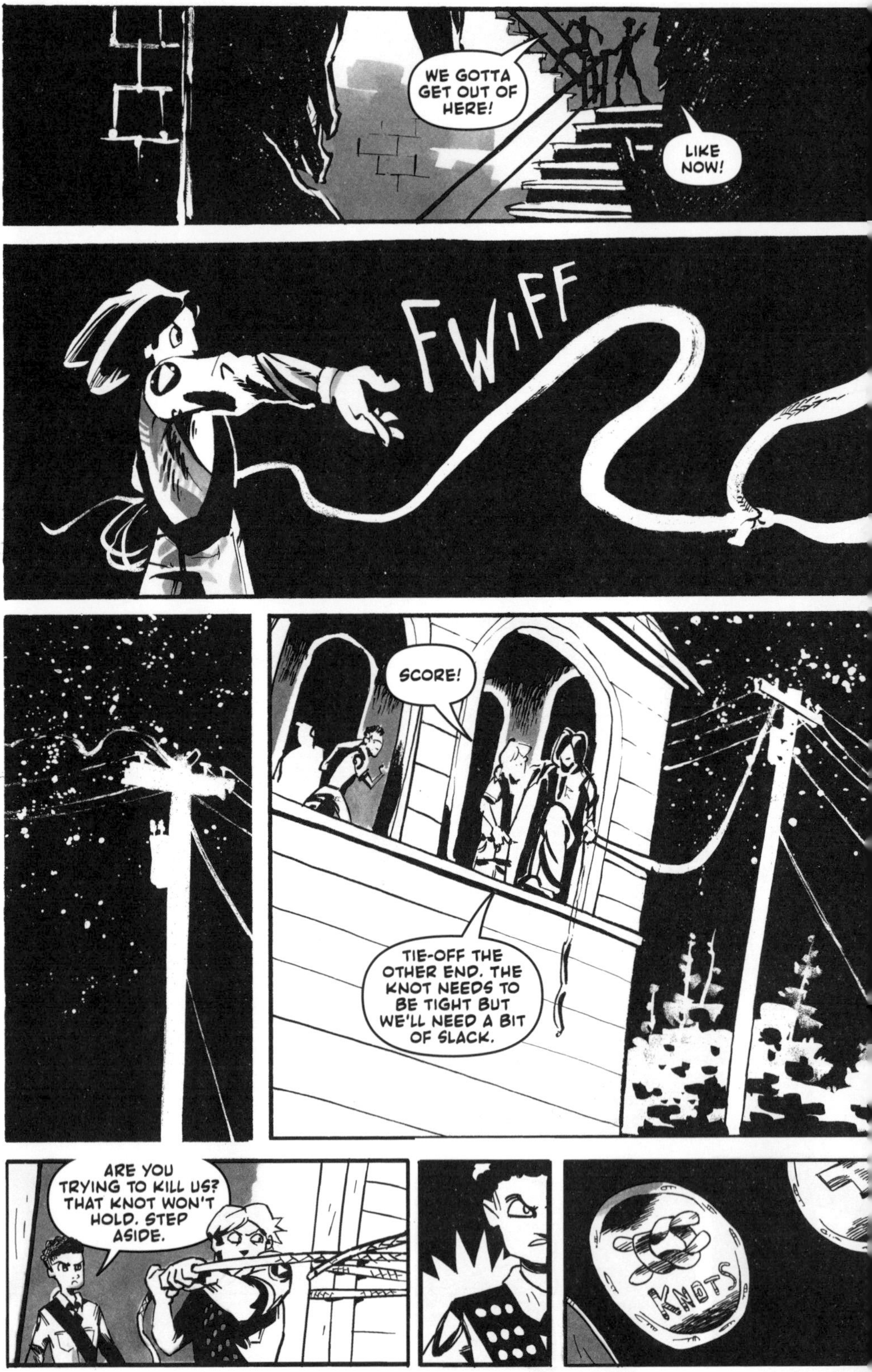
WE GOTTA GET OUT OF HERE!
LIKE NOW!
FWIFF
SCORE!
TIE-OFF THE OTHER END. THE KNOT NEEDS TO BE TIGHT BUT WE'LL NEED A BIT OF SLACK.
ARE YOU TRYING TO KILL US? THAT KNOT WON'T HOLD. STEP ASIDE.
KNOTS

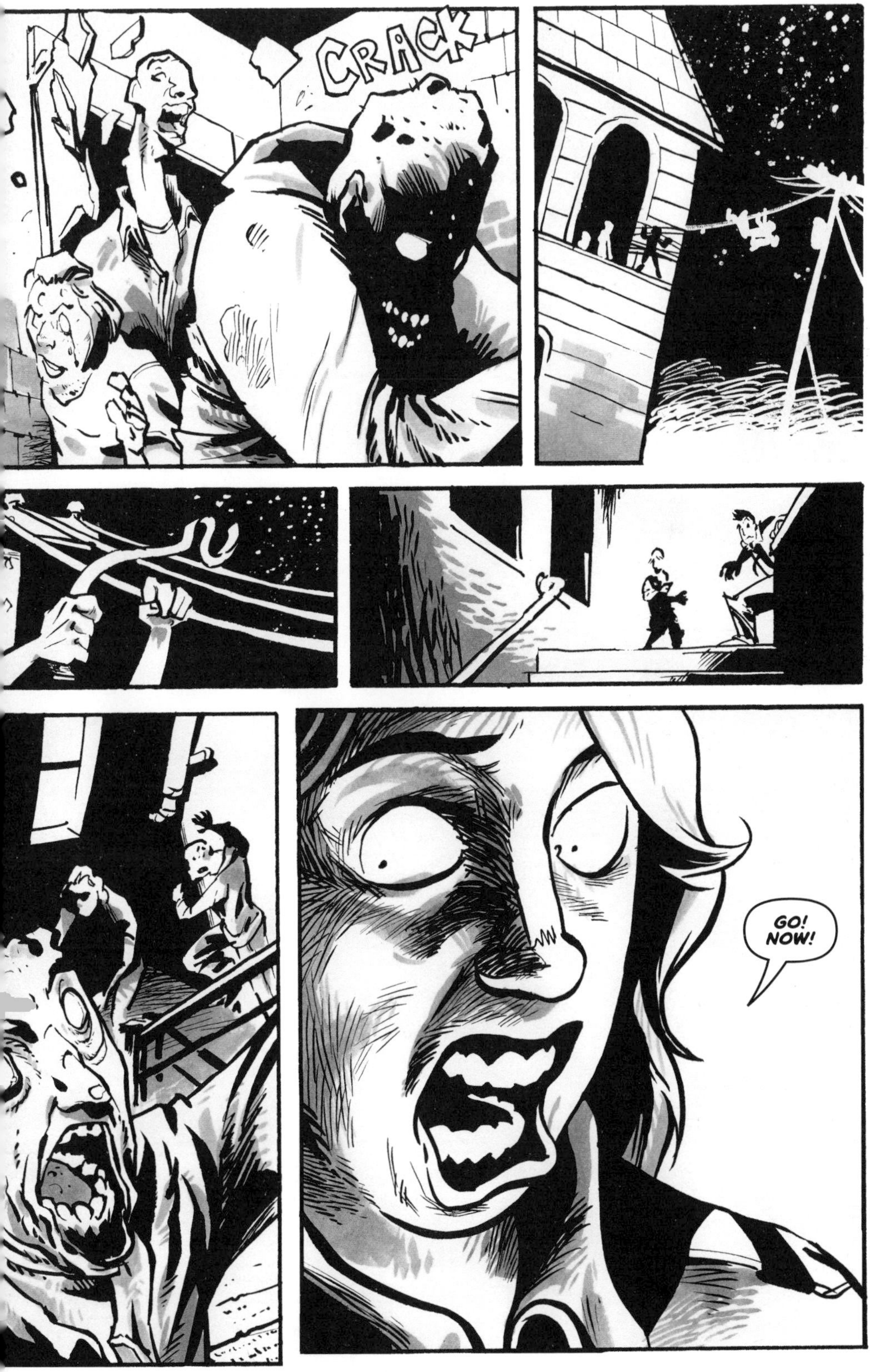
CRACK
GO!
NOW!

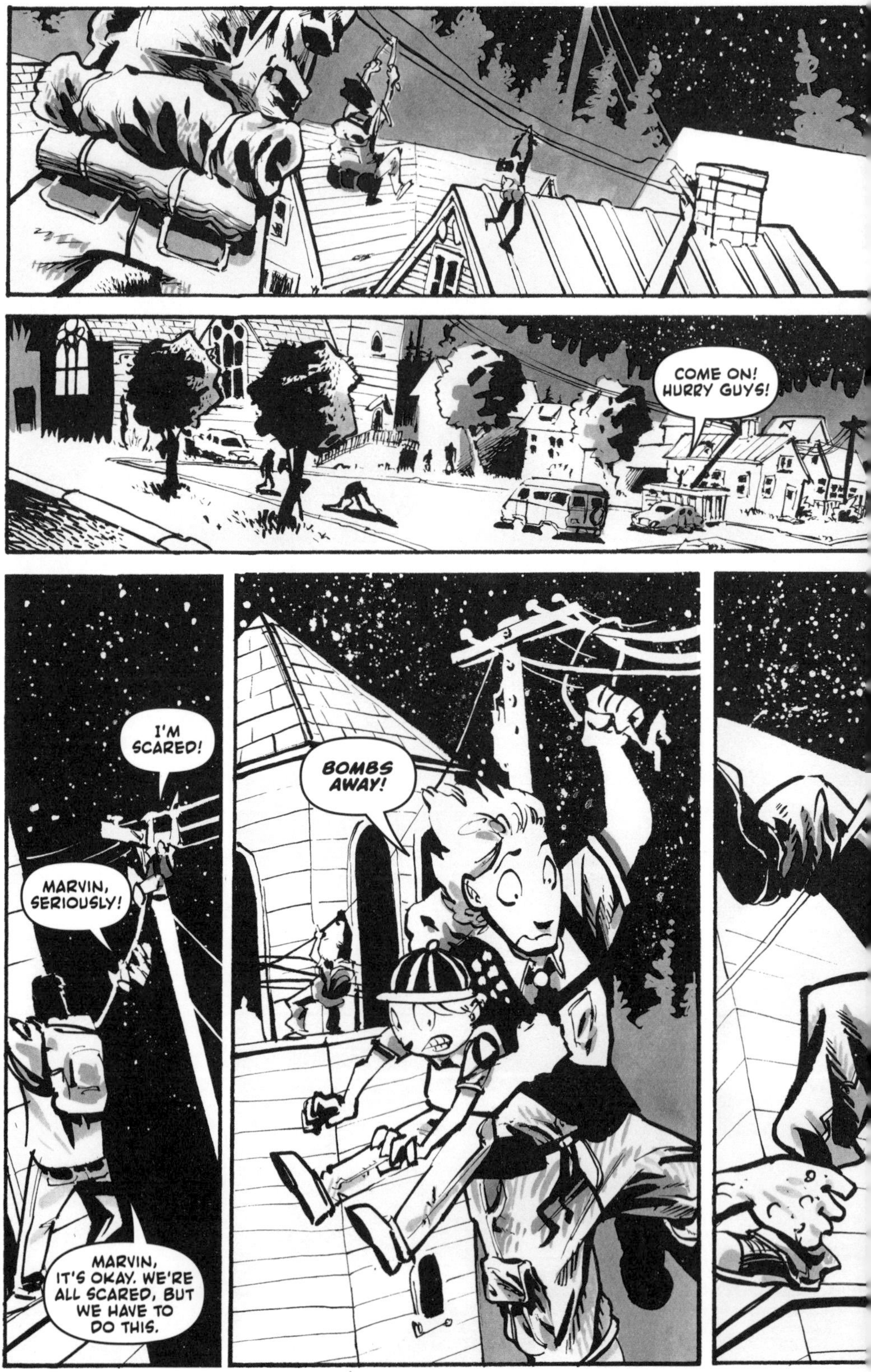
COME ON! HURRY GUYS!
I'M SCARED!
MARVIN, SERIOUSLY!
MARVIN, IT'S OKAY. WE'RE ALL SCARED, BUT WE HAVE TO DO THIS.
BOMBS AWAY!

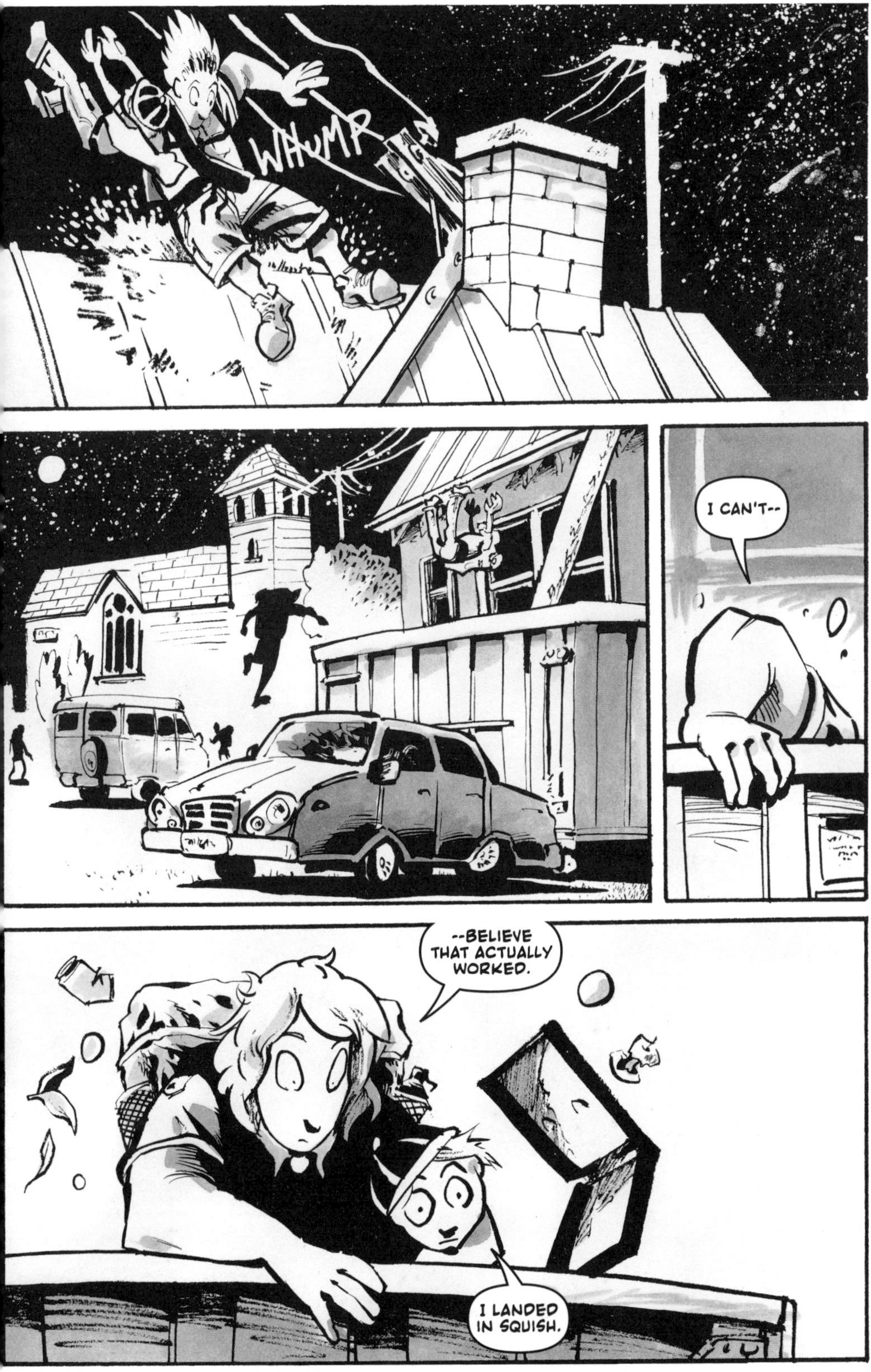
WHUMP
I CAN'T--
--BELIEVE THAT ACTUALLY WORKED.
I LANDED IN SQUISH.

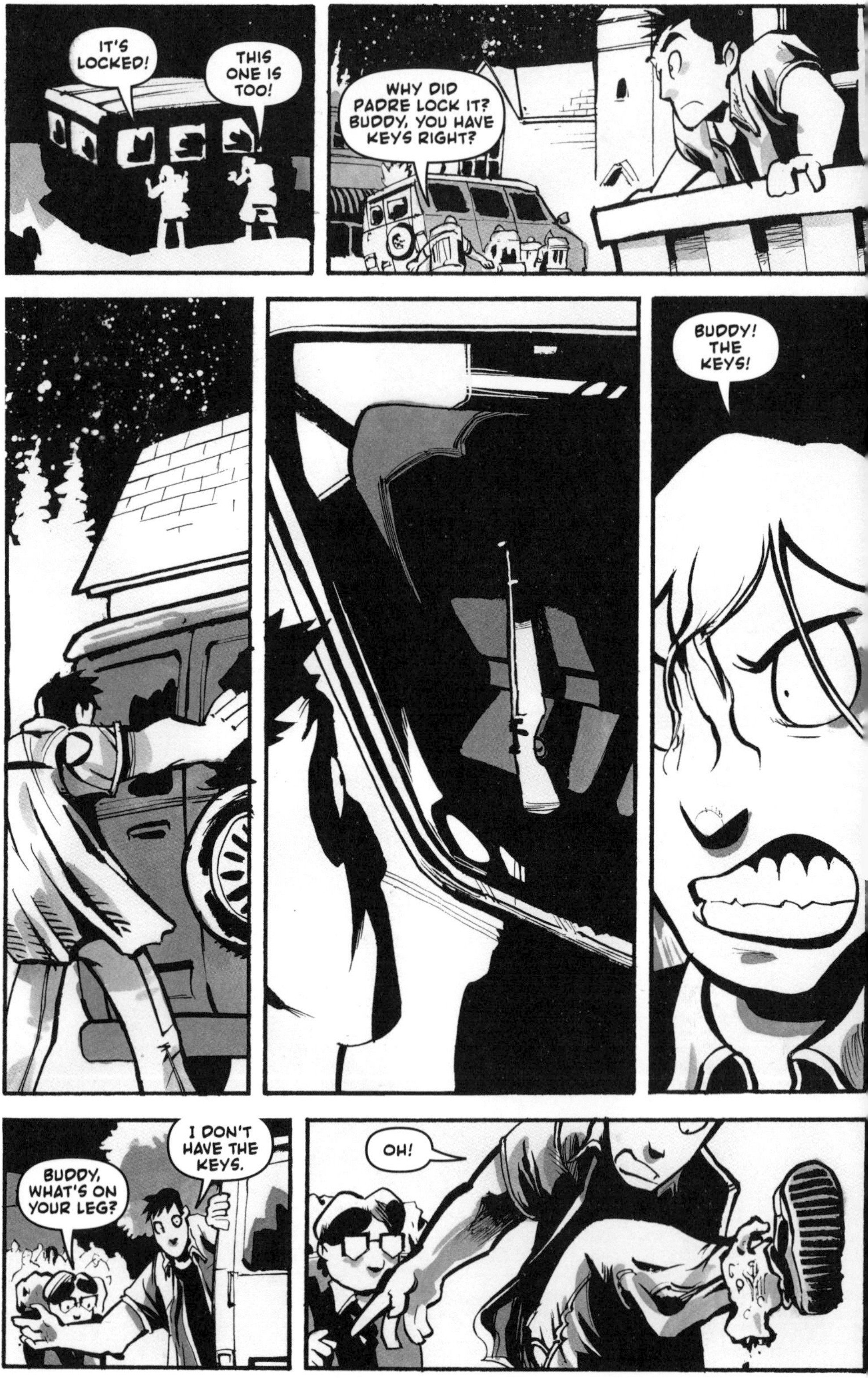
IT'S LOCKED!
THIS ONE IS TOO!
WHY DID PADRE LOCK IT? BUDDY, YOU HAVE KEYS RIGHT?
BUDDY! THE KEYS!
I DON'T HAVE THE KEYS.
BUDDY, WHAT'S ON YOUR LEG?
OH!

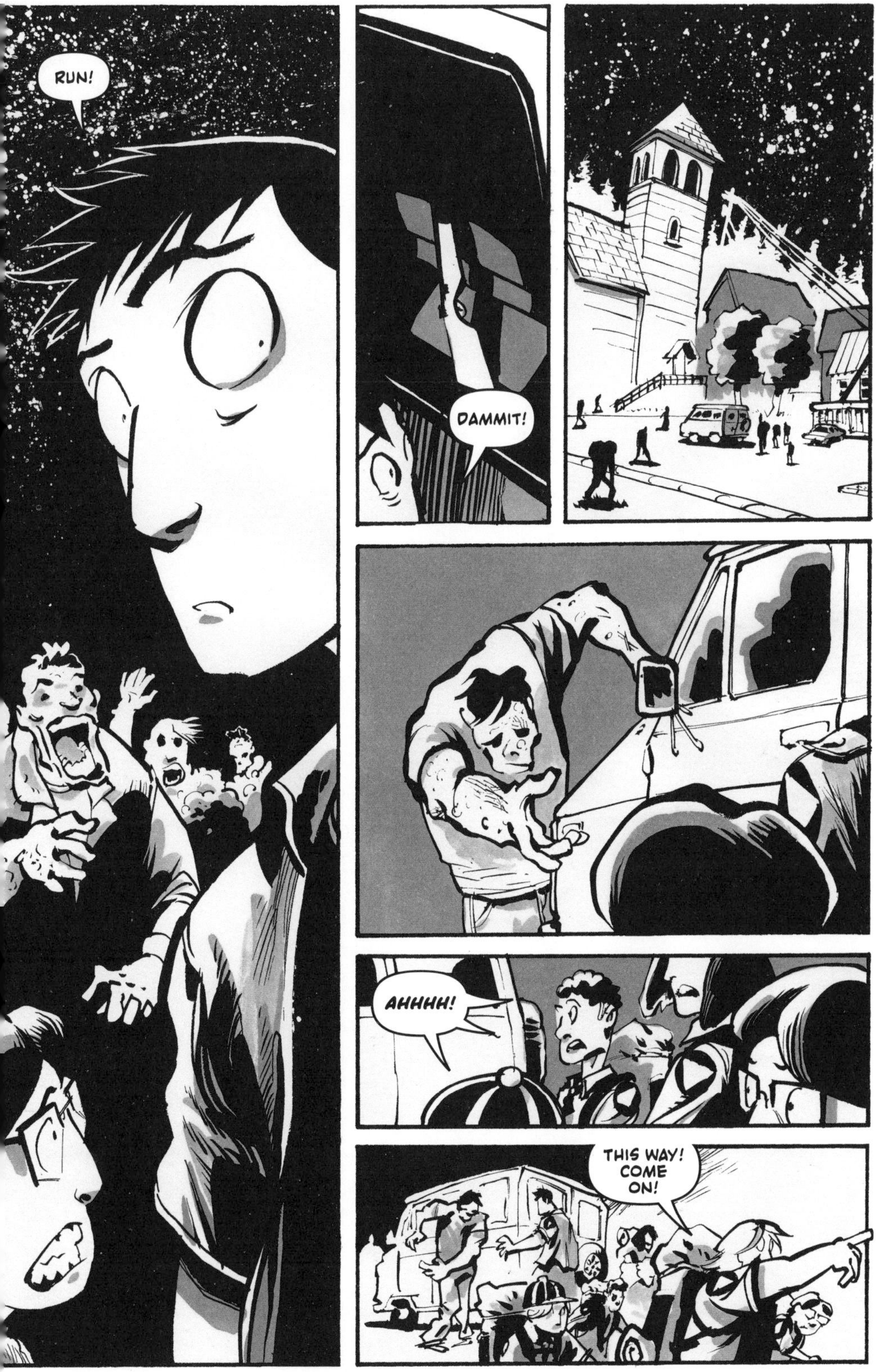
RUN!
DAMMIT!
AHHHH!
THIS WAY! COME ON!

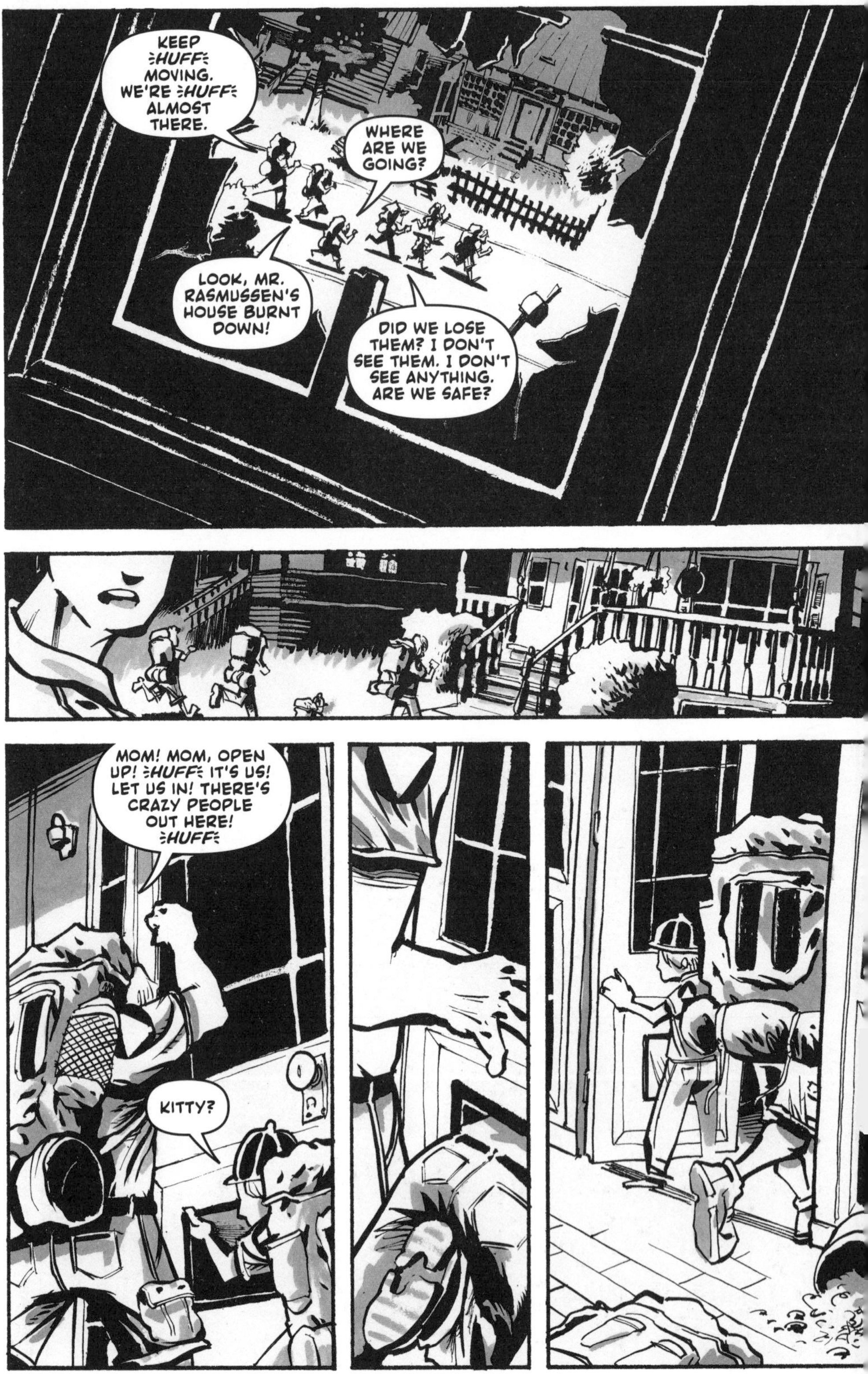
KEEP ≈HUFF≈ MOVING. WE'RE ≈HUFF≈ ALMOST THERE.
WHERE ARE WE GOING?
LOOK, MR. RASMUSSEN'S HOUSE BURNT DOWN!
DID WE LOSE THEM? I DON'T SEE THEM. I DON'T SEE ANYTHING. ARE WE SAFE?
MOM! MOM, OPEN UP! ≈HUFF≈ IT'S US! LET US IN! THERE'S CRAZY PEOPLE OUT HERE! ≈HUFF≈
KITTY?

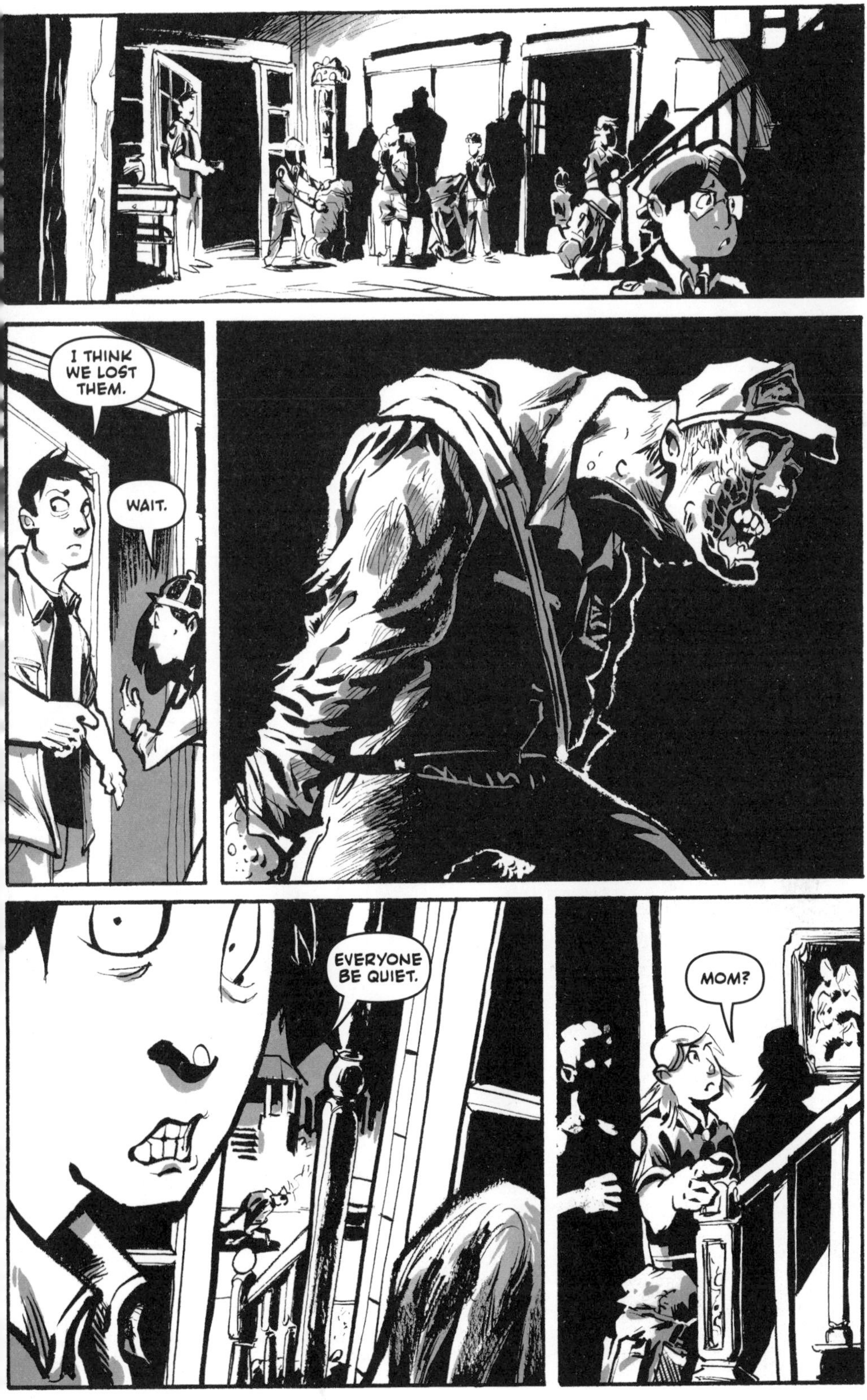
I THINK WE LOST THEM.
WAIT.
EVERYONE BE QUIET.
MOM?

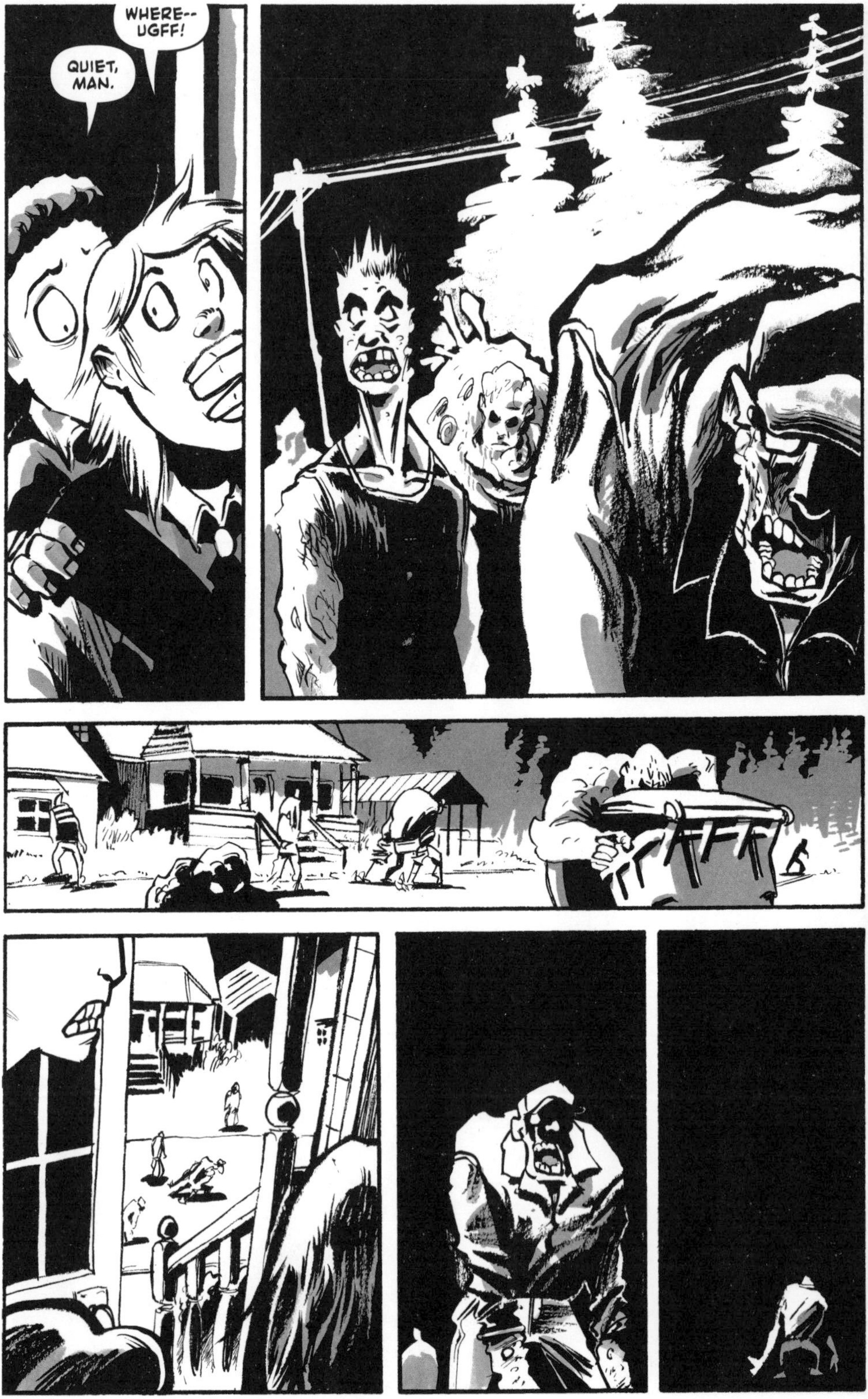
WHERE--
UGFF!
QUIET,
MAN.

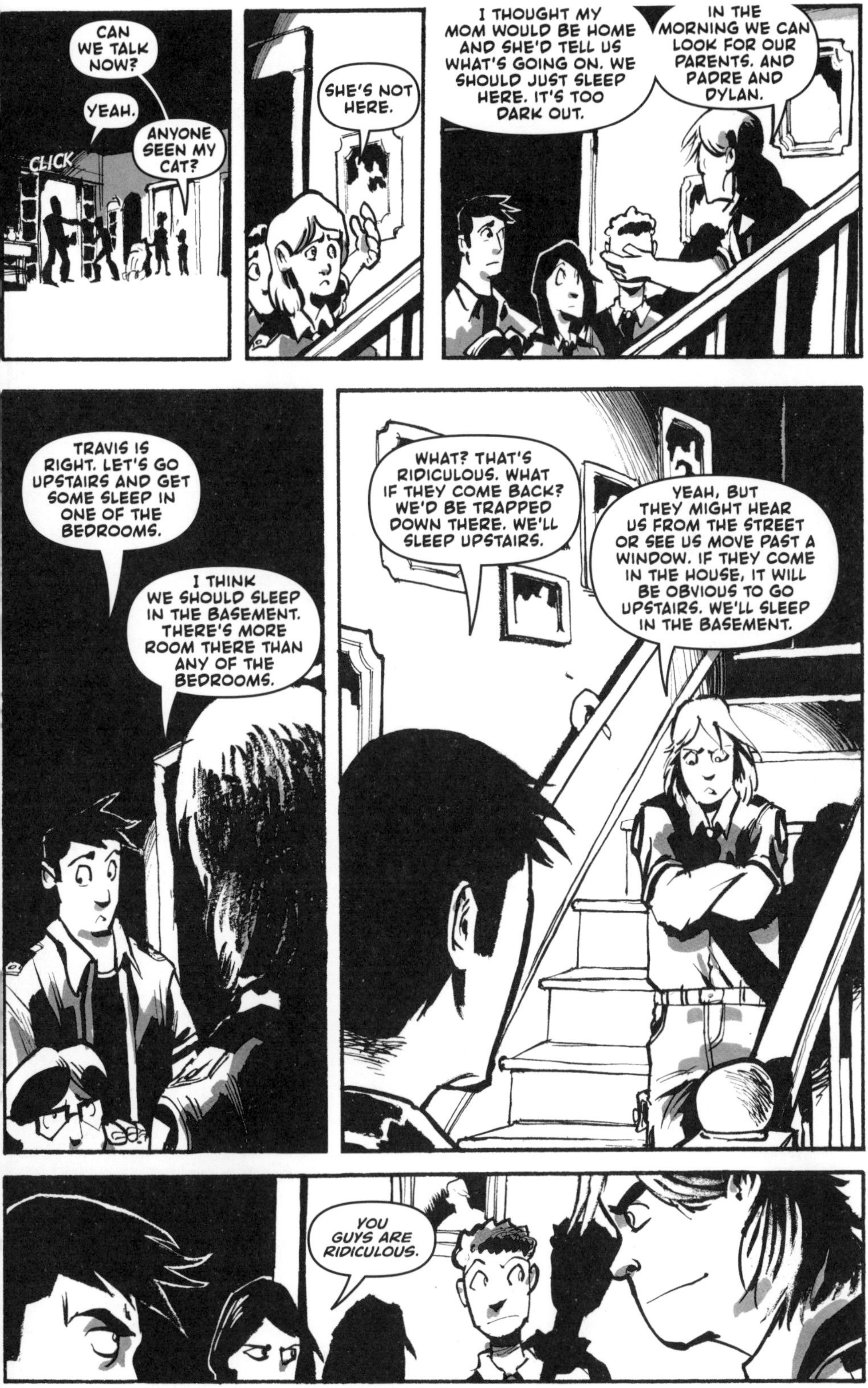
CAN WE TALK NOW?
YEAH.
ANYONE SEEN MY CAT?
CLICK
SHE'S NOT HERE.
I THOUGHT MY MOM WOULD BE HOME AND SHE'D TELL US WHAT'S GOING ON. WE SHOULD JUST SLEEP HERE. IT'S TOO DARK OUT.
IN THE MORNING WE CAN LOOK FOR OUR PARENTS. AND PADRE AND DYLAN.
TRAVIS IS RIGHT. LET'S GO UPSTAIRS AND GET SOME SLEEP IN ONE OF THE BEDROOMS.
I THINK WE SHOULD SLEEP IN THE BASEMENT. THERE'S MORE ROOM THERE THAN ANY OF THE BEDROOMS.
WHAT? THAT'S RIDICULOUS. WHAT IF THEY COME BACK? WE'D BE TRAPPED DOWN THERE. WE'LL SLEEP UPSTAIRS.
YEAH, BUT THEY MIGHT HEAR US FROM THE STREET OR SEE US MOVE PAST A WINDOW. IF THEY COME IN THE HOUSE, IT WILL BE OBVIOUS TO GO UPSTAIRS. WE'LL SLEEP IN THE BASEMENT.
YOU GUYS ARE RIDICULOUS.

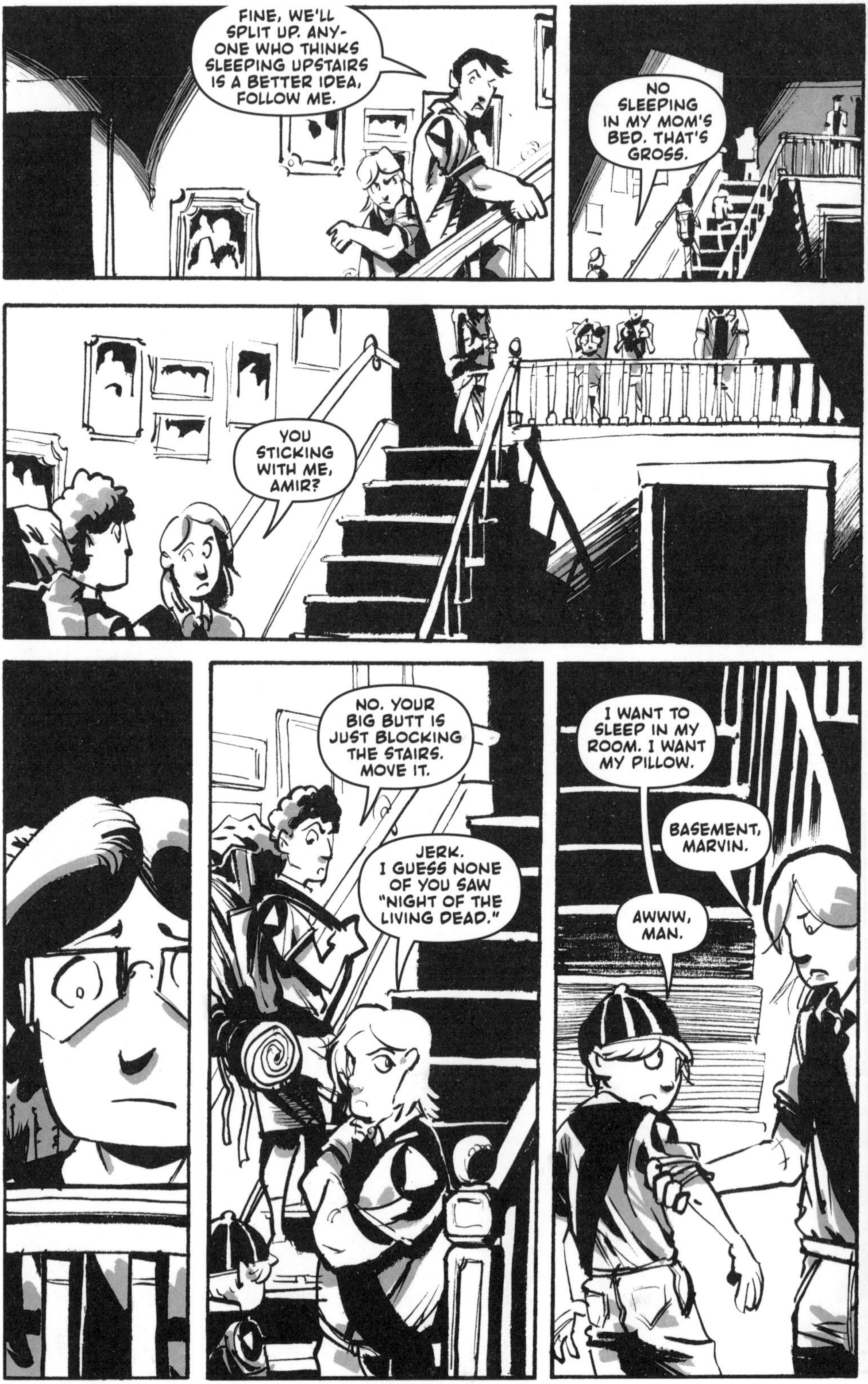
FINE, WE'LL SPLIT UP. ANYONE WHO THINKS SLEEPING UPSTAIRS IS A BETTER IDEA, FOLLOW ME.
NO SLEEPING IN MY MOM'S BED. THAT'S GROSS.
YOU STICKING WITH ME, AMIR?
NO. YOUR BIG BUTT IS JUST BLOCKING THE STAIRS. MOVE IT.
JERK. I GUESS NONE OF YOU SAW "NIGHT OF THE LIVING DEAD."
I WANT TO SLEEP IN MY ROOM. I WANT MY PILLOW.
BASEMENT, MARVIN.
AWWW, MAN.

HERE'S WHAT I THINK HAPPENED-- OKAY, TERRORISTS SMUGGLED A BOMB INTO ROSELAND, AND WERE HOLDING THE TOWN HOSTAGE.

WHY WOULD THEY DO THAT?

WHY WOULDN'T THEY DO THAT? THEY'RE TERRORISTS!

SO THOSE THINGS ARE TERRORISTS?

NO. THE BOMB WENT OFF AND IT MUTATED PEOPLE. THEY STARTED EATING EACH OTHER'S FACES AND ≷YAWN≷ SETTING DOGS ON FIRE.

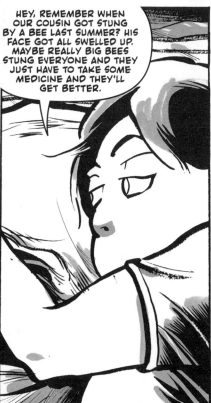

HEY, REMEMBER WHEN OUR COUSIN GOT STUNG BY A BEE LAST SUMMER? HIS FACE GOT ALL SWELLED UP. MAYBE REALLY BIG BEES STUNG EVERYONE AND THEY JUST HAVE TO TAKE SOME MEDICINE AND THEY'LL GET BETTER.

MARVIN, THAT'S STUPID. THAT'S SO STUPID. DON'T TALK ANYMORE. GO TO SLEEP.

WHATEVER TRAVIS. I'M SO TELLING... MOM... ZZZ.

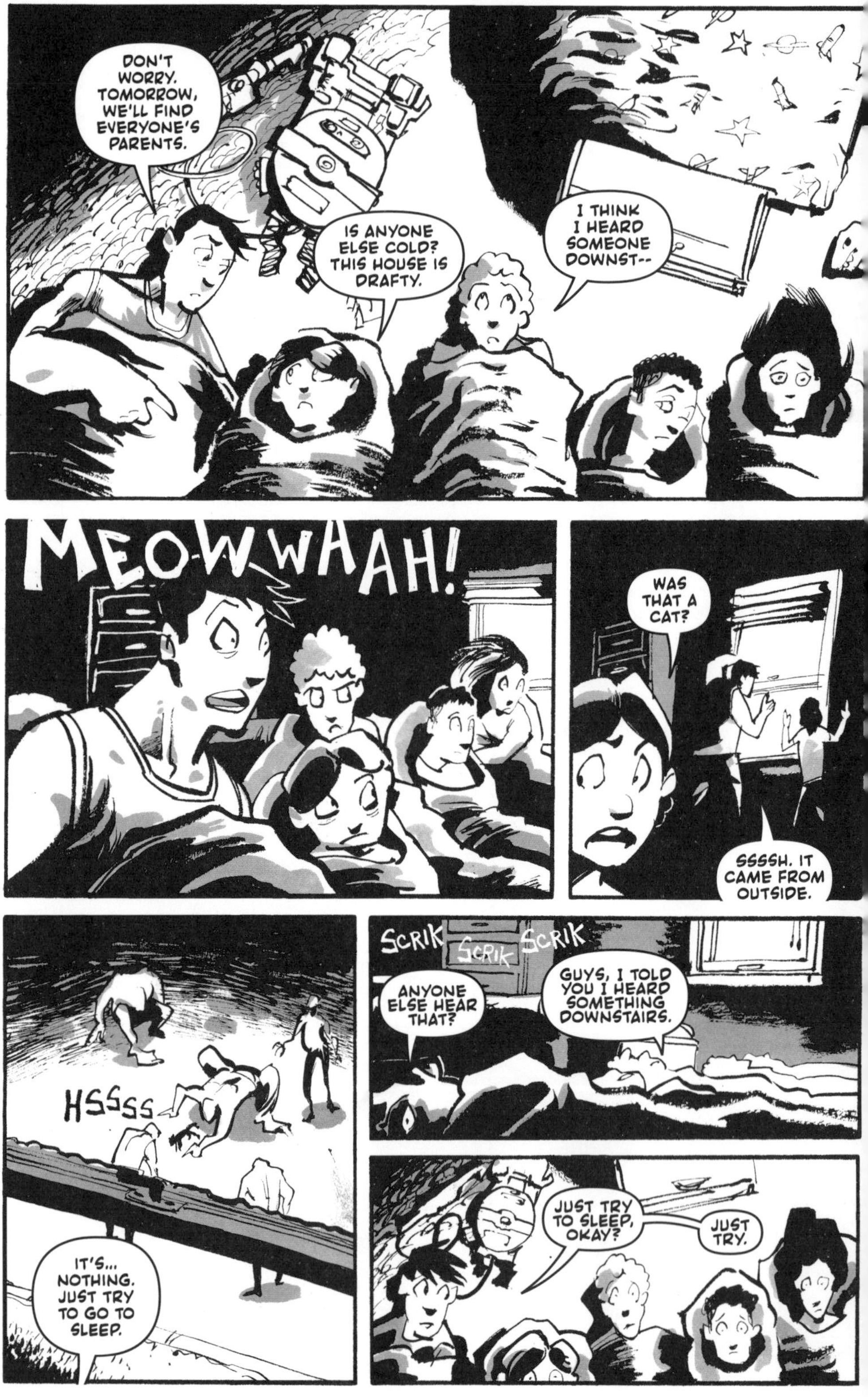
DON'T WORRY. TOMORROW, WE'LL FIND EVERYONE'S PARENTS.
IS ANYONE ELSE COLD? THIS HOUSE IS DRAFTY.
I THINK I HEARD SOMEONE DOWNST--
MEOWWAAH!
WAS THAT A CAT?
SSSSH. IT CAME FROM OUTSIDE.
HSSSS
IT'S... NOTHING. JUST TRY TO GO TO SLEEP.
SCRIK SCRIK SCRIK
ANYONE ELSE HEAR THAT?
GUYS, I TOLD YOU I HEARD SOMETHING DOWNSTAIRS.
JUST TRY TO SLEEP, OKAY?
JUST TRY.

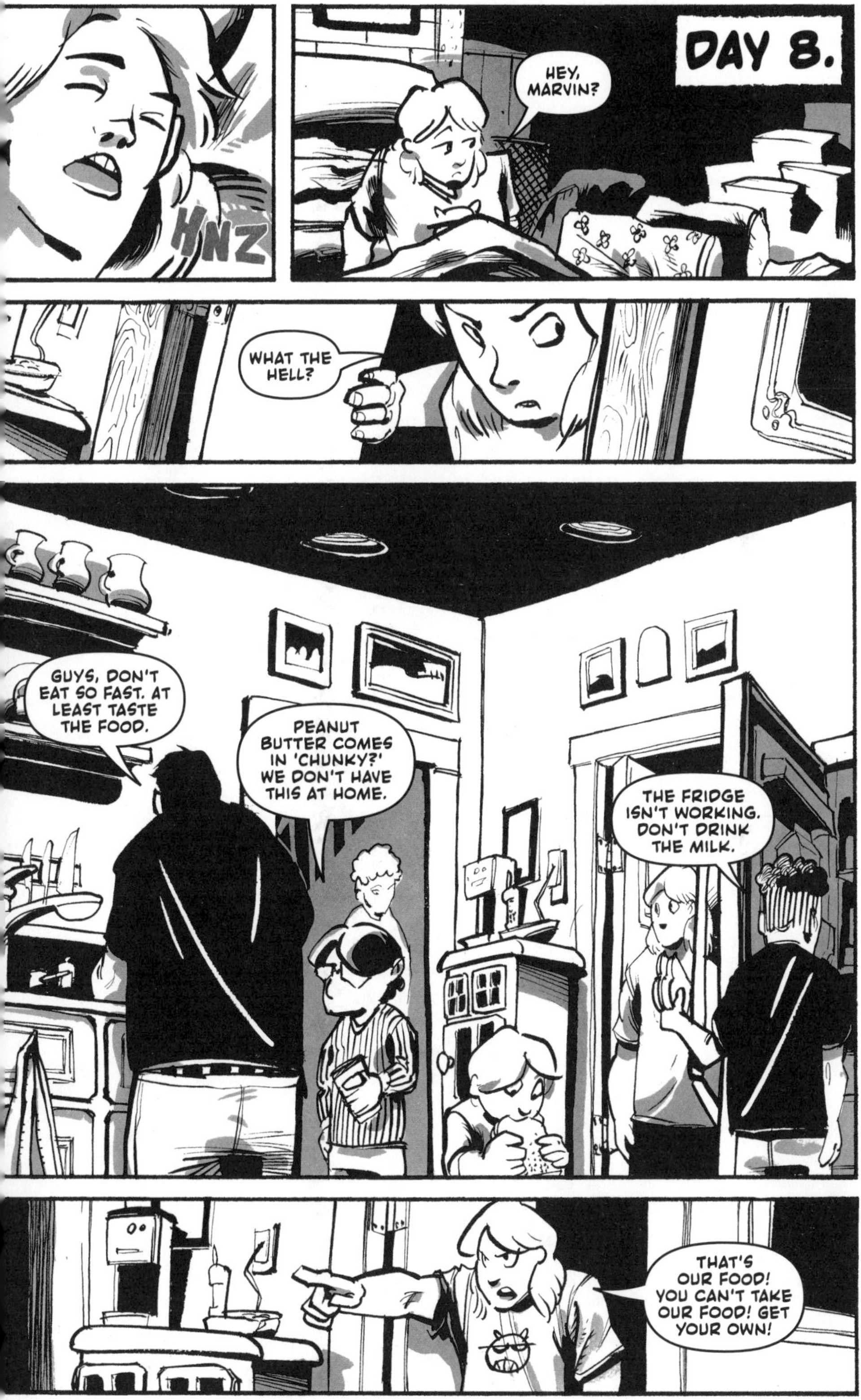
HNZ
DAY 8.
HEY, MARVIN?
WHAT THE HELL?
GUYS, DON'T EAT SO FAST. AT LEAST TASTE THE FOOD.
PEANUT BUTTER COMES IN 'CHUNKY?' WE DON'T HAVE THIS AT HOME.
THE FRIDGE ISN'T WORKING. DON'T DRINK THE MILK.
THAT'S OUR FOOD! YOU CAN'T TAKE OUR FOOD! GET YOUR OWN!

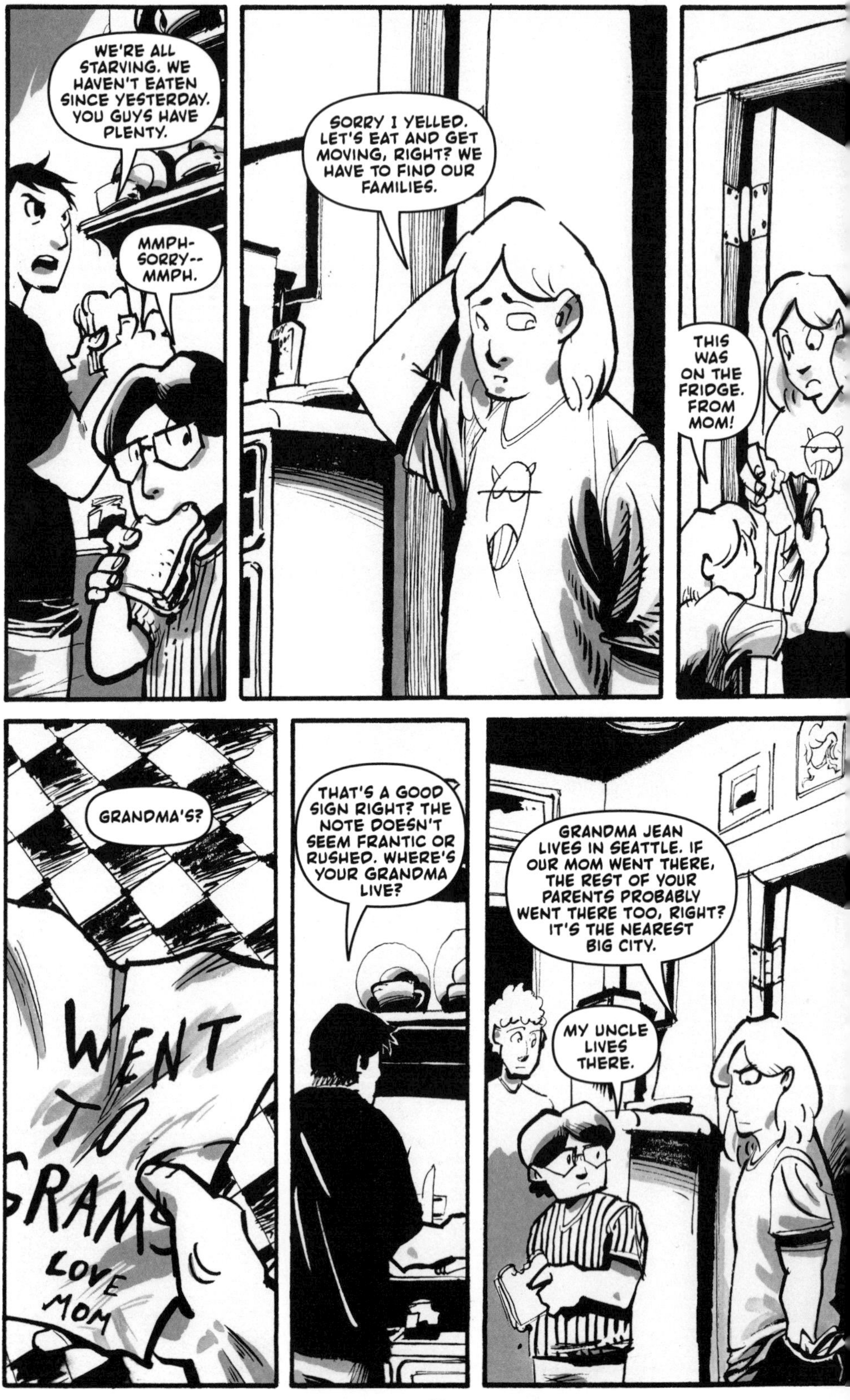
WE'RE ALL STARVING. WE HAVEN'T EATEN SINCE YESTERDAY. YOU GUYS HAVE PLENTY.
MMPH- SORRY-- MMPH.
SORRY I YELLED. LET'S EAT AND GET MOVING, RIGHT? WE HAVE TO FIND OUR FAMILIES.
THIS WAS ON THE FRIDGE. FROM MOM!
GRANDMA'S?
WENT TO GRAMS
LOVE MOM
THAT'S A GOOD SIGN RIGHT? THE NOTE DOESN'T SEEM FRANTIC OR RUSHED. WHERE'S YOUR GRANDMA LIVE?
GRANDMA JEAN LIVES IN SEATTLE. IF OUR MOM WENT THERE, THE REST OF YOUR PARENTS PROBABLY WENT THERE TOO, RIGHT? IT'S THE NEAREST BIG CITY.
MY UNCLE LIVES THERE.

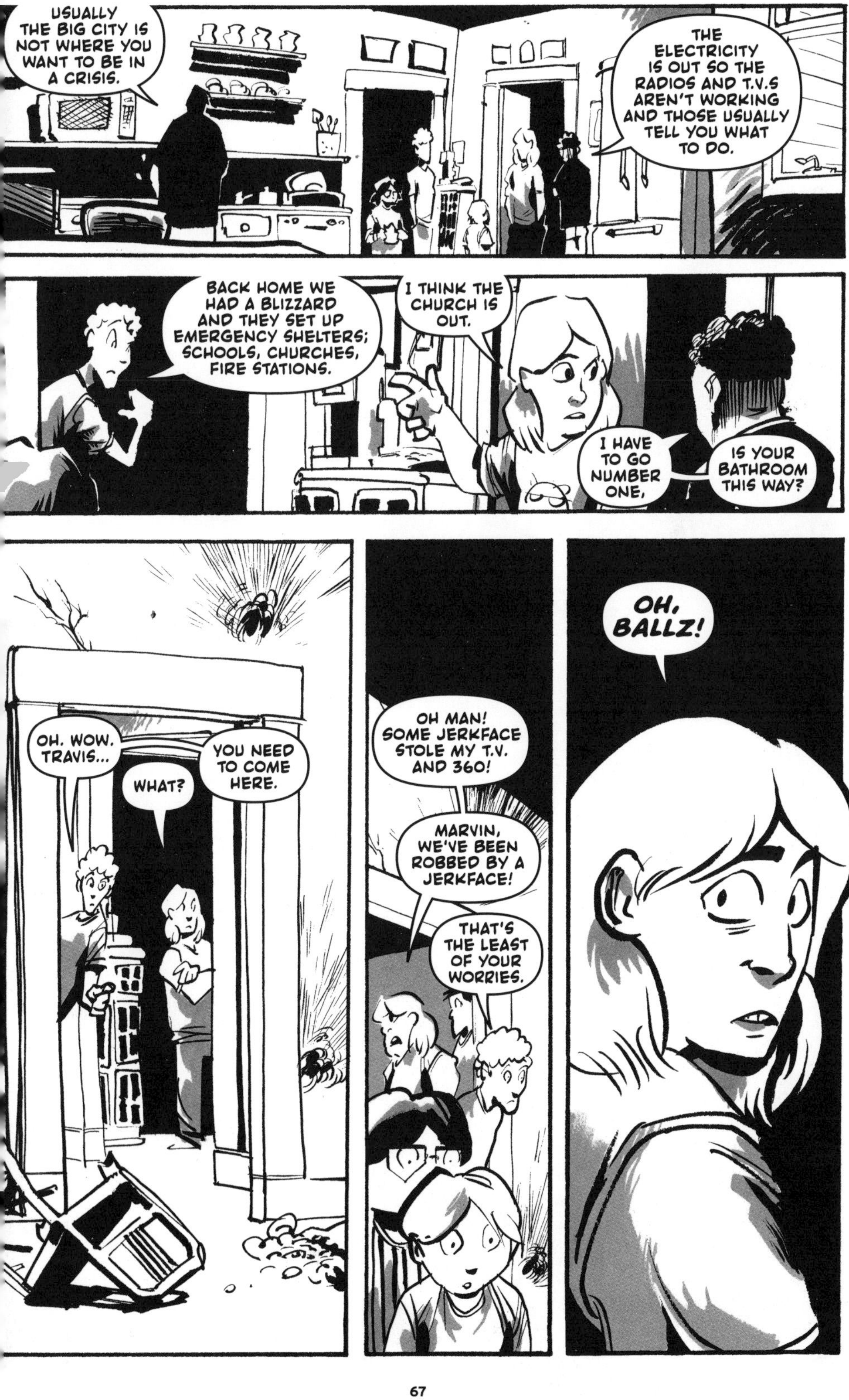
USUALLY THE BIG CITY IS NOT WHERE YOU WANT TO BE IN A CRISIS.
THE ELECTRICITY IS OUT SO THE RADIOS AND T.V.S AREN'T WORKING AND THOSE USUALLY TELL YOU WHAT TO DO.
BACK HOME WE HAD A BLIZZARD AND THEY SET UP EMERGENCY SHELTERS; SCHOOLS, CHURCHES, FIRE STATIONS.
I THINK THE CHURCH IS OUT.
I HAVE TO GO NUMBER ONE,
IS YOUR BATHROOM THIS WAY?
OH. WOW. TRAVIS...
WHAT?
YOU NEED TO COME HERE.
OH MAN! SOME JERKFACE STOLE MY T.V. AND 360!
MARVIN, WE'VE BEEN ROBBED BY A JERKFACE!
THAT'S THE LEAST OF YOUR WORRIES.
OH, BALLZ!

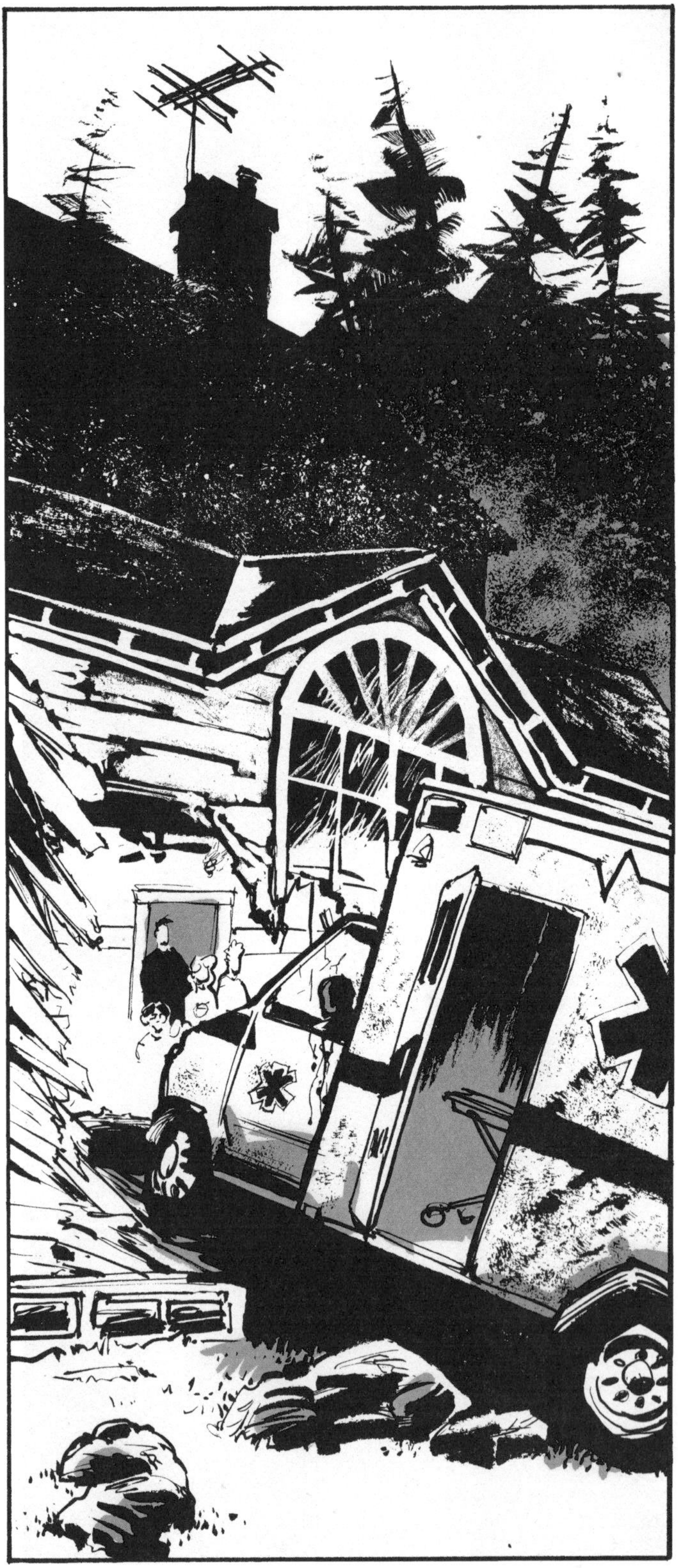

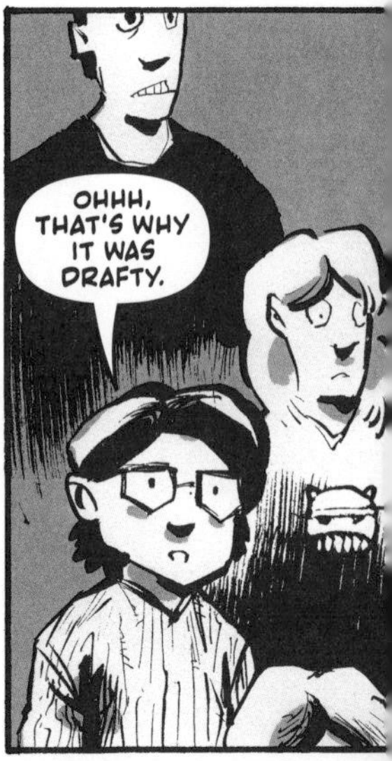
OHHH, THAT'S WHY IT WAS DRAFTY.

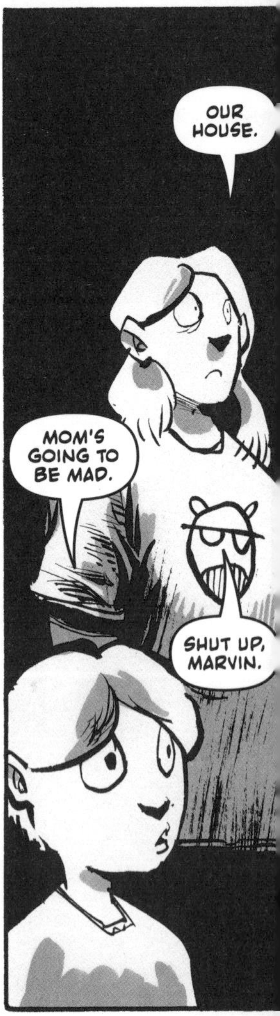
OUR HOUSE.
MOM'S GOING TO BE MAD.
SHUT UP, MARVIN.

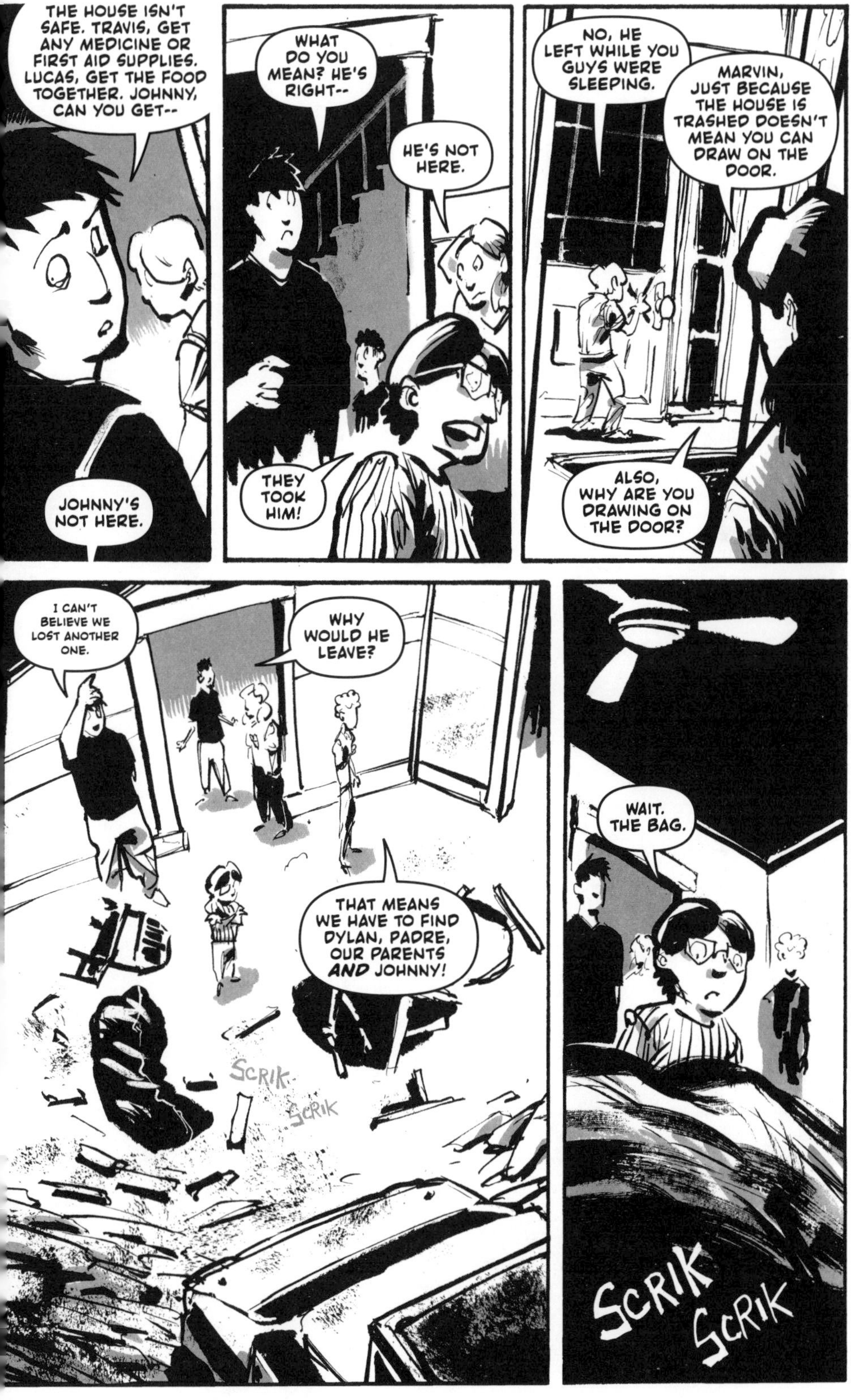
THE HOUSE ISN'T SAFE. TRAVIS, GET ANY MEDICINE OR FIRST AID SUPPLIES. LUCAS, GET THE FOOD TOGETHER. JOHNNY, CAN YOU GET--
JOHNNY'S NOT HERE.
WHAT DO YOU MEAN? HE'S RIGHT--
HE'S NOT HERE.
THEY TOOK HIM!
NO, HE LEFT WHILE YOU GUYS WERE SLEEPING.
MARVIN, JUST BECAUSE THE HOUSE IS TRASHED DOESN'T MEAN YOU CAN DRAW ON THE DOOR.
ALSO, WHY ARE YOU DRAWING ON THE DOOR?
I CAN'T BELIEVE WE LOST ANOTHER ONE.
WHY WOULD HE LEAVE?
THAT MEANS WE HAVE TO FIND DYLAN, PADRE, OUR PARENTS AND JOHNNY!
SCRIK
SCRIK
WAIT. THE BAG.
SCRIK
SCRIK

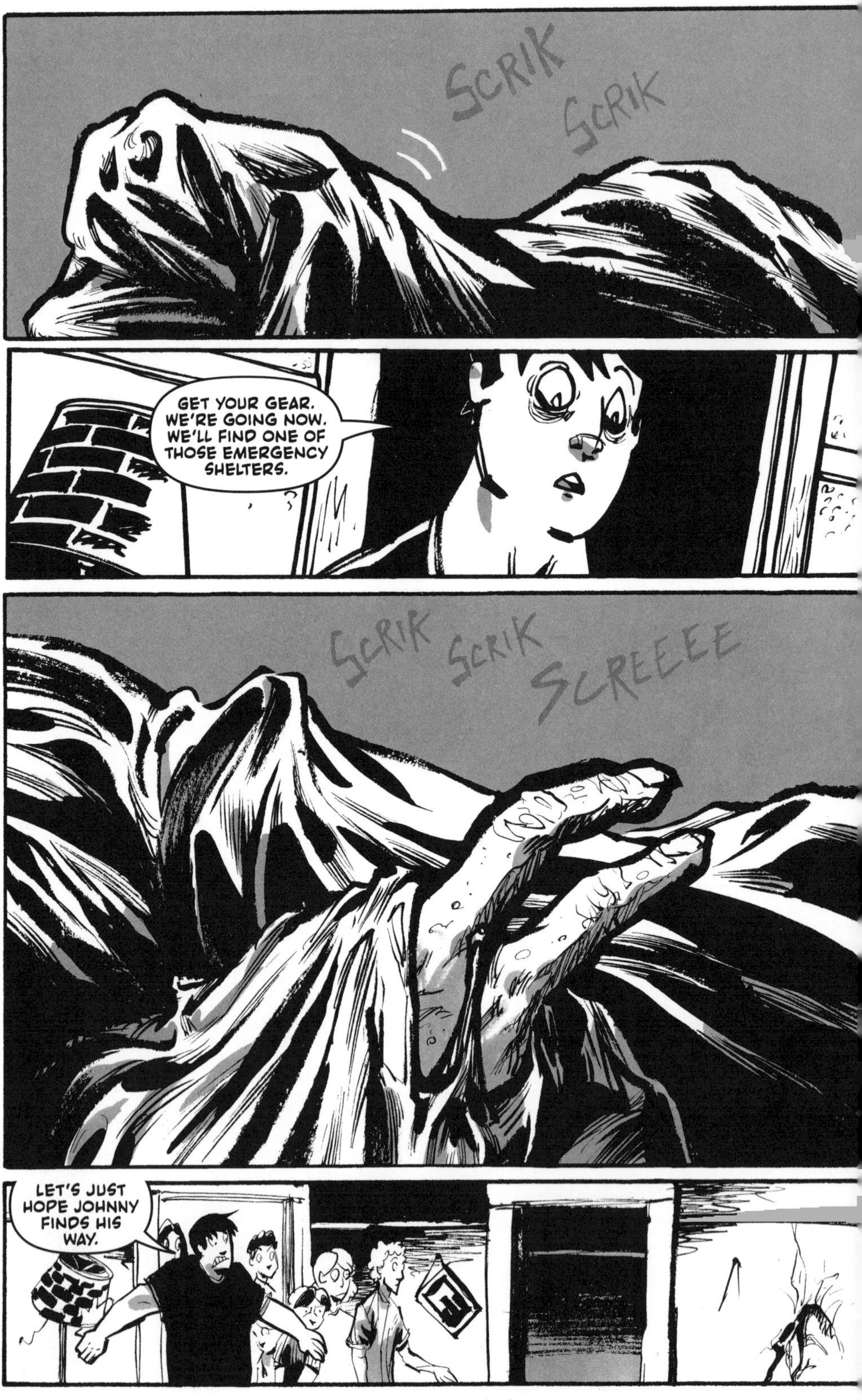
SCRIK
SCRIK
GET YOUR GEAR. WE'RE GOING NOW. WE'LL FIND ONE OF THOSE EMERGENCY SHELTERS.
SCRIK
SCRIK
SCREEEE
LET'S JUST HOPE JOHNNY FINDS HIS WAY.

HOW TO MAKE A PB&J SANDWICH

BY PRABIR AND MARVIN

U WILL NEED:

BREAD!

PB.!

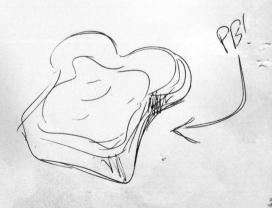

J!

STEP 1!

THE SECRET IS TO MAKE THE PEANUT BUTTER THICKEST AT THE FOUR EDGES OF THE BREAD.

PB!

STEP 2!

MAKE THE JELLY Thickest IN THE MIDDLE OF THE BREAD.

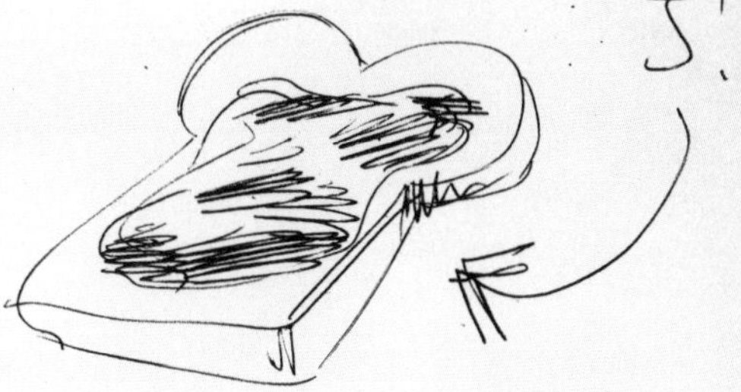
J!

STEP 3!

WHEN YOU PUT THE TWO PIECES OF BREAD TOGETHER THE THICK PEANUT BUTTER EDGES HELP SEAL IN THE JELLY!

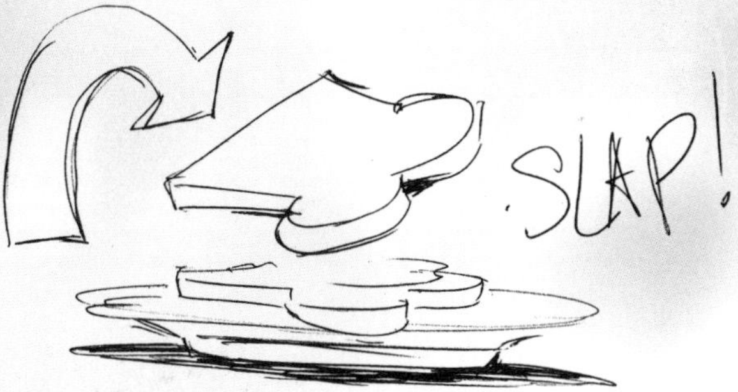
SLAP!

THAT WAY IT DOESN'T SQUIRT OUT AND GET OVER YOUR UNIFORM OR HANDS!

I HATE HAVING MESSY HANDS!

TRAVIS IS A JERK!

CHAPTER THREE

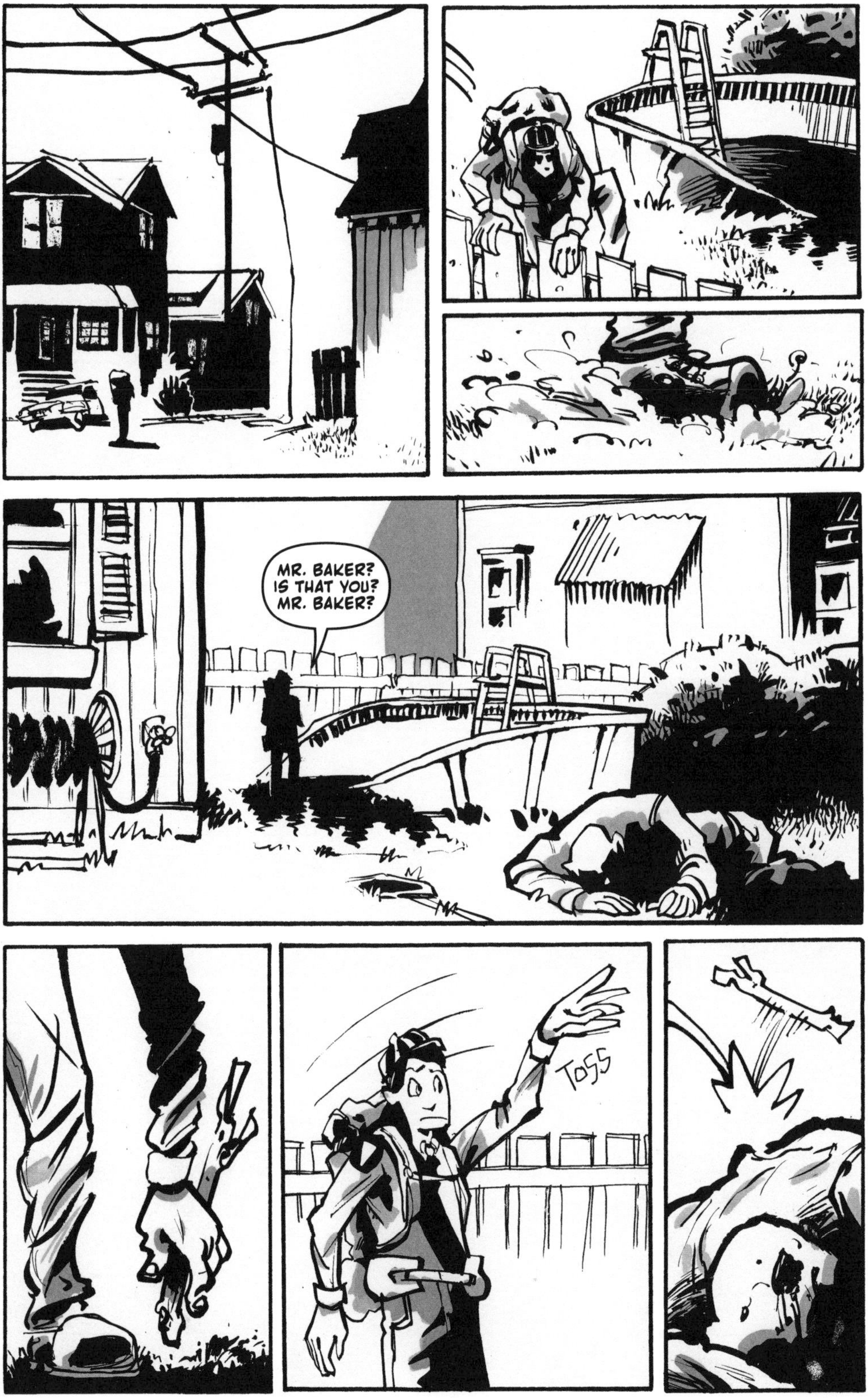
MR. BAKER?
IS THAT YOU?
MR. BAKER?
TOSS

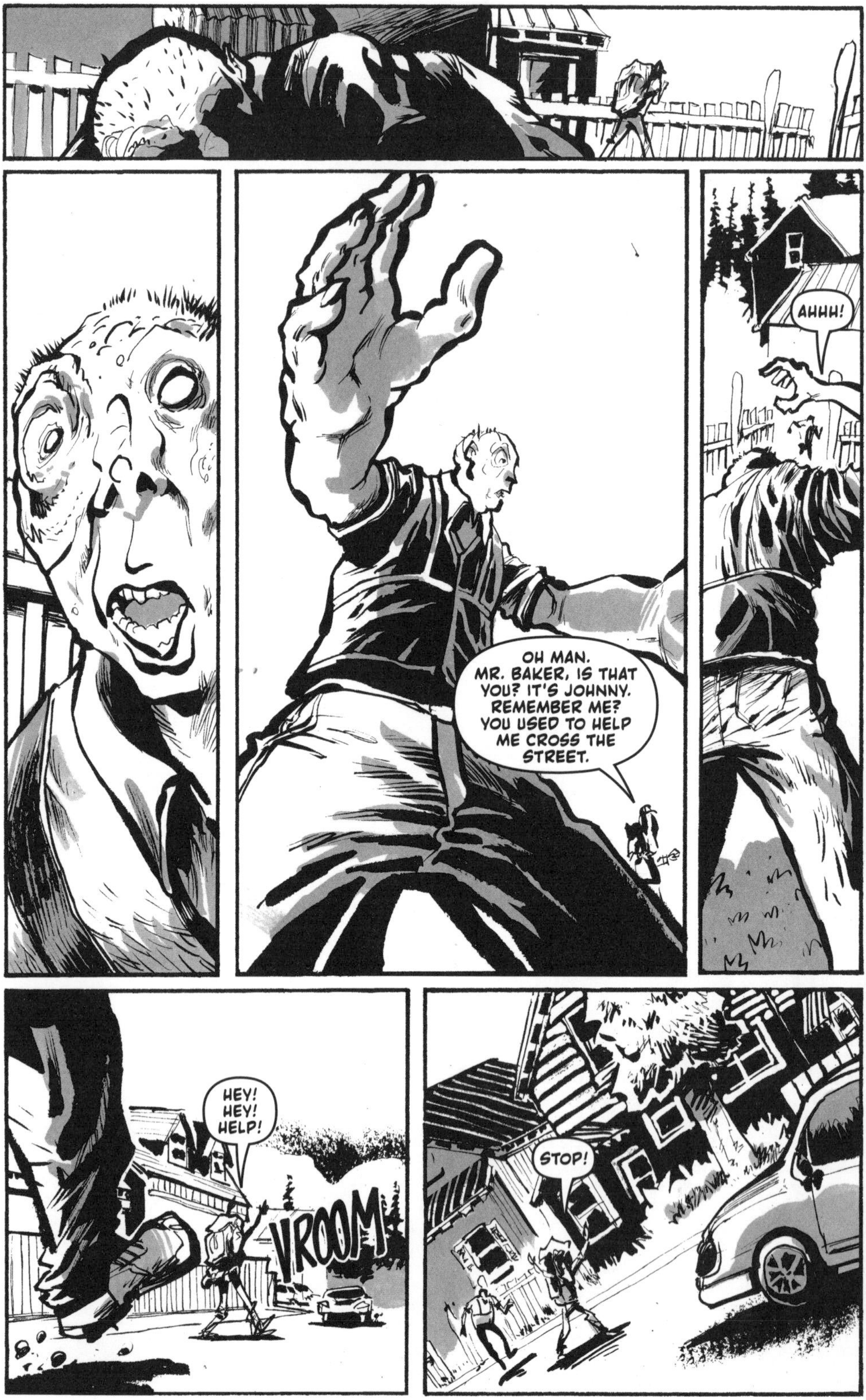
AHHH!
OH MAN. MR. BAKER, IS THAT YOU? IT'S JOHNNY. REMEMBER ME? YOU USED TO HELP ME CROSS THE STREET.
HEY! HEY! HELP!
VROOM
STOP!

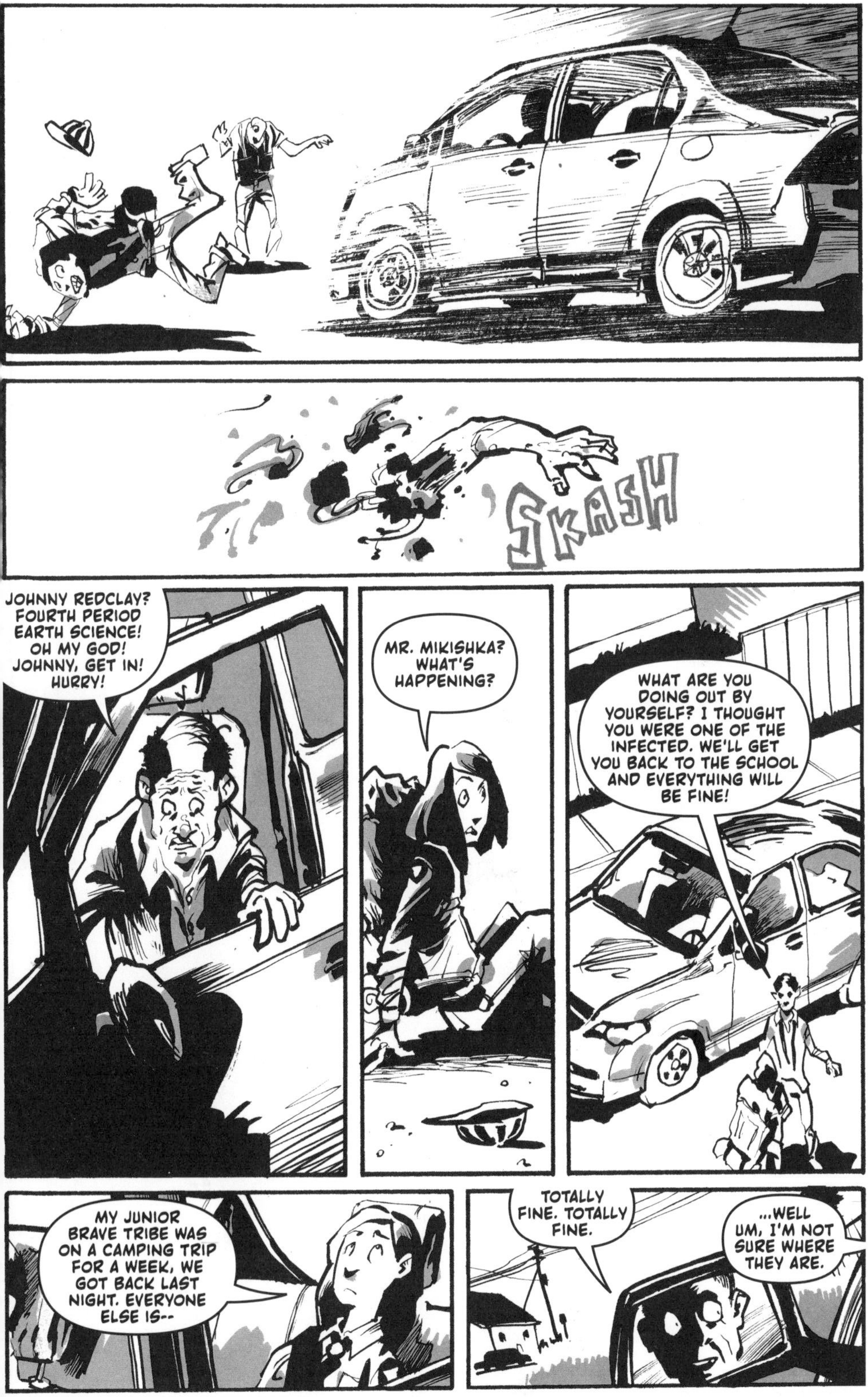
SKASH
JOHNNY REDCLAY? FOURTH PERIOD EARTH SCIENCE! OH MY GOD! JOHNNY, GET IN! HURRY!
MR. MIKISHKA? WHAT'S HAPPENING?
WHAT ARE YOU DOING OUT BY YOURSELF? I THOUGHT YOU WERE ONE OF THE INFECTED. WE'LL GET YOU BACK TO THE SCHOOL AND EVERYTHING WILL BE FINE!
MY JUNIOR BRAVE TRIBE WAS ON A CAMPING TRIP FOR A WEEK, WE GOT BACK LAST NIGHT. EVERYONE ELSE IS--
TOTALLY FINE. TOTALLY FINE.
...WELL UM, I'M NOT SURE WHERE THEY ARE.

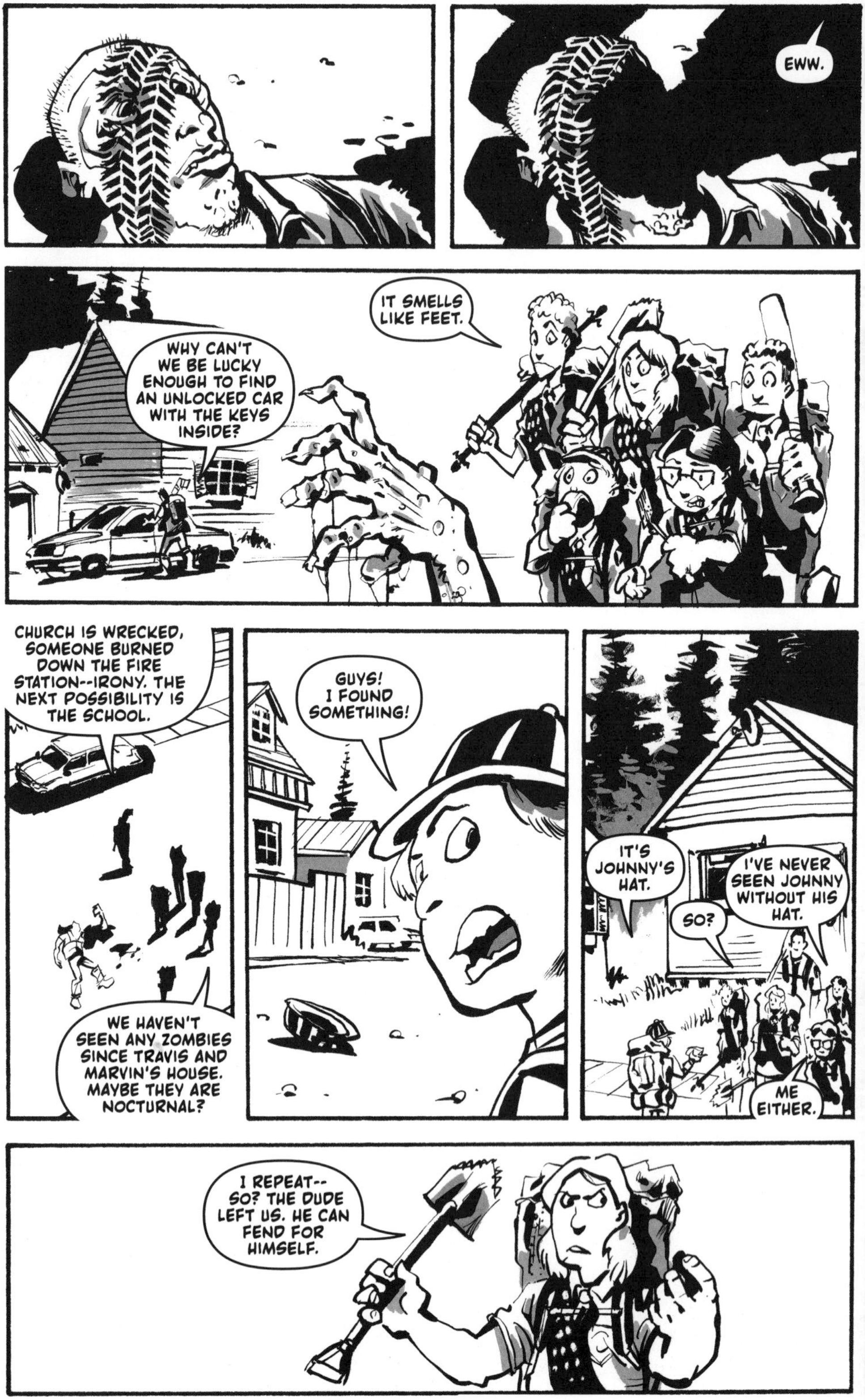

EWW.
IT SMELLS LIKE FEET.
WHY CAN'T WE BE LUCKY ENOUGH TO FIND AN UNLOCKED CAR WITH THE KEYS INSIDE?
CHURCH IS WRECKED, SOMEONE BURNED DOWN THE FIRE STATION--IRONY. THE NEXT POSSIBILITY IS THE SCHOOL.
WE HAVEN'T SEEN ANY ZOMBIES SINCE TRAVIS AND MARVIN'S HOUSE. MAYBE THEY ARE NOCTURNAL?
GUYS! I FOUND SOMETHING!
IT'S JOHNNY'S HAT.
I'VE NEVER SEEN JOHNNY WITHOUT HIS HAT.
SO?
ME EITHER.
I REPEAT--SO? THE DUDE LEFT US. HE CAN FEND FOR HIMSELF.

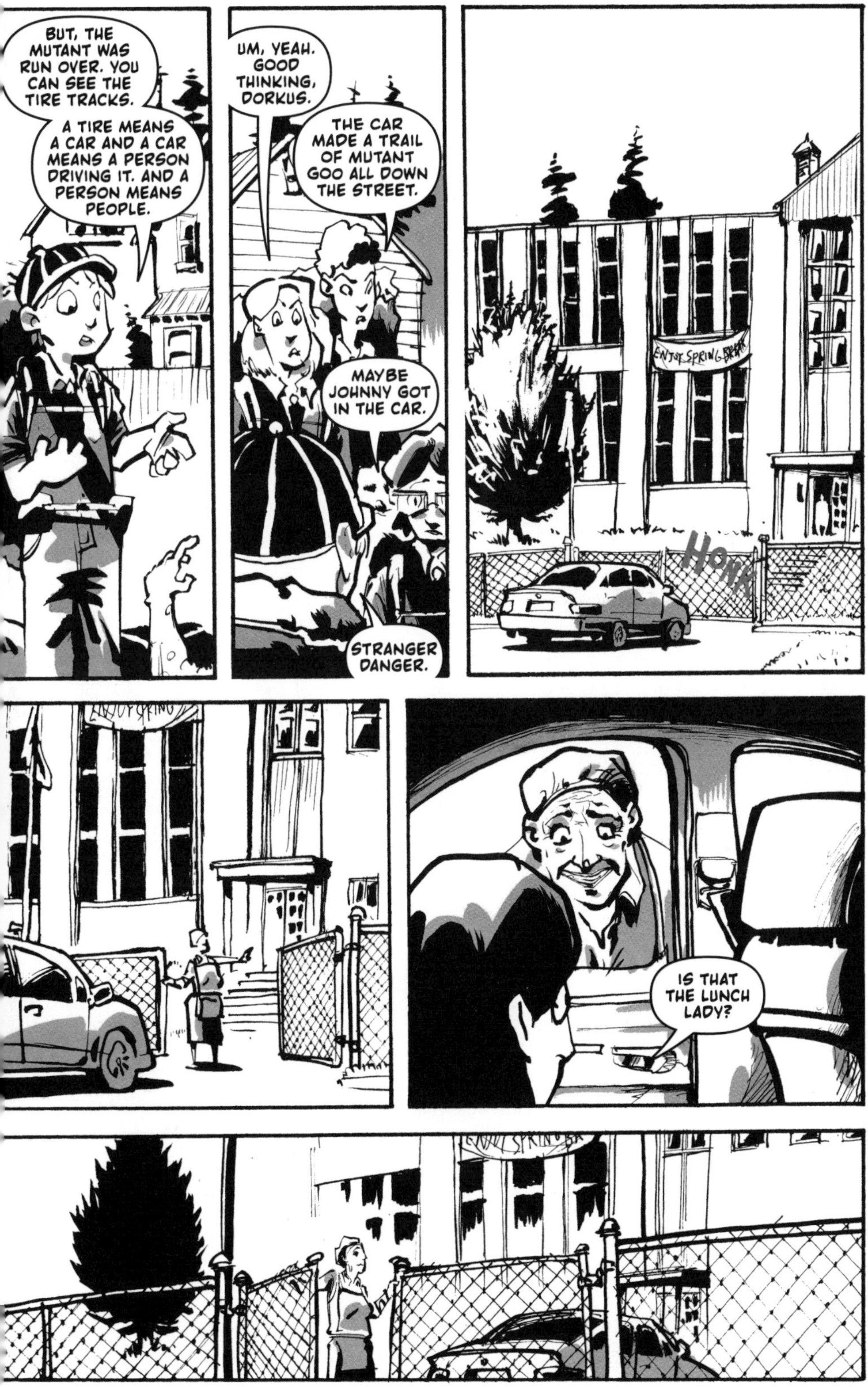
BUT, THE MUTANT WAS RUN OVER. YOU CAN SEE THE TIRE TRACKS.
A TIRE MEANS A CAR AND A CAR MEANS A PERSON DRIVING IT. AND A PERSON MEANS PEOPLE.
UM, YEAH. GOOD THINKING, DORKUS.
THE CAR MADE A TRAIL OF MUTANT GOO ALL DOWN THE STREET.
MAYBE JOHNNY GOT IN THE CAR.
STRANGER DANGER.
HONK
IS THAT THE LUNCH LADY?

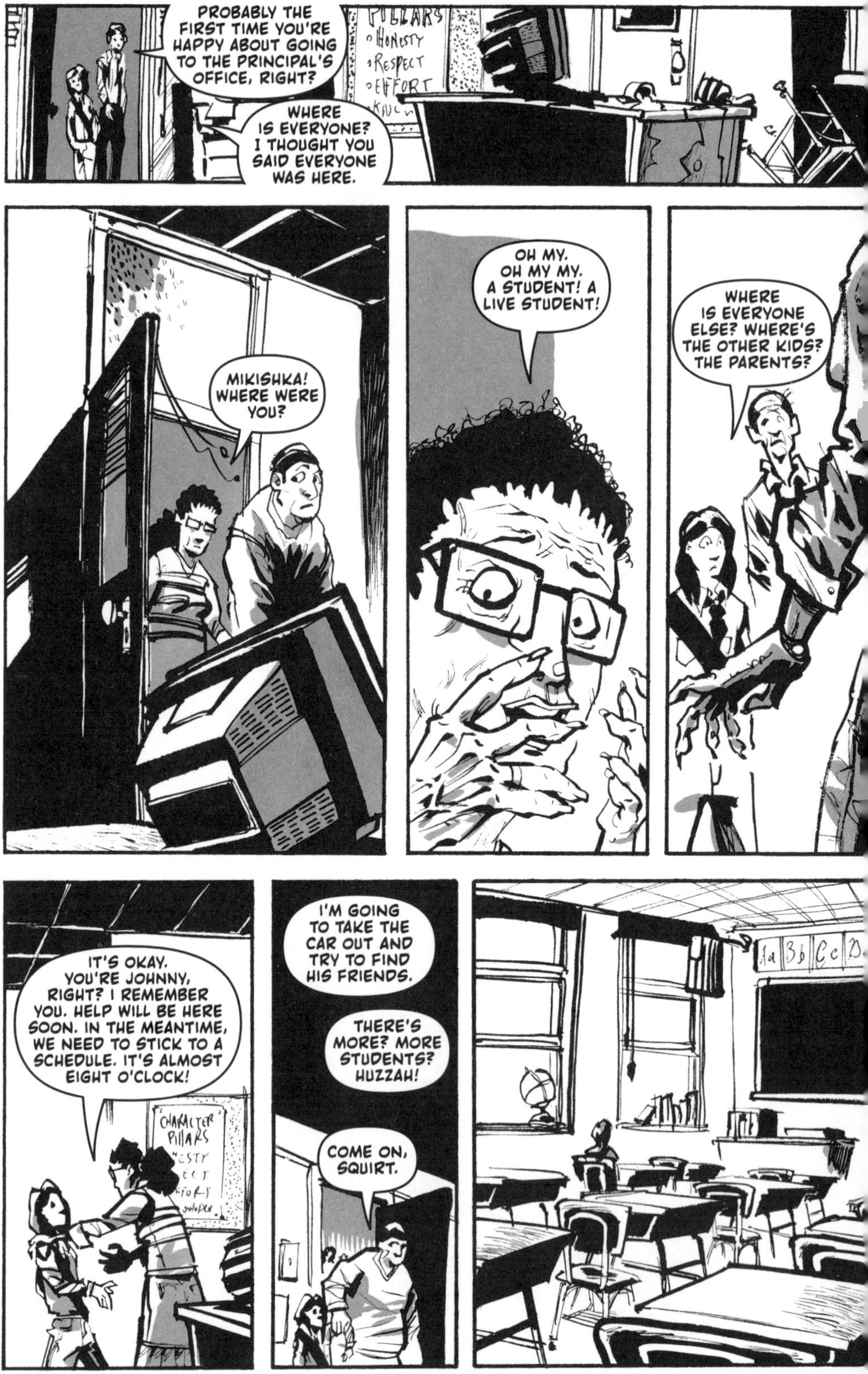
PILLARS
HONESTY
RESPECT
EFFORT
PROBABLY THE FIRST TIME YOU'RE HAPPY ABOUT GOING TO THE PRINCIPAL'S OFFICE, RIGHT?
WHERE IS EVERYONE? I THOUGHT YOU SAID EVERYONE WAS HERE.
MIKISHKA! WHERE WERE YOU?
OH MY. OH MY MY. A STUDENT! A LIVE STUDENT!
WHERE IS EVERYONE ELSE? WHERE'S THE OTHER KIDS? THE PARENTS?
IT'S OKAY. YOU'RE JOHNNY, RIGHT? I REMEMBER YOU. HELP WILL BE HERE SOON. IN THE MEANTIME, WE NEED TO STICK TO A SCHEDULE. IT'S ALMOST EIGHT O'CLOCK!
CHARACTER PILLARS
I'M GOING TO TAKE THE CAR OUT AND TRY TO FIND HIS FRIENDS.
THERE'S MORE? MORE STUDENTS? HUZZAH!
COME ON, SQUIRT.
Aa Bb Cc

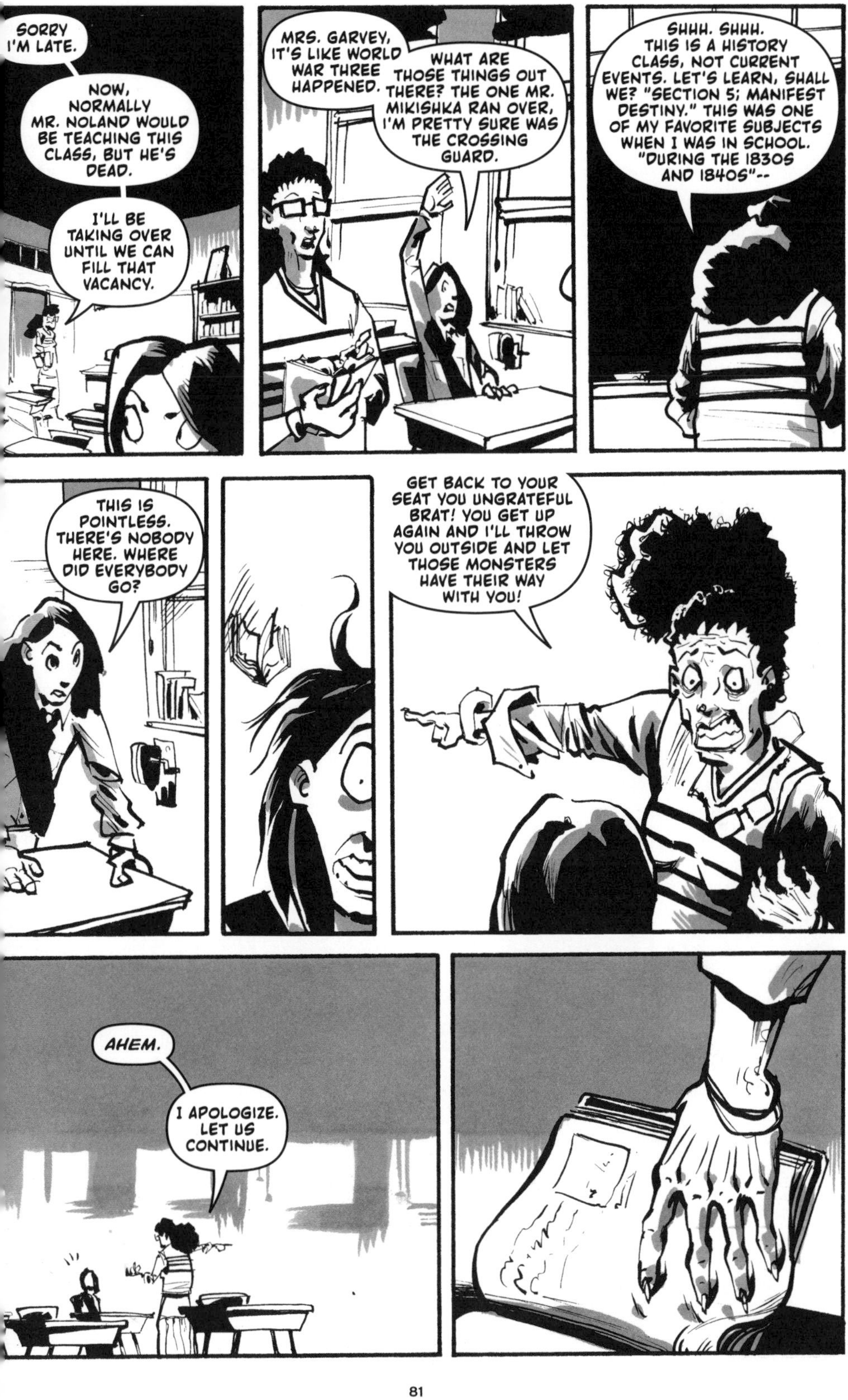
SORRY I'M LATE.
NOW, NORMALLY MR. NOLAND WOULD BE TEACHING THIS CLASS, BUT HE'S DEAD.
I'LL BE TAKING OVER UNTIL WE CAN FILL THAT VACANCY.
MRS. GARVEY, IT'S LIKE WORLD WAR THREE HAPPENED.
WHAT ARE THOSE THINGS OUT THERE? THE ONE MR. MIKISHKA RAN OVER, I'M PRETTY SURE WAS THE CROSSING GUARD.
SHHH. SHHH. THIS IS A HISTORY CLASS, NOT CURRENT EVENTS. LET'S LEARN, SHALL WE? "SECTION 5; MANIFEST DESTINY." THIS WAS ONE OF MY FAVORITE SUBJECTS WHEN I WAS IN SCHOOL. "DURING THE 1830S AND 1840S"--
THIS IS POINTLESS. THERE'S NOBODY HERE. WHERE DID EVERYBODY GO?
GET BACK TO YOUR SEAT YOU UNGRATEFUL BRAT! YOU GET UP AGAIN AND I'LL THROW YOU OUTSIDE AND LET THOSE MONSTERS HAVE THEIR WAY WITH YOU!
AHEM.
I APOLOGIZE. LET US CONTINUE.

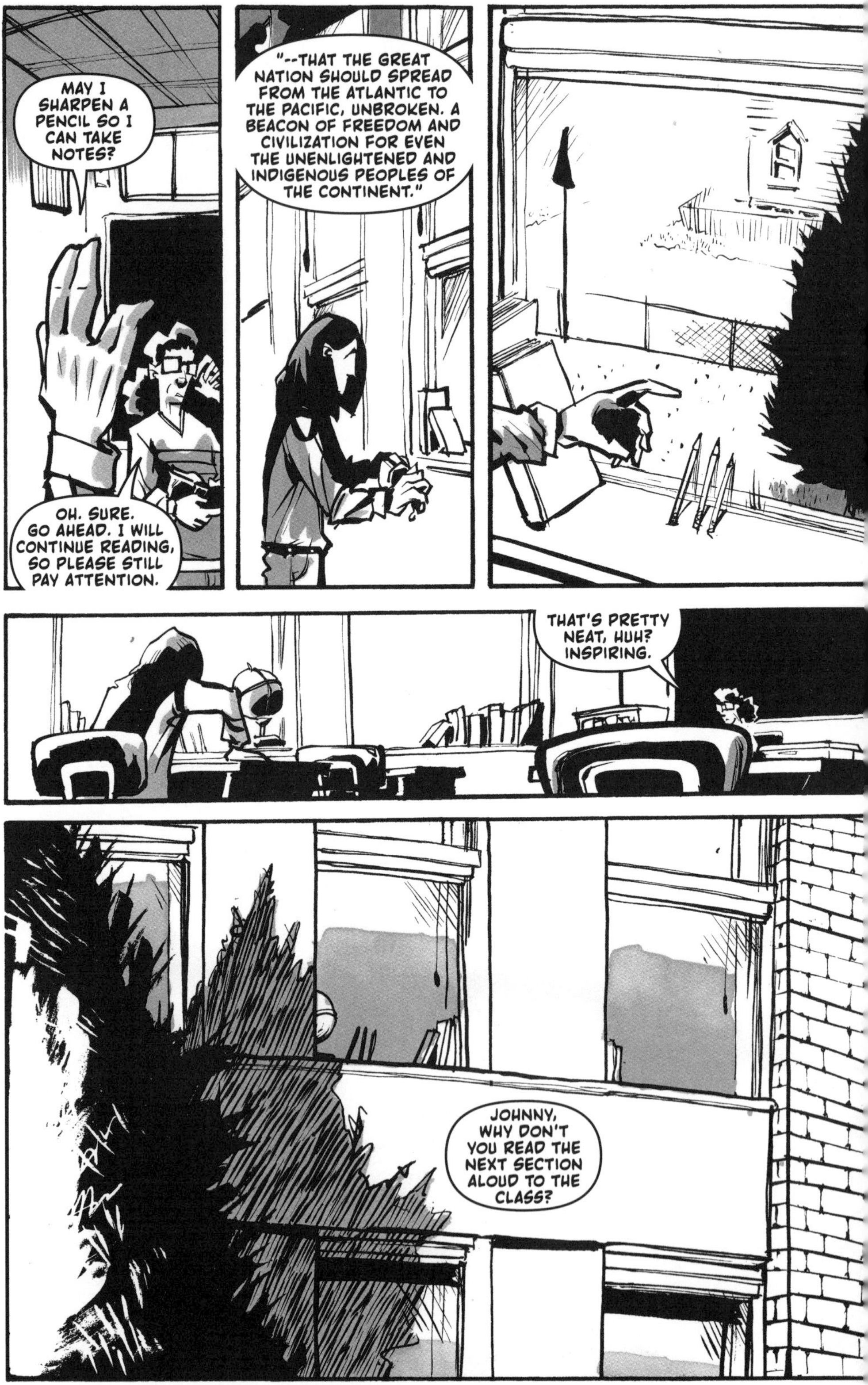
MAY I SHARPEN A PENCIL SO I CAN TAKE NOTES?
OH. SURE. GO AHEAD. I WILL CONTINUE READING, SO PLEASE STILL PAY ATTENTION.
"--THAT THE GREAT NATION SHOULD SPREAD FROM THE ATLANTIC TO THE PACIFIC, UNBROKEN. A BEACON OF FREEDOM AND CIVILIZATION FOR EVEN THE UNENLIGHTENED AND INDIGENOUS PEOPLES OF THE CONTINENT."
THAT'S PRETTY NEAT, HUH? INSPIRING.
JOHNNY, WHY DON'T YOU READ THE NEXT SECTION ALOUD TO THE CLASS?

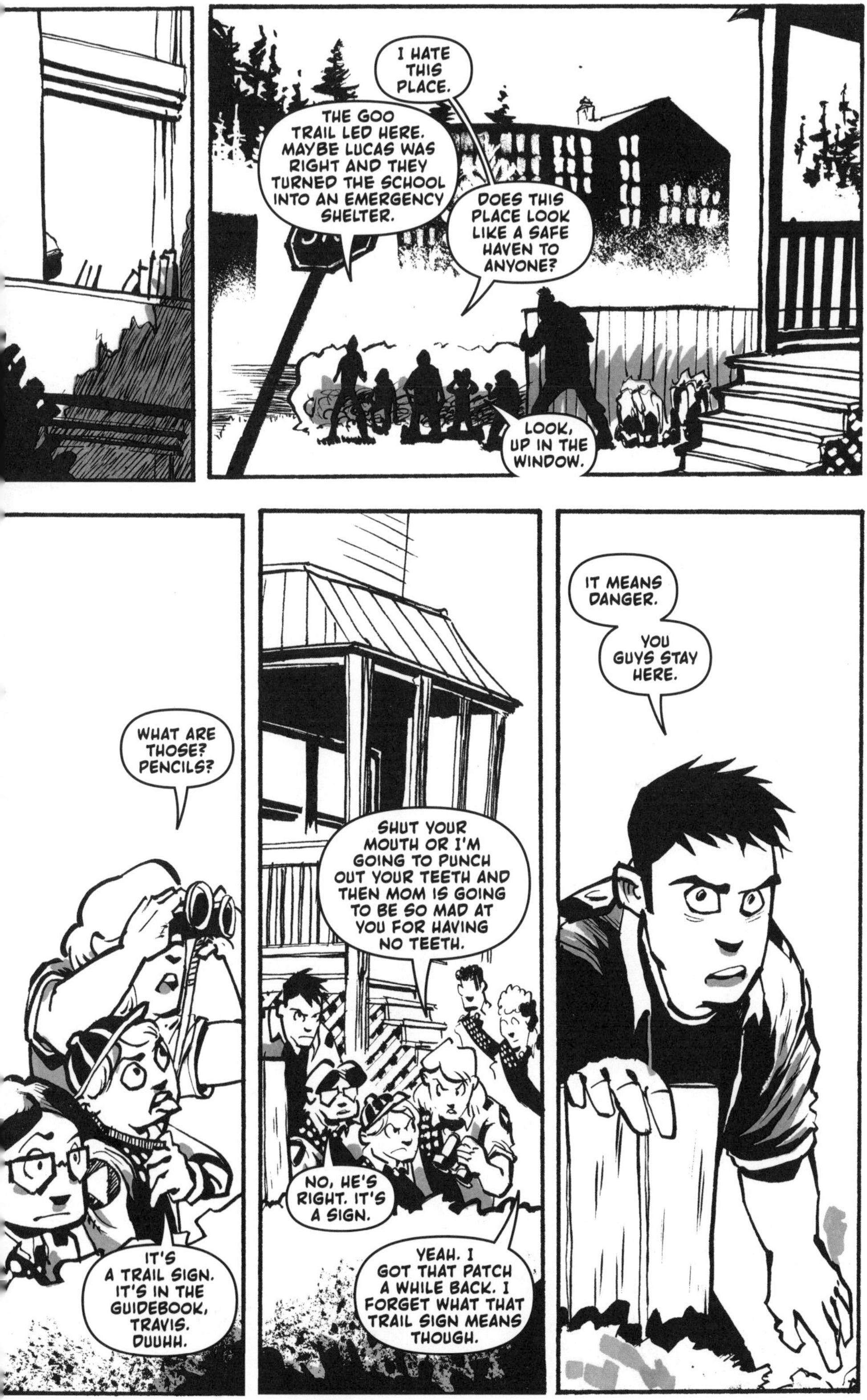
THE GOO TRAIL LED HERE. MAYBE LUCAS WAS RIGHT AND THEY TURNED THE SCHOOL INTO AN EMERGENCY SHELTER.
I HATE THIS PLACE.
DOES THIS PLACE LOOK LIKE A SAFE HAVEN TO ANYONE?
LOOK, UP IN THE WINDOW.
WHAT ARE THOSE? PENCILS?
IT'S A TRAIL SIGN. IT'S IN THE GUIDEBOOK, TRAVIS. DUUHH.
SHUT YOUR MOUTH OR I'M GOING TO PUNCH OUT YOUR TEETH AND THEN MOM IS GOING TO BE SO MAD AT YOU FOR HAVING NO TEETH.
NO, HE'S RIGHT. IT'S A SIGN.
YEAH. I GOT THAT PATCH A WHILE BACK. I FORGET WHAT THAT TRAIL SIGN MEANS THOUGH.
IT MEANS DANGER.
YOU GUYS STAY HERE.

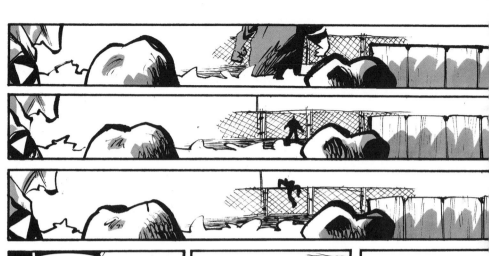

OH, HI. I'M BUDDY LANDON. I WENT TO THIS SCHOOL ABOUT TWELVE YEARS AGO. I USED TO ASK FOR EXTRA MAC AND CHEESE?

AHH!

SHAKE SHAKE SHAKE

CRACK

I THINK HE'S DEAD.

HE'S NOT--

YEAH, HE MIGHT BE DEAD.

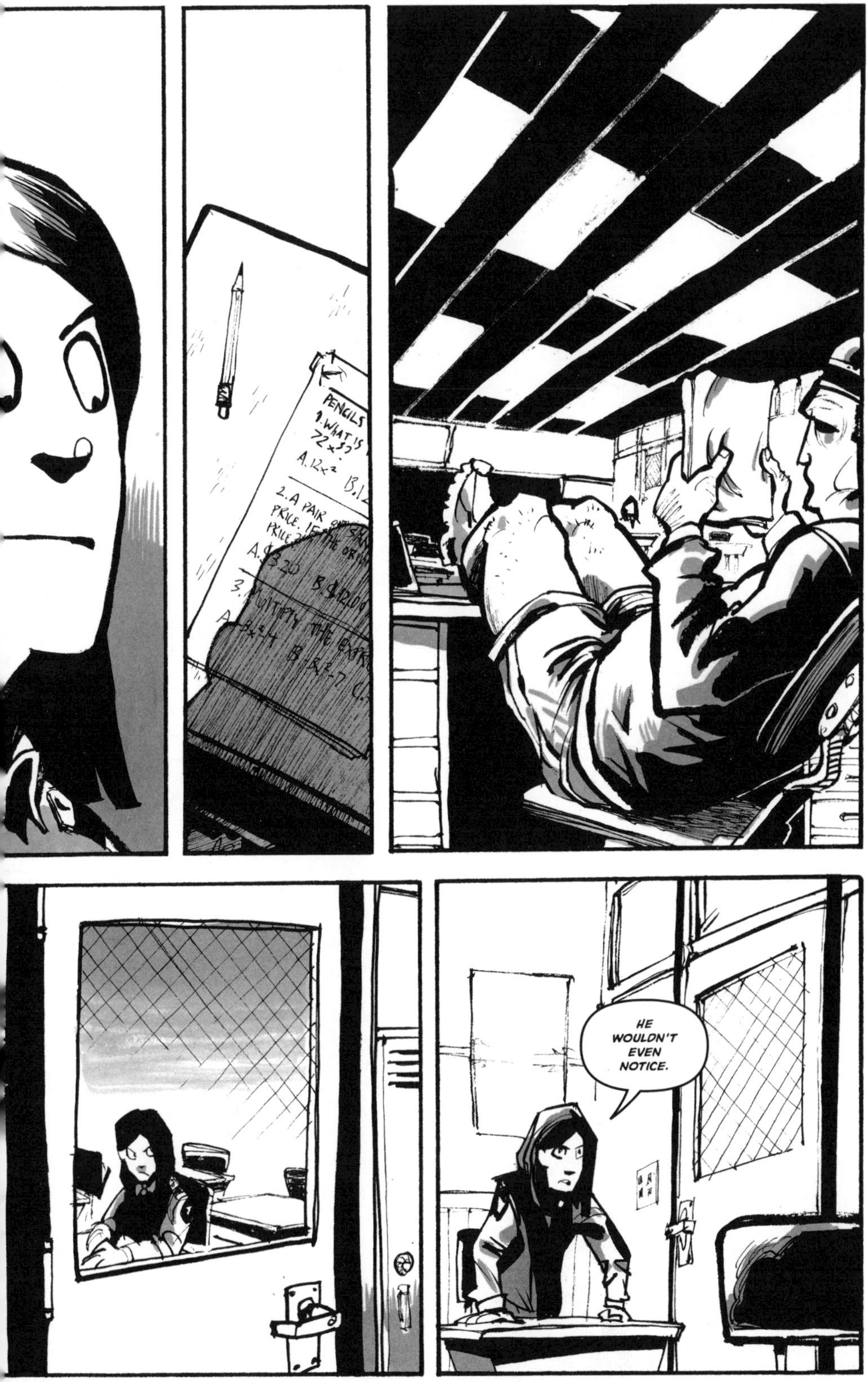
HE WOULDN'T EVEN NOTICE.

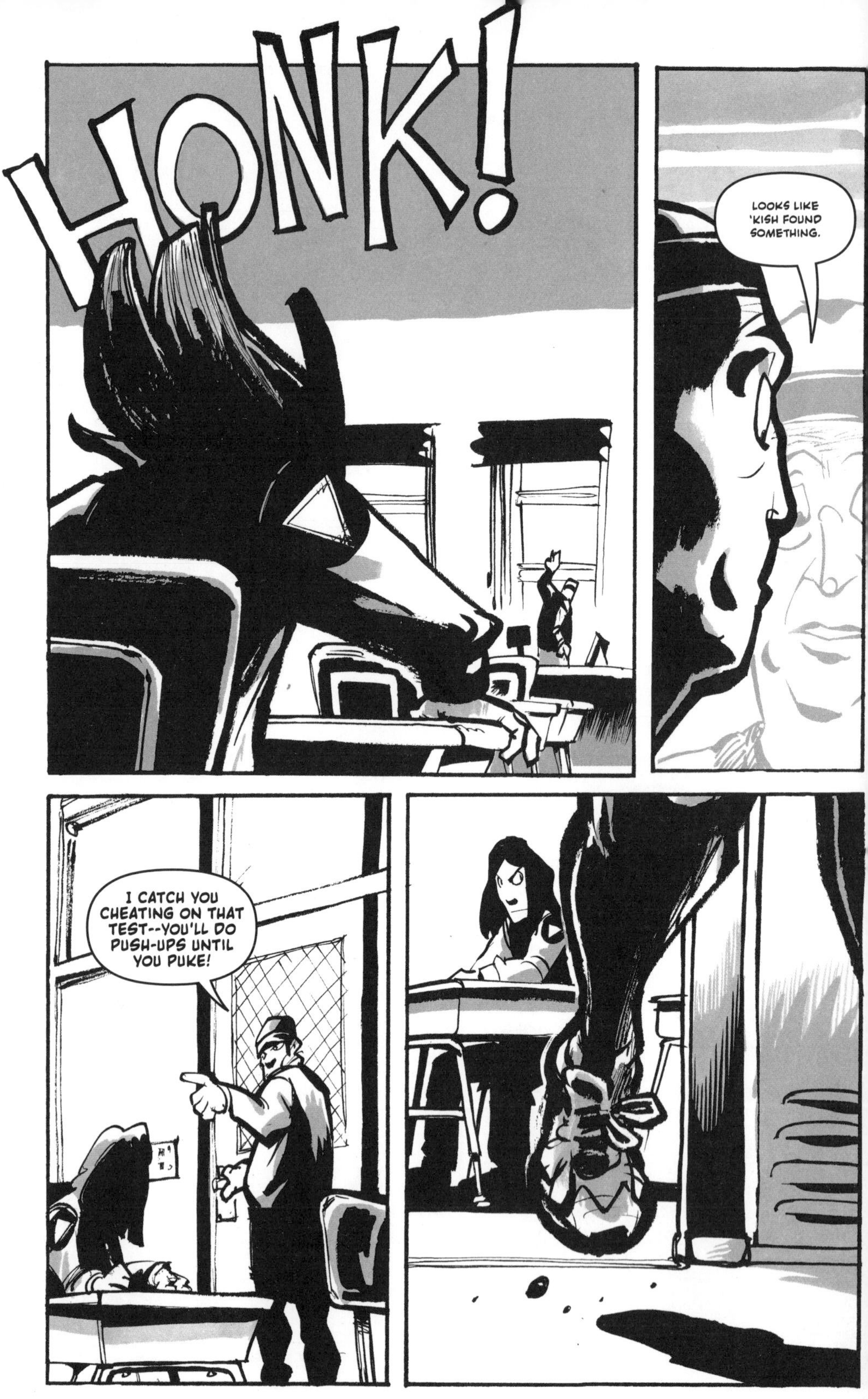
HONK!
LOOKS LIKE 'KISH FOUND SOMETHING.
I CATCH YOU CHEATING ON THAT TEST--YOU'LL DO PUSH-UPS UNTIL YOU PUKE!

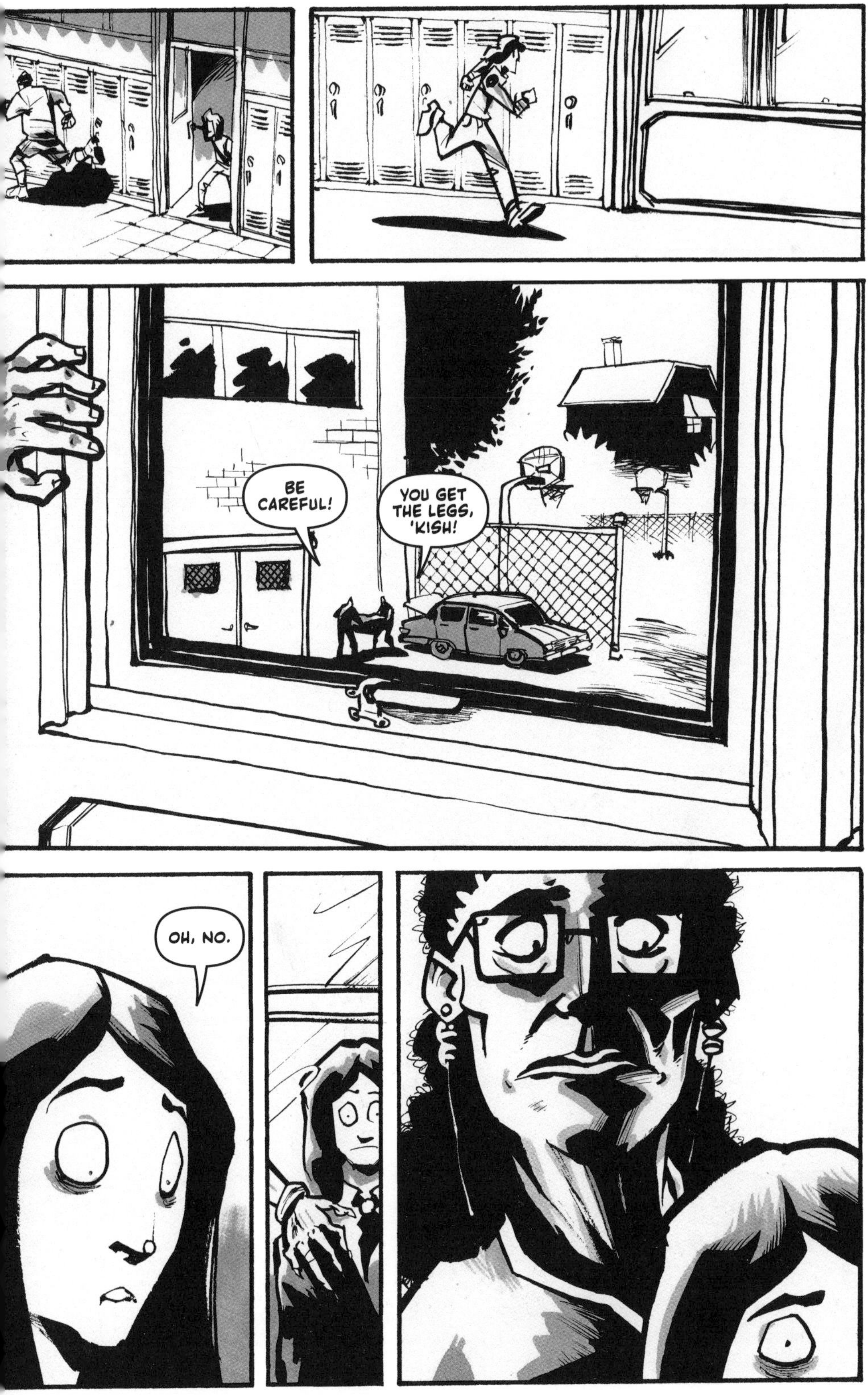
BE CAREFUL!
YOU GET THE LEGS, 'KISH!
OH, NO.

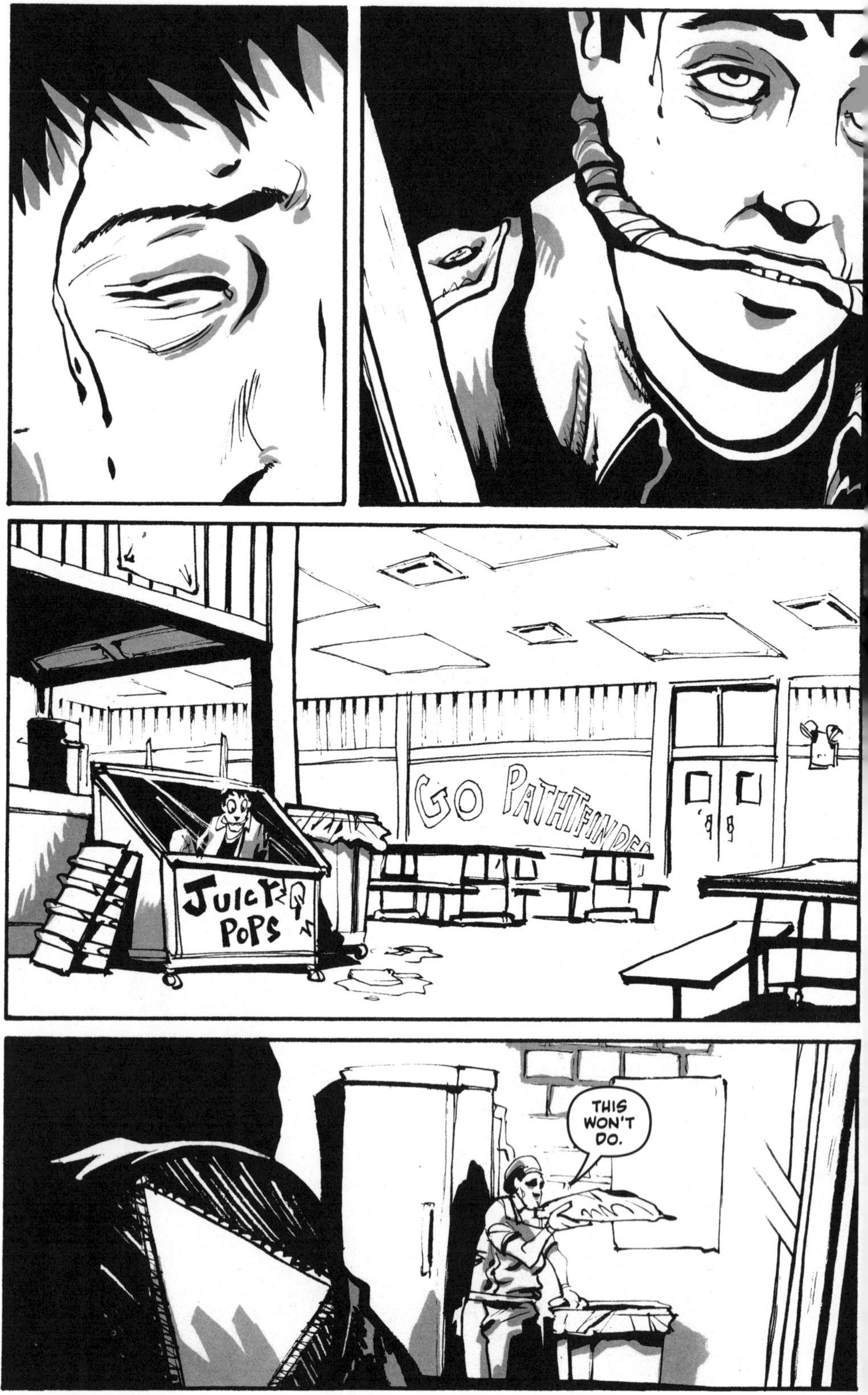
JUICY POPS
GO PATHTFINDER
THIS WON'T DO.

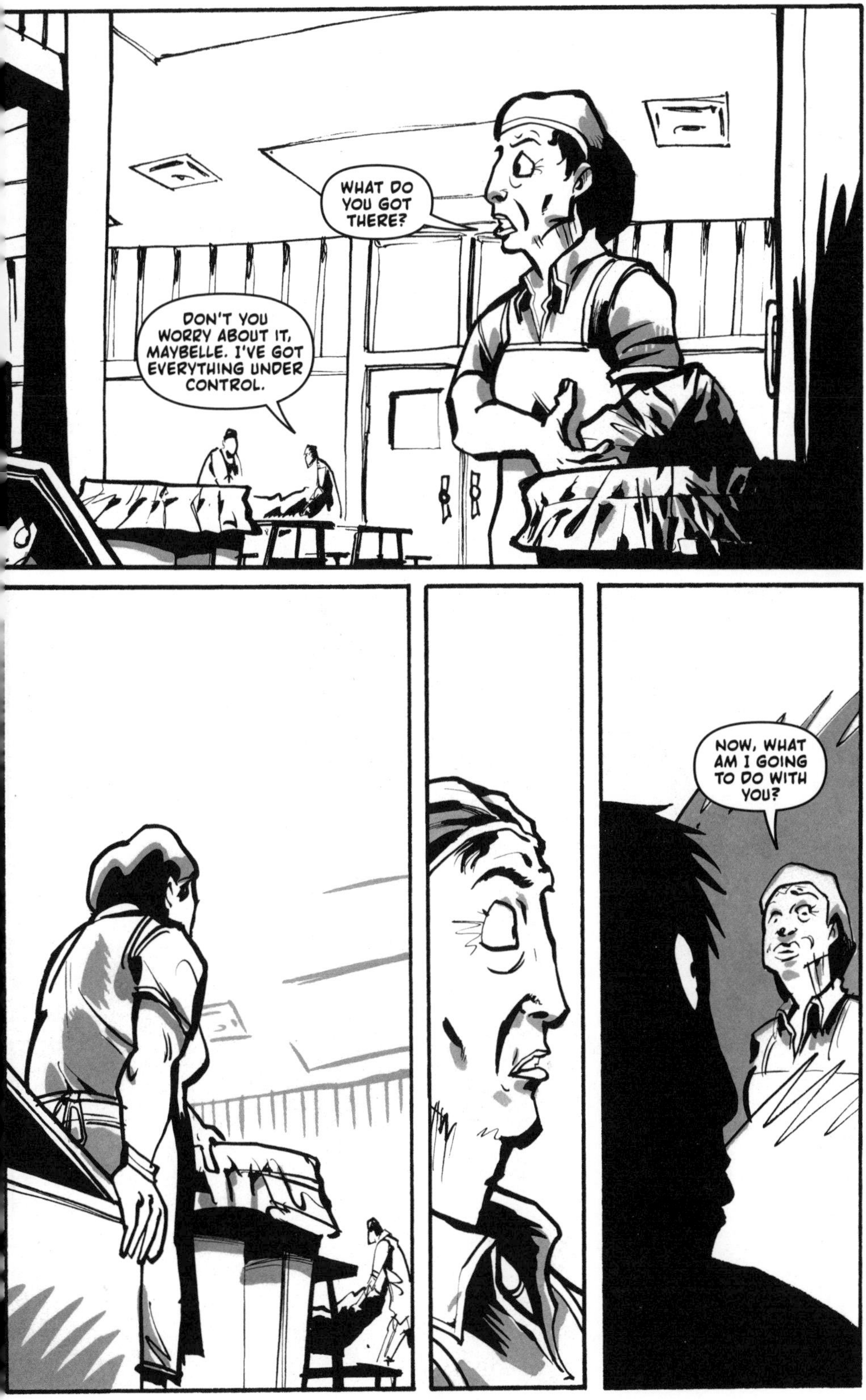
WHAT DO YOU GOT THERE?
DON'T YOU WORRY ABOUT IT, MAYBELLE. I'VE GOT EVERYTHING UNDER CONTROL.
NOW, WHAT AM I GOING TO DO WITH YOU?

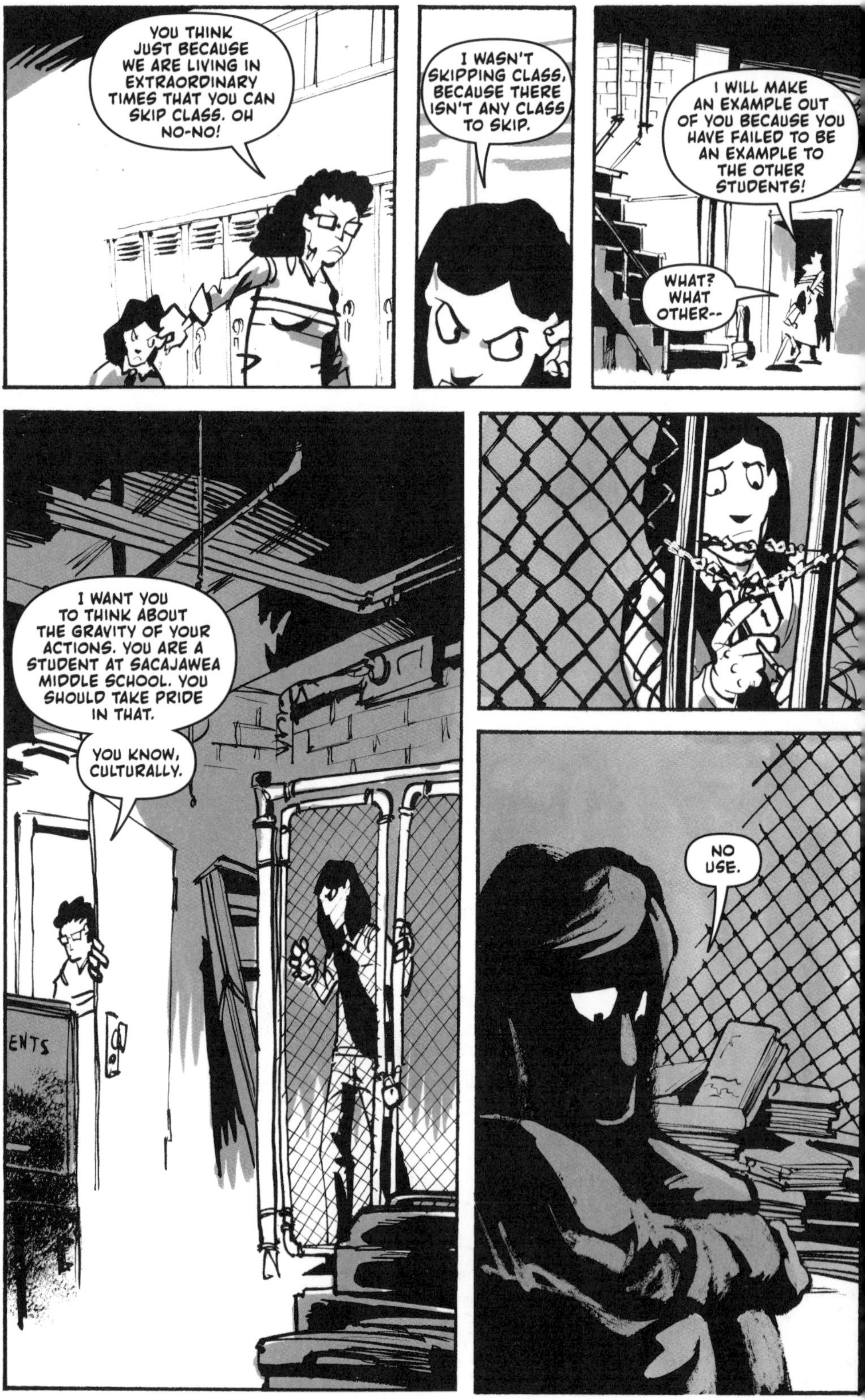
YOU THINK JUST BECAUSE WE ARE LIVING IN EXTRAORDINARY TIMES THAT YOU CAN SKIP CLASS. OH NO-NO!
I WASN'T SKIPPING CLASS, BECAUSE THERE ISN'T ANY CLASS TO SKIP.
I WILL MAKE AN EXAMPLE OUT OF YOU BECAUSE YOU HAVE FAILED TO BE AN EXAMPLE TO THE OTHER STUDENTS!
WHAT? WHAT OTHER--
I WANT YOU TO THINK ABOUT THE GRAVITY OF YOUR ACTIONS. YOU ARE A STUDENT AT SACAJAWEA MIDDLE SCHOOL. YOU SHOULD TAKE PRIDE IN THAT.
YOU KNOW, CULTURALLY.
ENTS
NO USE.

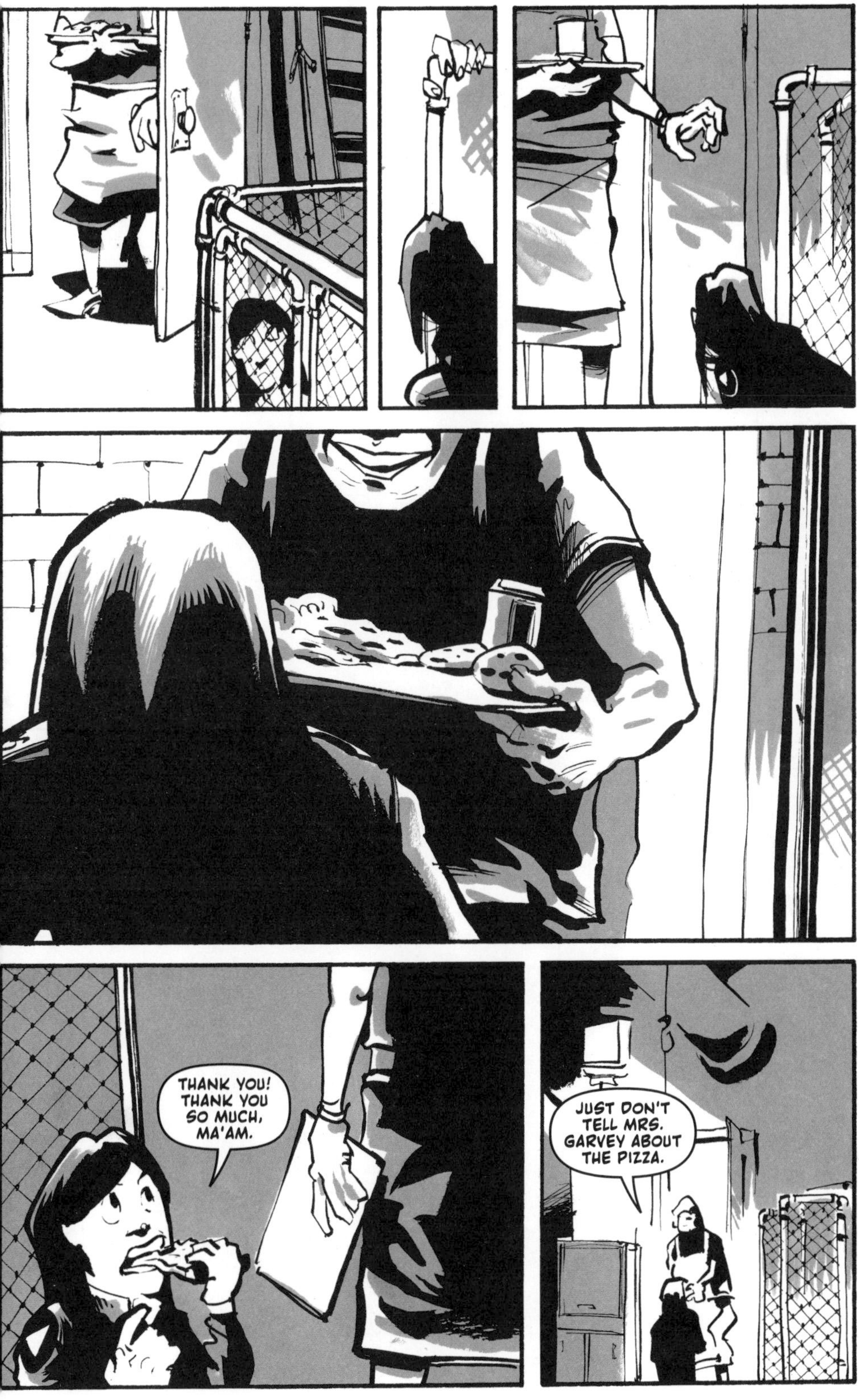
THANK YOU! THANK YOU SO MUCH, MA'AM.
JUST DON'T TELL MRS. GARVEY ABOUT THE PIZZA.

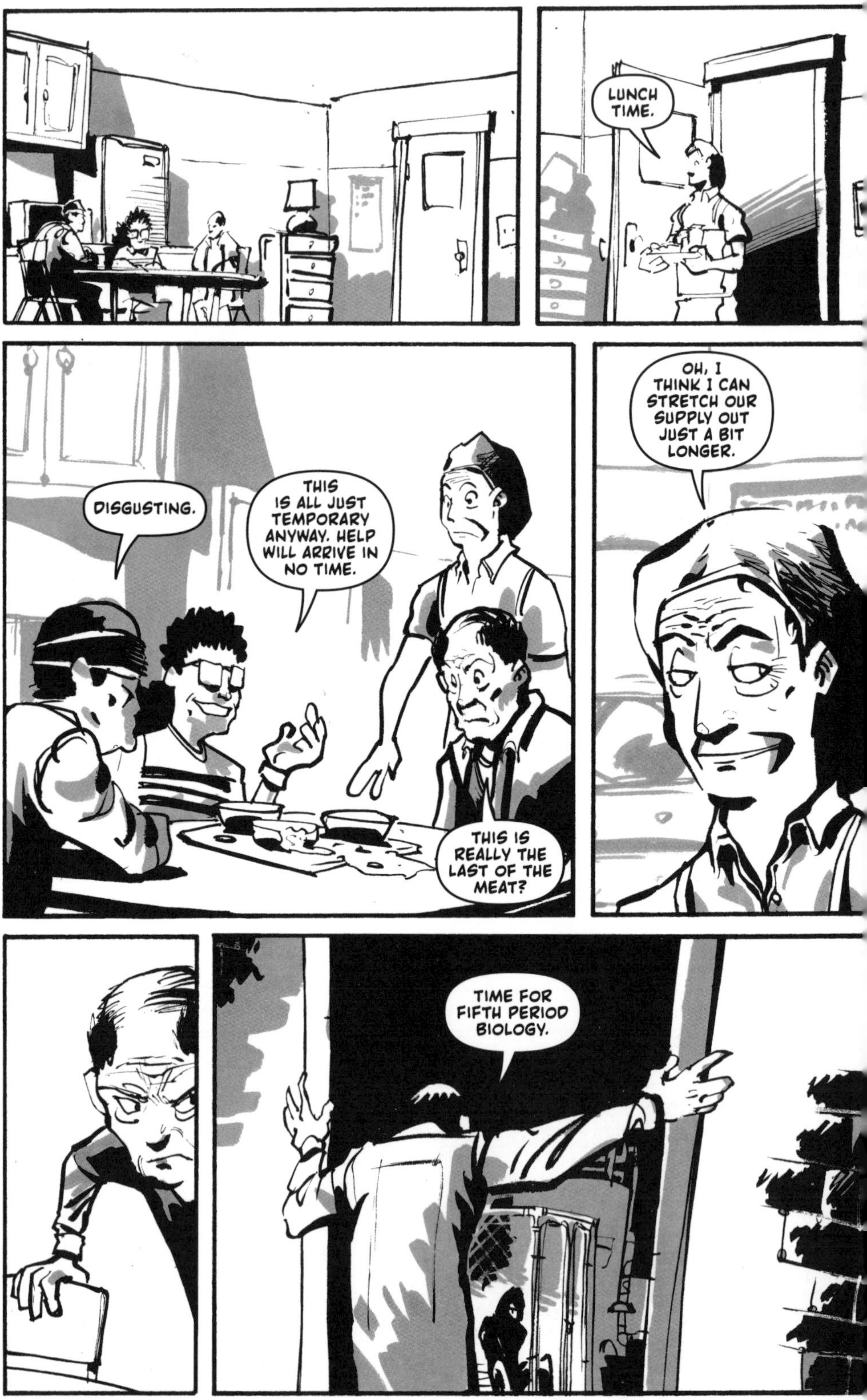
LUNCH TIME.
DISGUSTING.
THIS IS ALL JUST TEMPORARY ANYWAY. HELP WILL ARRIVE IN NO TIME.
THIS IS REALLY THE LAST OF THE MEAT?
OH, I THINK I CAN STRETCH OUR SUPPLY OUT JUST A BIT LONGER.
TIME FOR FIFTH PERIOD BIOLOGY.

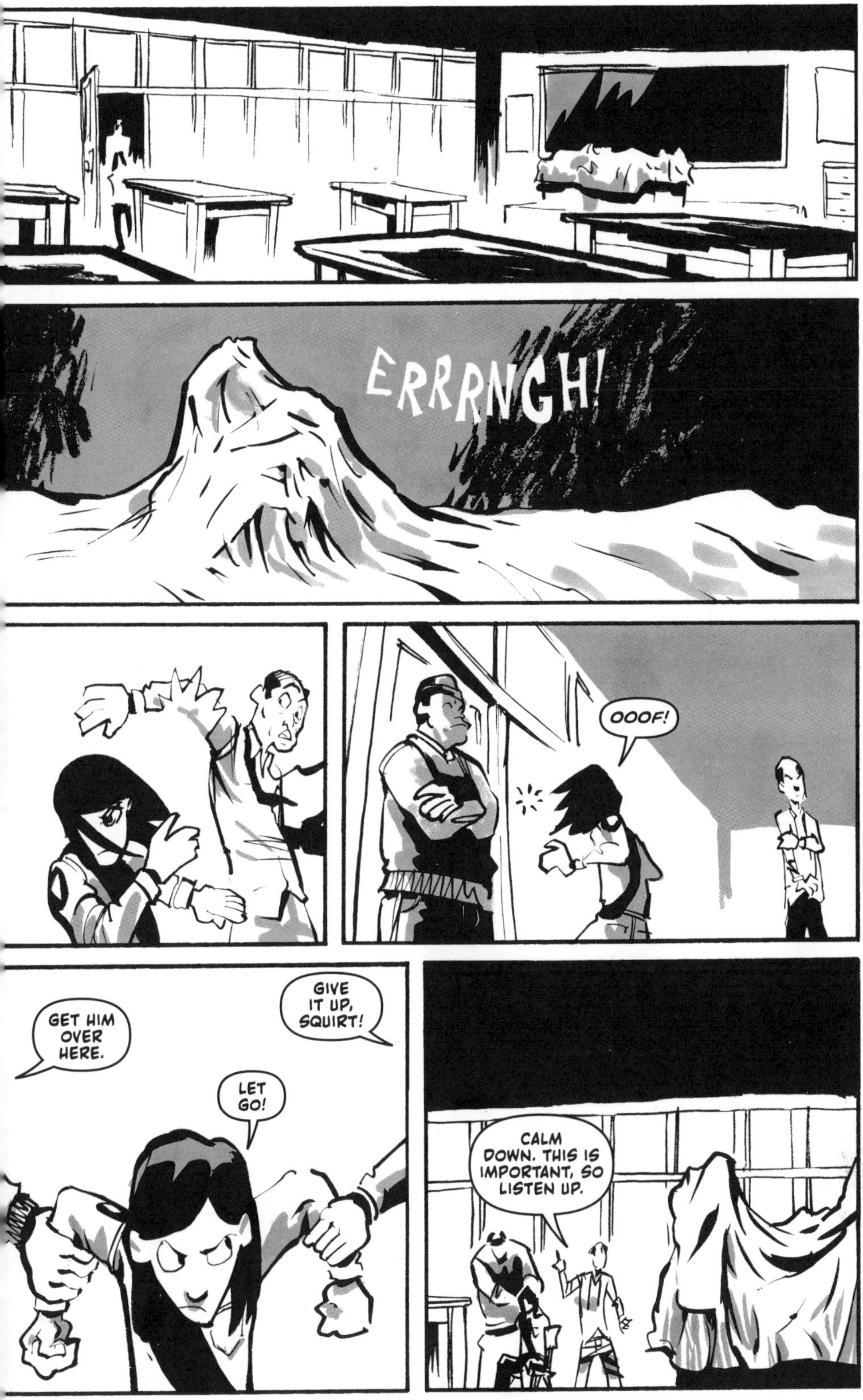
ERRRNGH!
OOOF!
GET HIM OVER HERE.
GIVE IT UP, SQUIRT!
LET GO!
CALM DOWN. THIS IS IMPORTANT, SO LISTEN UP.

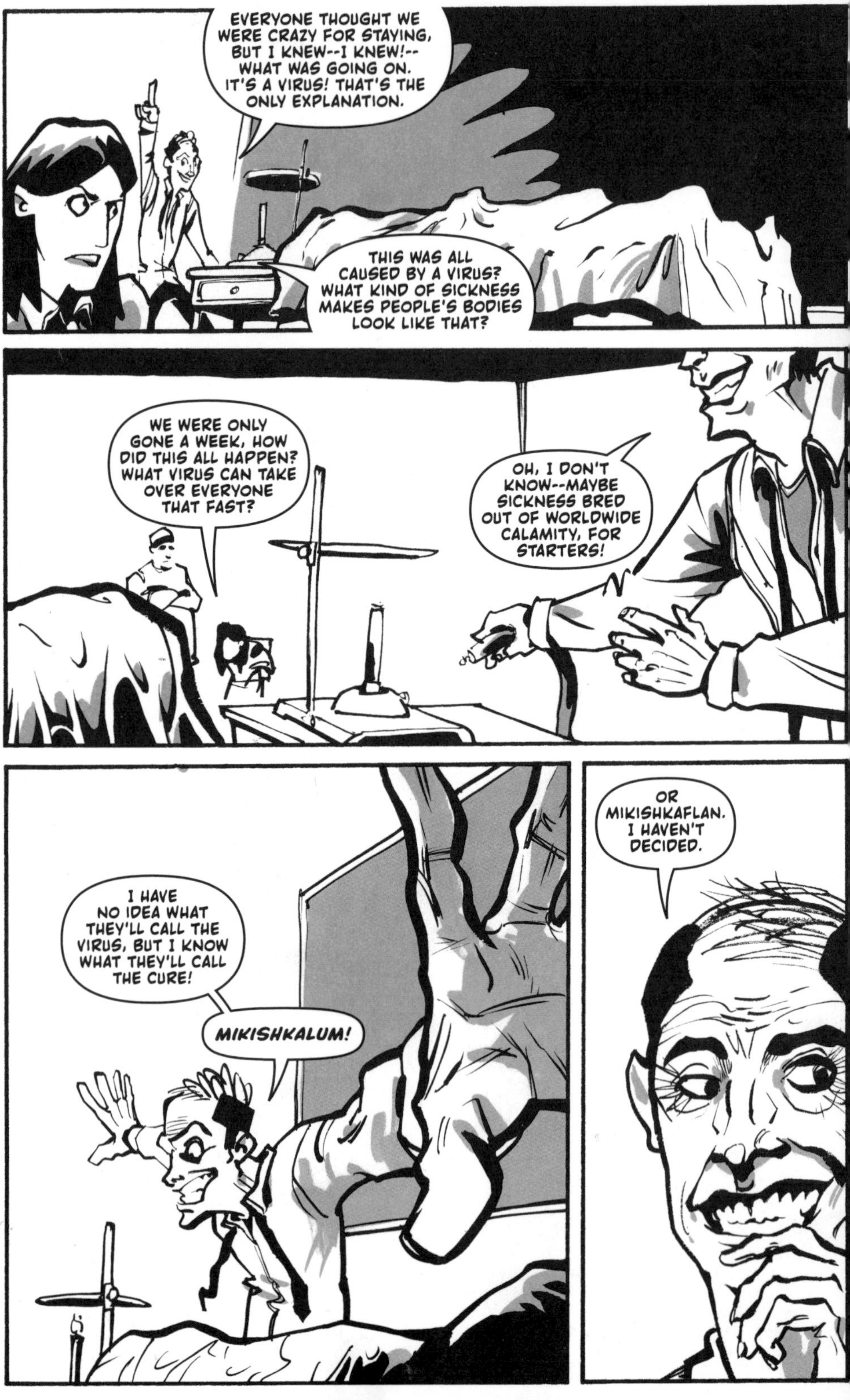

EVERYONE THOUGHT WE WERE CRAZY FOR STAYING, BUT I KNEW--I KNEW!-- WHAT WAS GOING ON. IT'S A VIRUS! THAT'S THE ONLY EXPLANATION.
THIS WAS ALL CAUSED BY A VIRUS? WHAT KIND OF SICKNESS MAKES PEOPLE'S BODIES LOOK LIKE THAT?
WE WERE ONLY GONE A WEEK, HOW DID THIS ALL HAPPEN? WHAT VIRUS CAN TAKE OVER EVERYONE THAT FAST?
OH, I DON'T KNOW--MAYBE SICKNESS BRED OUT OF WORLDWIDE CALAMITY, FOR STARTERS!
I HAVE NO IDEA WHAT THEY'LL CALL THE VIRUS, BUT I KNOW WHAT THEY'LL CALL THE CURE!
MIKISHKALUM!
OR MIKISHKAFLAN. I HAVEN'T DECIDED.

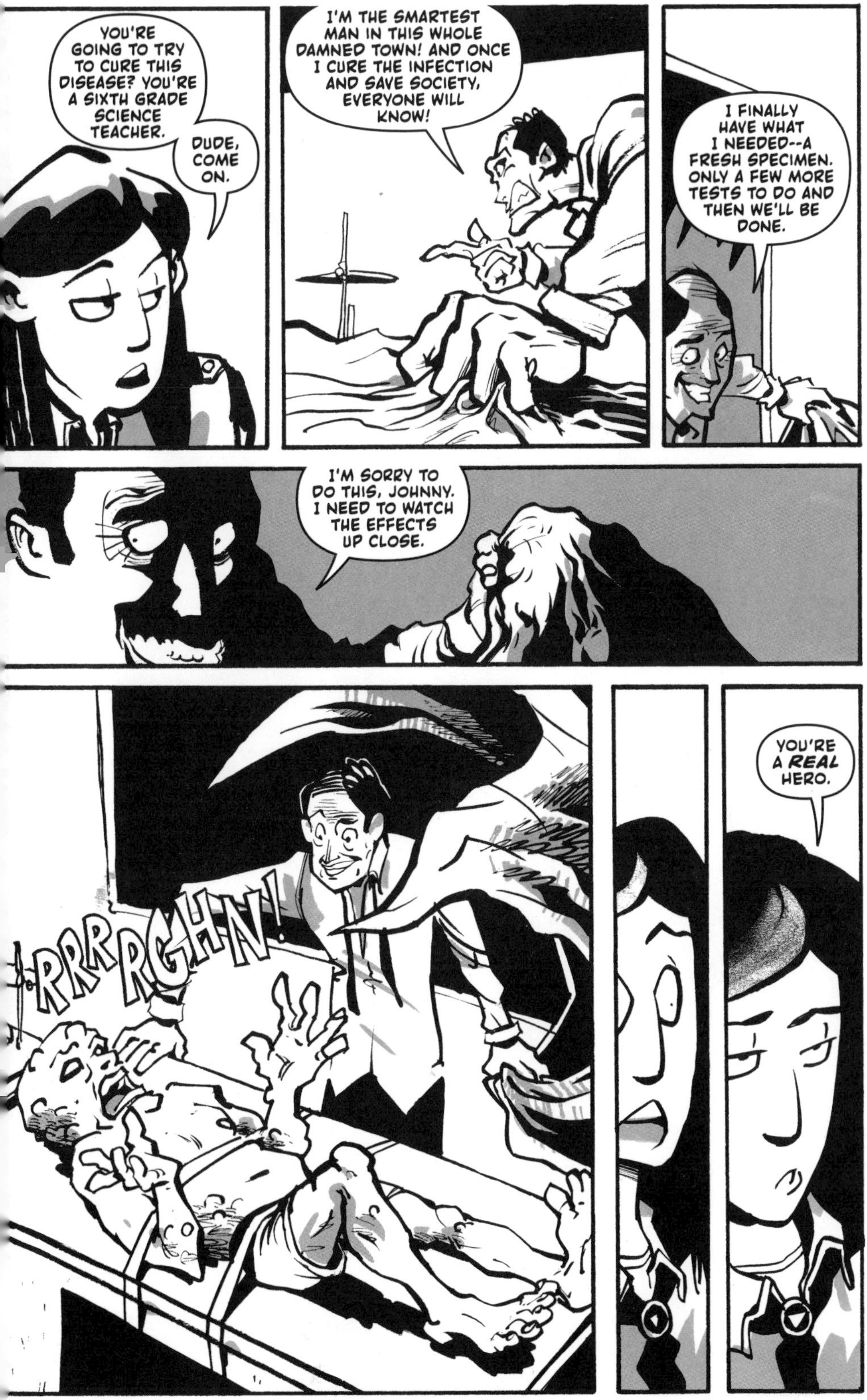
YOU'RE GOING TO TRY TO CURE THIS DISEASE? YOU'RE A SIXTH GRADE SCIENCE TEACHER.
DUDE, COME ON.
I'M THE SMARTEST MAN IN THIS WHOLE DAMNED TOWN! AND ONCE I CURE THE INFECTION AND SAVE SOCIETY, EVERYONE WILL KNOW!
I FINALLY HAVE WHAT I NEEDED--A FRESH SPECIMEN. ONLY A FEW MORE TESTS TO DO AND THEN WE'LL BE DONE.
I'M SORRY TO DO THIS, JOHNNY. I NEED TO WATCH THE EFFECTS UP CLOSE.
RRRRGHN!
YOU'RE A *REAL* HERO.

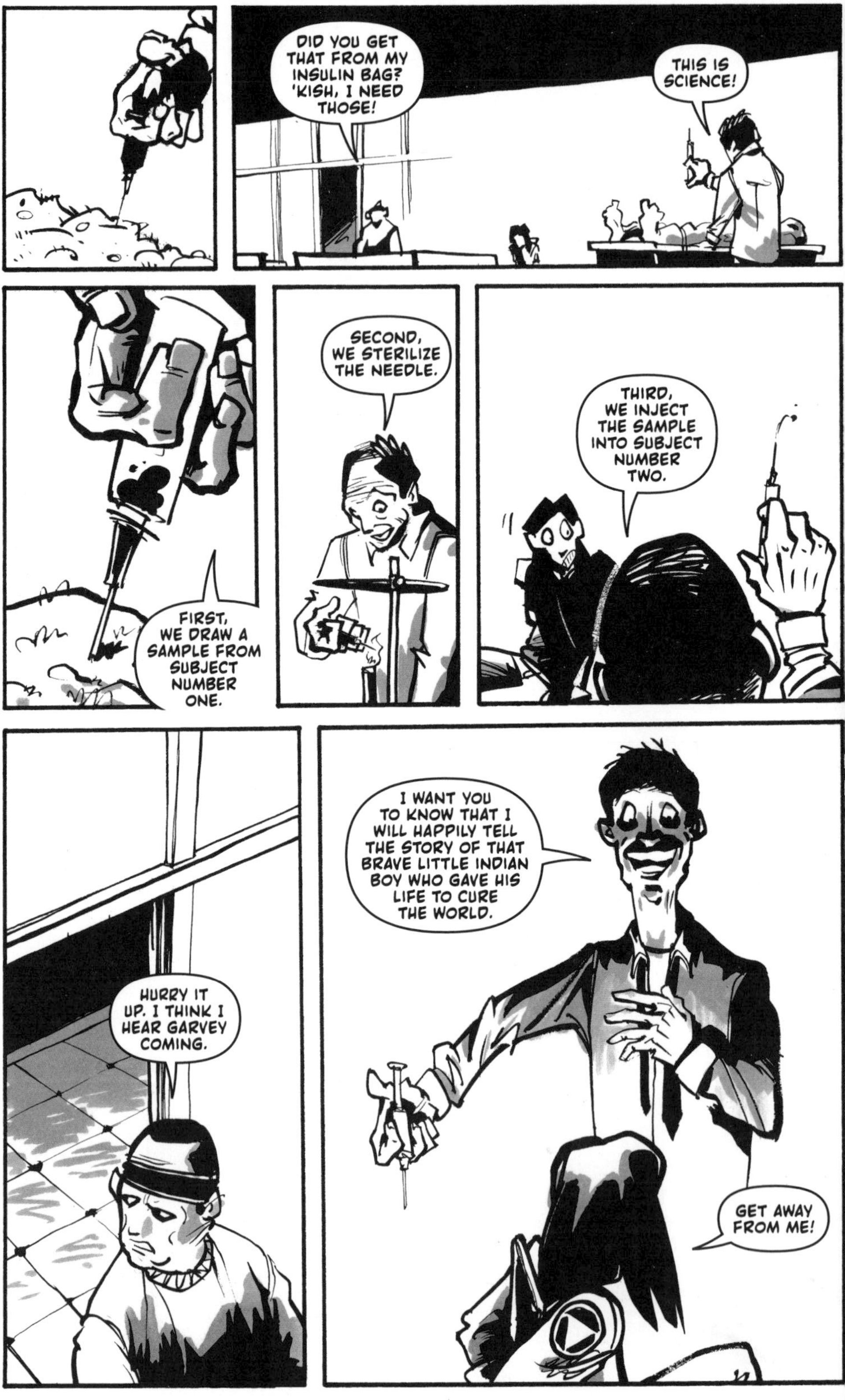

DID YOU GET THAT FROM MY INSULIN BAG? 'KISH, I NEED THOSE!
THIS IS SCIENCE!
FIRST, WE DRAW A SAMPLE FROM SUBJECT NUMBER ONE.
SECOND, WE STERILIZE THE NEEDLE.
THIRD, WE INJECT THE SAMPLE INTO SUBJECT NUMBER TWO.
HURRY IT UP. I THINK I HEAR GARVEY COMING.
I WANT YOU TO KNOW THAT I WILL HAPPILY TELL THE STORY OF THAT BRAVE LITTLE INDIAN BOY WHO GAVE HIS LIFE TO CURE THE WORLD.
GET AWAY FROM ME!

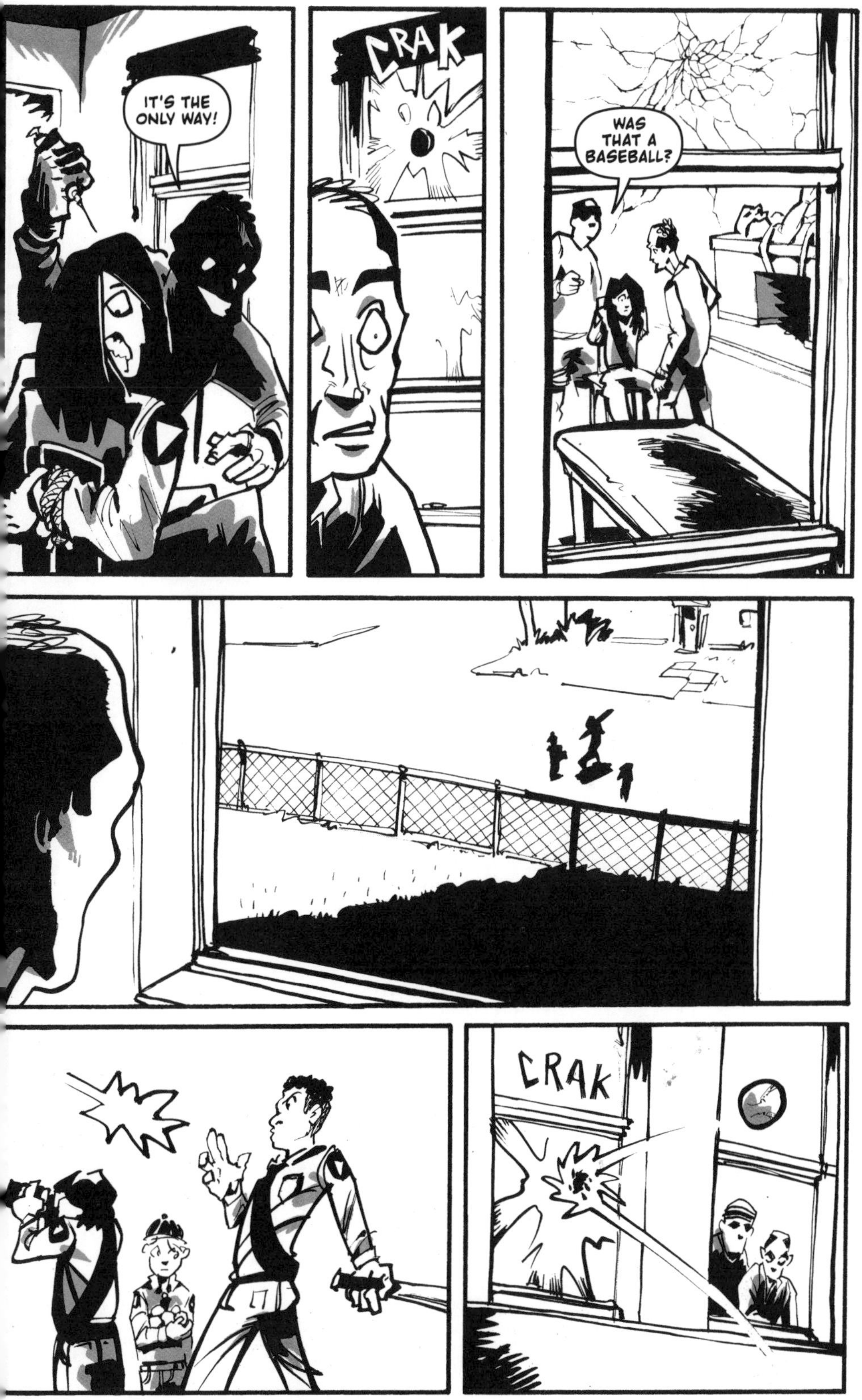
IT'S THE ONLY WAY!
CRAK
WAS THAT A BASEBALL?
CRAK

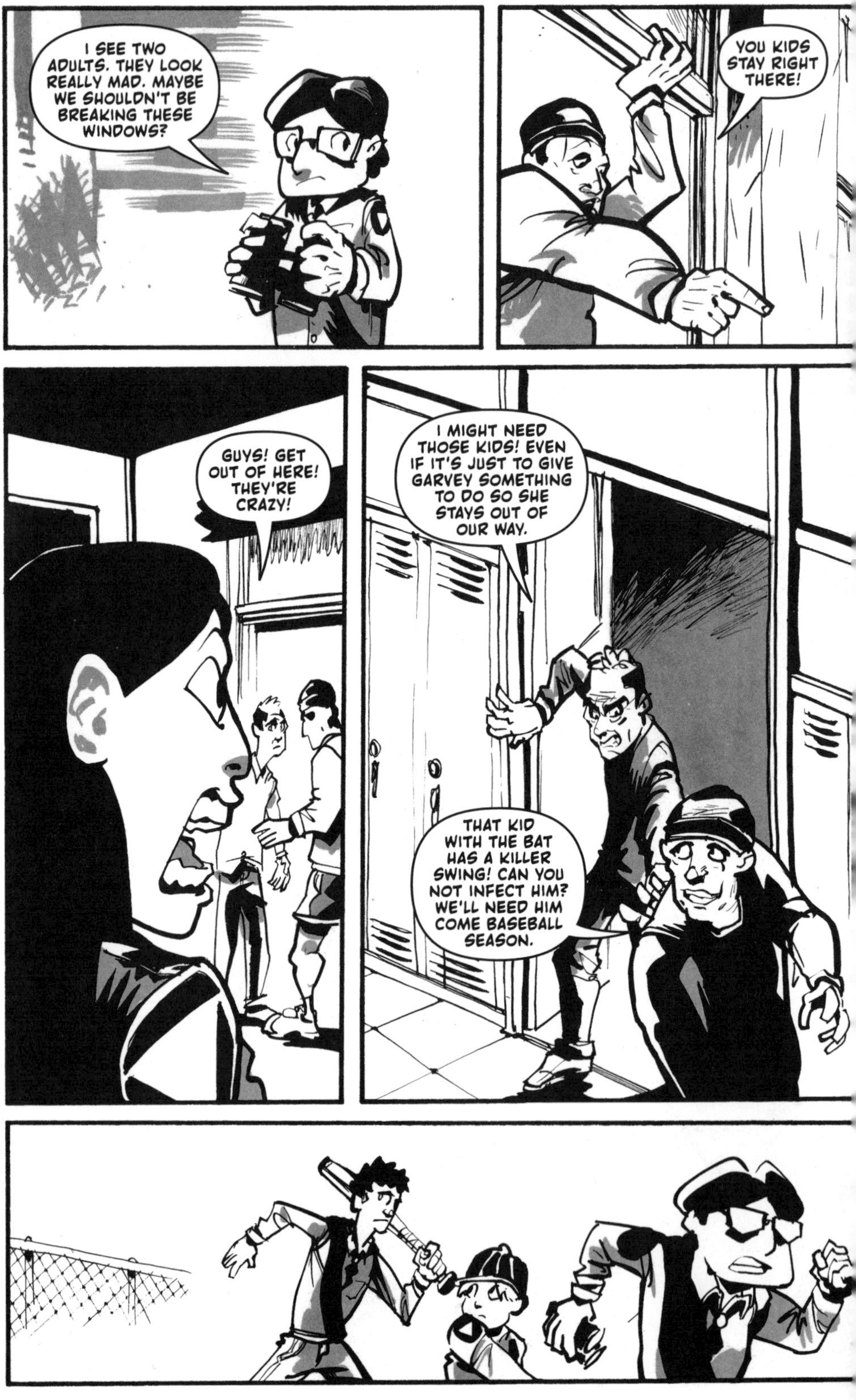
I SEE TWO ADULTS. THEY LOOK REALLY MAD. MAYBE WE SHOULDN'T BE BREAKING THESE WINDOWS?
YOU KIDS STAY RIGHT THERE!
GUYS! GET OUT OF HERE! THEY'RE CRAZY!
I MIGHT NEED THOSE KIDS! EVEN IF IT'S JUST TO GIVE GARVEY SOMETHING TO DO SO SHE STAYS OUT OF OUR WAY.
THAT KID WITH THE BAT HAS A KILLER SWING! CAN YOU NOT INFECT HIM? WE'LL NEED HIM COME BASEBALL SEASON.

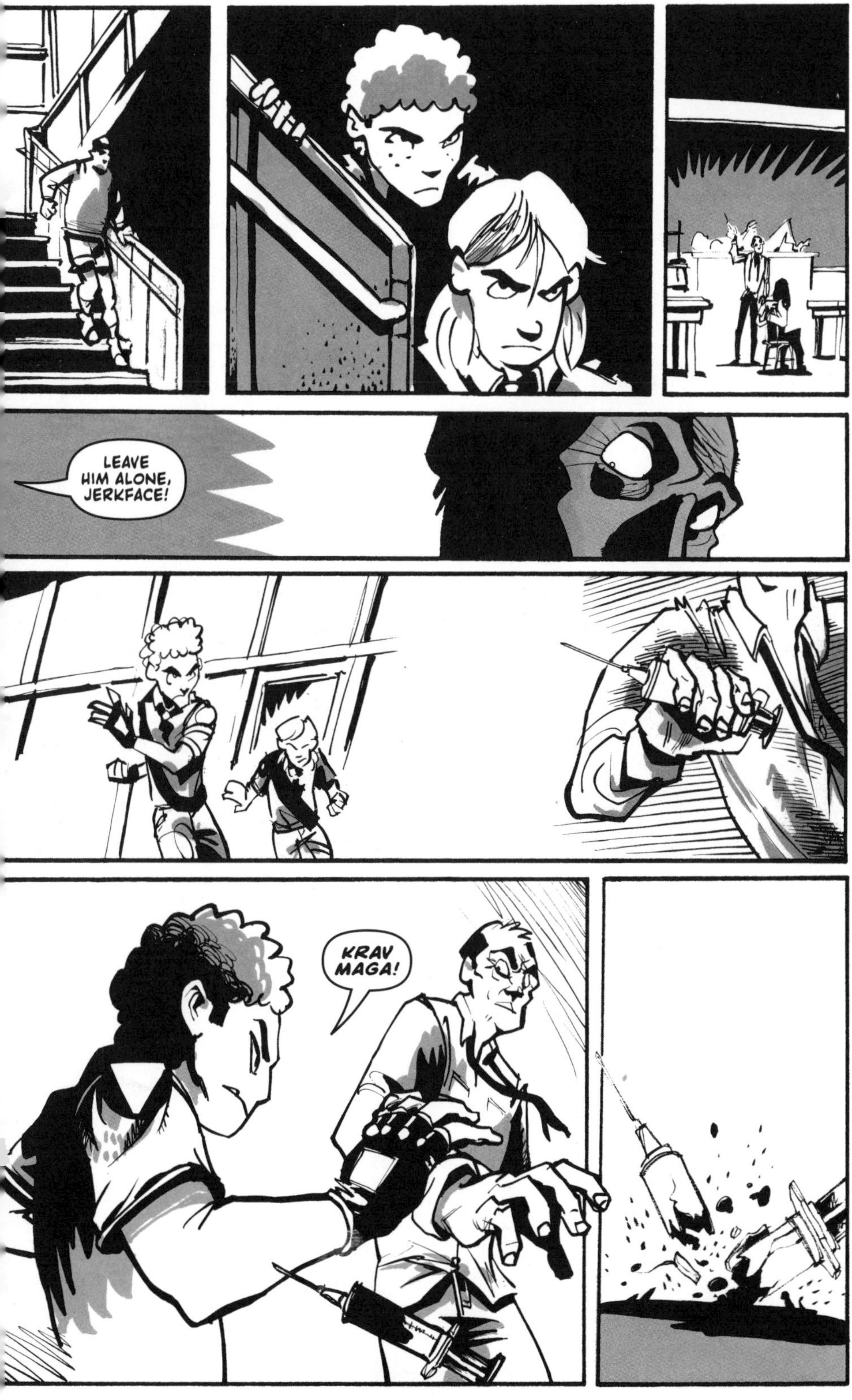
LEAVE HIM ALONE, JERKFACE!
KRAV MAGA!

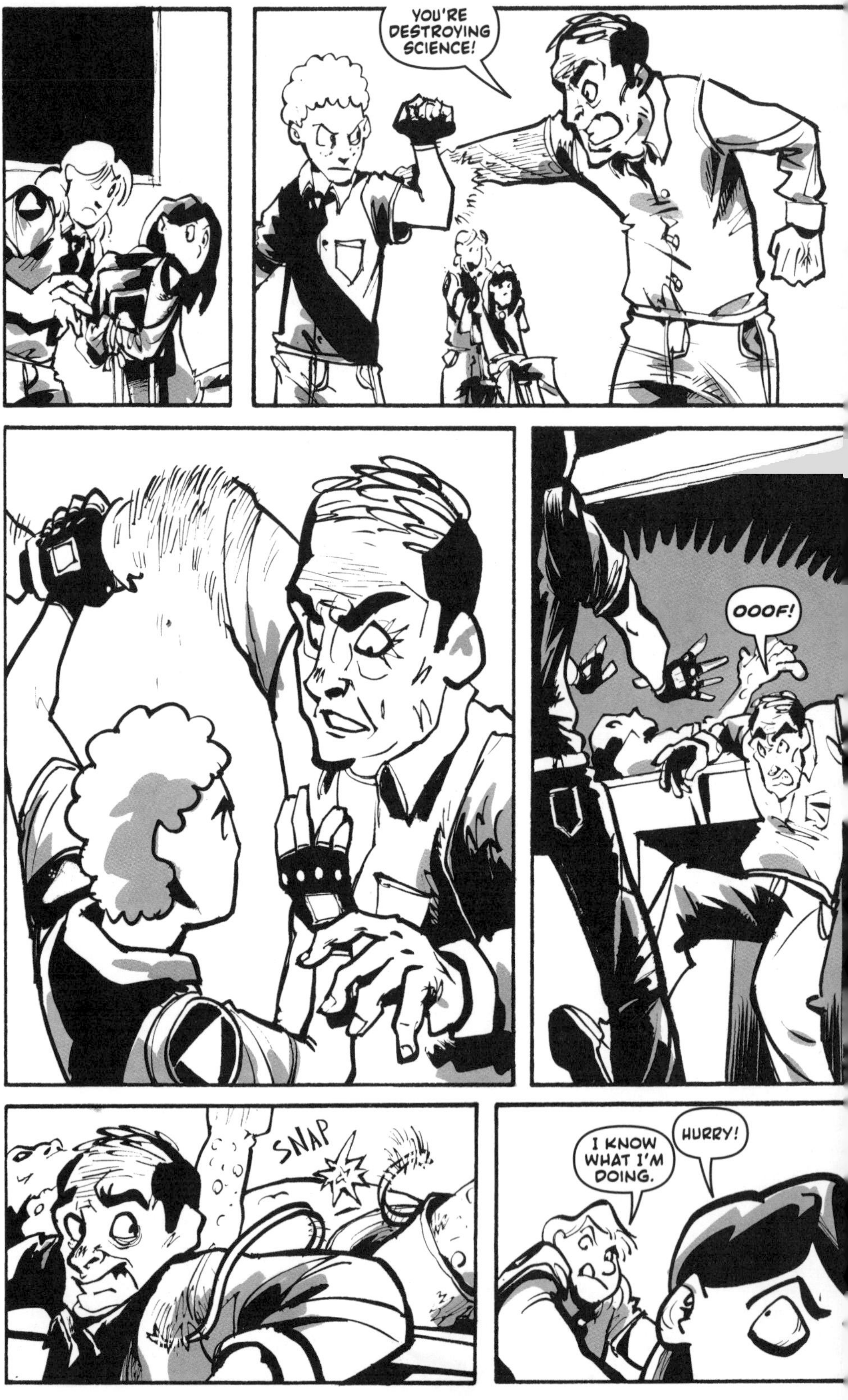
YOU'RE DESTROYING SCIENCE!
OOOF!
SNAP
I KNOW WHAT I'M DOING.
HURRY!

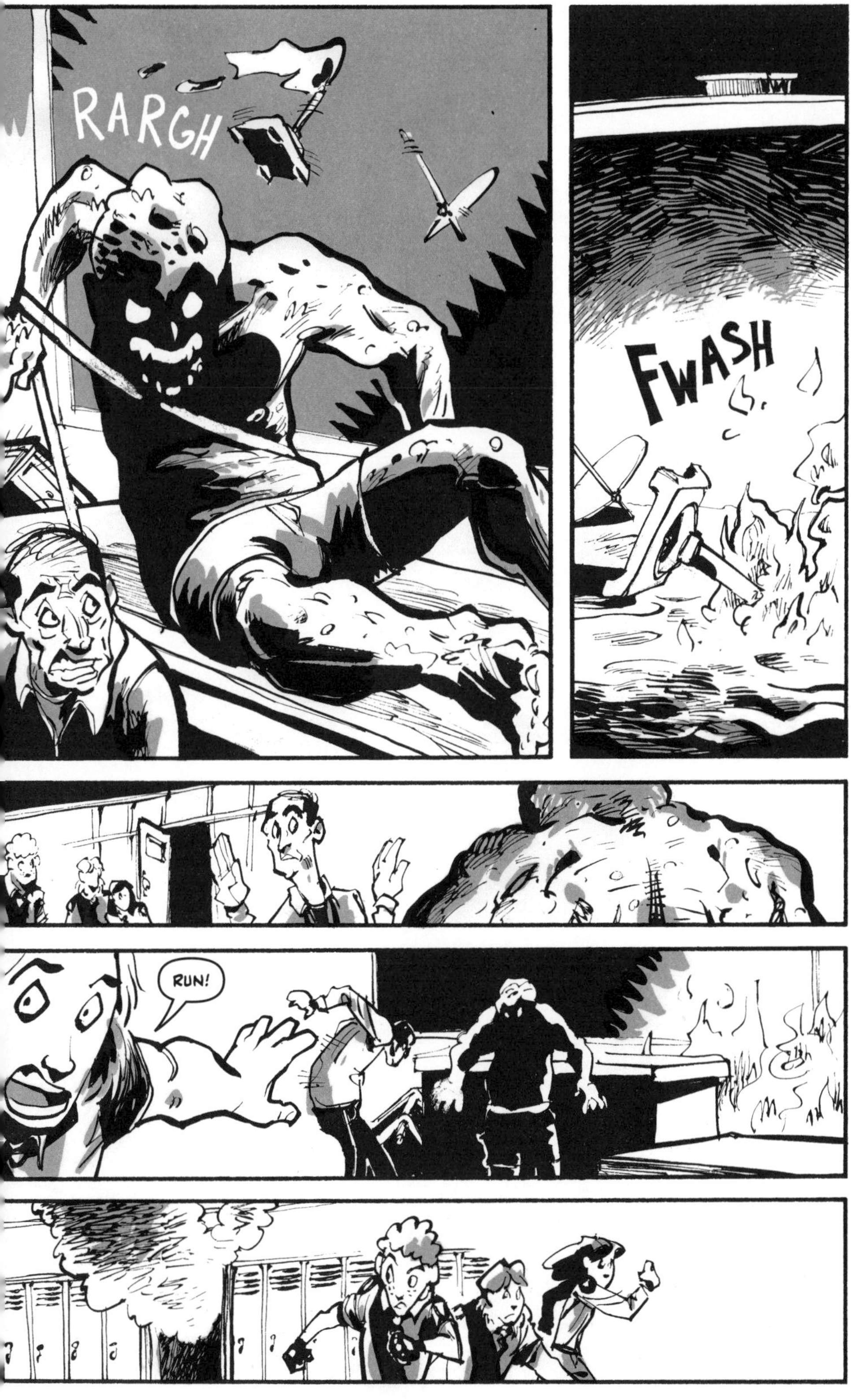
RARGH
FWASH
RUN!

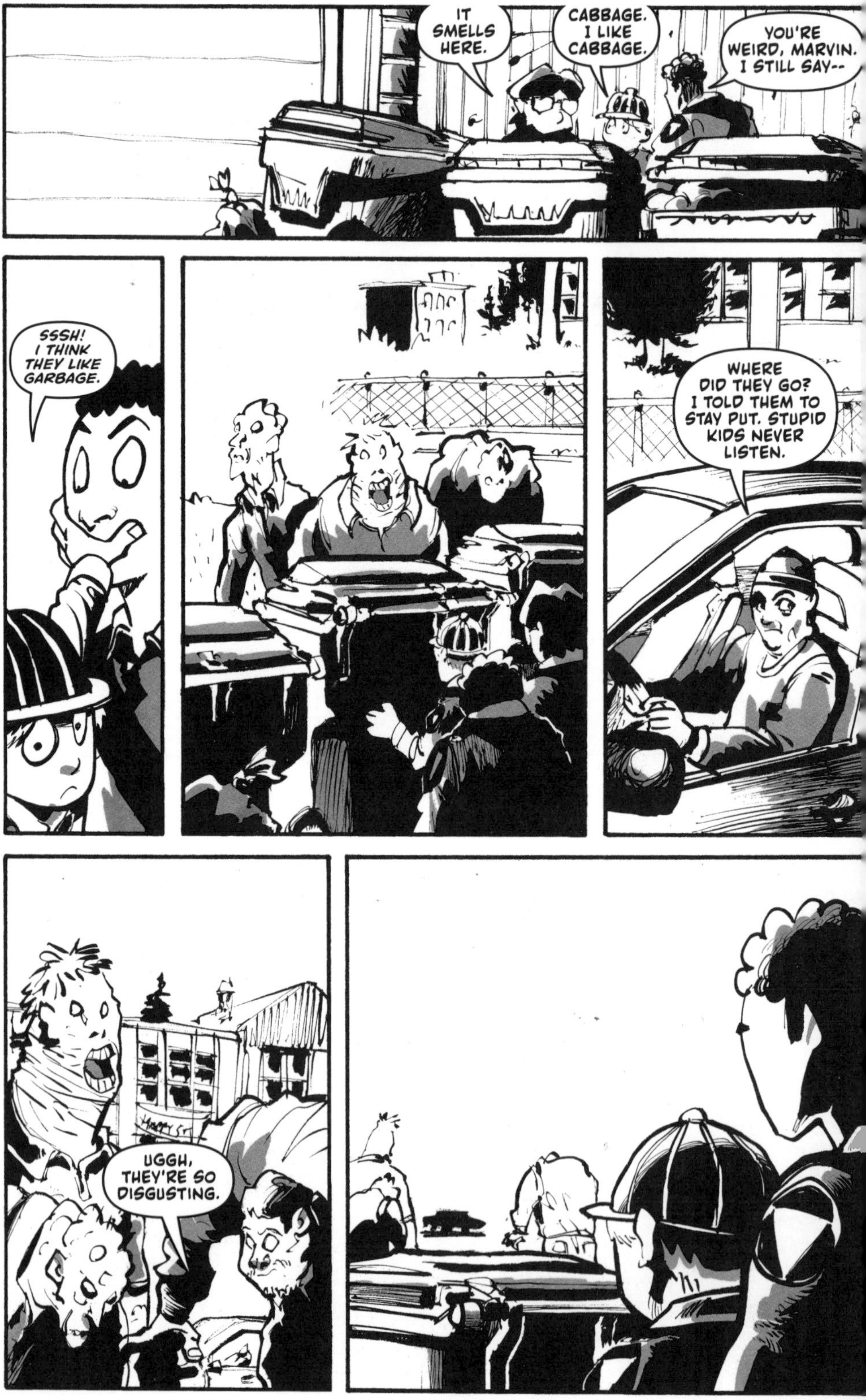
IT SMELLS HERE.
CABBAGE. I LIKE CABBAGE.
YOU'RE WEIRD, MARVIN. I STILL SAY--
SSSH! I THINK THEY LIKE GARBAGE.
WHERE DID THEY GO? I TOLD THEM TO STAY PUT. STUPID KIDS NEVER LISTEN.
UGGH, THEY'RE SO DISGUSTING.

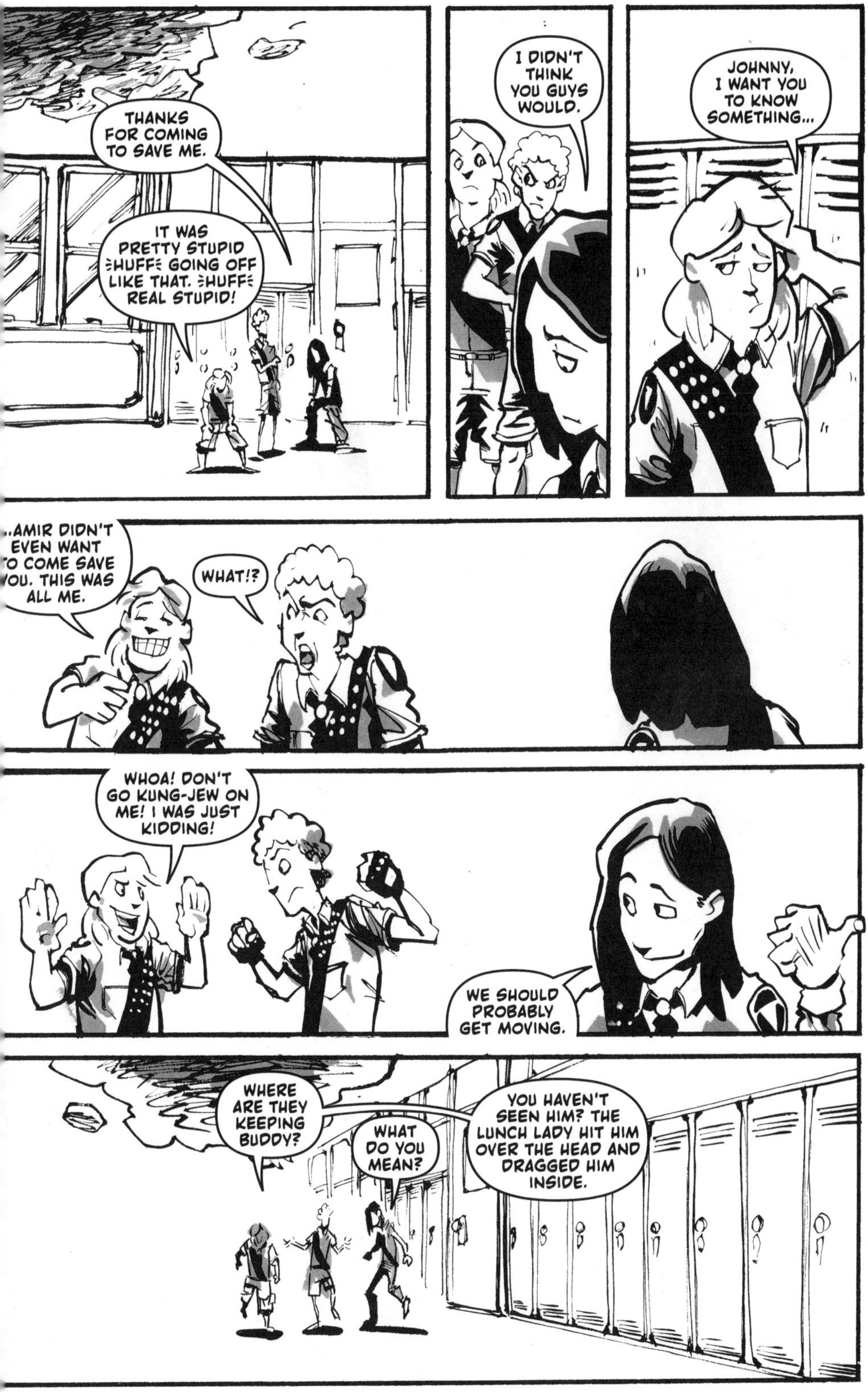
THANKS FOR COMING TO SAVE ME.
IT WAS PRETTY STUPID HUFF GOING OFF LIKE THAT. HUFF REAL STUPID!
I DIDN'T THINK YOU GUYS WOULD.
JOHNNY, I WANT YOU TO KNOW SOMETHING...
..AMIR DIDN'T EVEN WANT TO COME SAVE YOU. THIS WAS ALL ME.
WHAT!?
WHOA! DON'T GO KUNG-JEW ON ME! I WAS JUST KIDDING!
WE SHOULD PROBABLY GET MOVING.
WHERE ARE THEY KEEPING BUDDY?
WHAT DO YOU MEAN?
YOU HAVEN'T SEEN HIM? THE LUNCH LADY HIT HIM OVER THE HEAD AND DRAGGED HIM INSIDE.

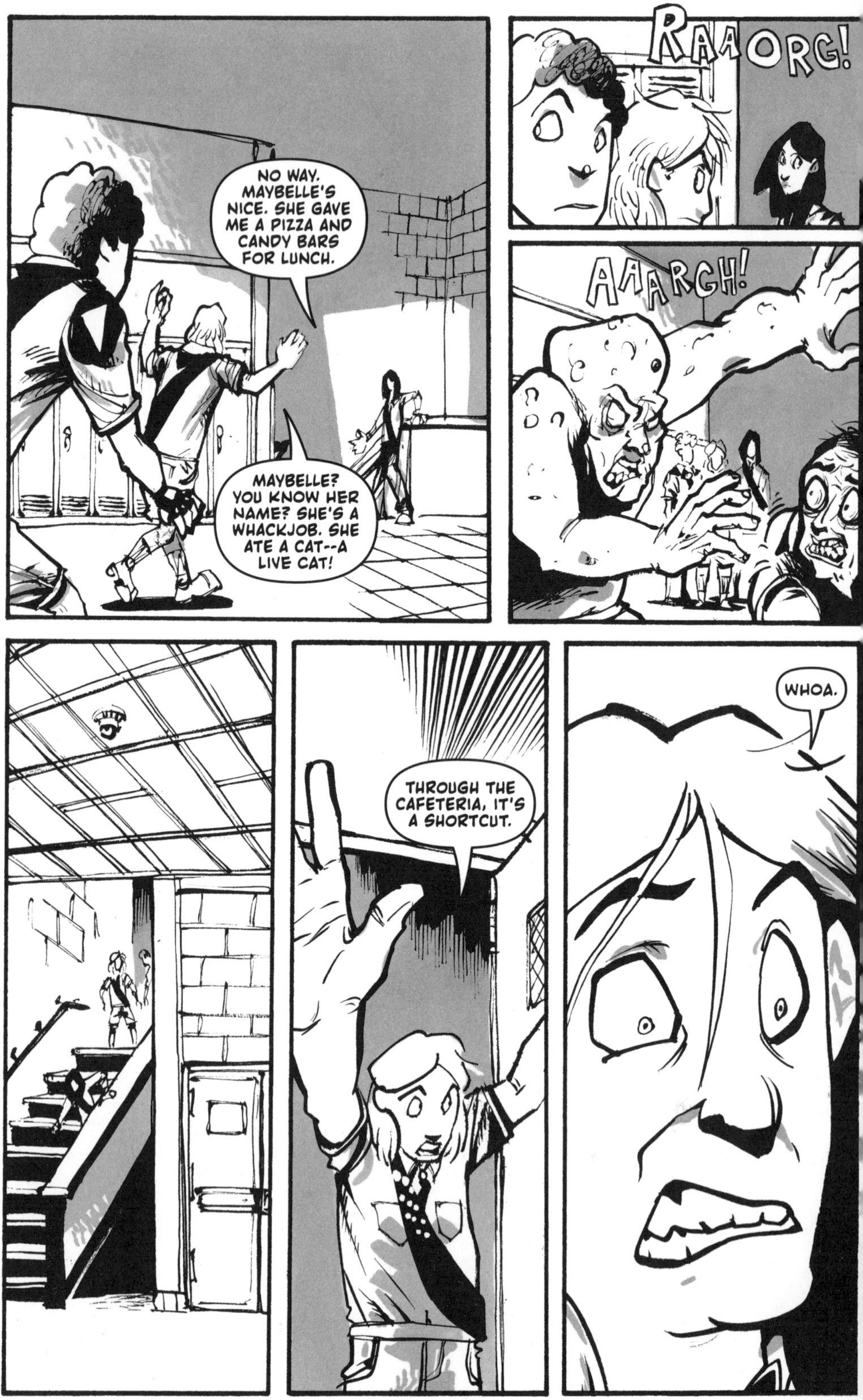
NO WAY. MAYBELLE'S NICE. SHE GAVE ME A PIZZA AND CANDY BARS FOR LUNCH.
MAYBELLE? YOU KNOW HER NAME? SHE'S A WHACKJOB. SHE ATE A CAT--A LIVE CAT!
RAAAORG!
AAARGH!
THROUGH THE CAFETERIA, IT'S A SHORTCUT.
WHOA.

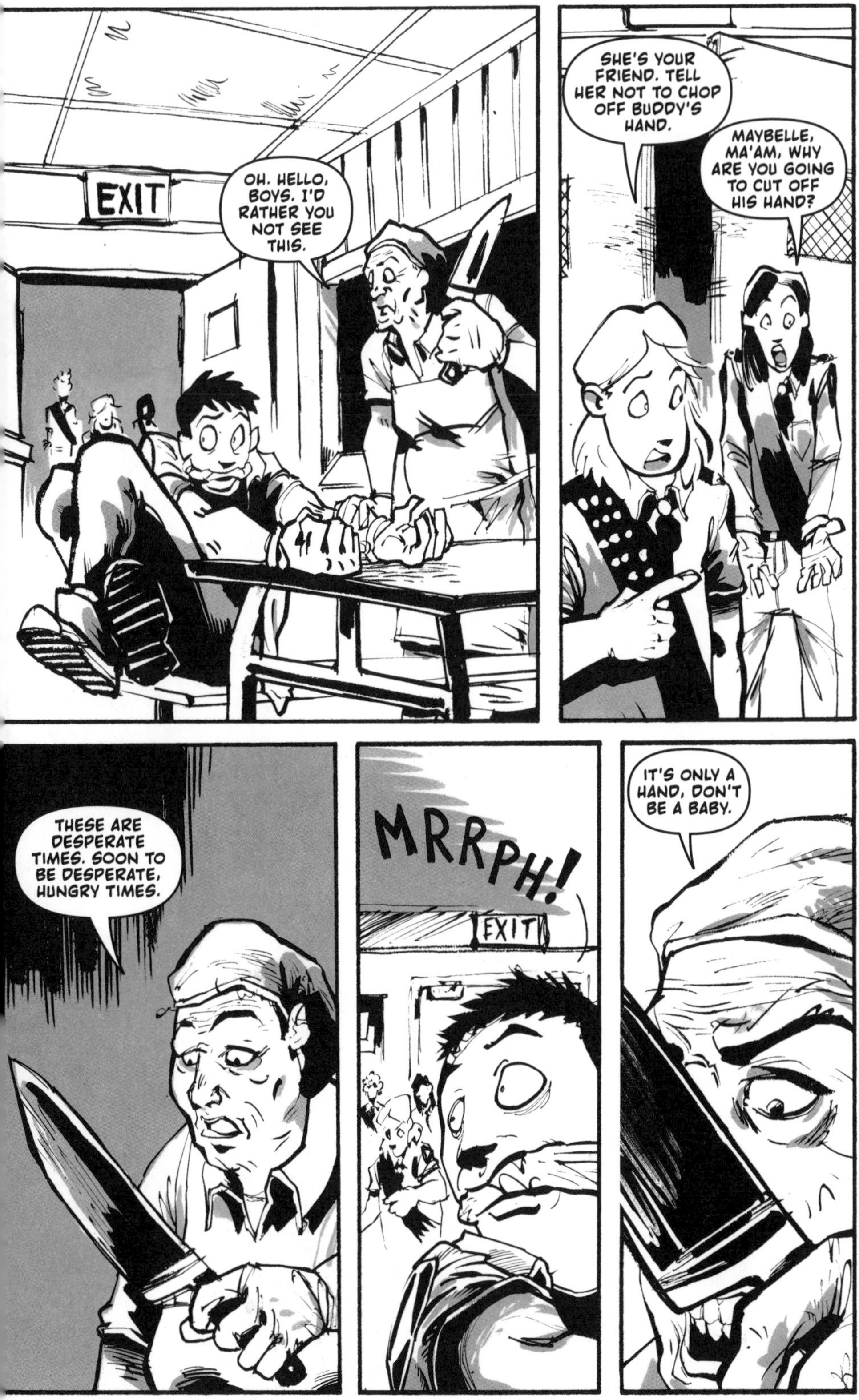
EXIT
OH. HELLO, BOYS. I'D RATHER YOU NOT SEE THIS.
SHE'S YOUR FRIEND. TELL HER NOT TO CHOP OFF BUDDY'S HAND.
MAYBELLE, MA'AM, WHY ARE YOU GOING TO CUT OFF HIS HAND?
THESE ARE DESPERATE TIMES. SOON TO BE DESPERATE, HUNGRY TIMES.
MRRPH!
EXIT
IT'S ONLY A HAND, DON'T BE A BABY.

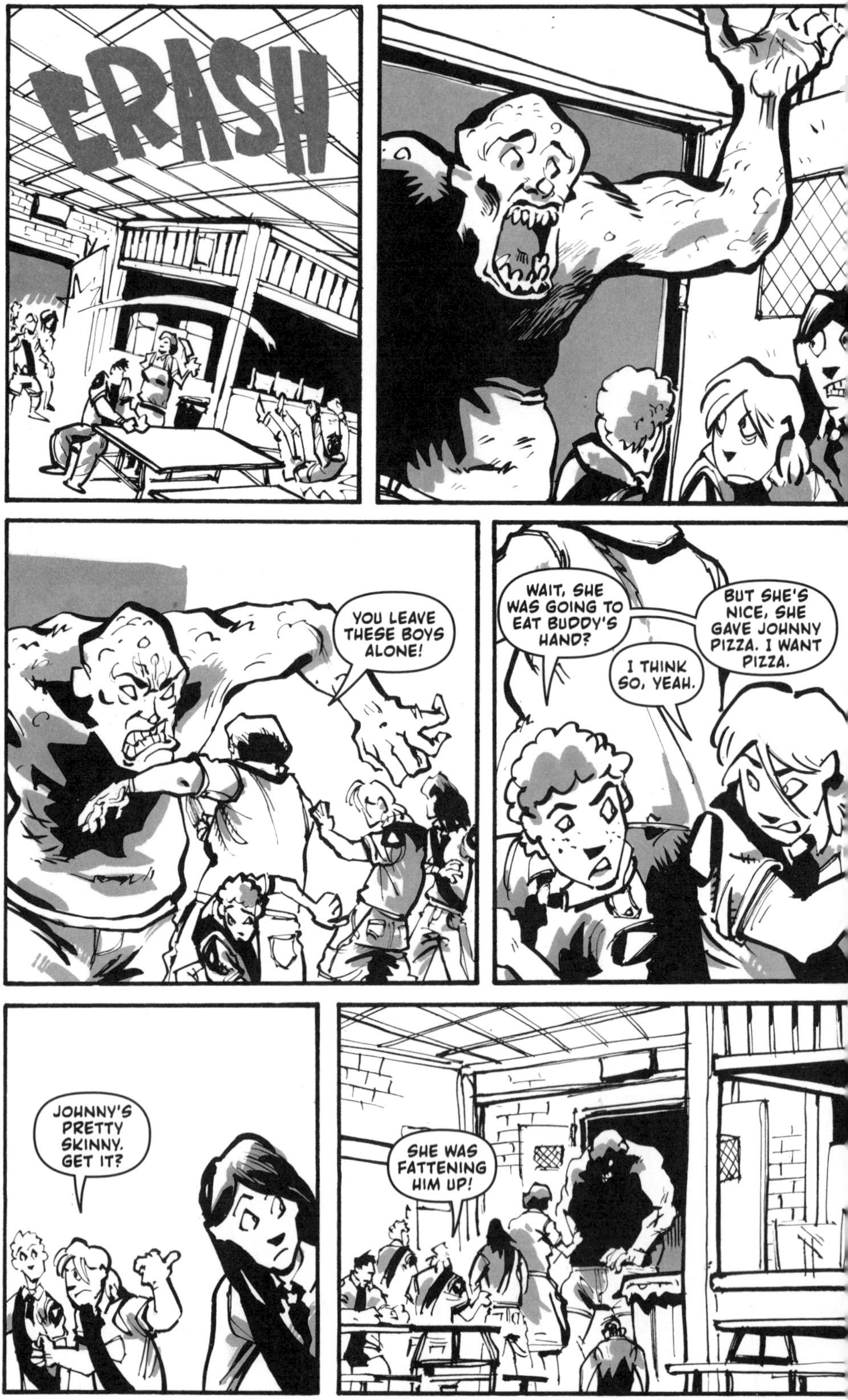
CRASH
YOU LEAVE THESE BOYS ALONE!
WAIT, SHE WAS GOING TO EAT BUDDY'S HAND?
I THINK SO, YEAH.
BUT SHE'S NICE, SHE GAVE JOHNNY PIZZA. I WANT PIZZA.
JOHNNY'S PRETTY SKINNY. GET IT?
SHE WAS FATTENING HIM UP!

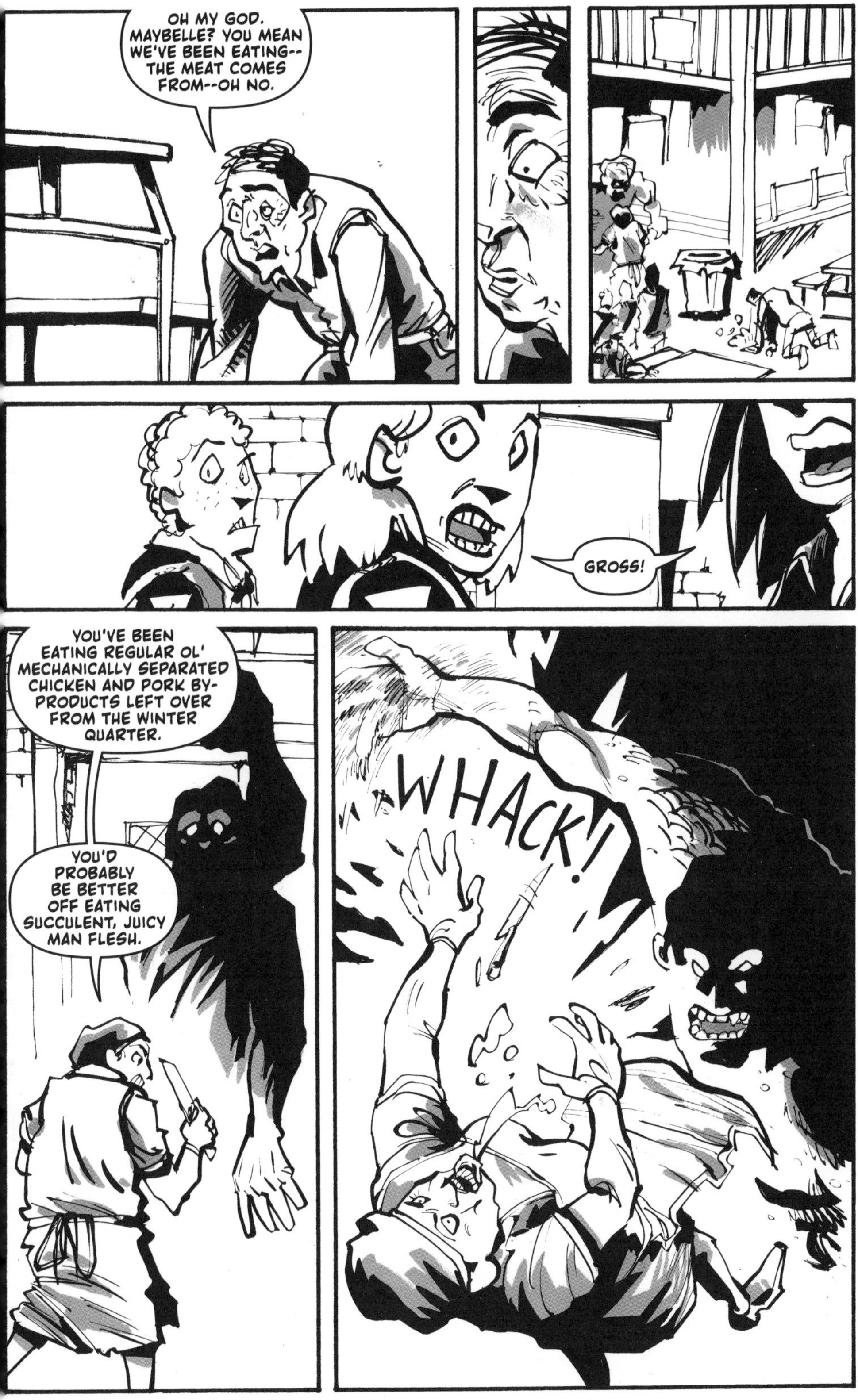
OH MY GOD. MAYBELLE? YOU MEAN WE'VE BEEN EATING-- THE MEAT COMES FROM--OH NO.
GROSS!
YOU'VE BEEN EATING REGULAR OL' MECHANICALLY SEPARATED CHICKEN AND PORK BY-PRODUCTS LEFT OVER FROM THE WINTER QUARTER.
YOU'D PROBABLY BE BETTER OFF EATING SUCCULENT, JUICY MAN FLESH.
WHACK!!

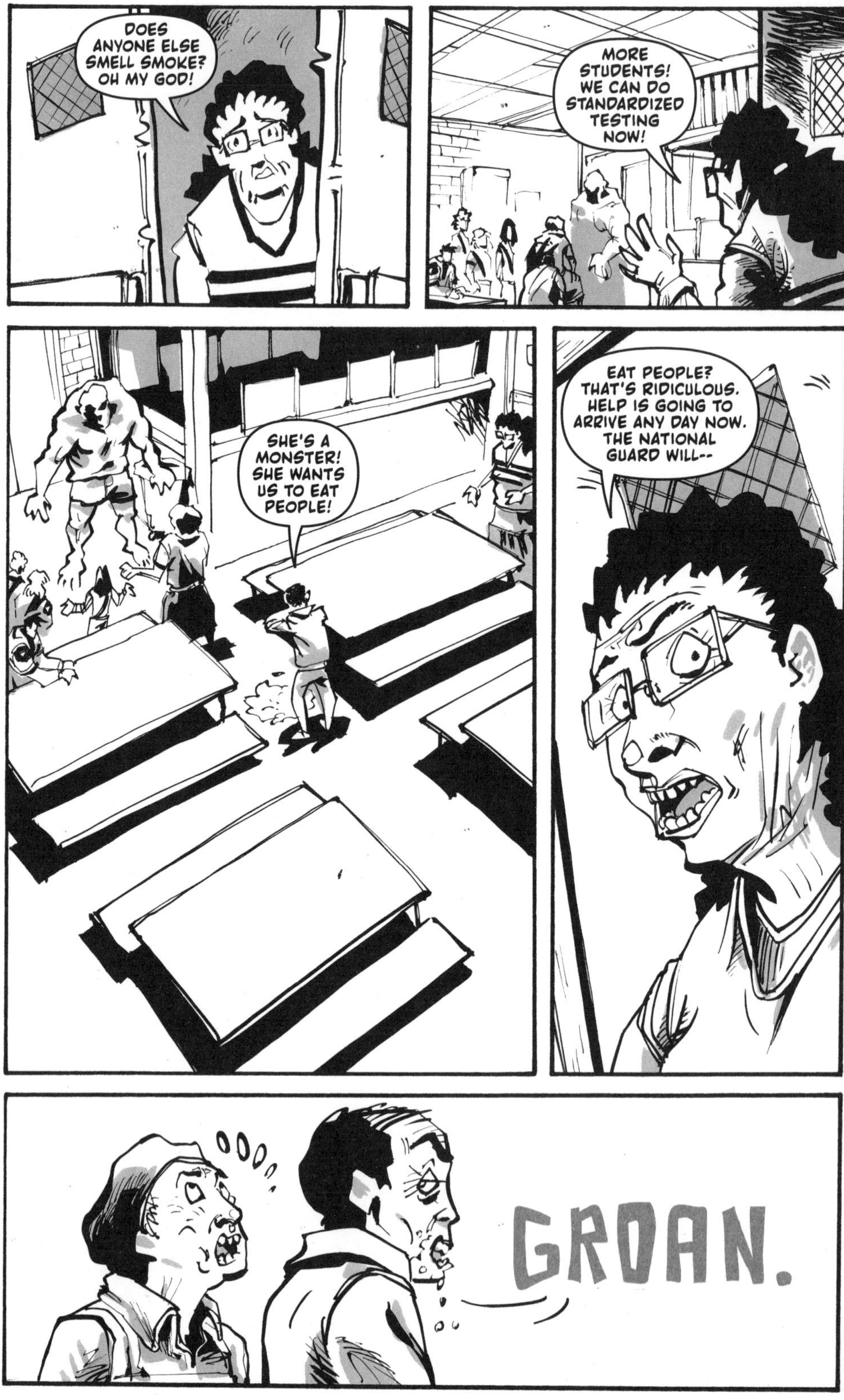
DOES ANYONE ELSE SMELL SMOKE? OH MY GOD!
MORE STUDENTS! WE CAN DO STANDARDIZED TESTING NOW!
SHE'S A MONSTER! SHE WANTS US TO EAT PEOPLE!
EAT PEOPLE? THAT'S RIDICULOUS. HELP IS GOING TO ARRIVE ANY DAY NOW. THE NATIONAL GUARD WILL--
GROAN.

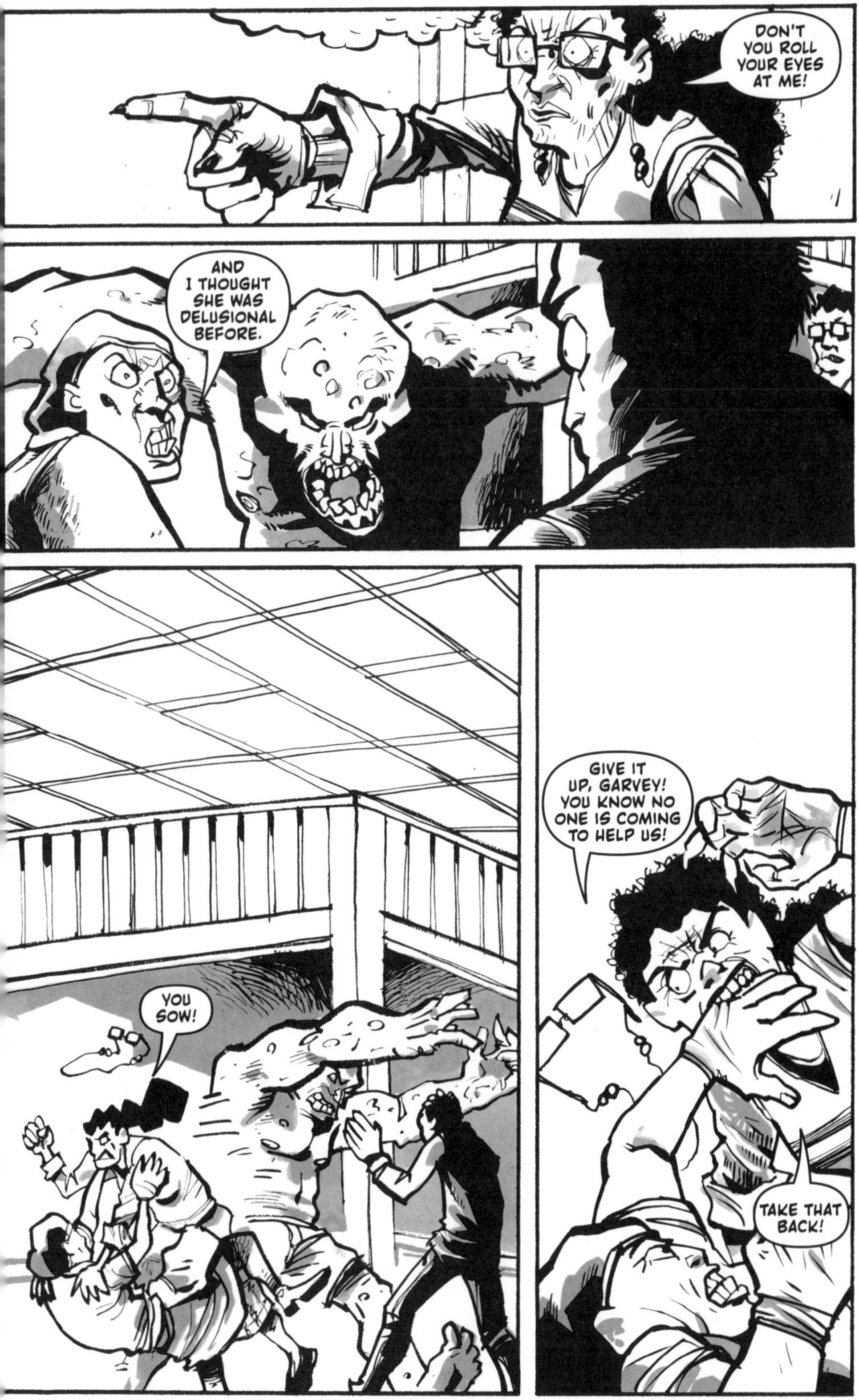
DON'T YOU ROLL YOUR EYES AT ME!
AND I THOUGHT SHE WAS DELUSIONAL BEFORE.
YOU SOW!
GIVE IT UP, GARVEY! YOU KNOW NO ONE IS COMING TO HELP US!
TAKE THAT BACK!

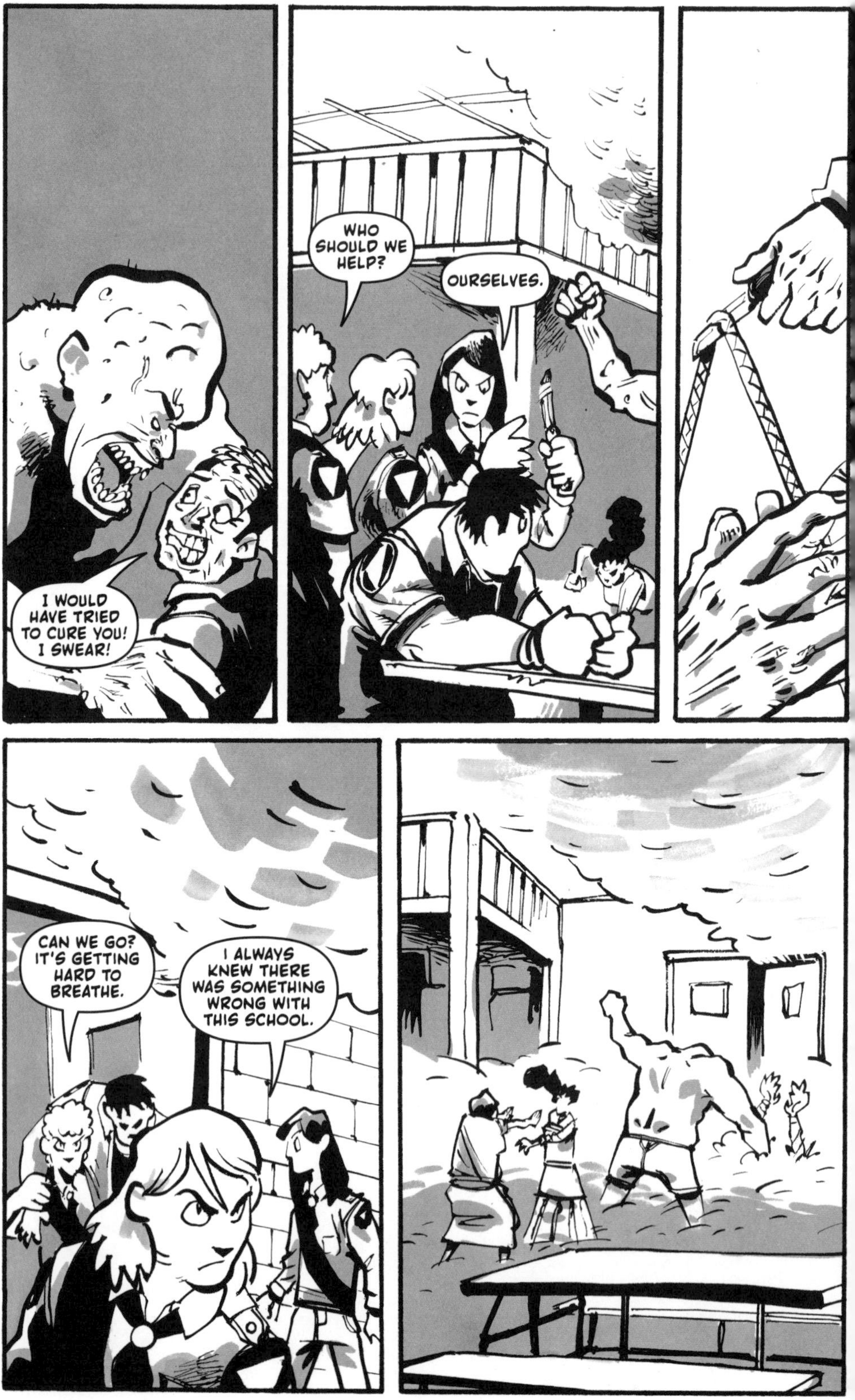
I WOULD HAVE TRIED TO CURE YOU! I SWEAR!
WHO SHOULD WE HELP?
OURSELVES.
CAN WE GO? IT'S GETTING HARD TO BREATHE.
I ALWAYS KNEW THERE WAS SOMETHING WRONG WITH THIS SCHOOL.

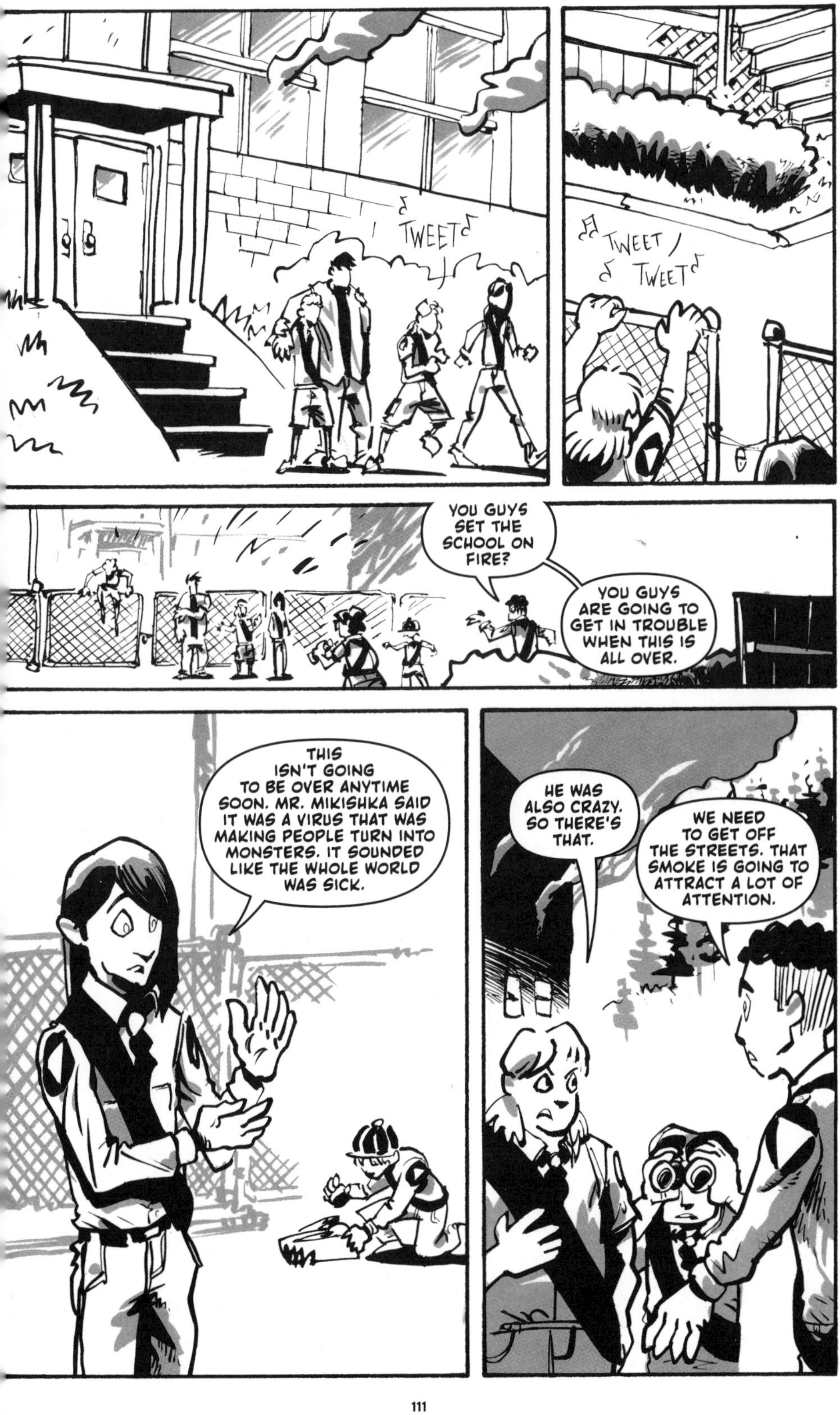
TWEET
TWEET / TWEET
YOU GUYS SET THE SCHOOL ON FIRE?
YOU GUYS ARE GOING TO GET IN TROUBLE WHEN THIS IS ALL OVER.
THIS ISN'T GOING TO BE OVER ANYTIME SOON. MR. MIKISHKA SAID IT WAS A VIRUS THAT WAS MAKING PEOPLE TURN INTO MONSTERS. IT SOUNDED LIKE THE WHOLE WORLD WAS SICK.
HE WAS ALSO CRAZY. SO THERE'S THAT.
WE NEED TO GET OFF THE STREETS. THAT SMOKE IS GOING TO ATTRACT A LOT OF ATTENTION.

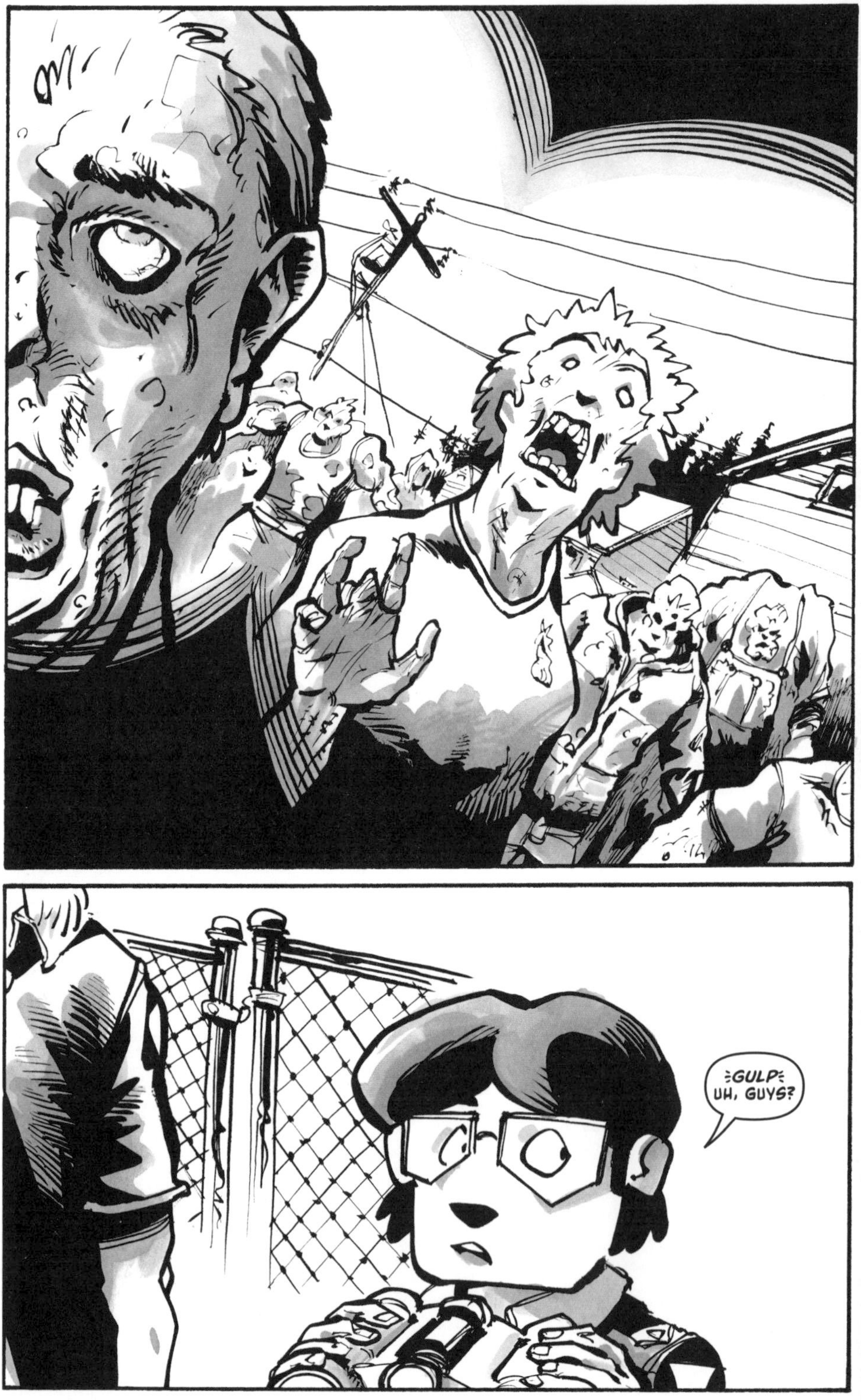
GULP
UH, GUYS?

THE BLACKFOOT STORY OF TWO BEARS

One evening an old Blackfoot told his grandson about a battle that goes on inside people.

He said, "My son, the battle is between two bears inside us all.

"One is Evil—It is anger, envy, jealousy, sorrow, regret, greed, arrogance, self-pity, guilt, resentment, inferiority, lies, false pride, superiority, and ego.

"The other is Good—It is joy, peace, love, hope, serenity, humility, kindness, benevolence, empathy, generosity, truth, compassion and faith."

The grandson thought about it for a minute and then asked his grandfather: "Which bear wins?"

The Blackfoot replied, "The one you feed."

✕

EVERYONE KNOWS
"DON'T FEED THE BEARS."
DUH.
        -MARVIN

GUYS, THIS STORY IS A BOGUS WHITE PEOPLE THING.
I MEAN COME ON!
            -JOHNNY

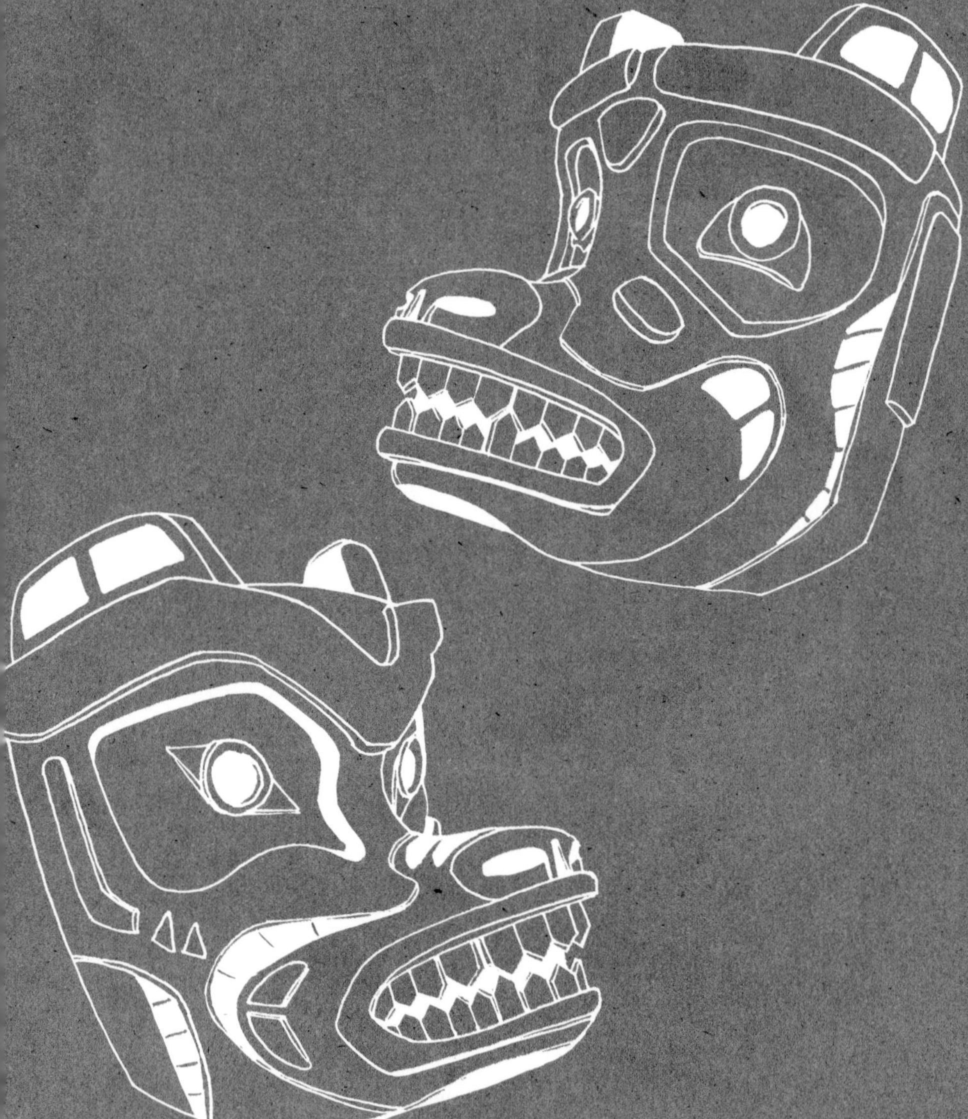

CHAPTER FOUR

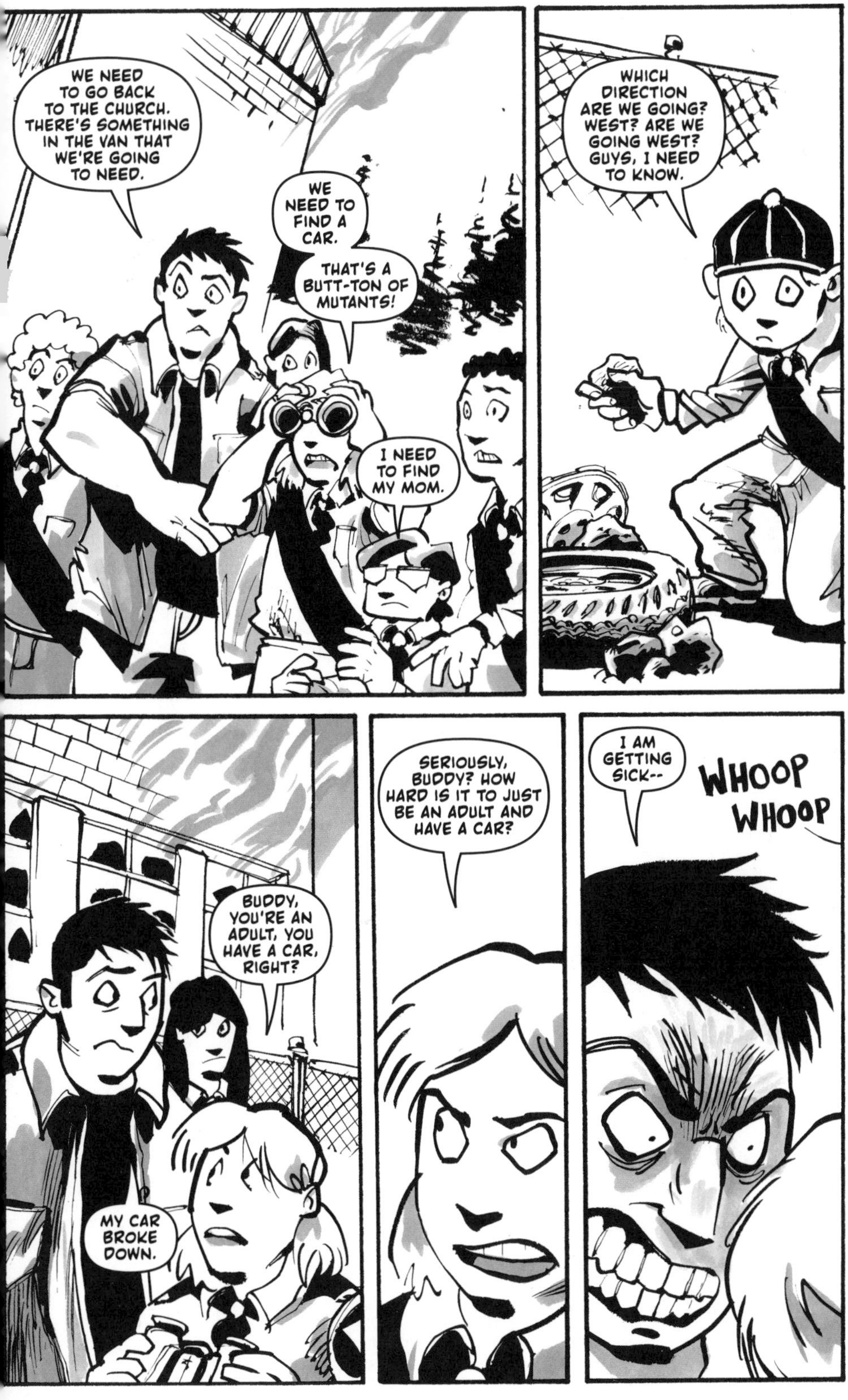
WE NEED TO GO BACK TO THE CHURCH. THERE'S SOMETHING IN THE VAN THAT WE'RE GOING TO NEED.
WE NEED TO FIND A CAR.
THAT'S A BUTT-TON OF MUTANTS!
I NEED TO FIND MY MOM.
WHICH DIRECTION ARE WE GOING? WEST? ARE WE GOING WEST? GUYS, I NEED TO KNOW.
BUDDY, YOU'RE AN ADULT, YOU HAVE A CAR, RIGHT?
MY CAR BROKE DOWN.
SERIOUSLY, BUDDY? HOW HARD IS IT TO JUST BE AN ADULT AND HAVE A CAR?
I AM GETTING SICK--
WHOOP WHOOP

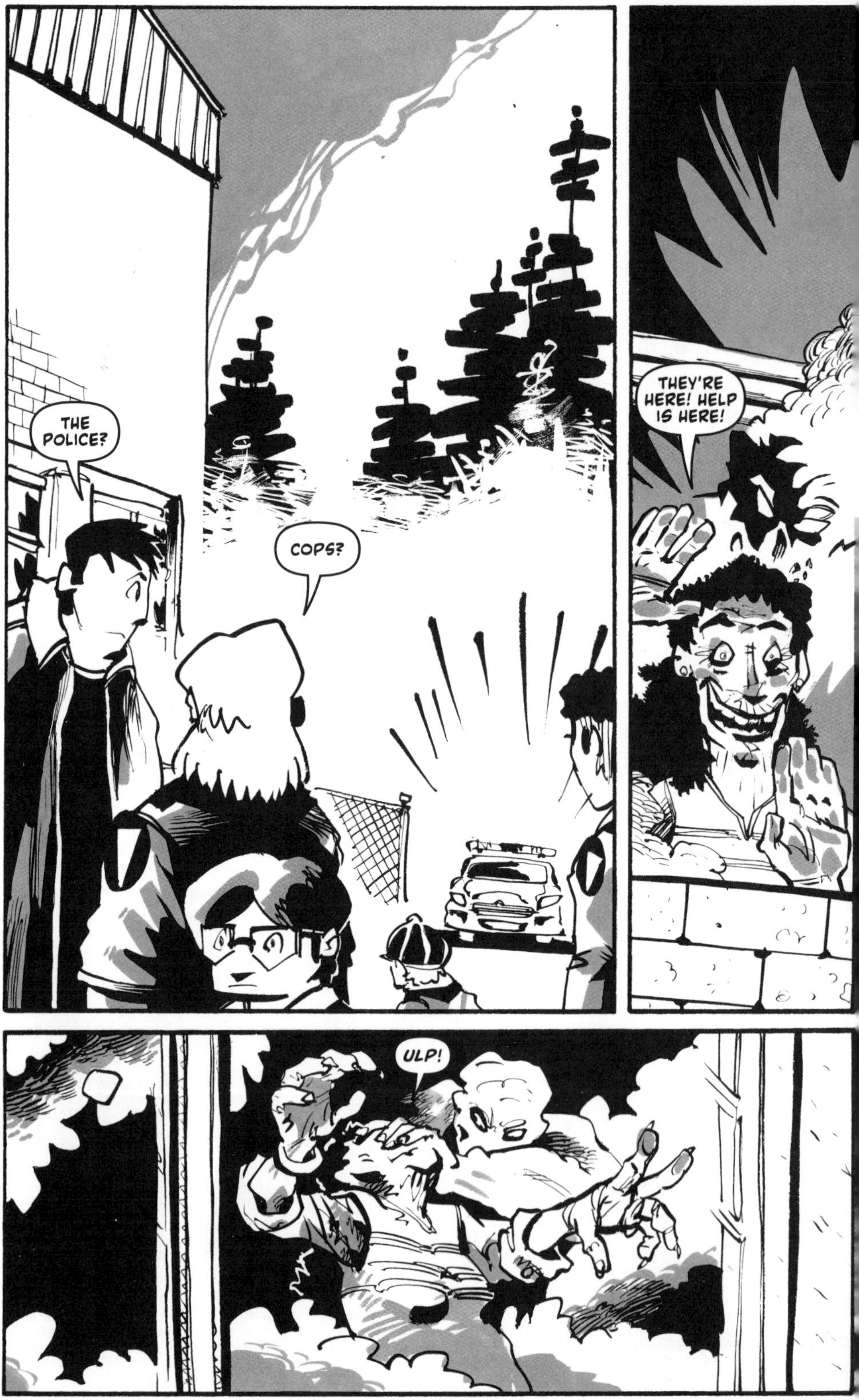
THE POLICE?
COPS?
THEY'RE HERE! HELP IS HERE!
ULP!

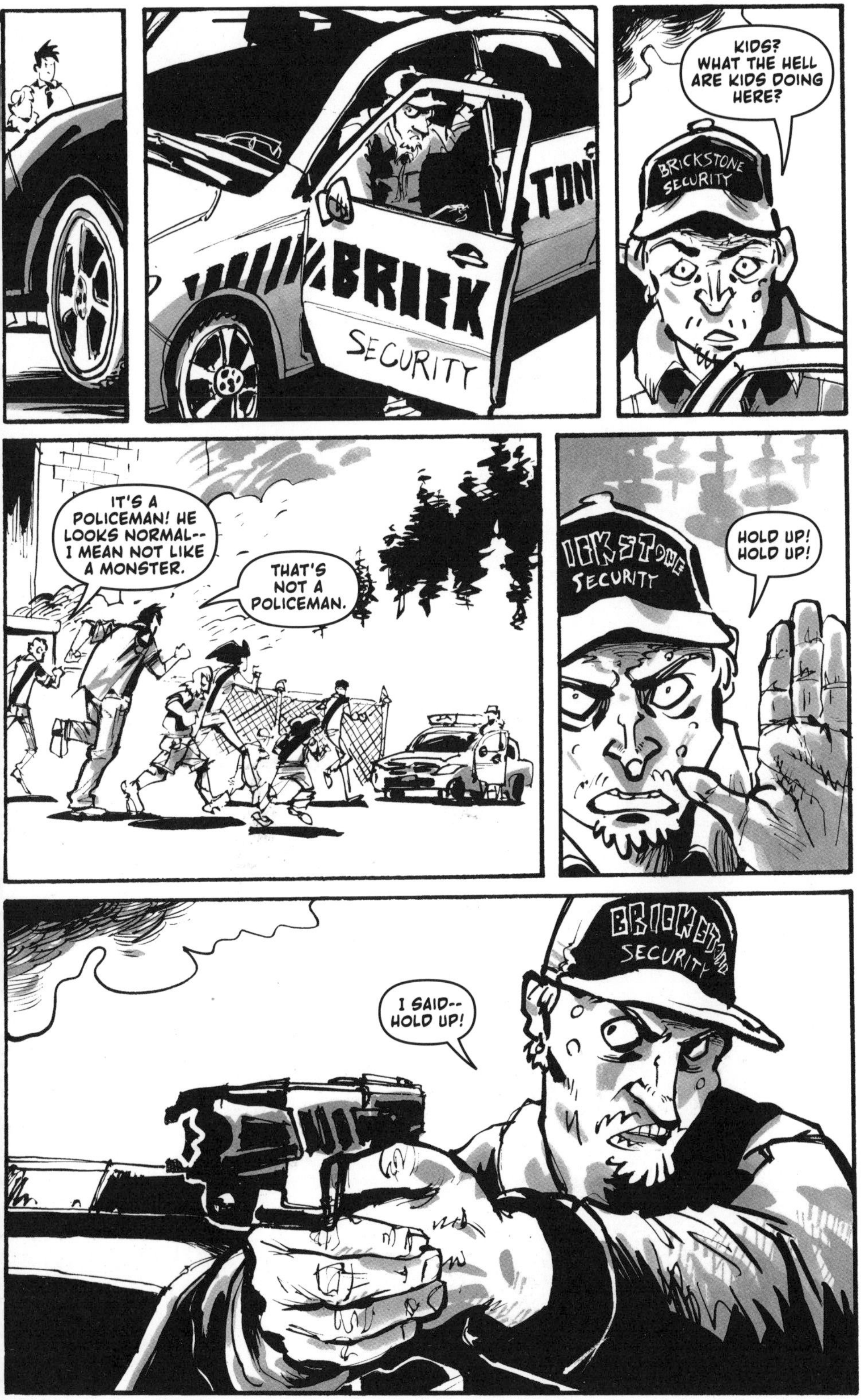
BRICK
SECURITY
TON
KIDS? WHAT THE HELL ARE KIDS DOING HERE?
BRICKSTONE SECURITY
IT'S A POLICEMAN! HE LOOKS NORMAL-- I MEAN NOT LIKE A MONSTER.
THAT'S NOT A POLICEMAN.
SECURITY
HOLD UP! HOLD UP!
SECURITY
I SAID-- HOLD UP!

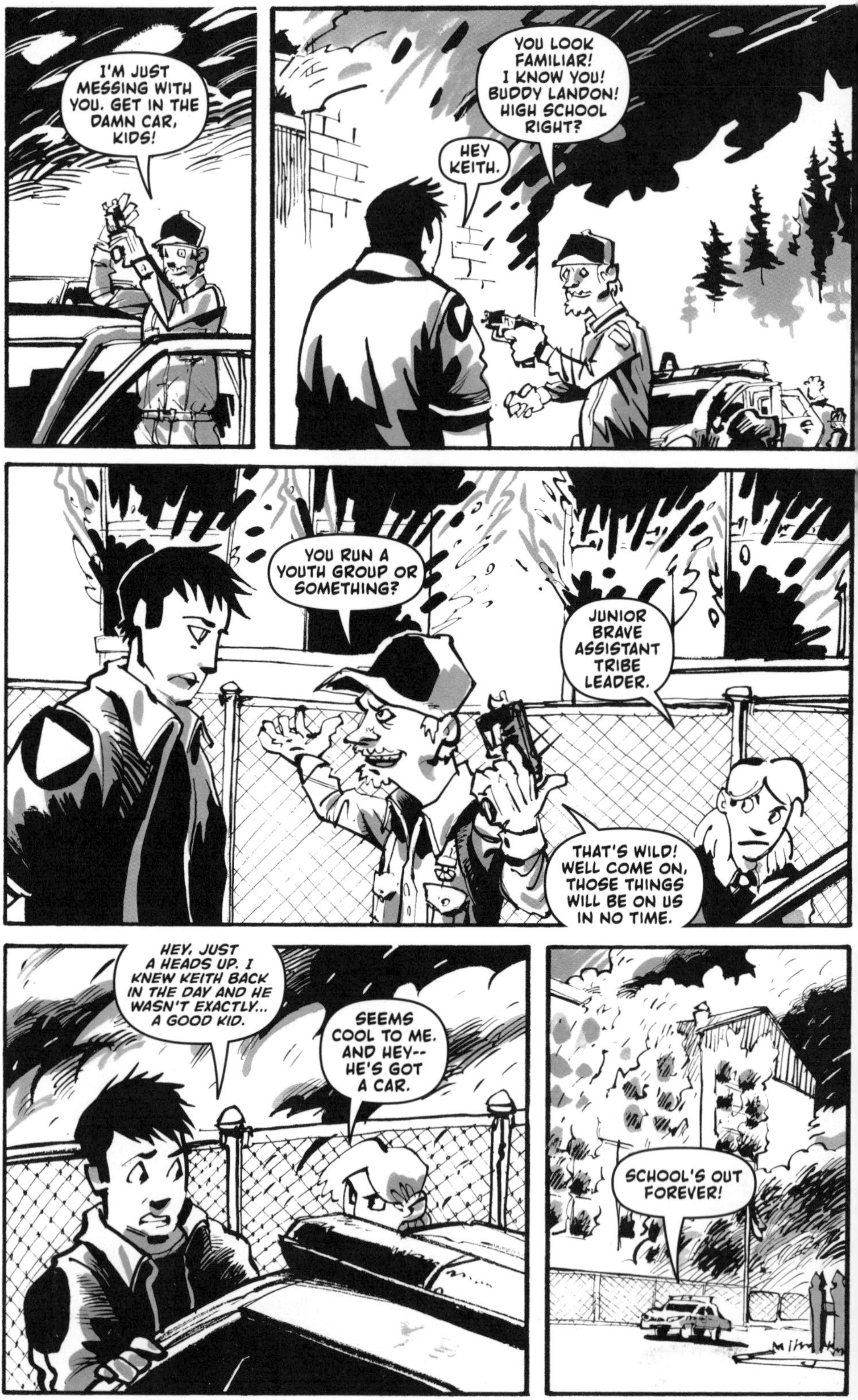
I'M JUST MESSING WITH YOU. GET IN THE DAMN CAR, KIDS!
YOU LOOK FAMILIAR! I KNOW YOU! BUDDY LANDON! HIGH SCHOOL RIGHT?
HEY KEITH.
YOU RUN A YOUTH GROUP OR SOMETHING?
JUNIOR BRAVE ASSISTANT TRIBE LEADER.
THAT'S WILD! WELL COME ON, THOSE THINGS WILL BE ON US IN NO TIME.
HEY, JUST A HEADS UP. I KNEW KEITH BACK IN THE DAY AND HE WASN'T EXACTLY... A GOOD KID.
SEEMS COOL TO ME. AND HEY-- HE'S GOT A CAR.
SCHOOL'S OUT FOREVER!

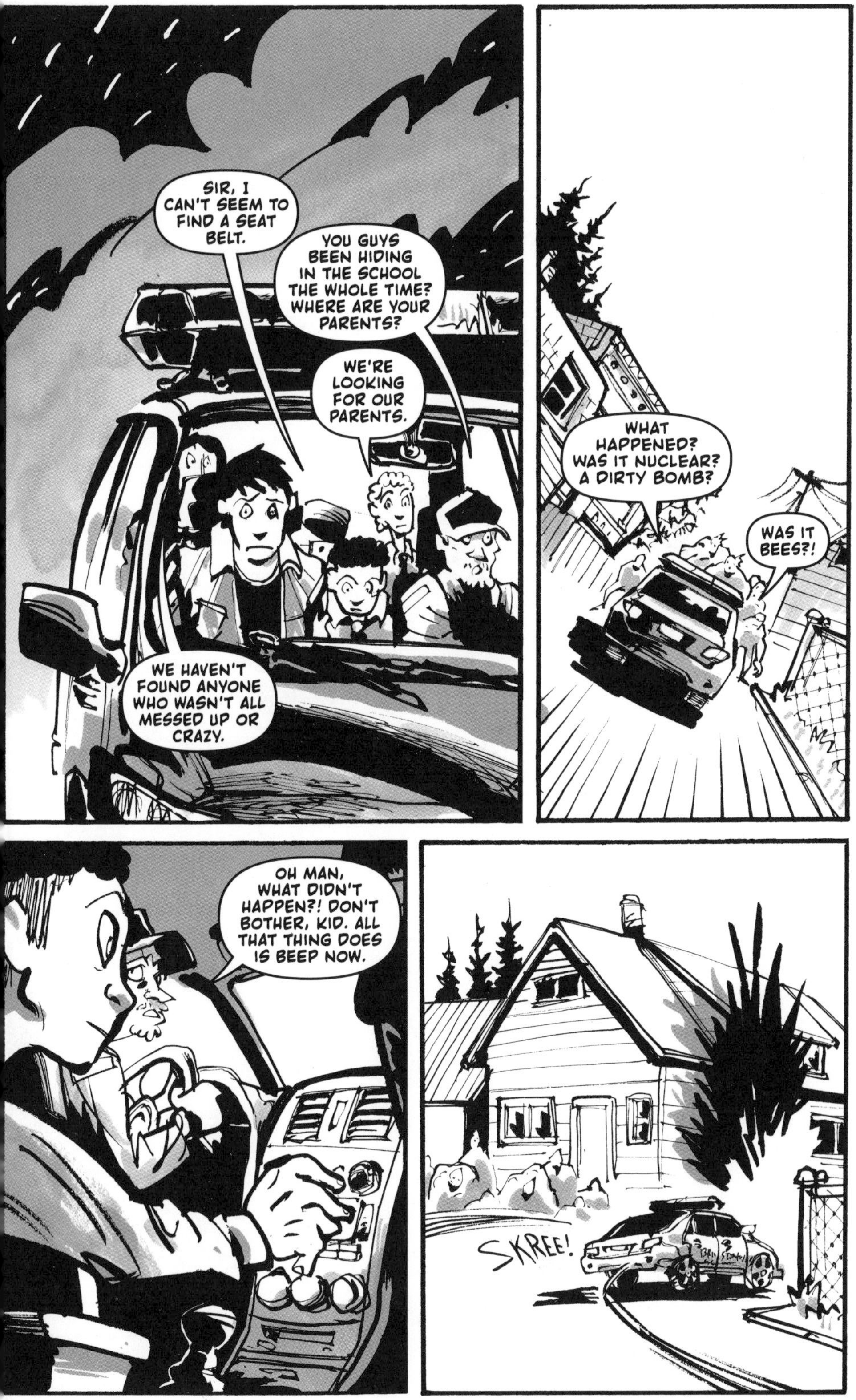
SIR, I CAN'T SEEM TO FIND A SEAT BELT.
YOU GUYS BEEN HIDING IN THE SCHOOL THE WHOLE TIME? WHERE ARE YOUR PARENTS?
WE'RE LOOKING FOR OUR PARENTS.
WE HAVEN'T FOUND ANYONE WHO WASN'T ALL MESSED UP OR CRAZY.
WHAT HAPPENED? WAS IT NUCLEAR? A DIRTY BOMB?
WAS IT BEES?!
OH MAN, WHAT DIDN'T HAPPEN?! DON'T BOTHER, KID. ALL THAT THING DOES IS BEEP NOW.
SKREE!

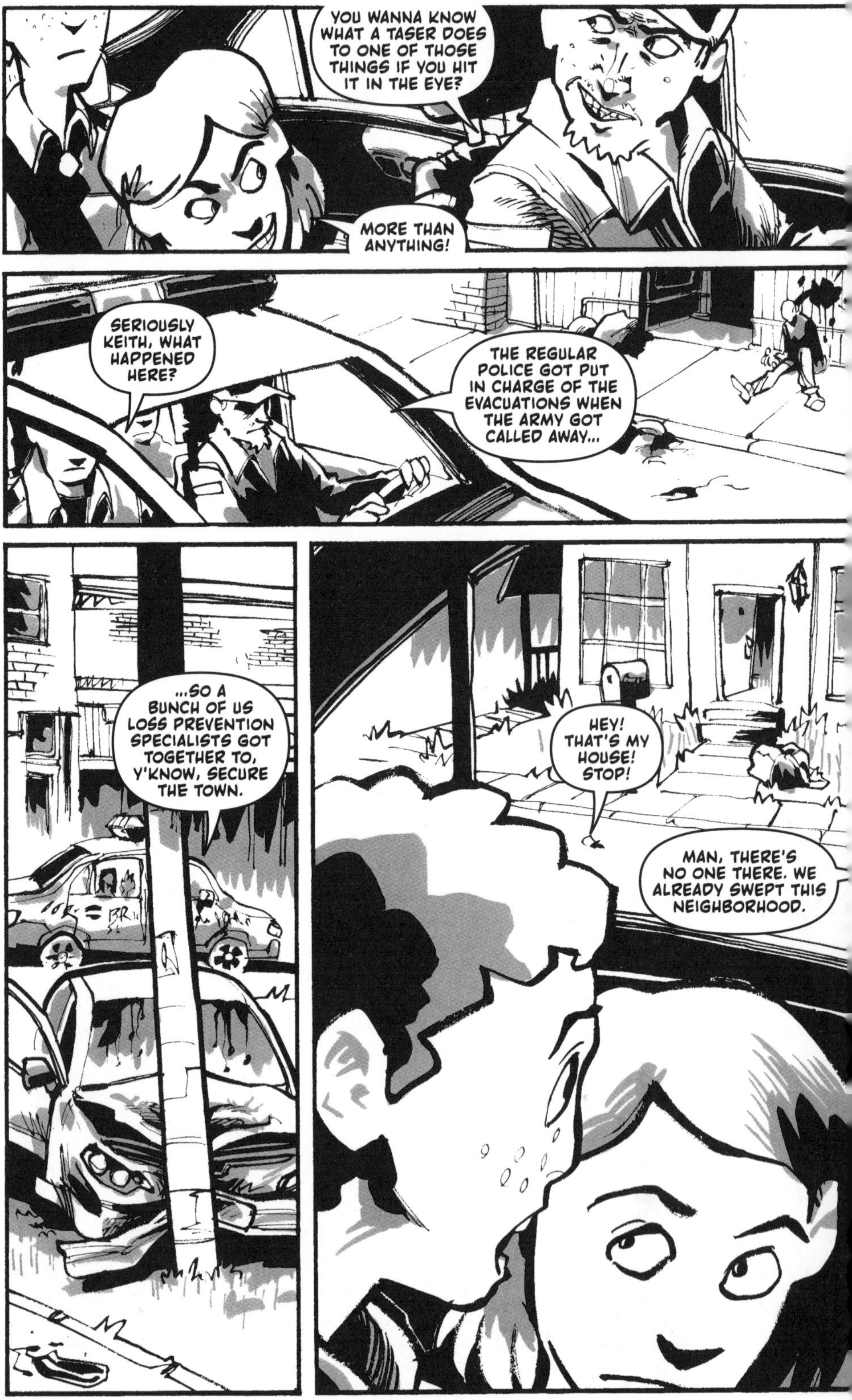
YOU WANNA KNOW WHAT A TASER DOES TO ONE OF THOSE THINGS IF YOU HIT IT IN THE EYE?
MORE THAN ANYTHING!
SERIOUSLY KEITH, WHAT HAPPENED HERE?
THE REGULAR POLICE GOT PUT IN CHARGE OF THE EVACUATIONS WHEN THE ARMY GOT CALLED AWAY...
...SO A BUNCH OF US LOSS PREVENTION SPECIALISTS GOT TOGETHER TO, Y'KNOW, SECURE THE TOWN.
HEY! THAT'S MY HOUSE! STOP!
MAN, THERE'S NO ONE THERE. WE ALREADY SWEPT THIS NEIGHBORHOOD.

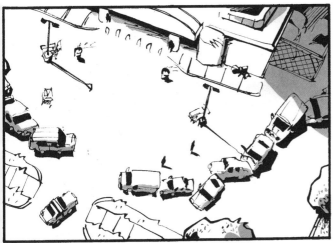

CHECK IT OUT DUDES, PRETTY COOL, HUH? THE STORE IS OURS.

LOOK WHAT I FOUND! JUNIOR BRAVES!

IF OUR FAMILIES AREN'T HERE, THAT MEANS THEY GOT EVACUATED, RIGHT? SO THEY'RE SAFE. OR MAYBE THEY'RE HERE.

YOU SHOULD HAVE SEEN THIS PLACE A COUPLE OF DAYS AGO, MAN. IT WAS A ZOO!

SEGEL
KRAV M
SEGEEKM@G

PEOPLE GRABBING EVERYTHING! NOT USEFUL STUFF EITHER, LIKE BATTERIES OR CIGARETTES.

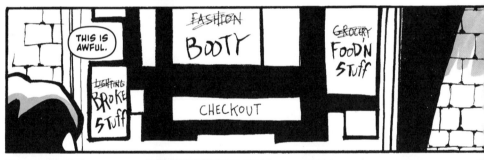

THIS IS AWFUL.

~~FASHION~~ BOOTY

~~GROCERY~~ FOOD'N STUFF

~~LIGHTING~~ BROKE STUFF

CHECKOUT

EVERYONE HERE IS IN A UNIFORM.

KEITH, WHERE ARE THE REGULAR PEOPLE?

THERE WERE SOME CITIZENS, BUT I THINK THEY ALL KINDA LEFT AFTER A FEW DAYS.

I GUESS THEY DIDN'T LIKE IT HERE.

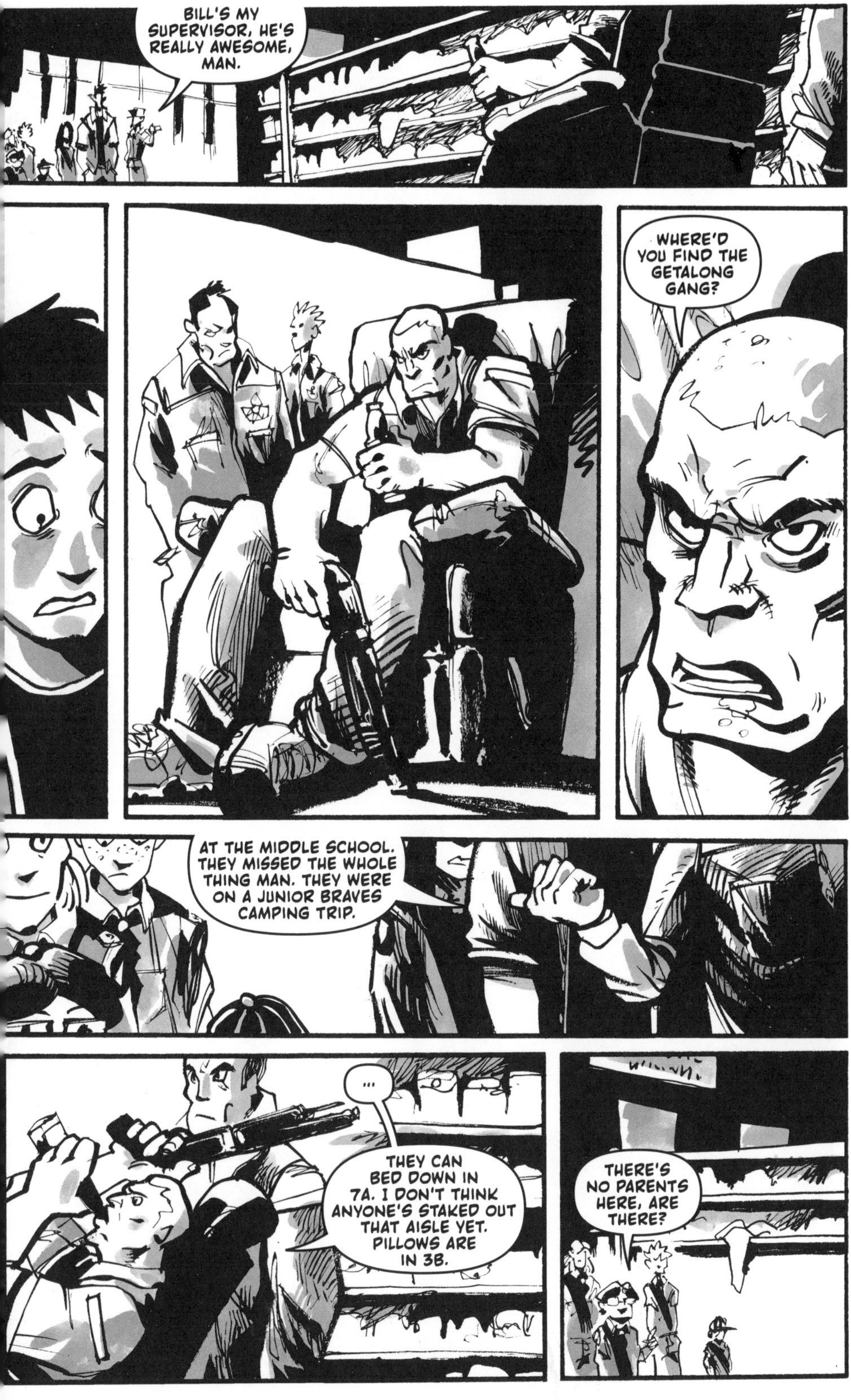
BILL'S MY SUPERVISOR, HE'S REALLY AWESOME, MAN.
WHERE'D YOU FIND THE GETALONG GANG?
AT THE MIDDLE SCHOOL. THEY MISSED THE WHOLE THING MAN. THEY WERE ON A JUNIOR BRAVES CAMPING TRIP.
...
THEY CAN BED DOWN IN 7A. I DON'T THINK ANYONE'S STAKED OUT THAT AISLE YET. PILLOWS ARE IN 3B.
THERE'S NO PARENTS HERE, ARE THERE?

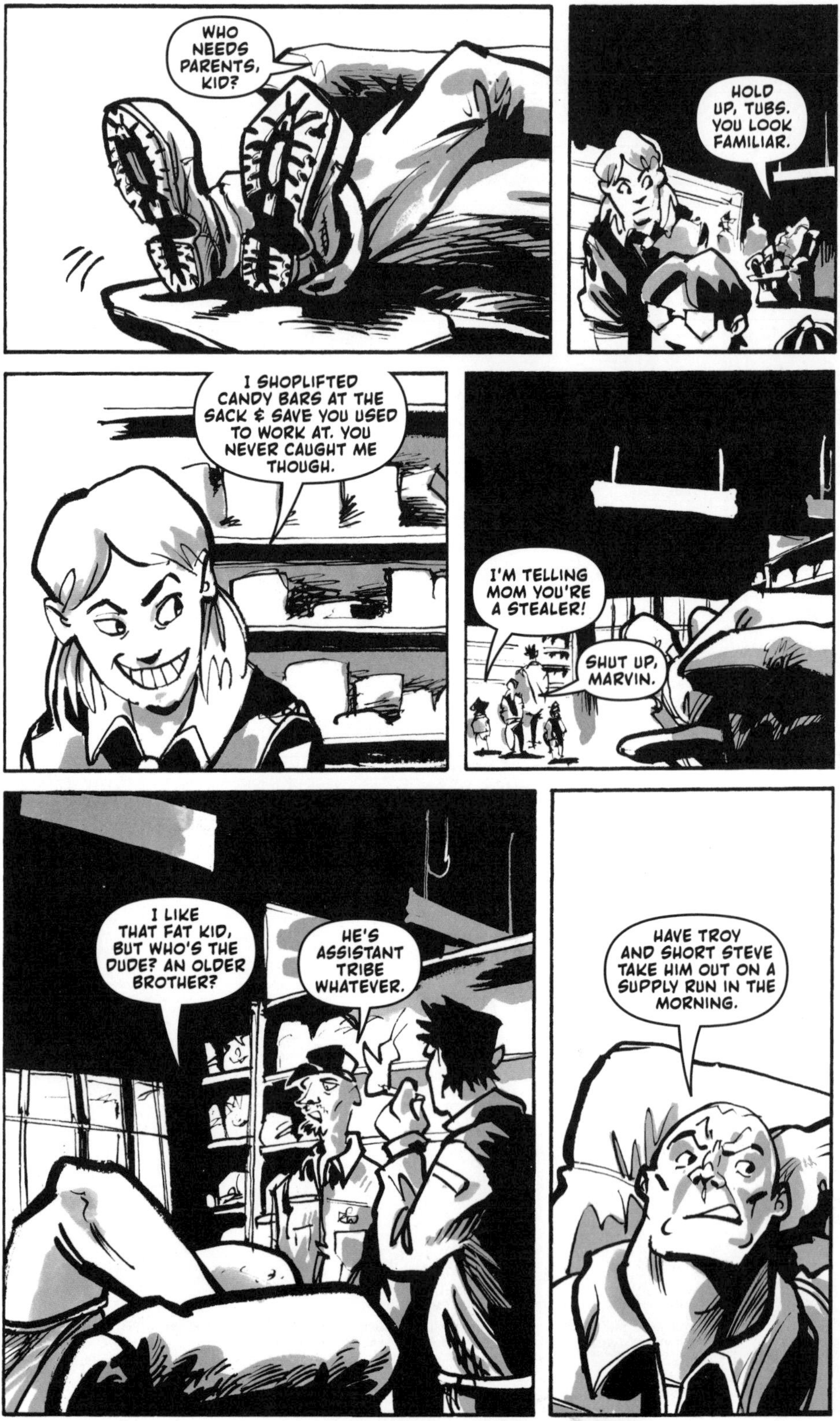
WHO NEEDS PARENTS, KID?
HOLD UP, TUBS. YOU LOOK FAMILIAR.
I SHOPLIFTED CANDY BARS AT THE SACK & SAVE YOU USED TO WORK AT. YOU NEVER CAUGHT ME THOUGH.
I'M TELLING MOM YOU'RE A STEALER!
SHUT UP, MARVIN.
I LIKE THAT FAT KID, BUT WHO'S THE DUDE? AN OLDER BROTHER?
HE'S ASSISTANT TRIBE WHATEVER.
HAVE TROY AND SHORT STEVE TAKE HIM OUT ON A SUPPLY RUN IN THE MORNING.

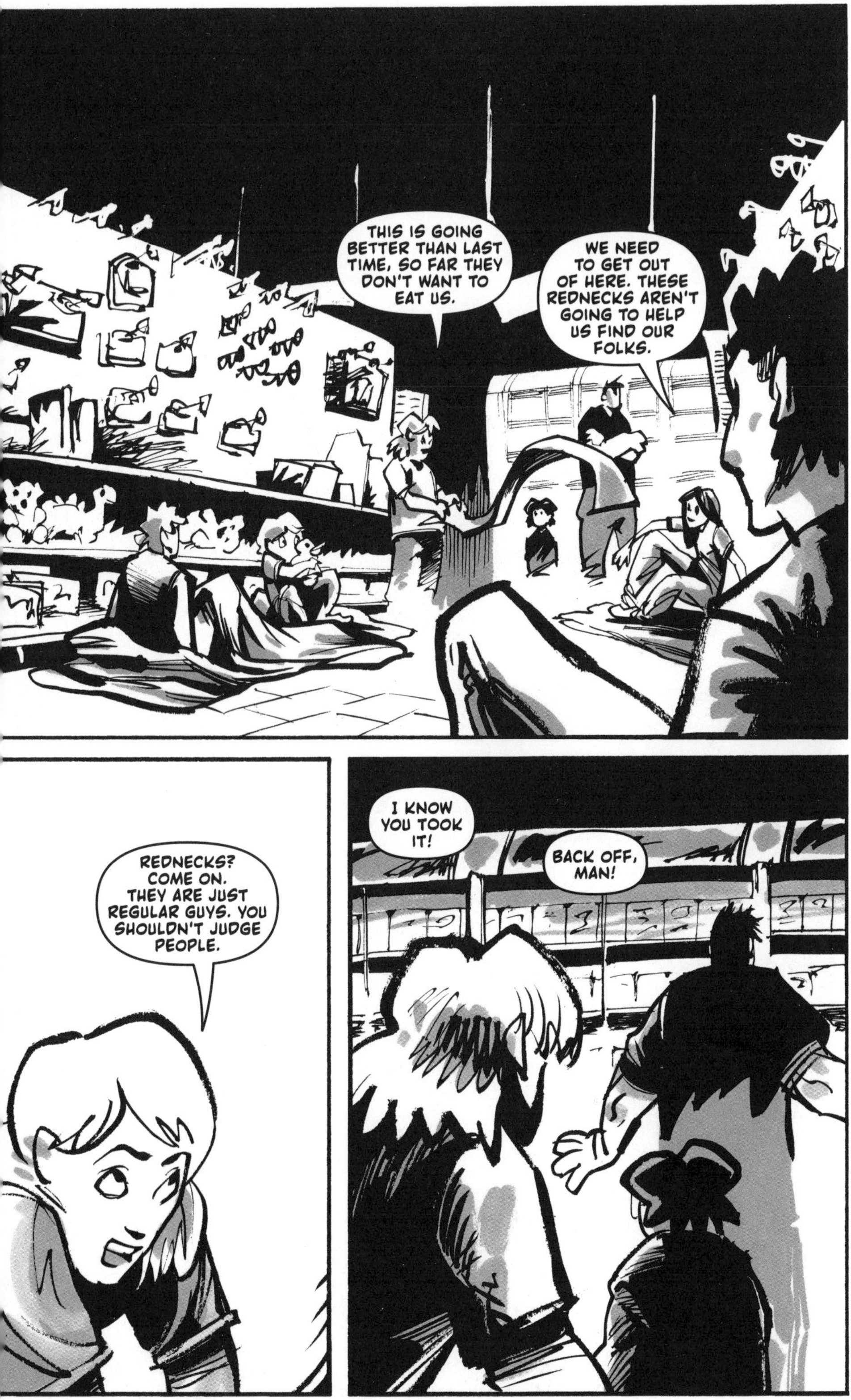
THIS IS GOING BETTER THAN LAST TIME, SO FAR THEY DON'T WANT TO EAT US.
WE NEED TO GET OUT OF HERE. THESE REDNECKS AREN'T GOING TO HELP US FIND OUR FOLKS.
REDNECKS? COME ON. THEY ARE JUST REGULAR GUYS. YOU SHOULDN'T JUDGE PEOPLE.
I KNOW YOU TOOK IT!
BACK OFF, MAN!

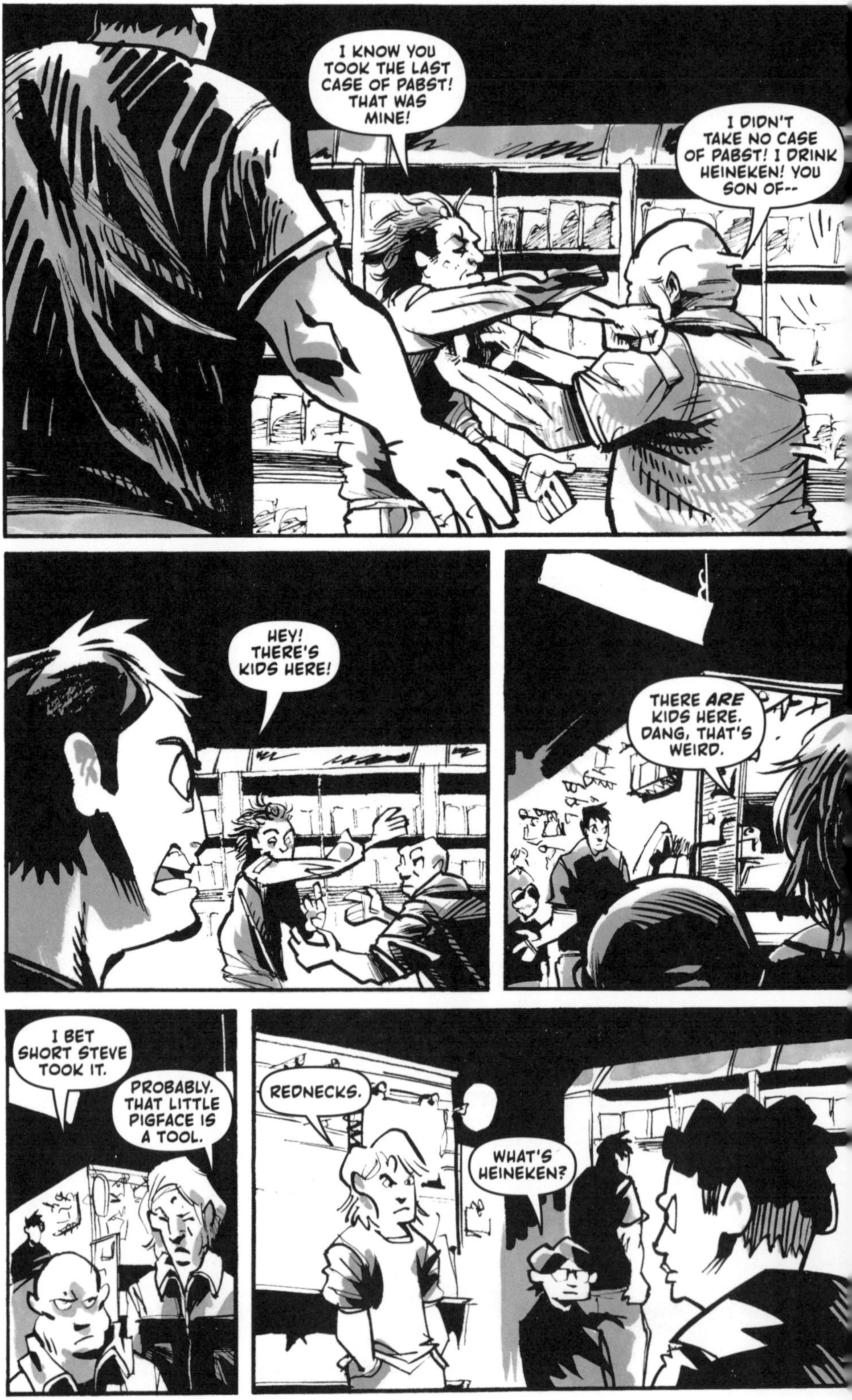
I KNOW YOU TOOK THE LAST CASE OF PABST! THAT WAS MINE!
I DIDN'T TAKE NO CASE OF PABST! I DRINK HEINEKEN! YOU SON OF--
HEY! THERE'S KIDS HERE!
THERE ARE KIDS HERE. DANG, THAT'S WEIRD.
I BET SHORT STEVE TOOK IT.
PROBABLY. THAT LITTLE PIGFACE IS A TOOL.
REDNECKS.
WHAT'S HEINEKEN?

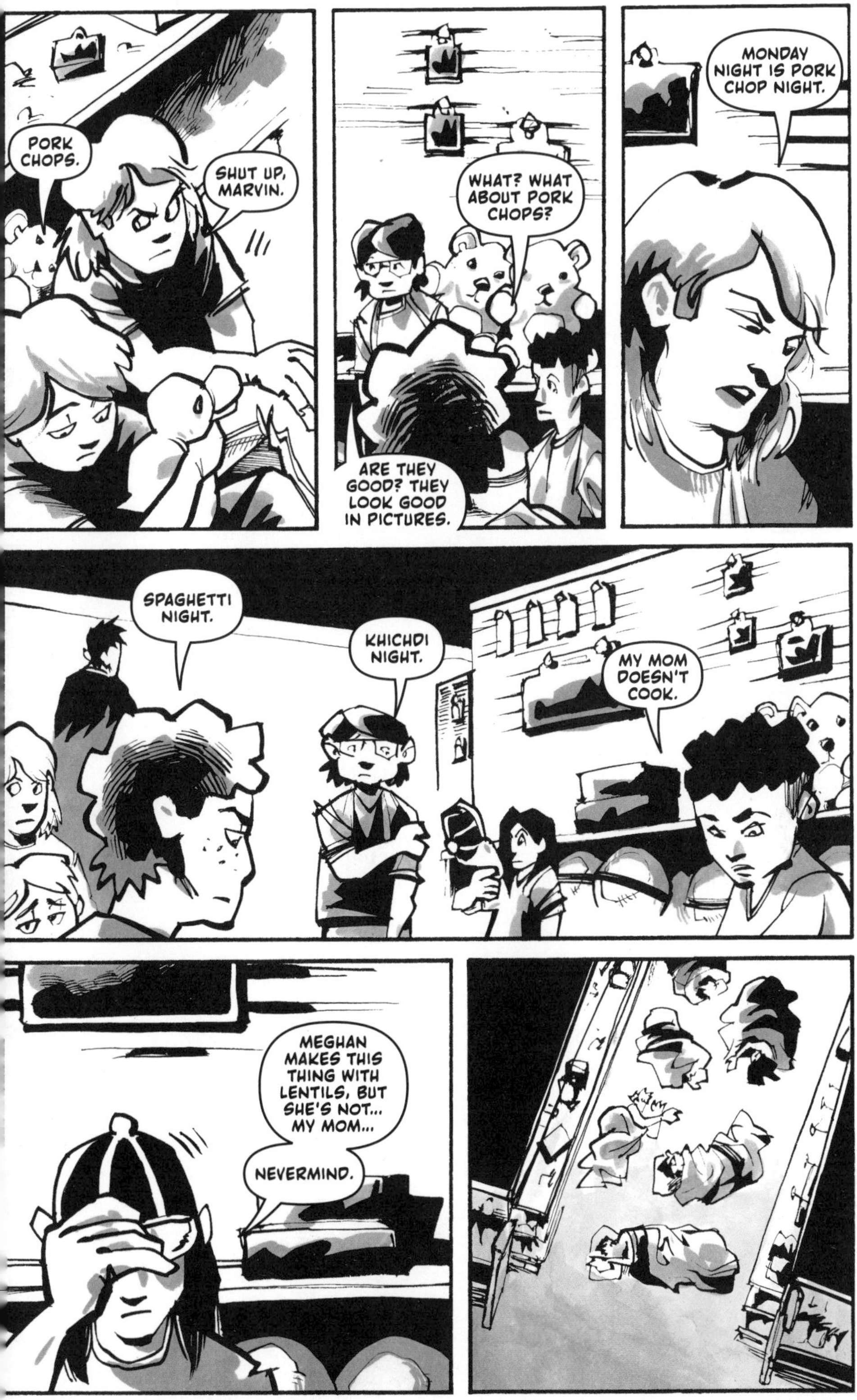
PORK CHOPS.
SHUT UP, MARVIN.
WHAT? WHAT ABOUT PORK CHOPS?
ARE THEY GOOD? THEY LOOK GOOD IN PICTURES.
MONDAY NIGHT IS PORK CHOP NIGHT.
SPAGHETTI NIGHT.
KHICHDI NIGHT.
MY MOM DOESN'T COOK.
MEGHAN MAKES THIS THING WITH LENTILS, BUT SHE'S NOT... MY MOM...
NEVERMIND.

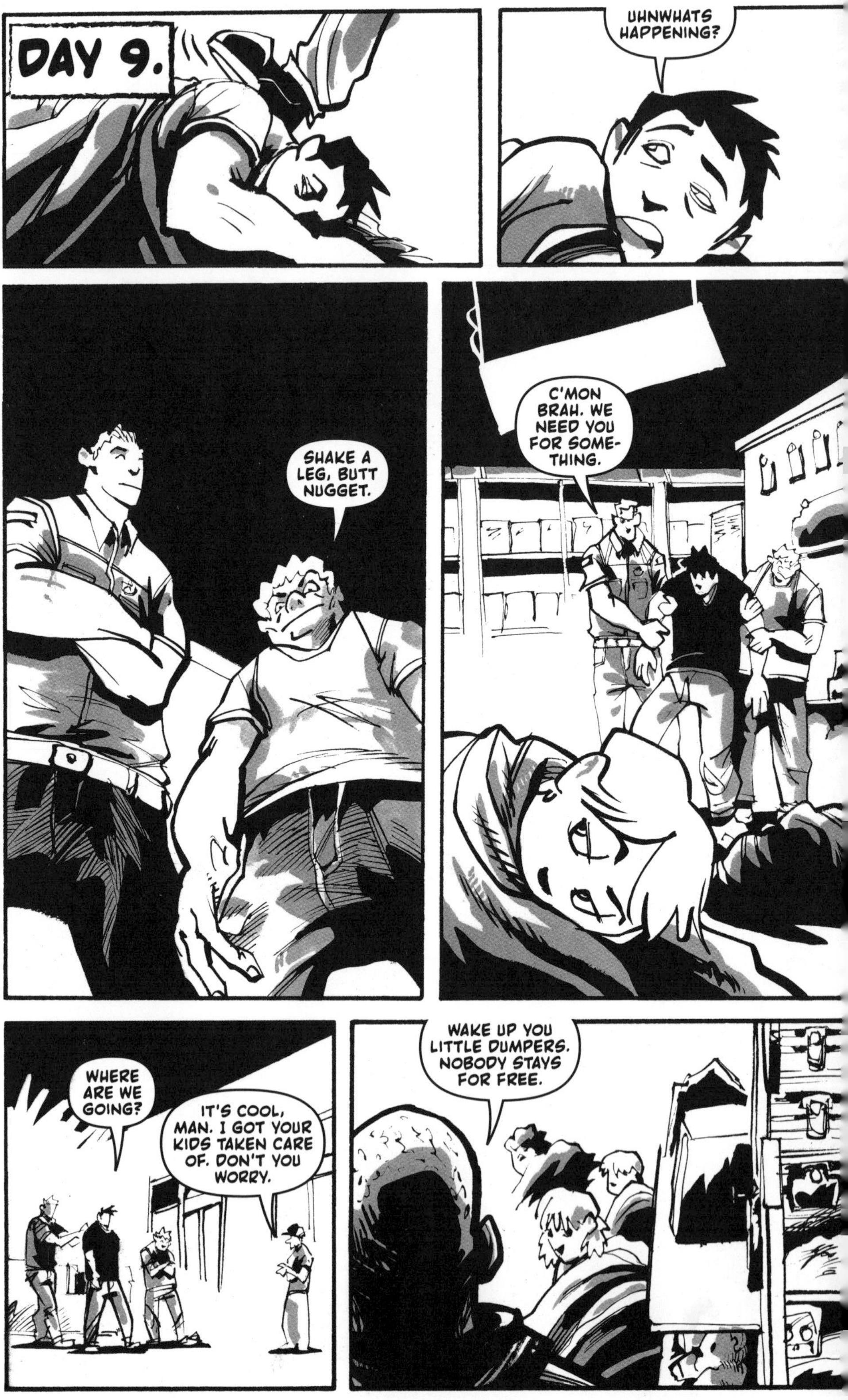
DAY 9.
UHNWHATS HAPPENING?
SHAKE A LEG, BUTT NUGGET.
C'MON BRAH. WE NEED YOU FOR SOME-THING.
WHERE ARE WE GOING?
IT'S COOL, MAN. I GOT YOUR KIDS TAKEN CARE OF. DON'T YOU WORRY.
WAKE UP YOU LITTLE DUMPERS. NOBODY STAYS FOR FREE.

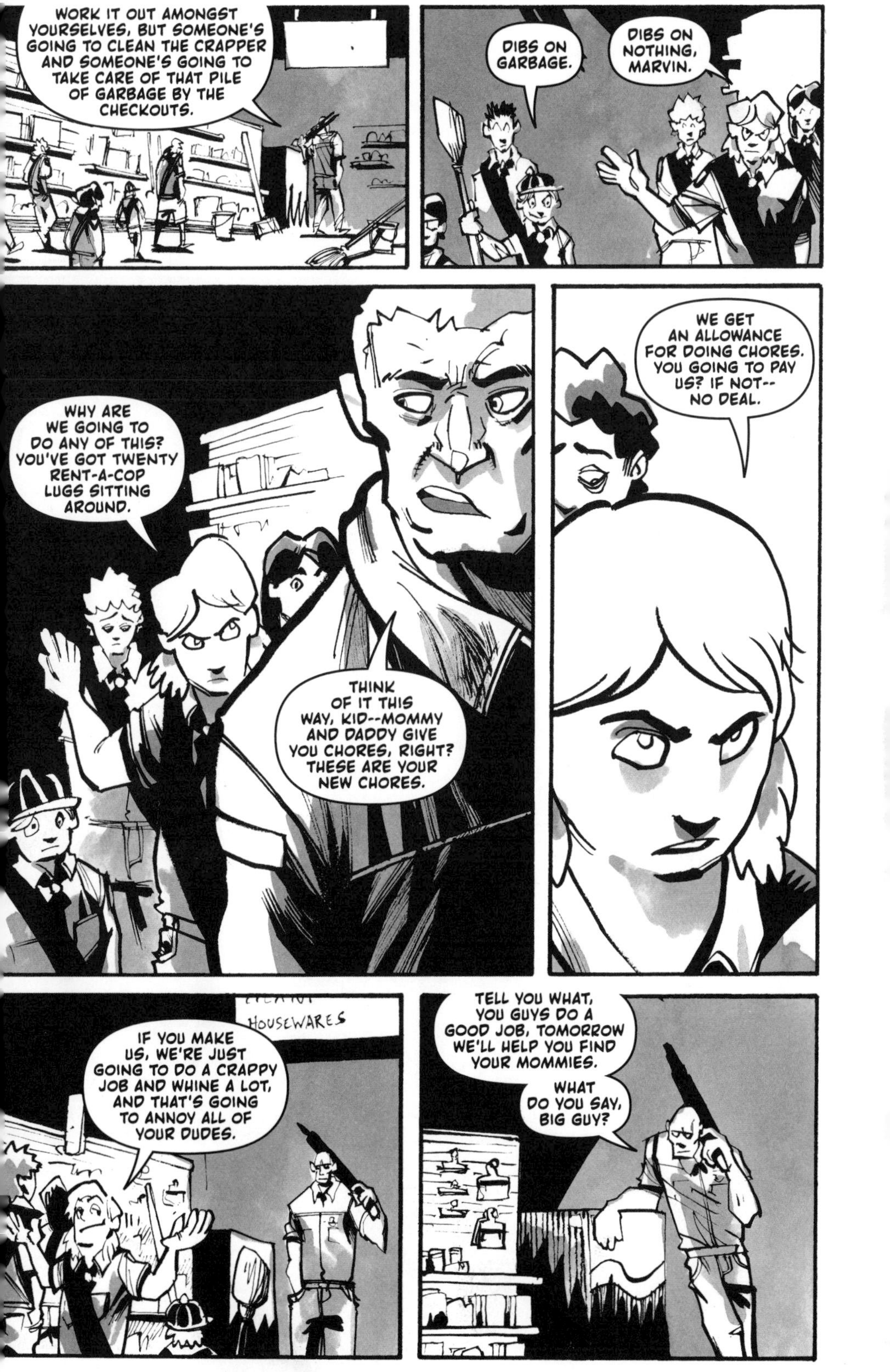
WORK IT OUT AMONGST YOURSELVES, BUT SOMEONE'S GOING TO CLEAN THE CRAPPER AND SOMEONE'S GOING TO TAKE CARE OF THAT PILE OF GARBAGE BY THE CHECKOUTS.
DIBS ON GARBAGE.
DIBS ON NOTHING, MARVIN.
WHY ARE WE GOING TO DO ANY OF THIS? YOU'VE GOT TWENTY RENT-A-COP LUGS SITTING AROUND.
THINK OF IT THIS WAY, KID--MOMMY AND DADDY GIVE YOU CHORES, RIGHT? THESE ARE YOUR NEW CHORES.
WE GET AN ALLOWANCE FOR DOING CHORES. YOU GOING TO PAY US? IF NOT--NO DEAL.
HOUSEWARES
IF YOU MAKE US, WE'RE JUST GOING TO DO A CRAPPY JOB AND WHINE A LOT, AND THAT'S GOING TO ANNOY ALL OF YOUR DUDES.
TELL YOU WHAT, YOU GUYS DO A GOOD JOB, TOMORROW WE'LL HELP YOU FIND YOUR MOMMIES.
WHAT DO YOU SAY, BIG GUY?

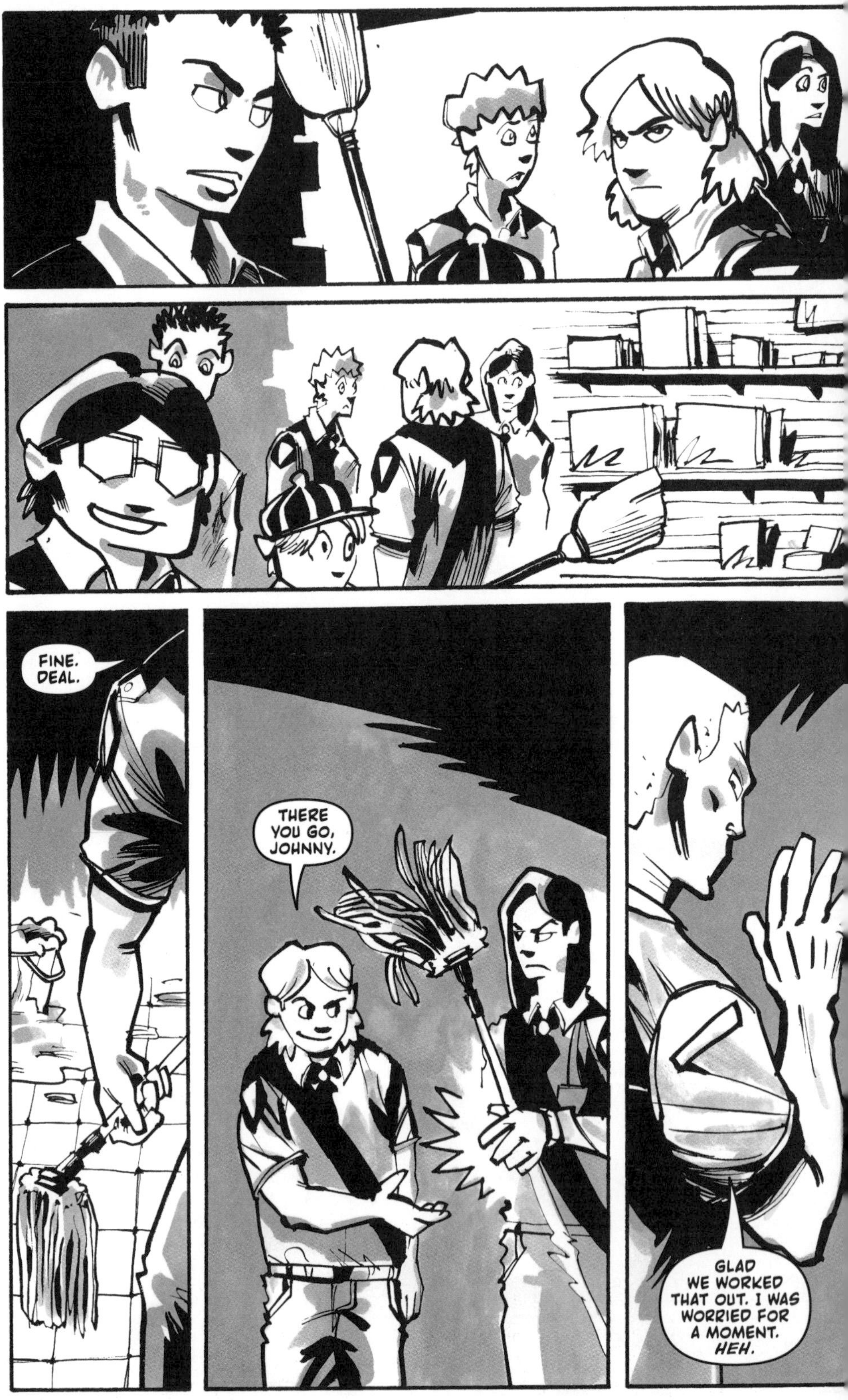
FINE. DEAL.
THERE YOU GO, JOHNNY.
GLAD WE WORKED THAT OUT. I WAS WORRIED FOR A MOMENT. HEH.

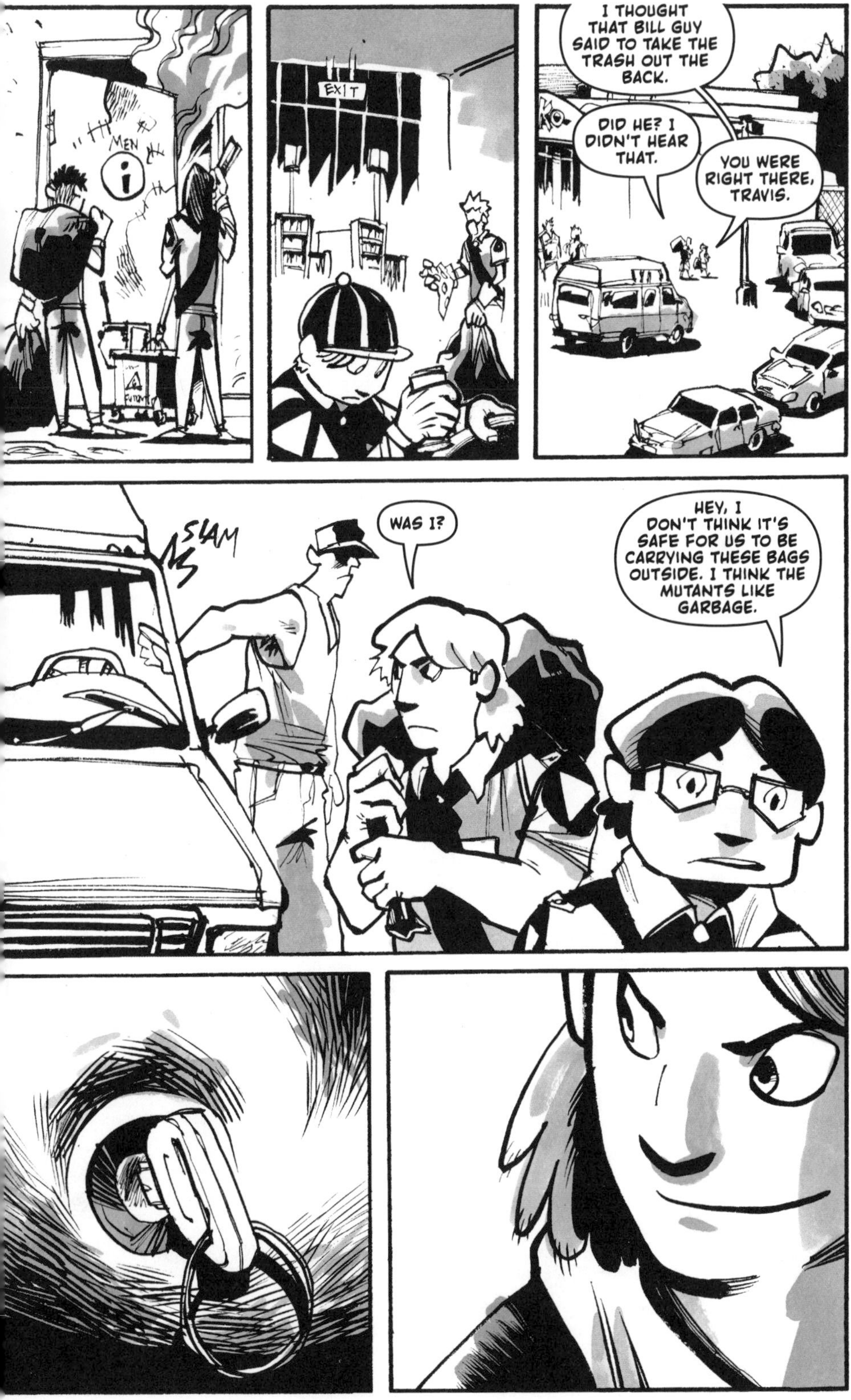
MEN
EXIT
I THOUGHT THAT BILL GUY SAID TO TAKE THE TRASH OUT THE BACK.
DID HE? I DIDN'T HEAR THAT.
YOU WERE RIGHT THERE, TRAVIS.
SLAM
WAS I?
HEY, I DON'T THINK IT'S SAFE FOR US TO BE CARRYING THESE BAGS OUTSIDE. I THINK THE MUTANTS LIKE GARBAGE.

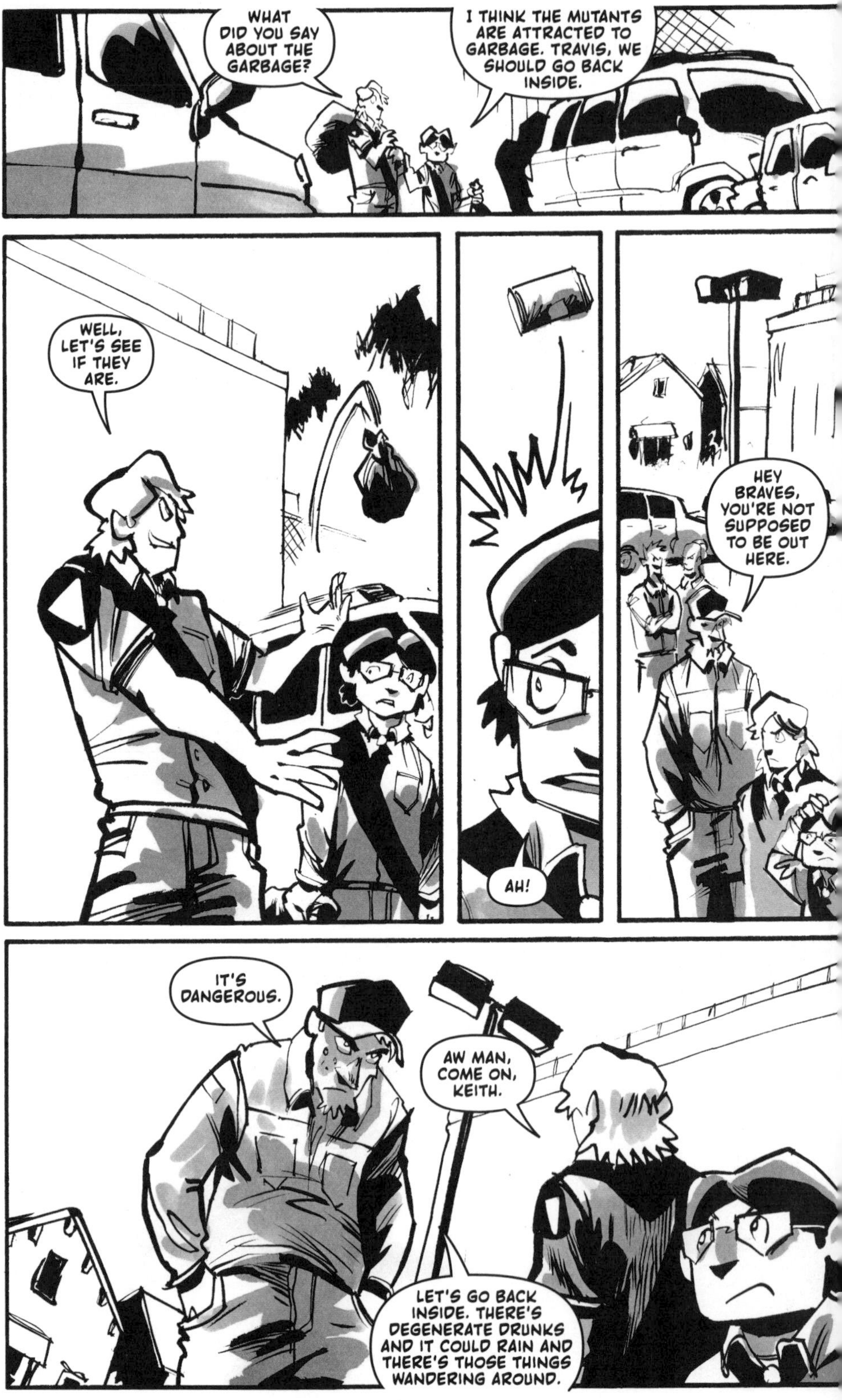
WHAT DID YOU SAY ABOUT THE GARBAGE?
I THINK THE MUTANTS ARE ATTRACTED TO GARBAGE. TRAVIS, WE SHOULD GO BACK INSIDE.
WELL, LET'S SEE IF THEY ARE.
AH!
HEY BRAVES, YOU'RE NOT SUPPOSED TO BE OUT HERE.
IT'S DANGEROUS.
AW MAN, COME ON, KEITH.
LET'S GO BACK INSIDE. THERE'S DEGENERATE DRUNKS AND IT COULD RAIN AND THERE'S THOSE THINGS WANDERING AROUND.

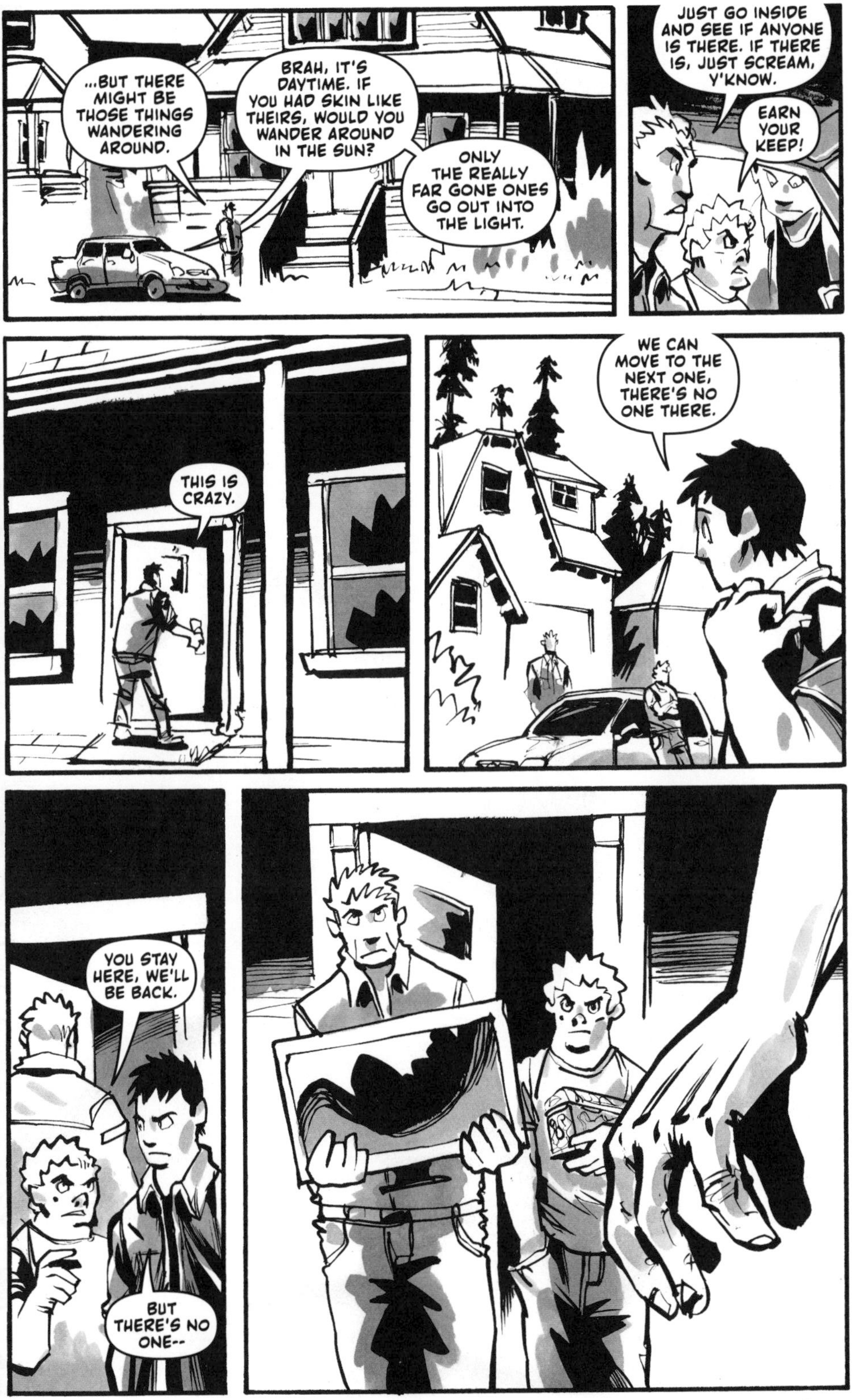
...BUT THERE MIGHT BE THOSE THINGS WANDERING AROUND.
BRAH, IT'S DAYTIME. IF YOU HAD SKIN LIKE THEIRS, WOULD YOU WANDER AROUND IN THE SUN?
ONLY THE REALLY FAR GONE ONES GO OUT INTO THE LIGHT.
JUST GO INSIDE AND SEE IF ANYONE IS THERE. IF THERE IS, JUST SCREAM, Y'KNOW.
EARN YOUR KEEP!
THIS IS CRAZY.
WE CAN MOVE TO THE NEXT ONE, THERE'S NO ONE THERE.
YOU STAY HERE, WE'LL BE BACK.
BUT THERE'S NO ONE--

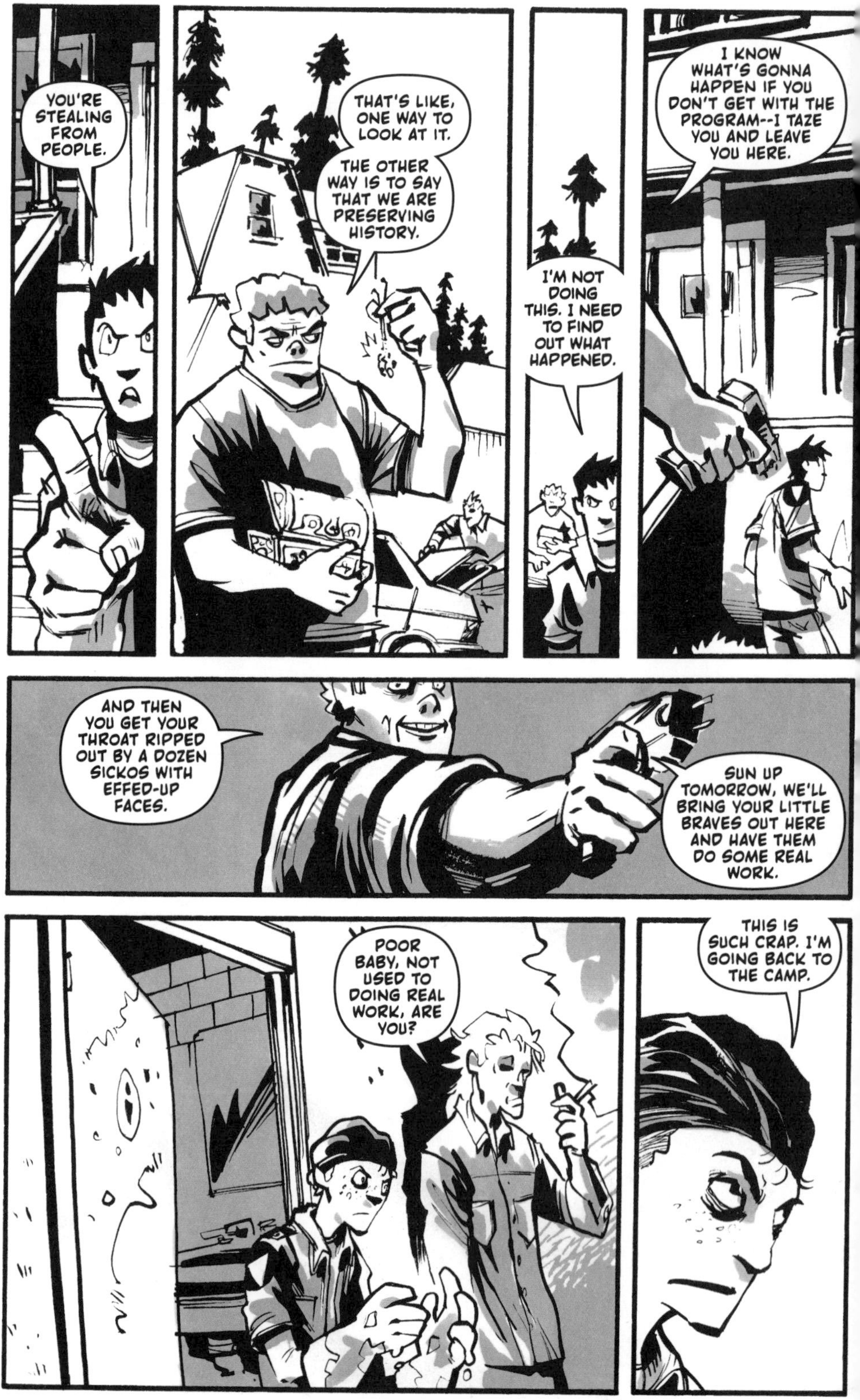
YOU'RE STEALING FROM PEOPLE.
THAT'S LIKE, ONE WAY TO LOOK AT IT.
THE OTHER WAY IS TO SAY THAT WE ARE PRESERVING HISTORY.
I'M NOT DOING THIS. I NEED TO FIND OUT WHAT HAPPENED.
I KNOW WHAT'S GONNA HAPPEN IF YOU DON'T GET WITH THE PROGRAM--I TAZE YOU AND LEAVE YOU HERE.
AND THEN YOU GET YOUR THROAT RIPPED OUT BY A DOZEN SICKOS WITH EFFED-UP FACES.
SUN UP TOMORROW, WE'LL BRING YOUR LITTLE BRAVES OUT HERE AND HAVE THEM DO SOME REAL WORK.
POOR BABY, NOT USED TO DOING REAL WORK, ARE YOU?
THIS IS SUCH CRAP. I'M GOING BACK TO THE CAMP.

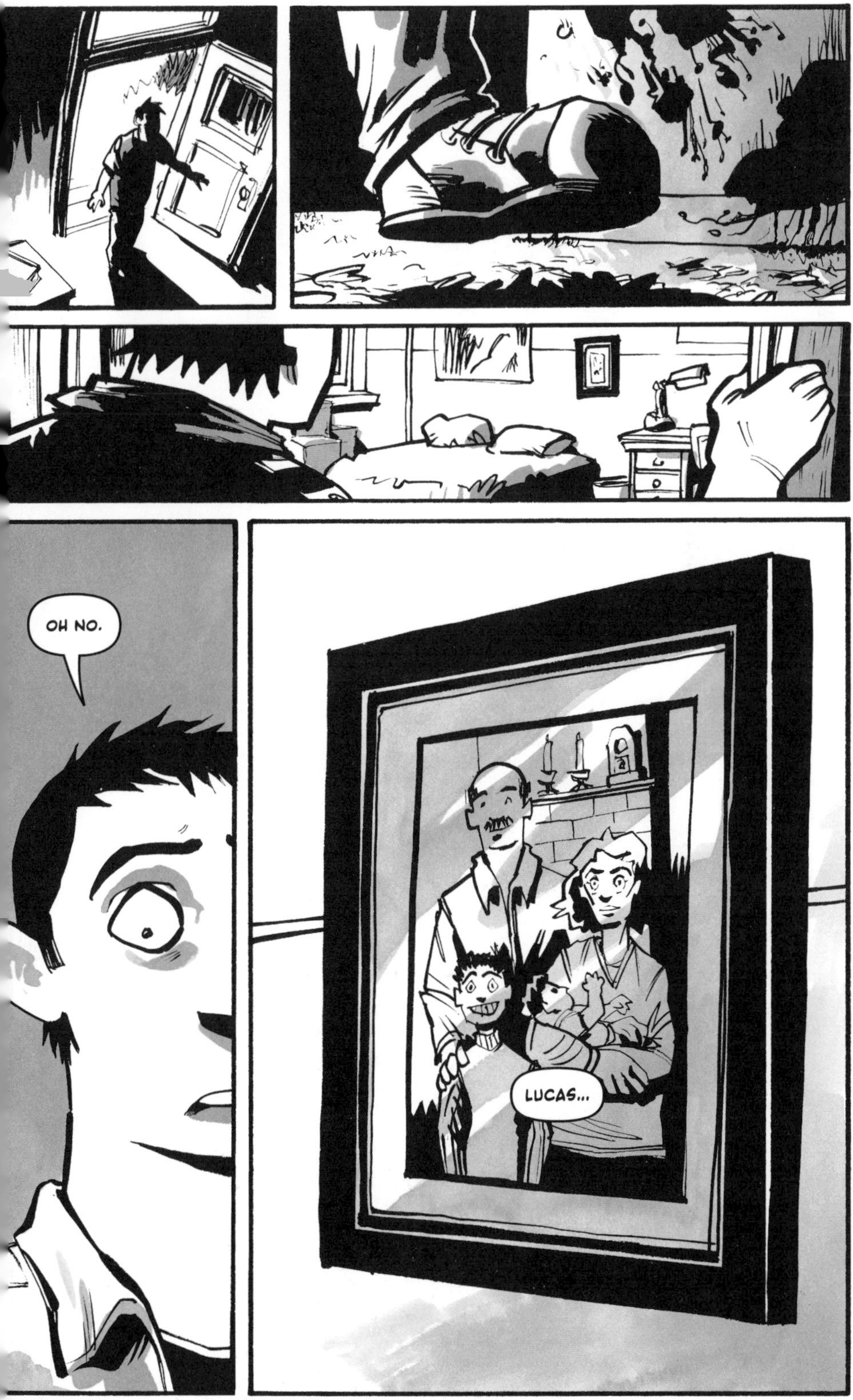
OH NO.
LUCAS...

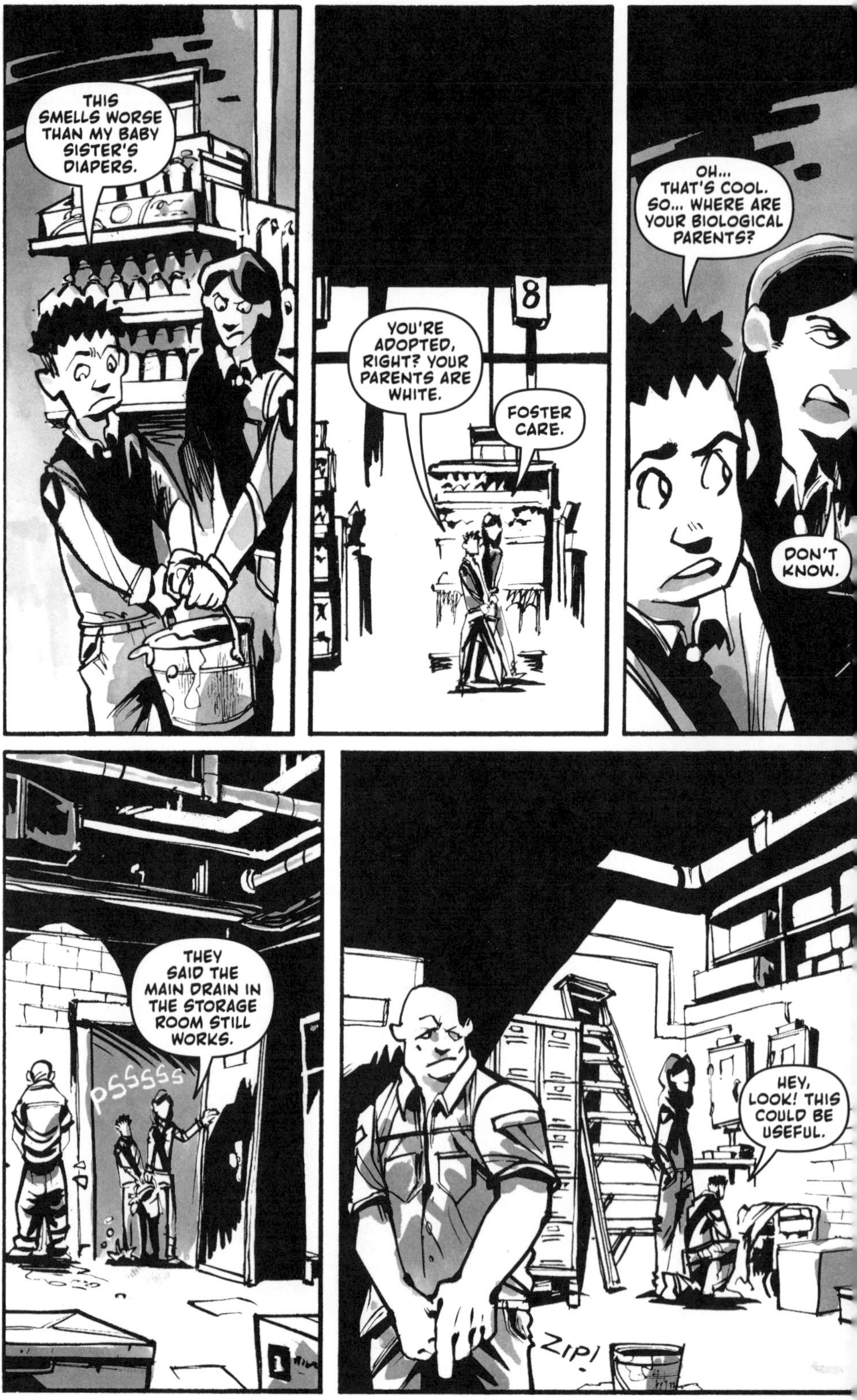
THIS SMELLS WORSE THAN MY BABY SISTER'S DIAPERS.
YOU'RE ADOPTED, RIGHT? YOUR PARENTS ARE WHITE.
FOSTER CARE.
8
OH... THAT'S COOL. SO... WHERE ARE YOUR BIOLOGICAL PARENTS?
DON'T KNOW.
THEY SAID THE MAIN DRAIN IN THE STORAGE ROOM STILL WORKS.
PSSSSS
1
HEY, LOOK! THIS COULD BE USEFUL.
ZIP!

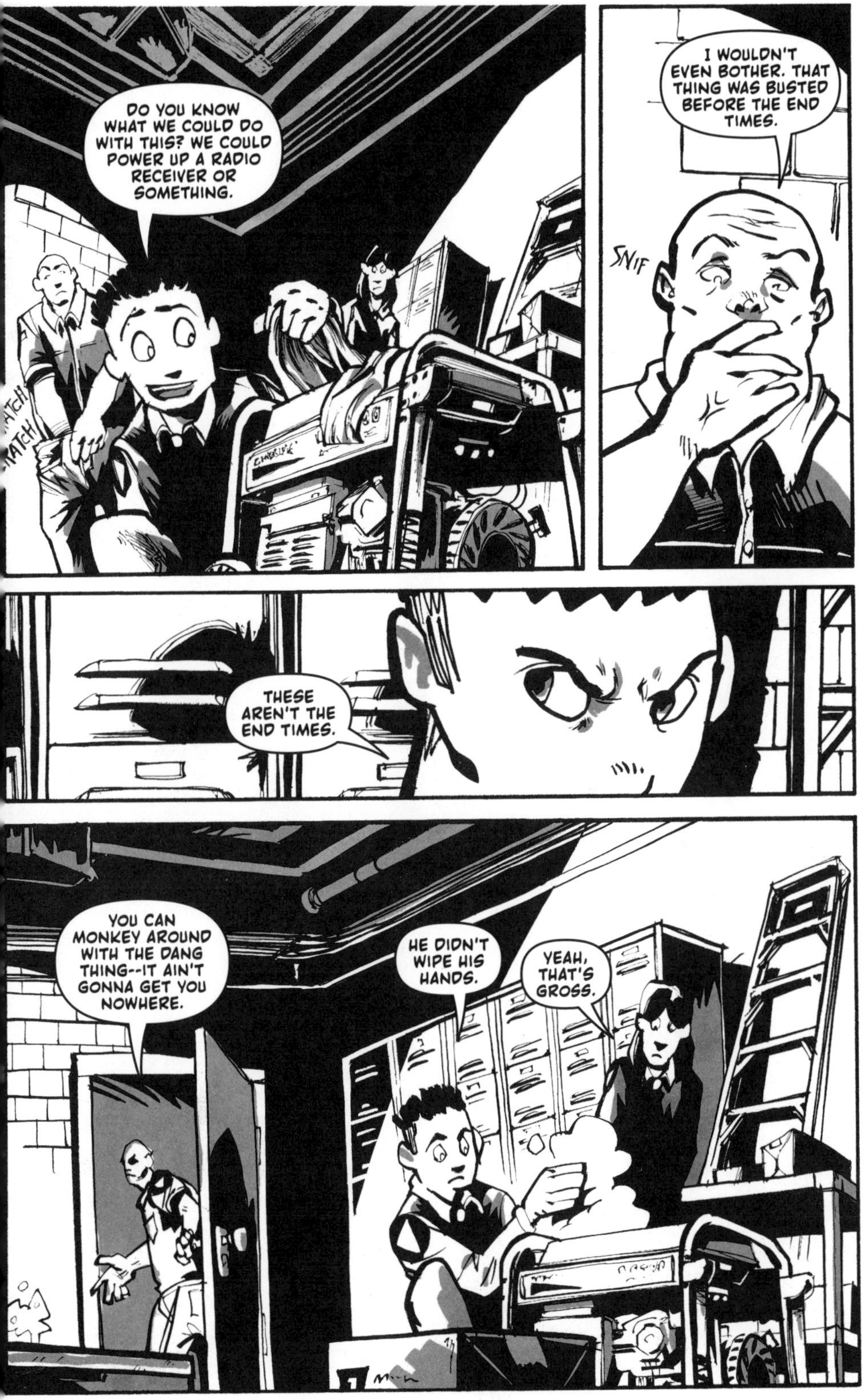
DO YOU KNOW WHAT WE COULD DO WITH THIS? WE COULD POWER UP A RADIO RECEIVER OR SOMETHING.
I WOULDN'T EVEN BOTHER. THAT THING WAS BUSTED BEFORE THE END TIMES.
SNIF
THESE AREN'T THE END TIMES.
YOU CAN MONKEY AROUND WITH THE DANG THING--IT AIN'T GONNA GET YOU NOWHERE.
HE DIDN'T WIPE HIS HANDS.
YEAH, THAT'S GROSS.

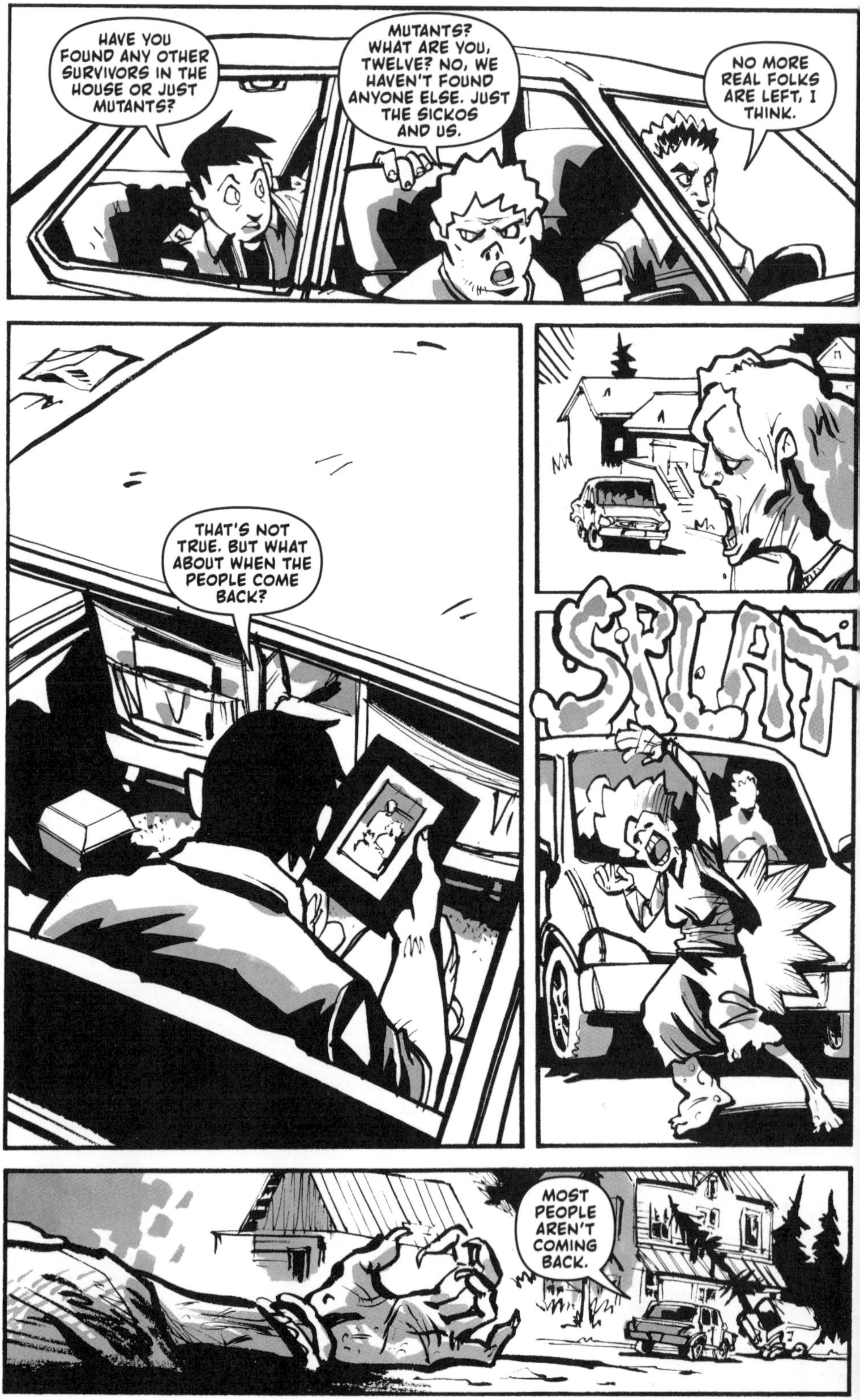
HAVE YOU FOUND ANY OTHER SURVIVORS IN THE HOUSE OR JUST MUTANTS?
MUTANTS? WHAT ARE YOU, TWELVE? NO, WE HAVEN'T FOUND ANYONE ELSE. JUST THE SICKOS AND US.
NO MORE REAL FOLKS ARE LEFT, I THINK.
THAT'S NOT TRUE. BUT WHAT ABOUT WHEN THE PEOPLE COME BACK?
SPLAT
MOST PEOPLE AREN'T COMING BACK.

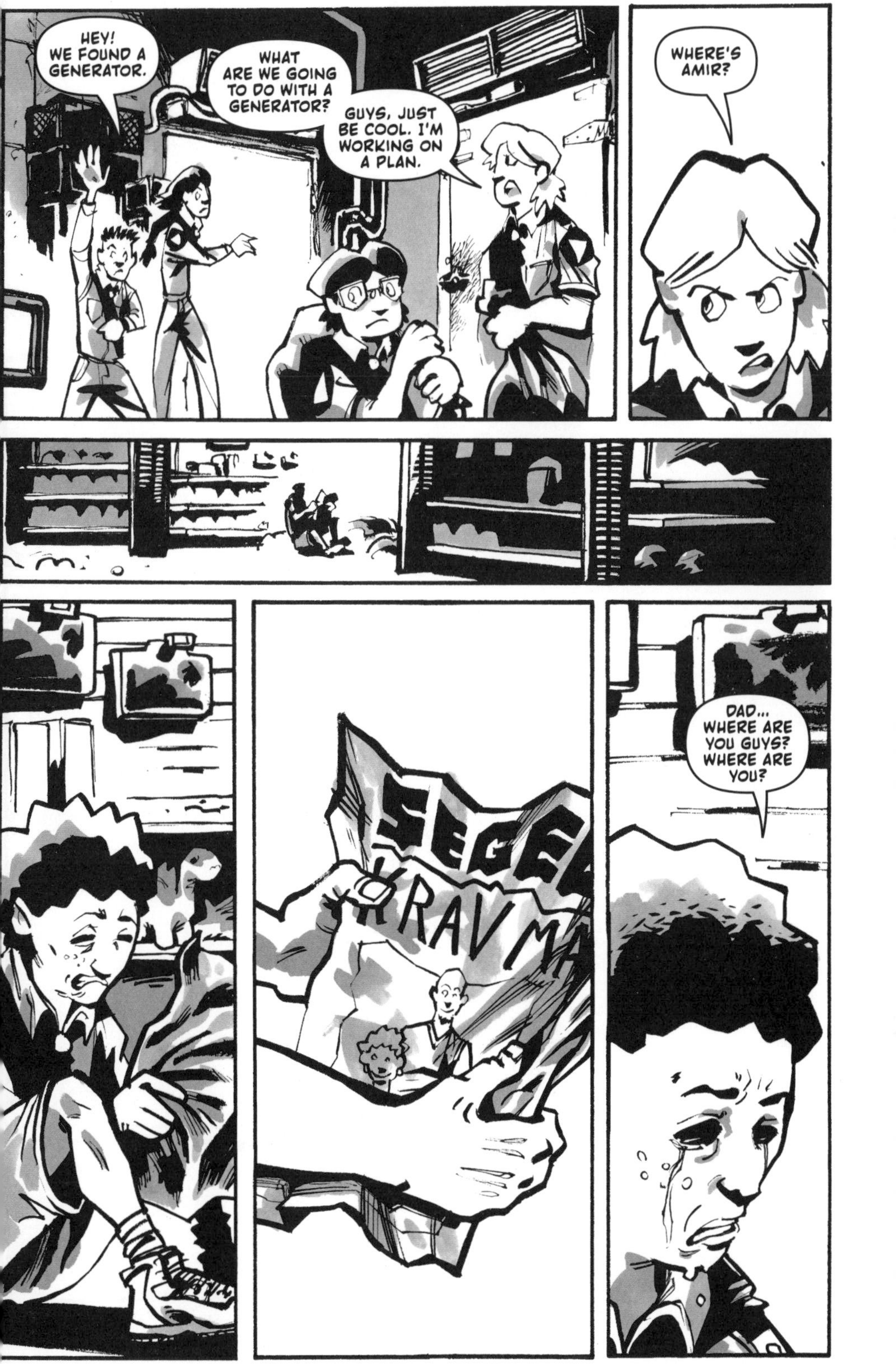
HEY! WE FOUND A GENERATOR.
WHAT ARE WE GOING TO DO WITH A GENERATOR?
GUYS, JUST BE COOL. I'M WORKING ON A PLAN.
WHERE'S AMIR?
DAD... WHERE ARE YOU GUYS? WHERE ARE YOU?

How to Dress a Wound

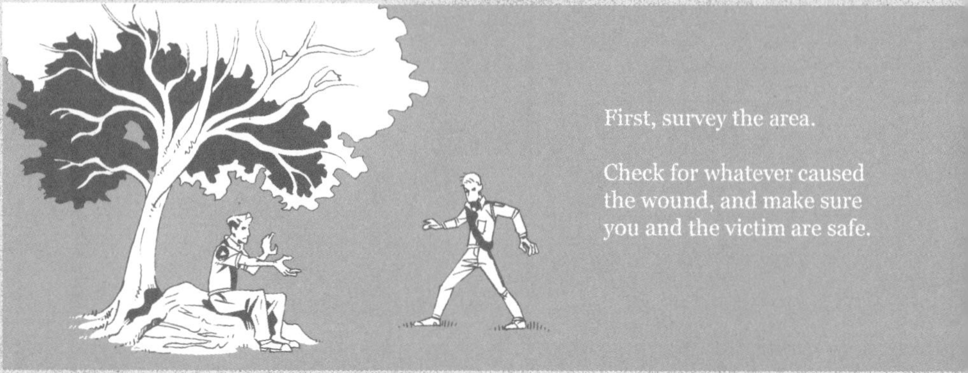
First, survey the area.
Check for whatever caused the wound, and make sure you and the victim are safe.

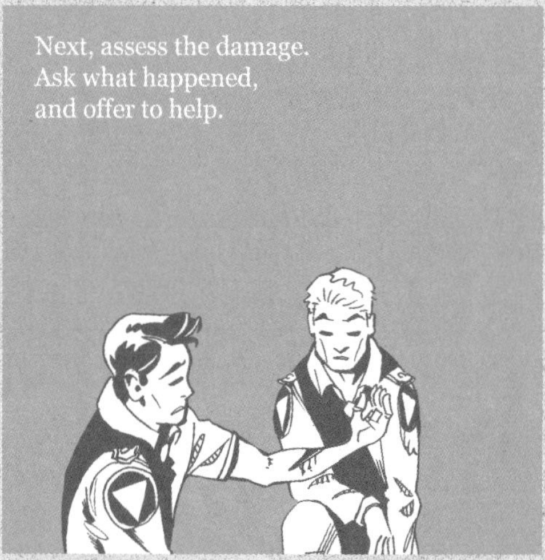
Next, assess the damage. Ask what happened, and offer to help.

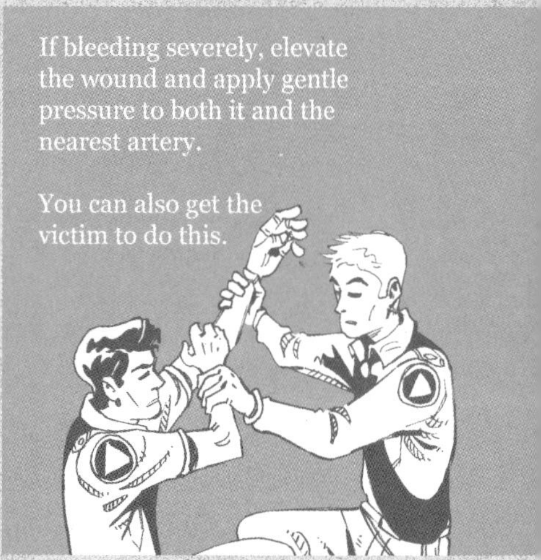
If bleeding severely, elevate the wound and apply gentle pressure to both it and the nearest artery.
You can also get the victim to do this.

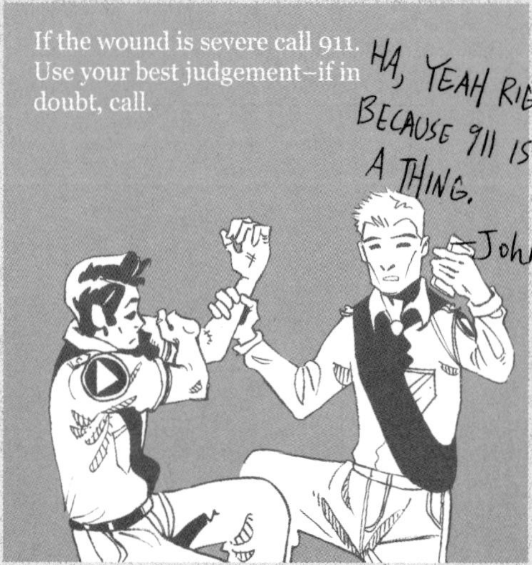
If the wound is severe call 911. Use your best judgement–if in doubt, call.
HA, YEAH RIGHT. BECAUSE 911 IS STill A THING.
—Johnny

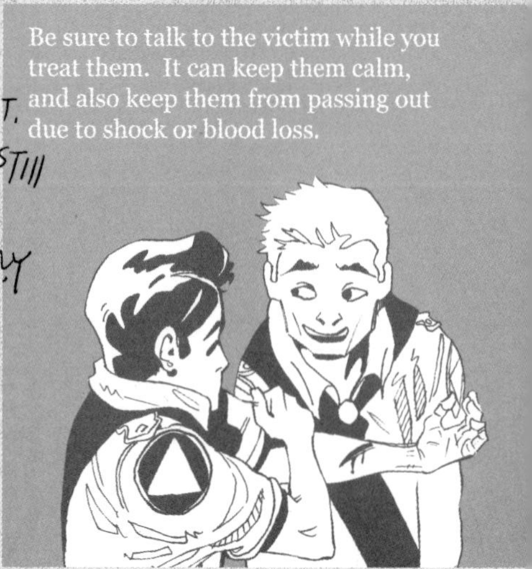
Be sure to talk to the victim while you treat them. It can keep them calm, and also keep them from passing out due to shock or blood loss.

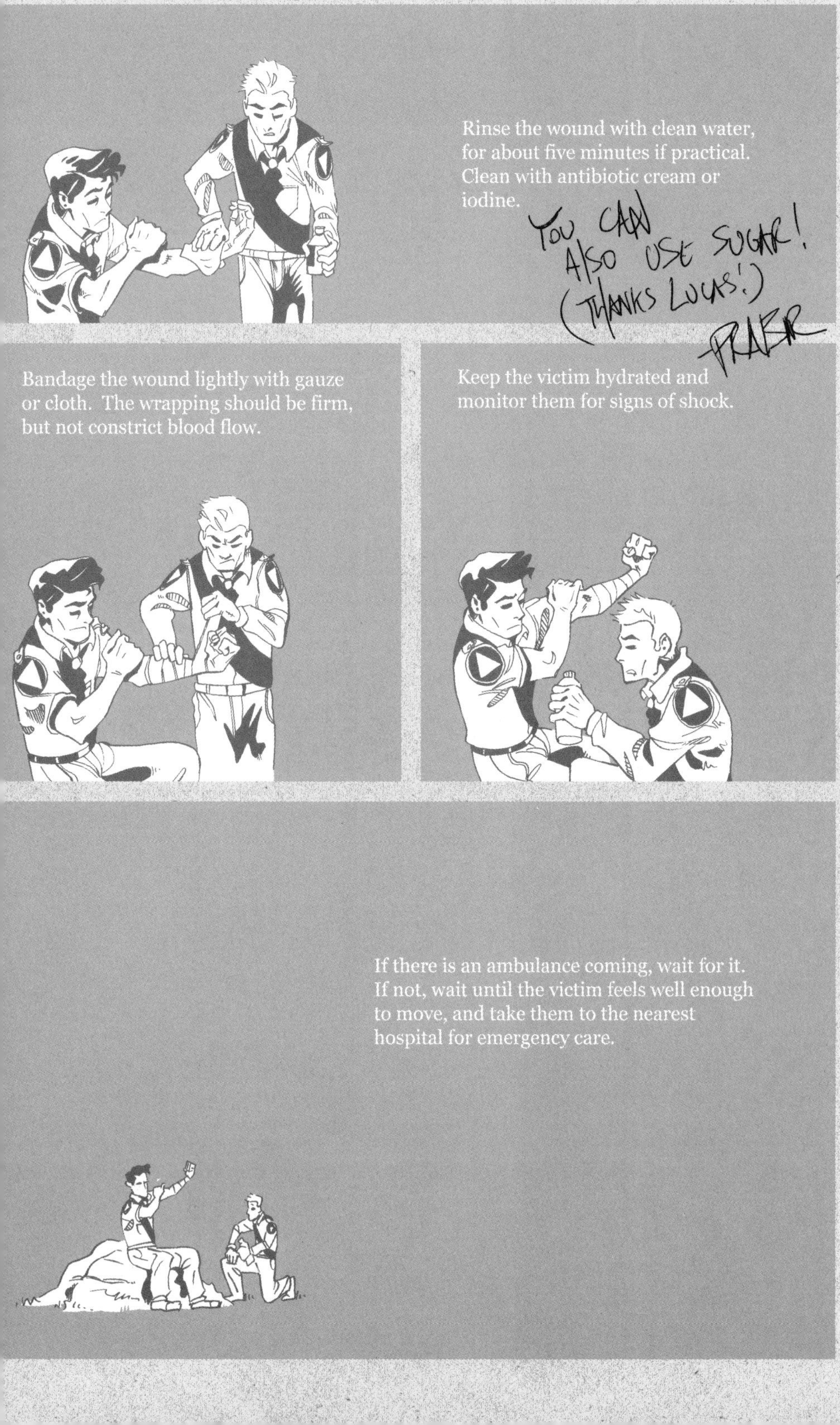
Rinse the wound with clean water, for about five minutes if practical. Clean with antibiotic cream or iodine.
YOU CAN ALSO USE SUGAR! (THANKS LUCAS!) PRABAR
Bandage the wound lightly with gauze or cloth. The wrapping should be firm, but not constrict blood flow.
Keep the victim hydrated and monitor them for signs of shock.
If there is an ambulance coming, wait for it. If not, wait until the victim feels well enough to move, and take them to the nearest hospital for emergency care.

CHAPTER FIVE

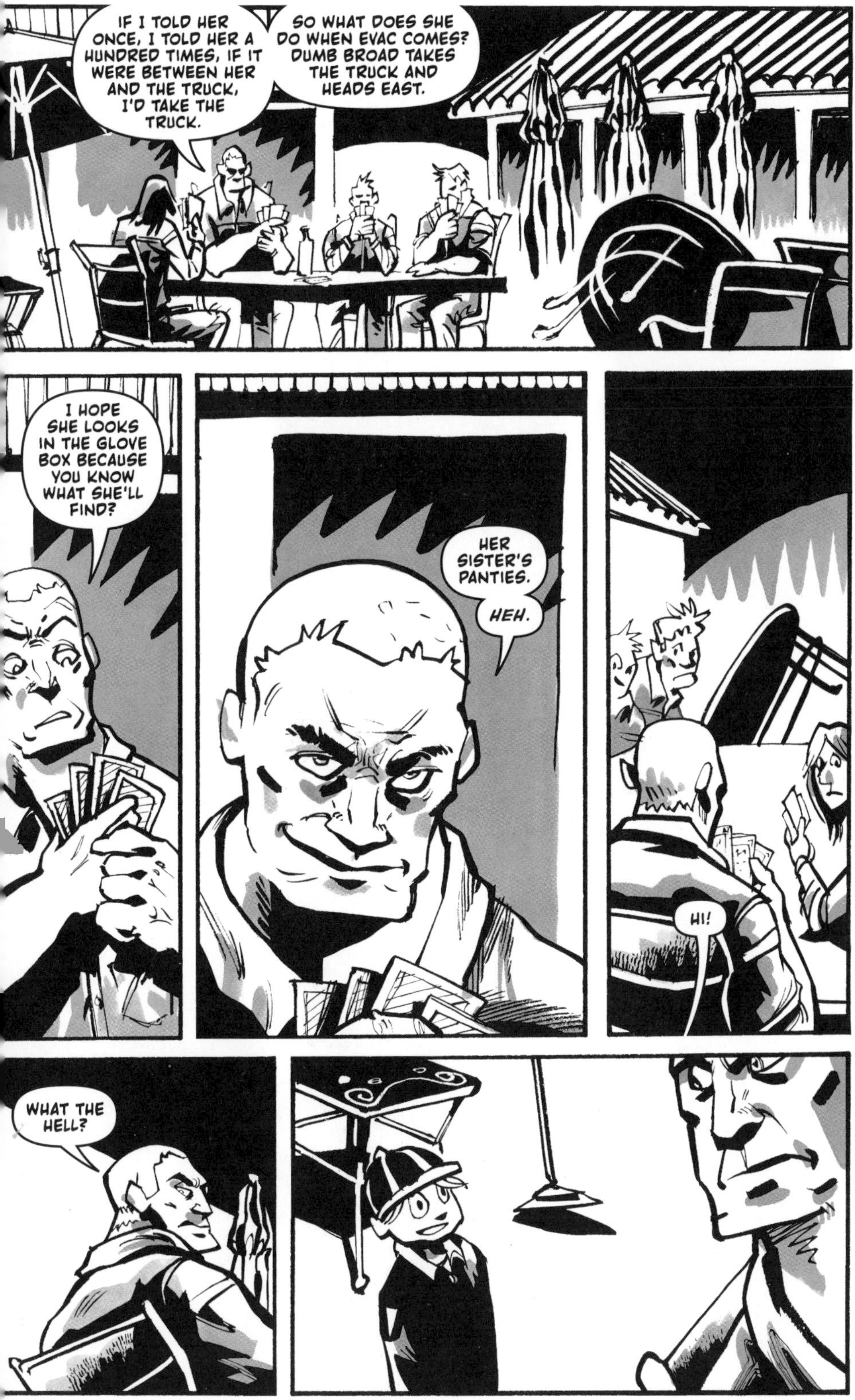
IF I TOLD HER ONCE, I TOLD HER A HUNDRED TIMES, IF IT WERE BETWEEN HER AND THE TRUCK, I'D TAKE THE TRUCK.
SO WHAT DOES SHE DO WHEN EVAC COMES? DUMB BROAD TAKES THE TRUCK AND HEADS EAST.
I HOPE SHE LOOKS IN THE GLOVE BOX BECAUSE YOU KNOW WHAT SHE'LL FIND?
HER SISTER'S PANTIES.
HEH.
HI!
WHAT THE HELL?

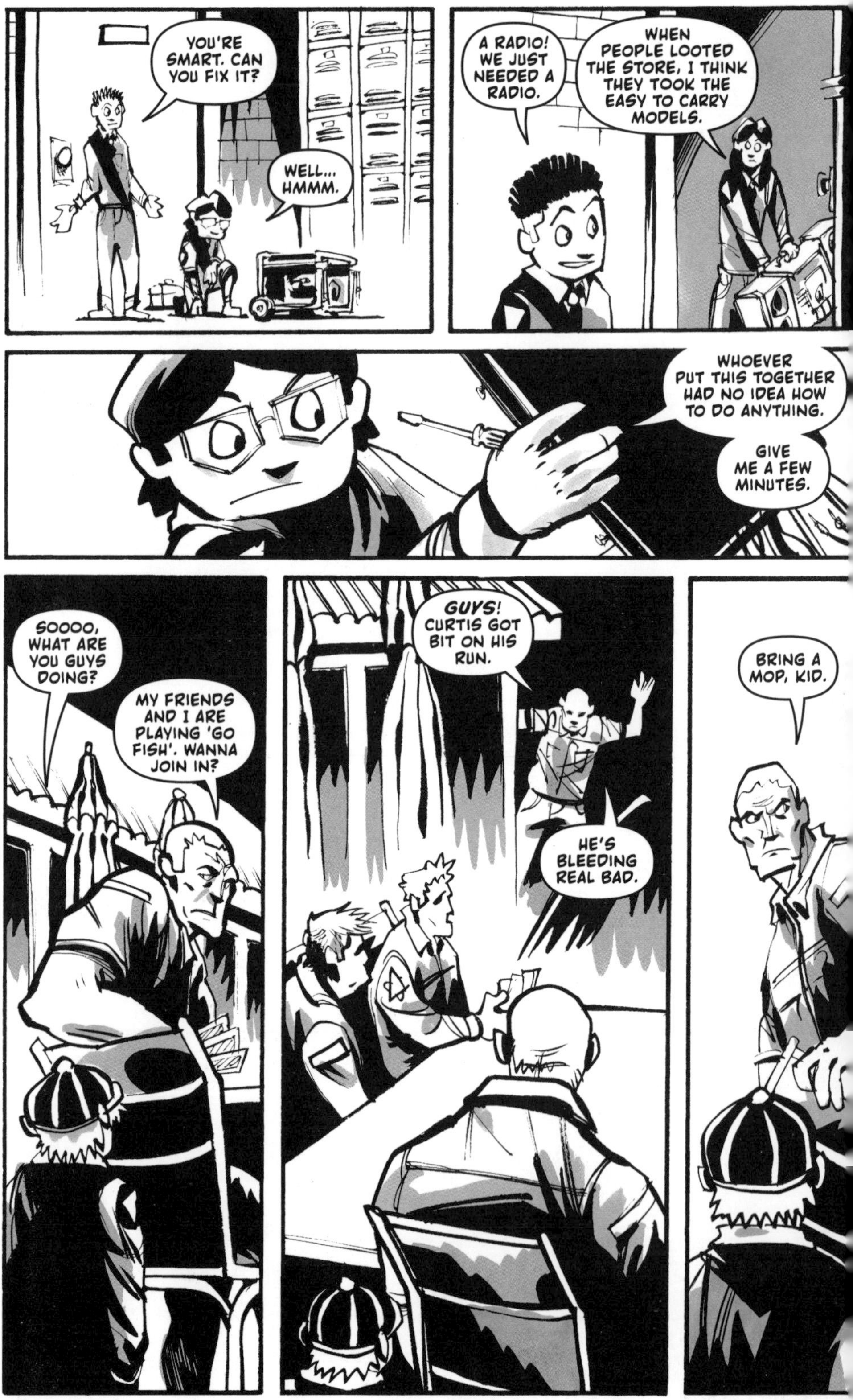
YOU'RE SMART. CAN YOU FIX IT?
WELL... HMMM.
A RADIO! WE JUST NEEDED A RADIO.
WHEN PEOPLE LOOTED THE STORE, I THINK THEY TOOK THE EASY TO CARRY MODELS.
WHOEVER PUT THIS TOGETHER HAD NO IDEA HOW TO DO ANYTHING.
GIVE ME A FEW MINUTES.
SOOOO, WHAT ARE YOU GUYS DOING?
MY FRIENDS AND I ARE PLAYING 'GO FISH'. WANNA JOIN IN?
GUYS! CURTIS GOT BIT ON HIS RUN.
HE'S BLEEDING REAL BAD.
BRING A MOP, KID.

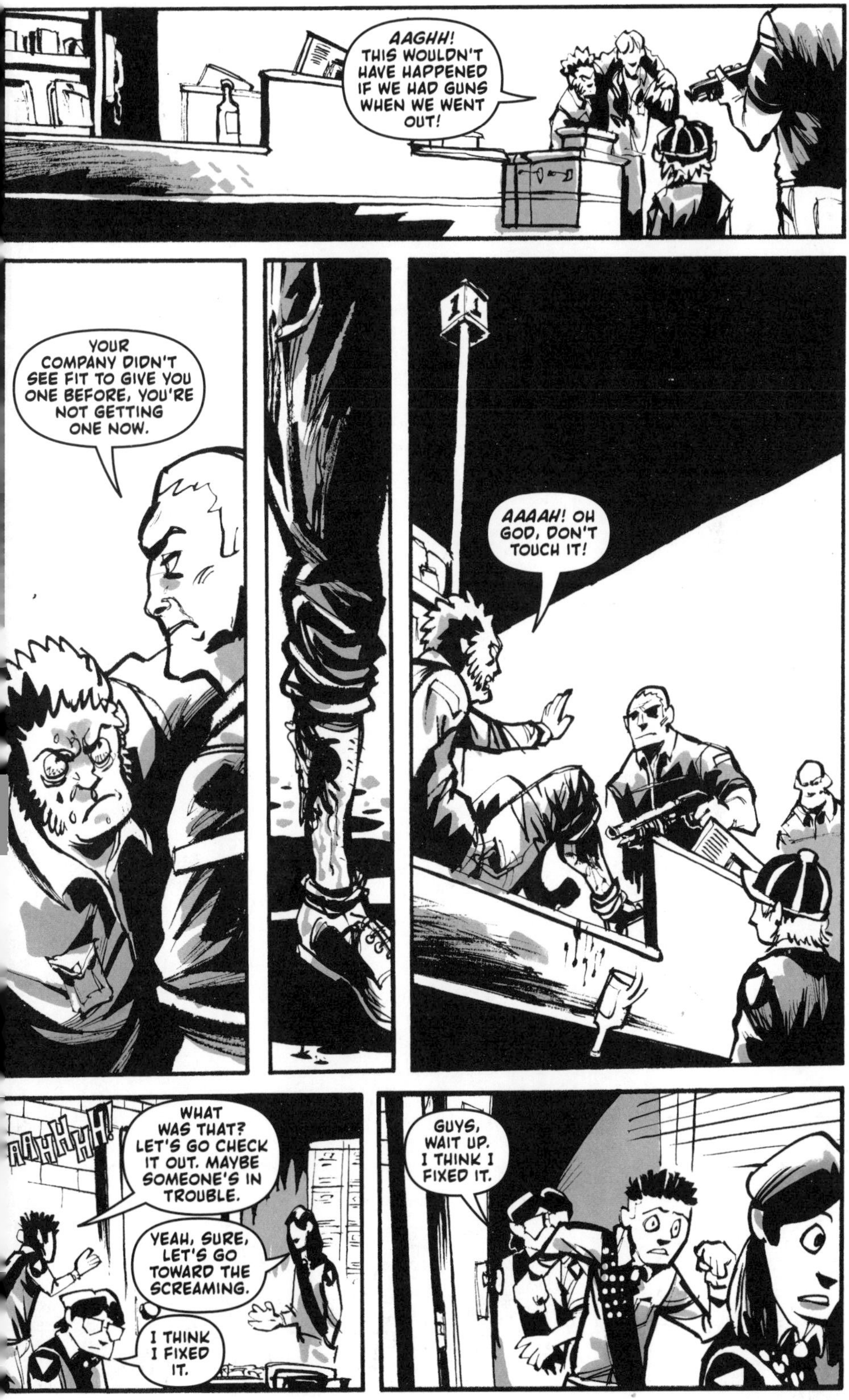
AAGHH! THIS WOULDN'T HAVE HAPPENED IF WE HAD GUNS WHEN WE WENT OUT!
YOUR COMPANY DIDN'T SEE FIT TO GIVE YOU ONE BEFORE, YOU'RE NOT GETTING ONE NOW.
AAAAH! OH GOD, DON'T TOUCH IT!
AAHHHH!
WHAT WAS THAT? LET'S GO CHECK IT OUT. MAYBE SOMEONE'S IN TROUBLE.
YEAH, SURE, LET'S GO TOWARD THE SCREAMING.
I THINK I FIXED IT.
GUYS, WAIT UP. I THINK I FIXED IT.

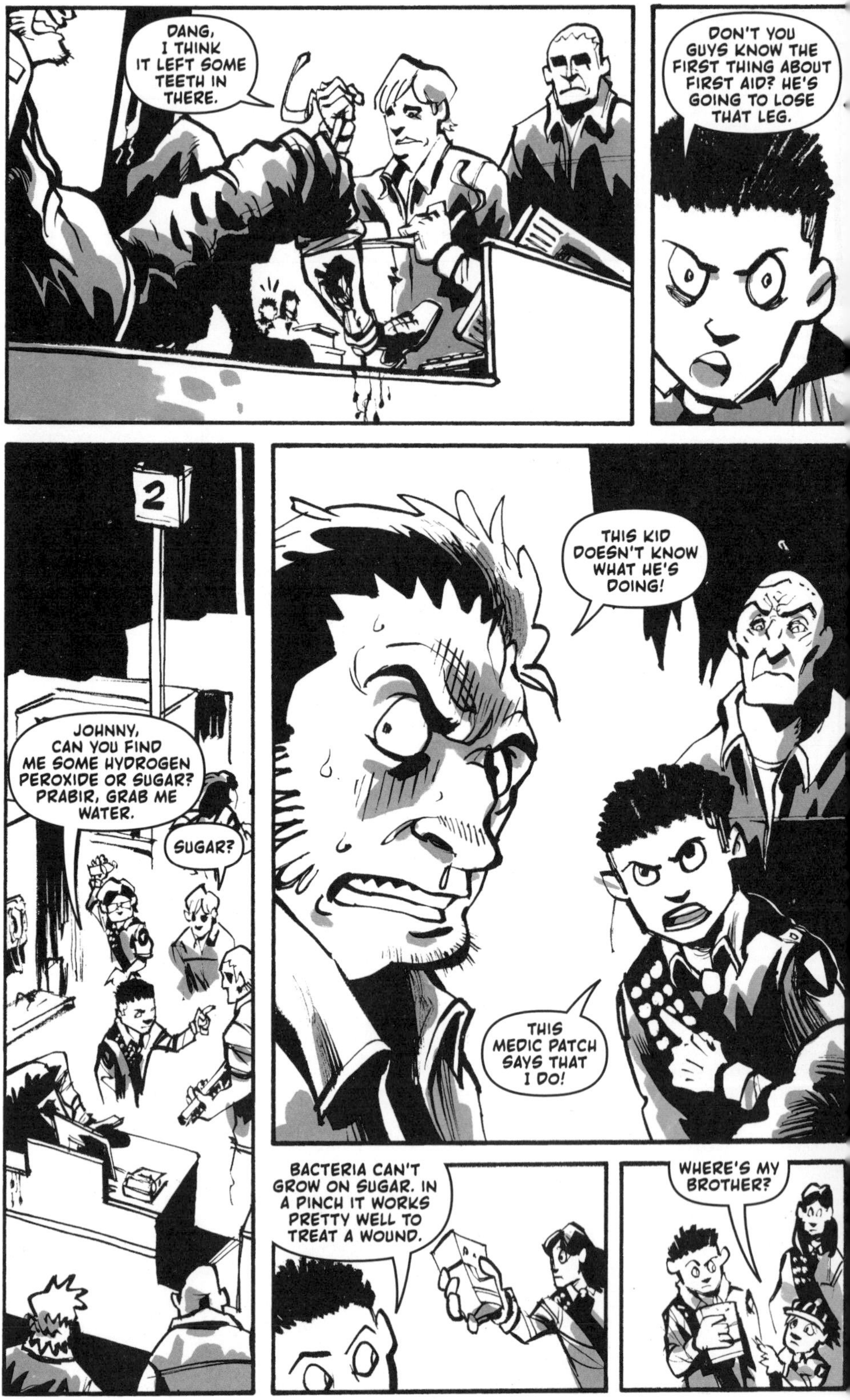
DANG, I THINK IT LEFT SOME TEETH IN THERE.
DON'T YOU GUYS KNOW THE FIRST THING ABOUT FIRST AID? HE'S GOING TO LOSE THAT LEG.
2
JOHNNY, CAN YOU FIND ME SOME HYDROGEN PEROXIDE OR SUGAR? PRABIR, GRAB ME WATER.
SUGAR?
THIS KID DOESN'T KNOW WHAT HE'S DOING!
THIS MEDIC PATCH SAYS THAT I DO!
BACTERIA CAN'T GROW ON SUGAR. IN A PINCH IT WORKS PRETTY WELL TO TREAT A WOUND.
WHERE'S MY BROTHER?

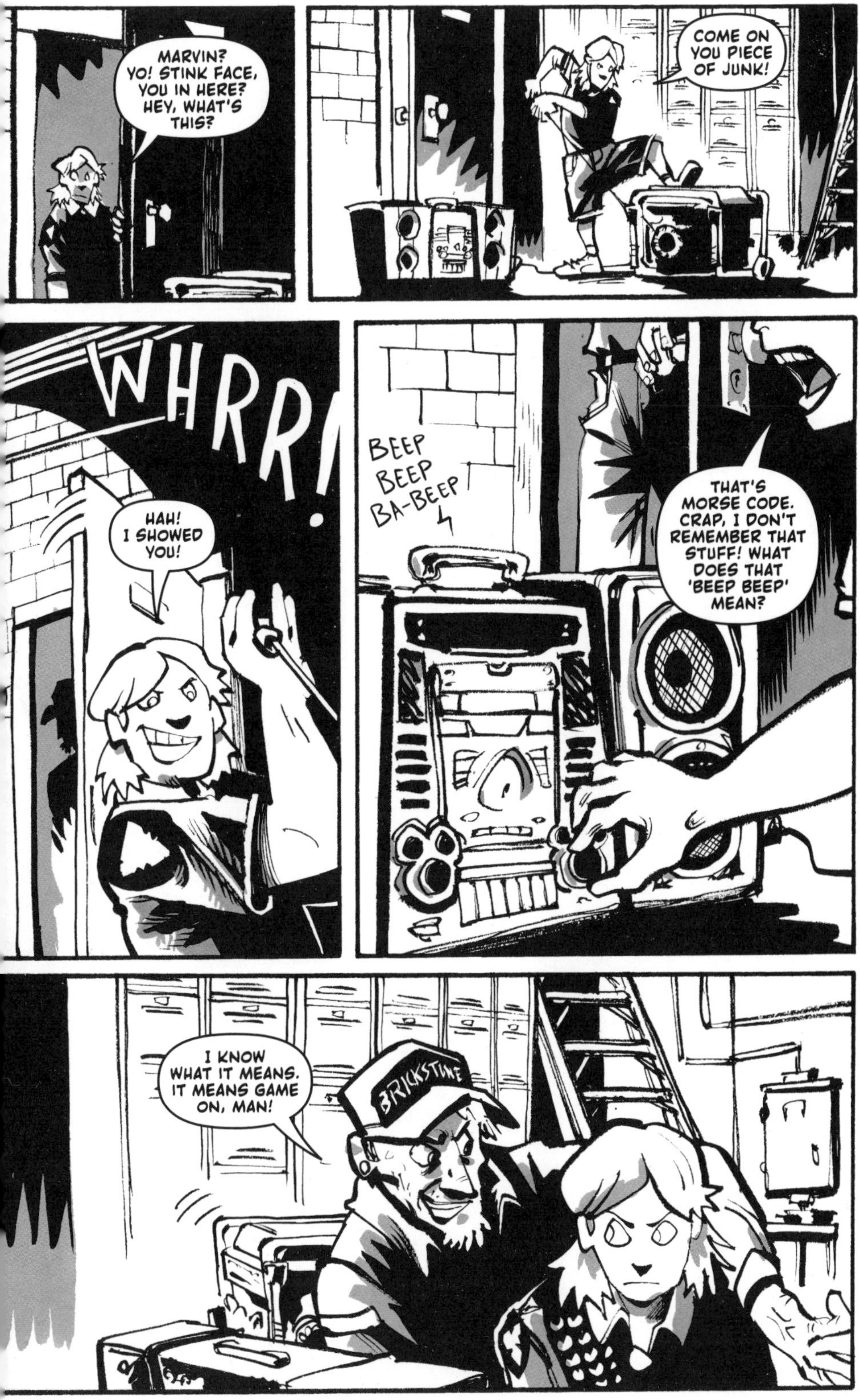
MARVIN? YO! STINK FACE, YOU IN HERE? HEY, WHAT'S THIS?
COME ON YOU PIECE OF JUNK!
WHRR!
HAH! I SHOWED YOU!
BEEP BEEP BA-BEEP
THAT'S MORSE CODE. CRAP, I DON'T REMEMBER THAT STUFF! WHAT DOES THAT 'BEEP BEEP' MEAN?
I KNOW WHAT IT MEANS. IT MEANS GAME ON, MAN!
BRICKSTONE

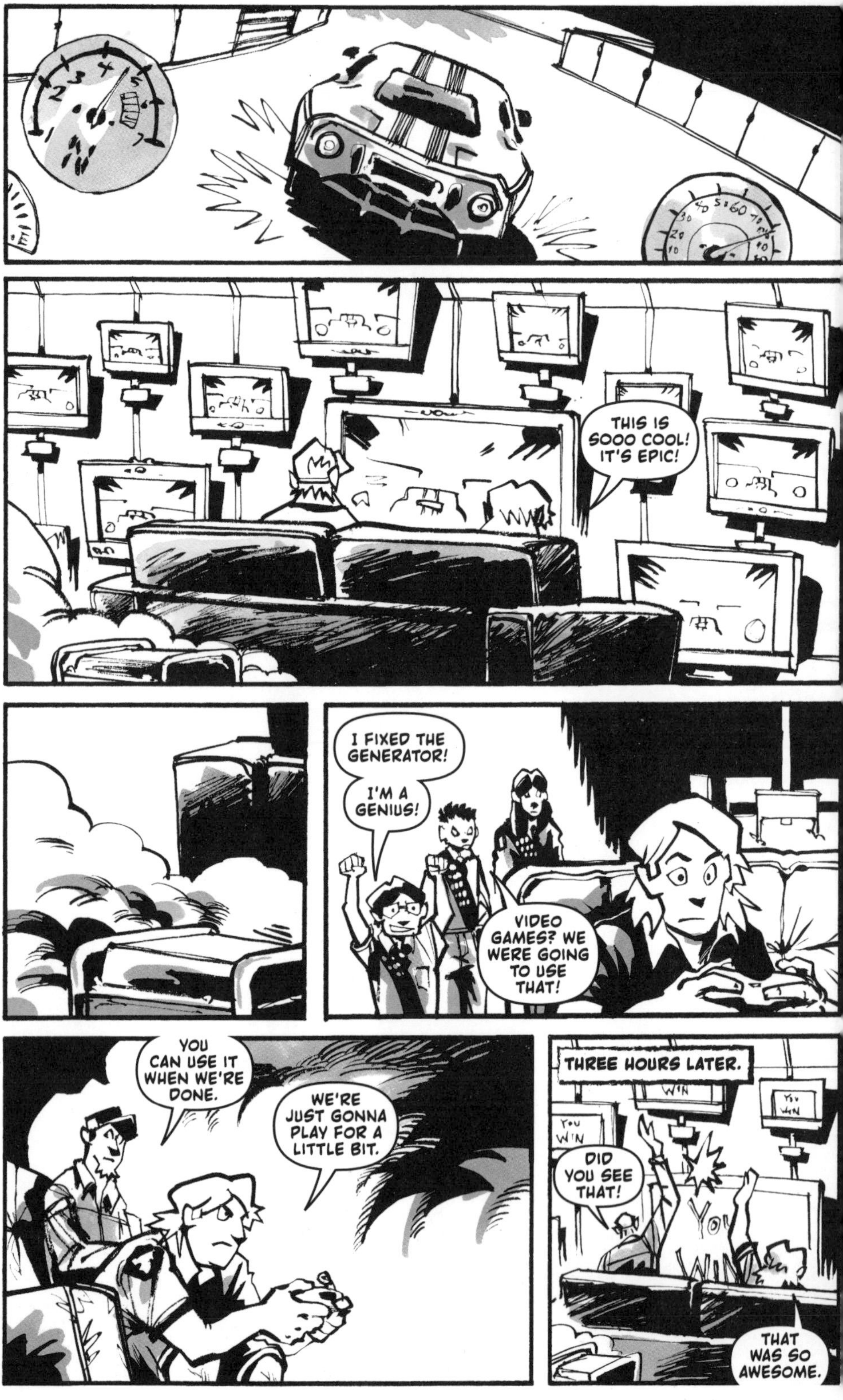
THIS IS SOOO COOL! IT'S EPIC!
I FIXED THE GENERATOR!
I'M A GENIUS!
VIDEO GAMES? WE WERE GOING TO USE THAT!
YOU CAN USE IT WHEN WE'RE DONE.
WE'RE JUST GONNA PLAY FOR A LITTLE BIT.
THREE HOURS LATER.
YOU WIN
YOU WIN
DID YOU SEE THAT!
THAT WAS SO AWESOME.

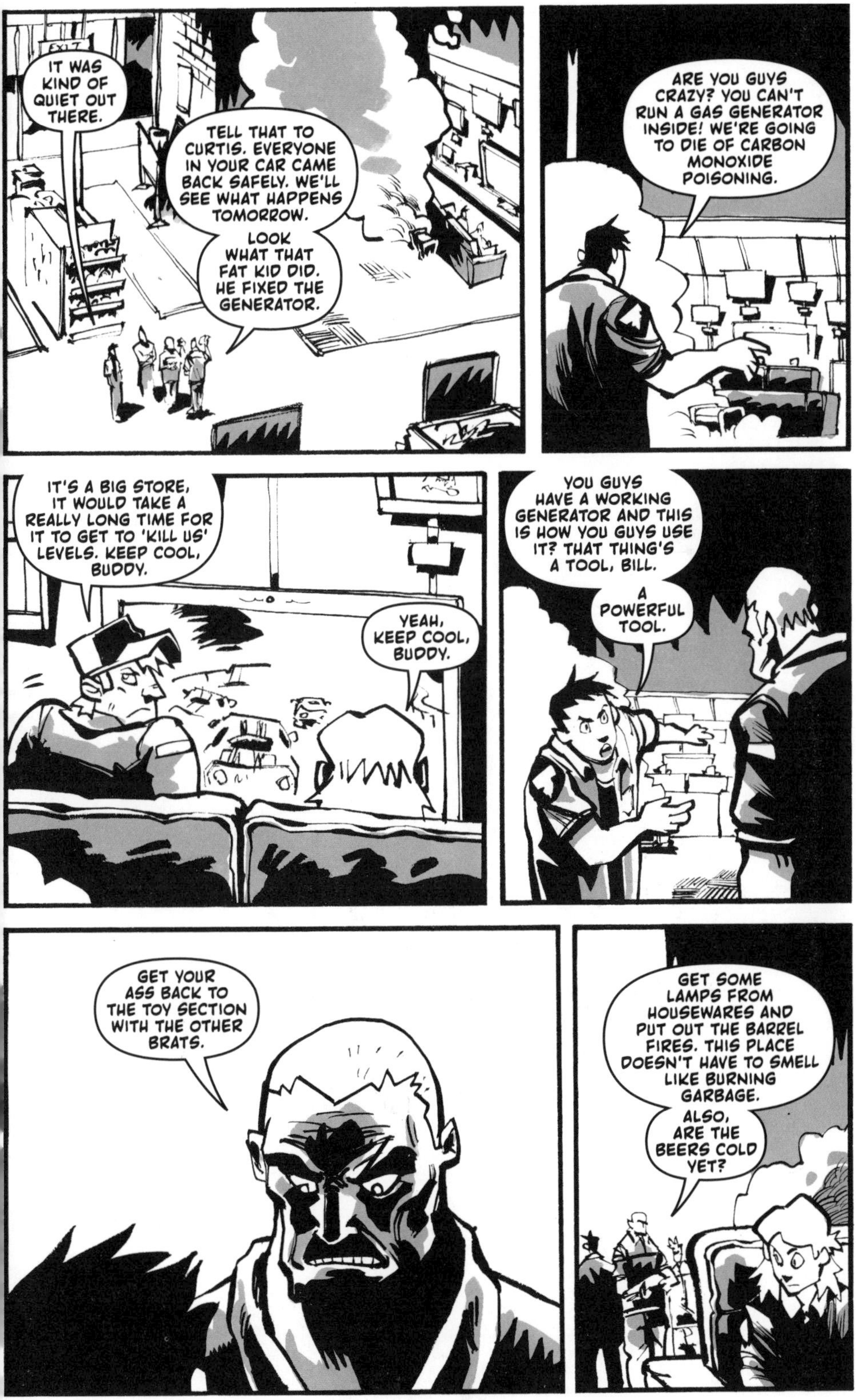

EXIT
IT WAS KIND OF QUIET OUT THERE.
TELL THAT TO CURTIS. EVERYONE IN YOUR CAR CAME BACK SAFELY. WE'LL SEE WHAT HAPPENS TOMORROW.
LOOK WHAT THAT FAT KID DID. HE FIXED THE GENERATOR.
ARE YOU GUYS CRAZY? YOU CAN'T RUN A GAS GENERATOR INSIDE! WE'RE GOING TO DIE OF CARBON MONOXIDE POISONING.
IT'S A BIG STORE, IT WOULD TAKE A REALLY LONG TIME FOR IT TO GET TO 'KILL US' LEVELS. KEEP COOL, BUDDY.
YEAH, KEEP COOL, BUDDY.
YOU GUYS HAVE A WORKING GENERATOR AND THIS IS HOW YOU GUYS USE IT? THAT THING'S A TOOL, BILL.
A POWERFUL TOOL.
GET YOUR ASS BACK TO THE TOY SECTION WITH THE OTHER BRATS.
GET SOME LAMPS FROM HOUSEWARES AND PUT OUT THE BARREL FIRES. THIS PLACE DOESN'T HAVE TO SMELL LIKE BURNING GARBAGE.
ALSO, ARE THE BEERS COLD YET?

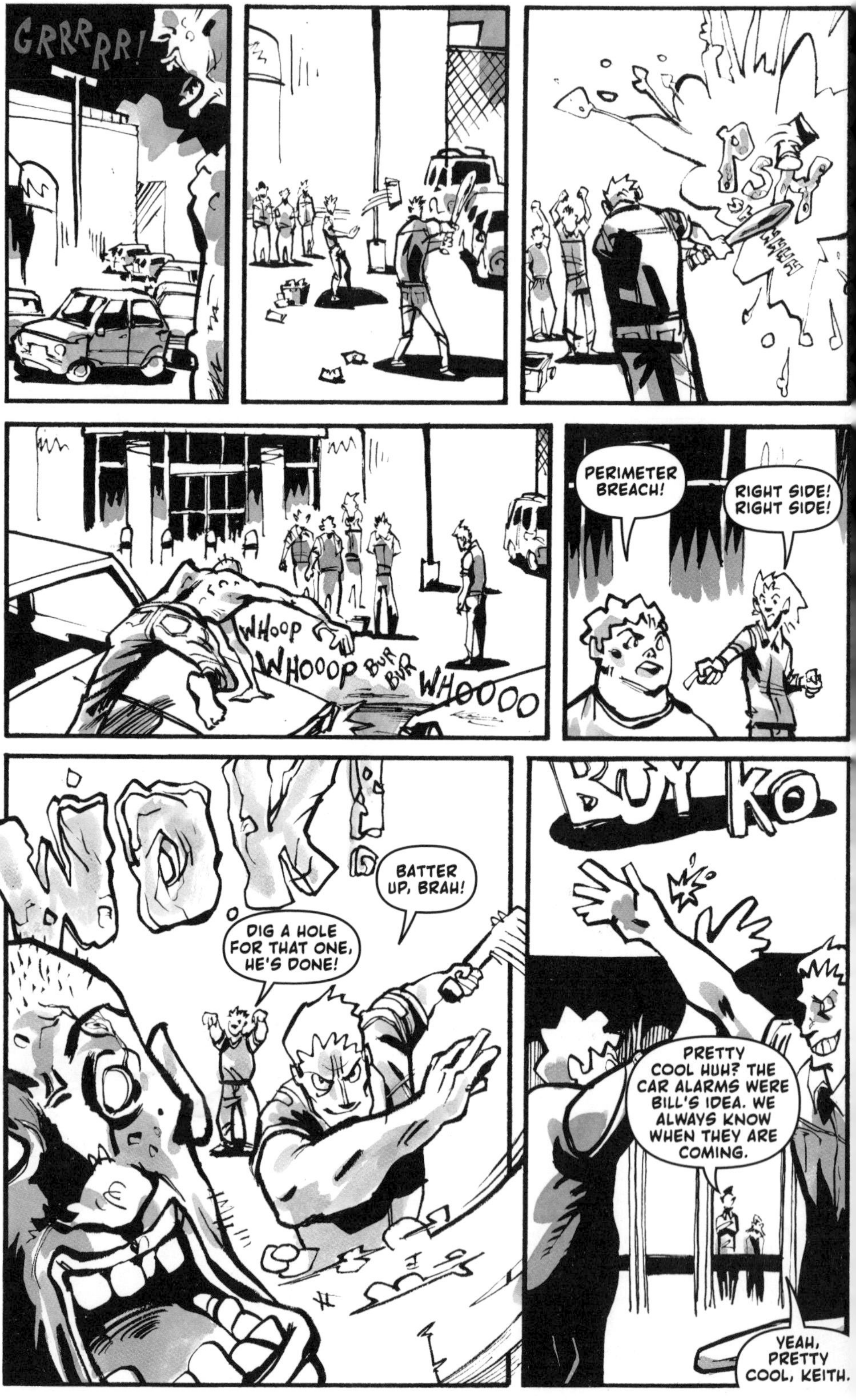
GRRRRR!
PSHH
PERIMETER BREACH!
RIGHT SIDE! RIGHT SIDE!
WHOOP
WHOOOP BUR BUR
WHOOOOO
BATTER UP, BRAH!
DIG A HOLE FOR THAT ONE, HE'S DONE!
BUY KO
PRETTY COOL HUH? THE CAR ALARMS WERE BILL'S IDEA. WE ALWAYS KNOW WHEN THEY ARE COMING.
YEAH, PRETTY COOL, KEITH.

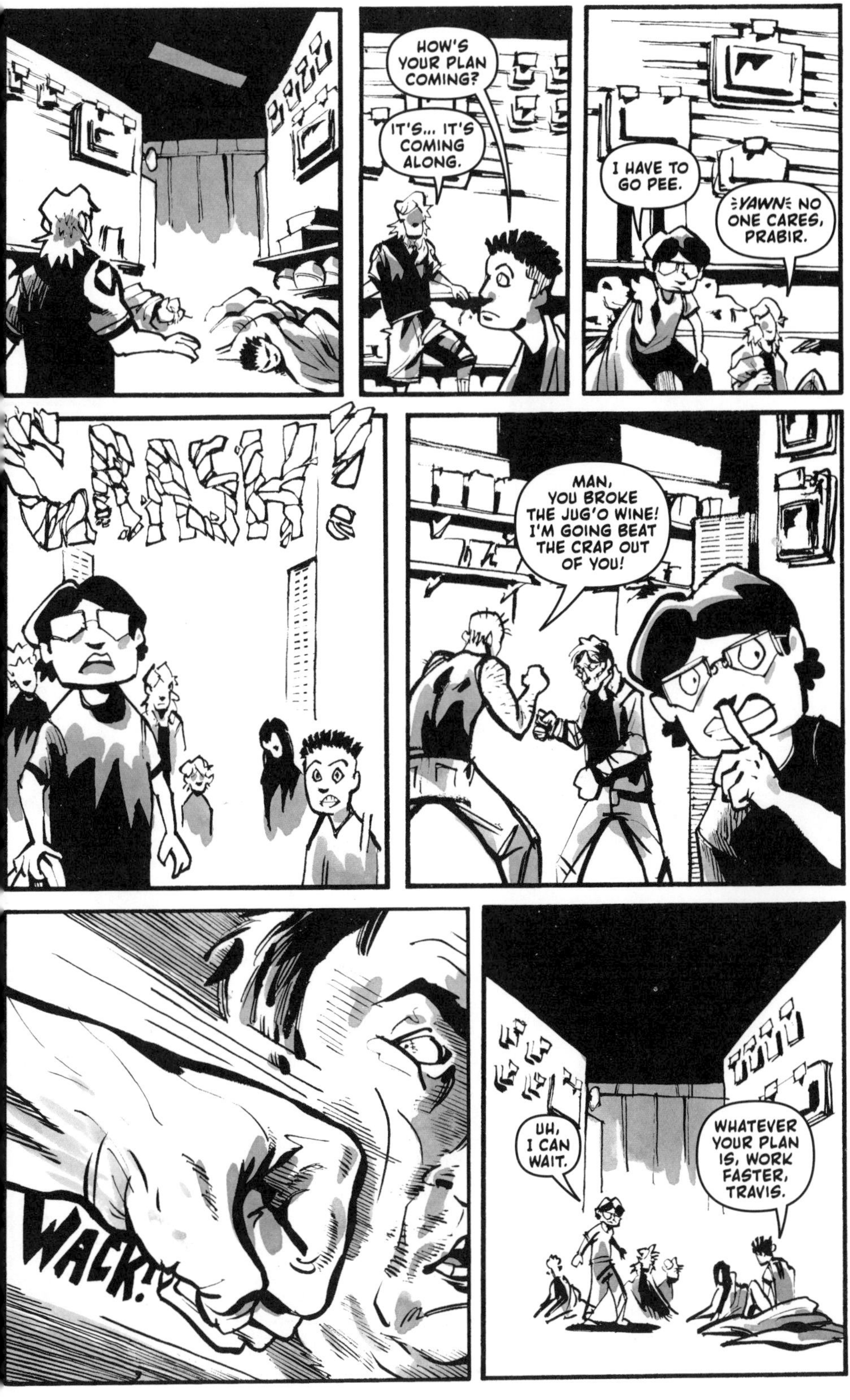
HOW'S YOUR PLAN COMING?
IT'S... IT'S COMING ALONG.
I HAVE TO GO PEE.
≷YAWN≶ NO ONE CARES, PRABIR.
MAN, YOU BROKE THE JUG'O WINE! I'M GOING BEAT THE CRAP OUT OF YOU!
WACK!
UH, I CAN WAIT.
WHATEVER YOUR PLAN IS, WORK FASTER, TRAVIS.

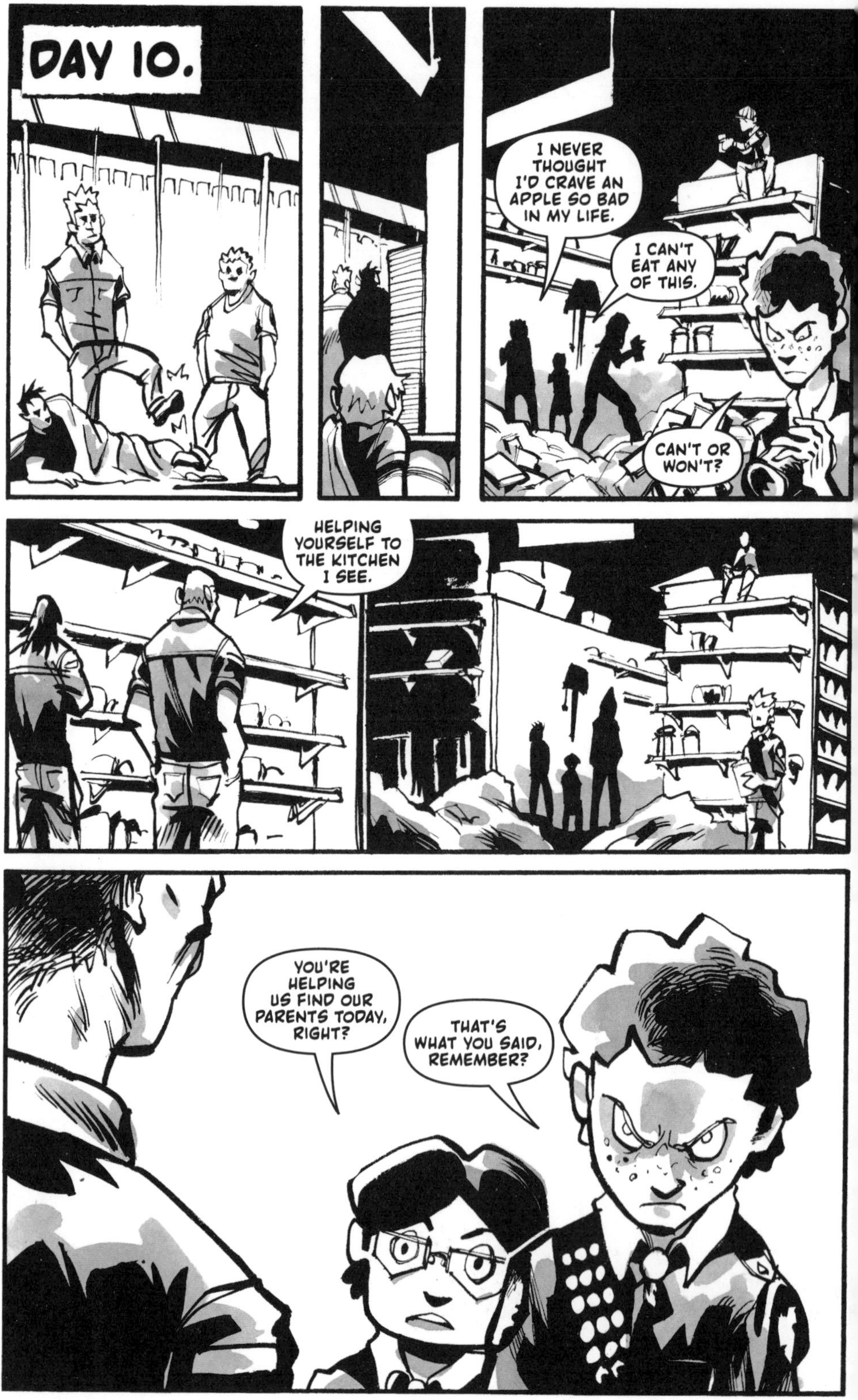
DAY 10.
I NEVER THOUGHT I'D CRAVE AN APPLE SO BAD IN MY LIFE.
I CAN'T EAT ANY OF THIS.
CAN'T OR WON'T?
HELPING YOURSELF TO THE KITCHEN I SEE.
YOU'RE HELPING US FIND OUR PARENTS TODAY, RIGHT?
THAT'S WHAT YOU SAID, REMEMBER?

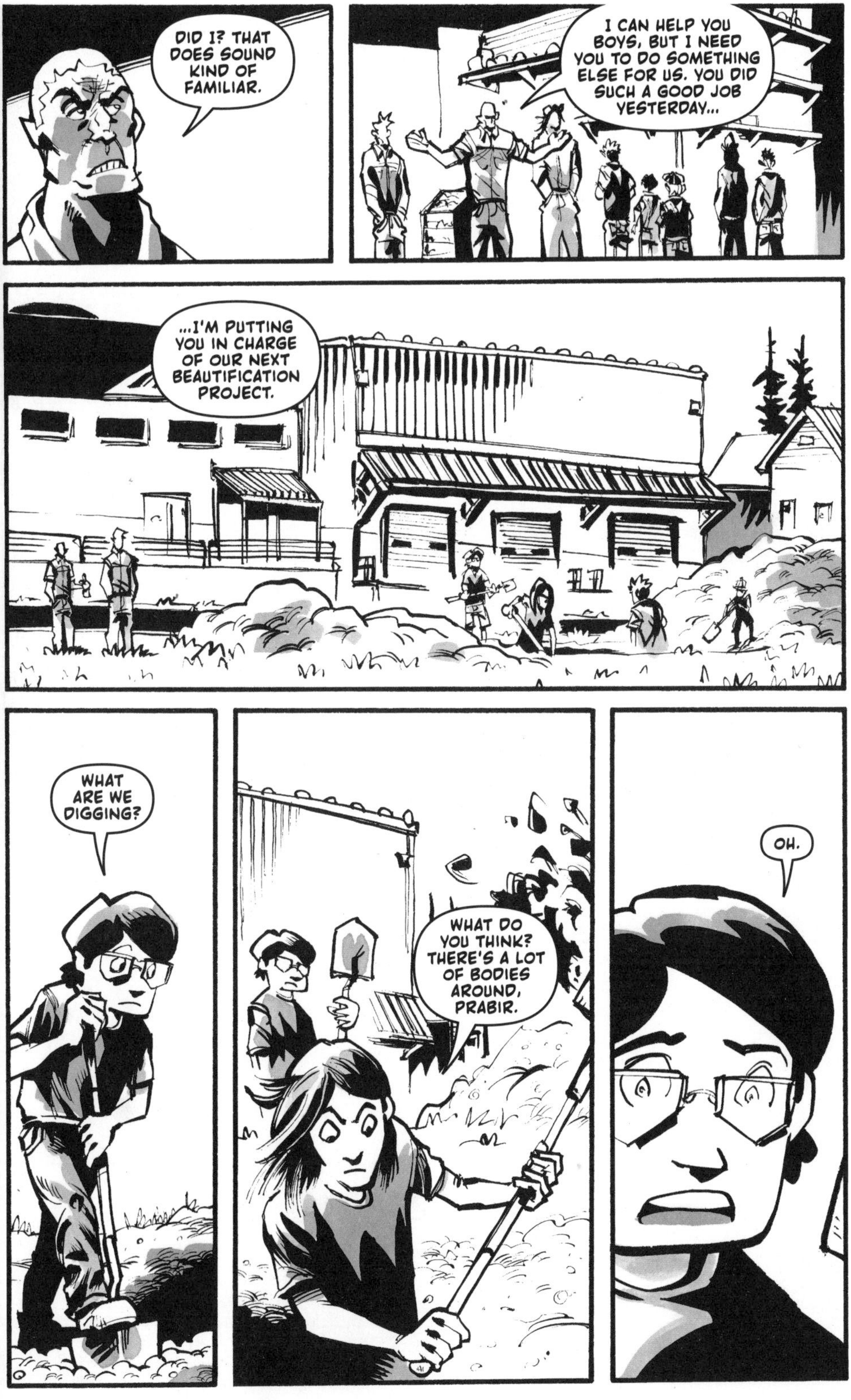
DID I? THAT DOES SOUND KIND OF FAMILIAR.
I CAN HELP YOU BOYS, BUT I NEED YOU TO DO SOMETHING ELSE FOR US. YOU DID SUCH A GOOD JOB YESTERDAY...
...I'M PUTTING YOU IN CHARGE OF OUR NEXT BEAUTIFICATION PROJECT.
WHAT ARE WE DIGGING?
WHAT DO YOU THINK? THERE'S A LOT OF BODIES AROUND, PRABIR.
OH.

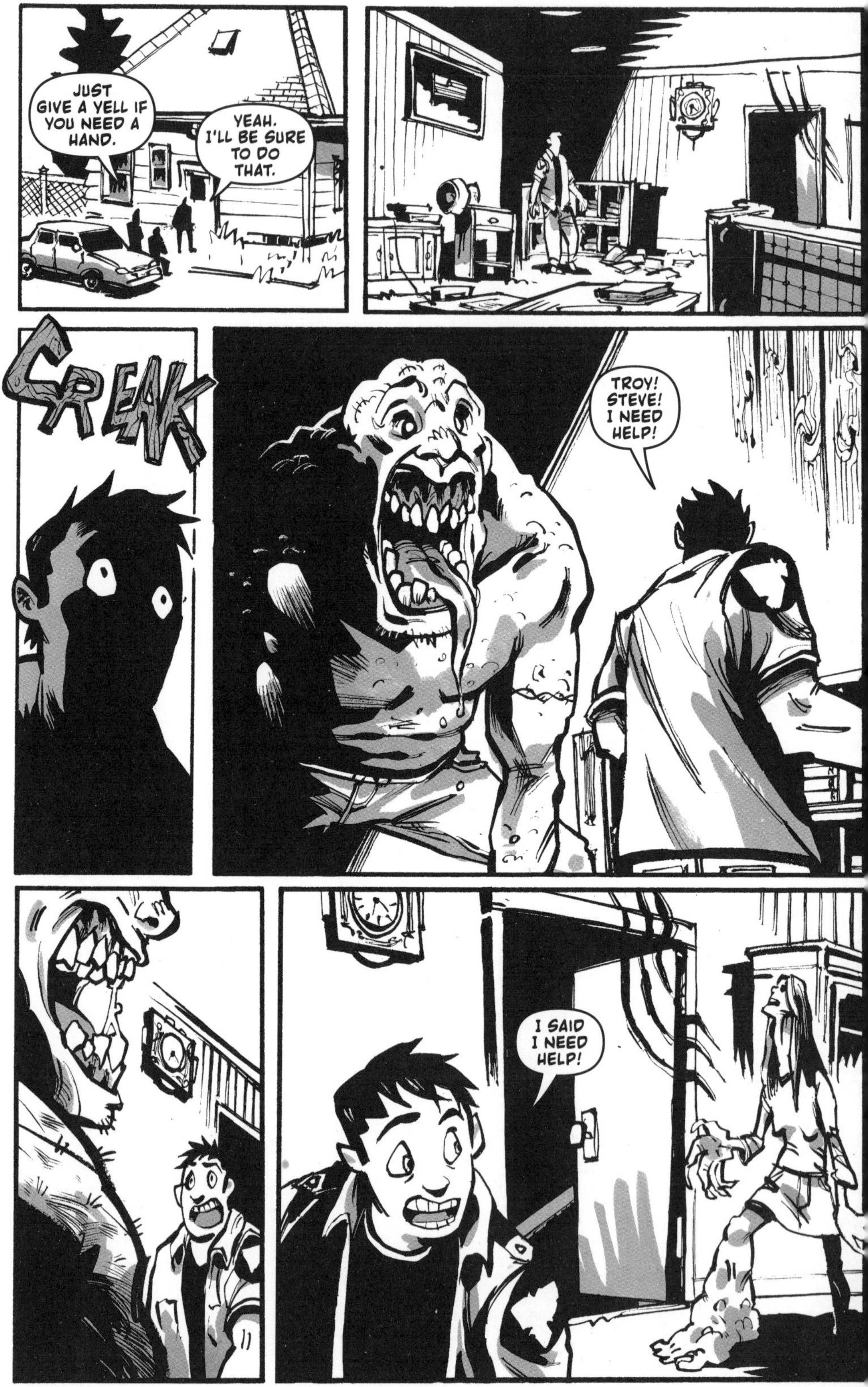
JUST GIVE A YELL IF YOU NEED A HAND.
YEAH. I'LL BE SURE TO DO THAT.
CREAK
TROY! STEVE! I NEED HELP!
I SAID I NEED HELP!

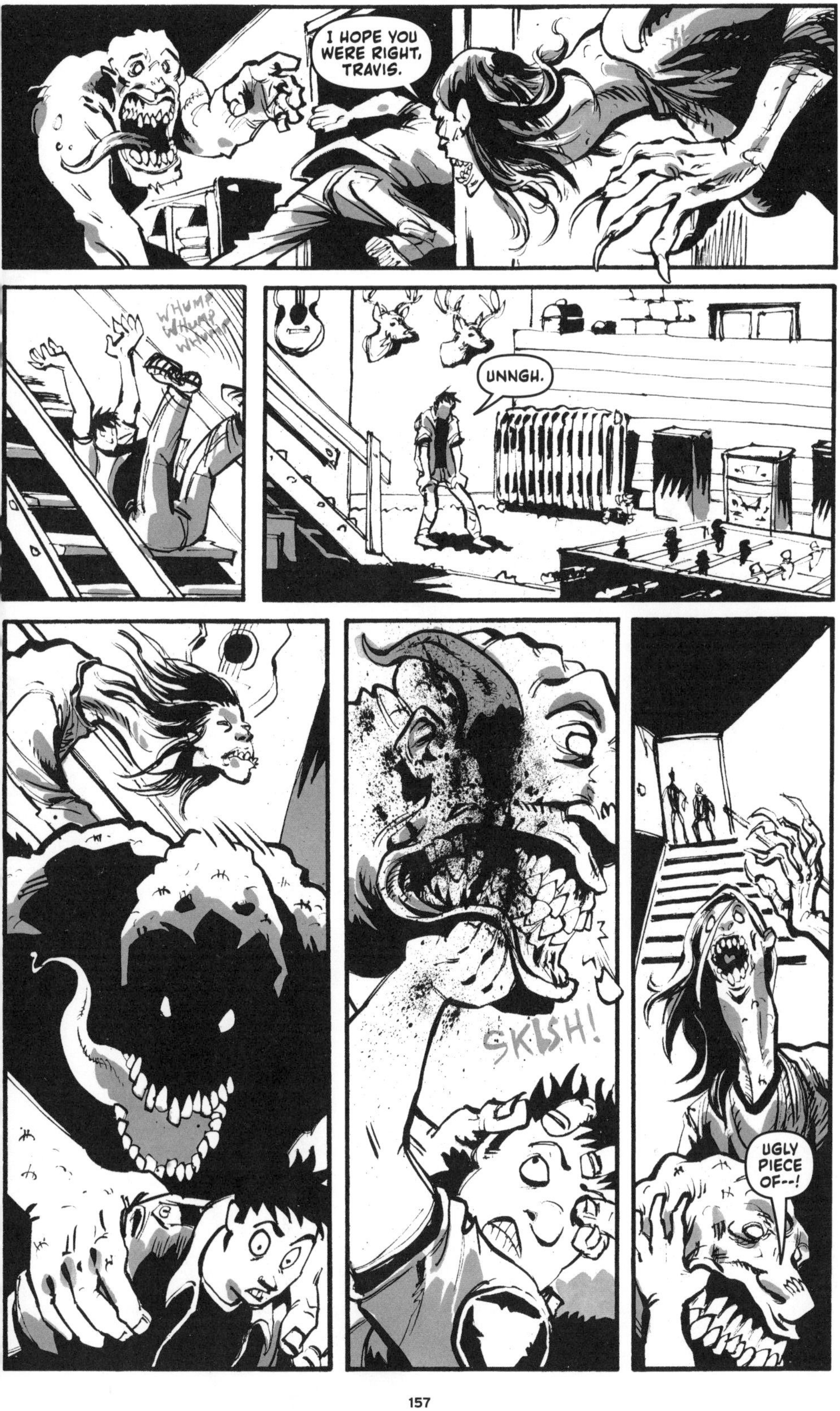
I HOPE YOU WERE RIGHT, TRAVIS.
WHUMP
WHUMP
WHUMP
UNNGH.
SKLSH!
UGLY PIECE OF--!

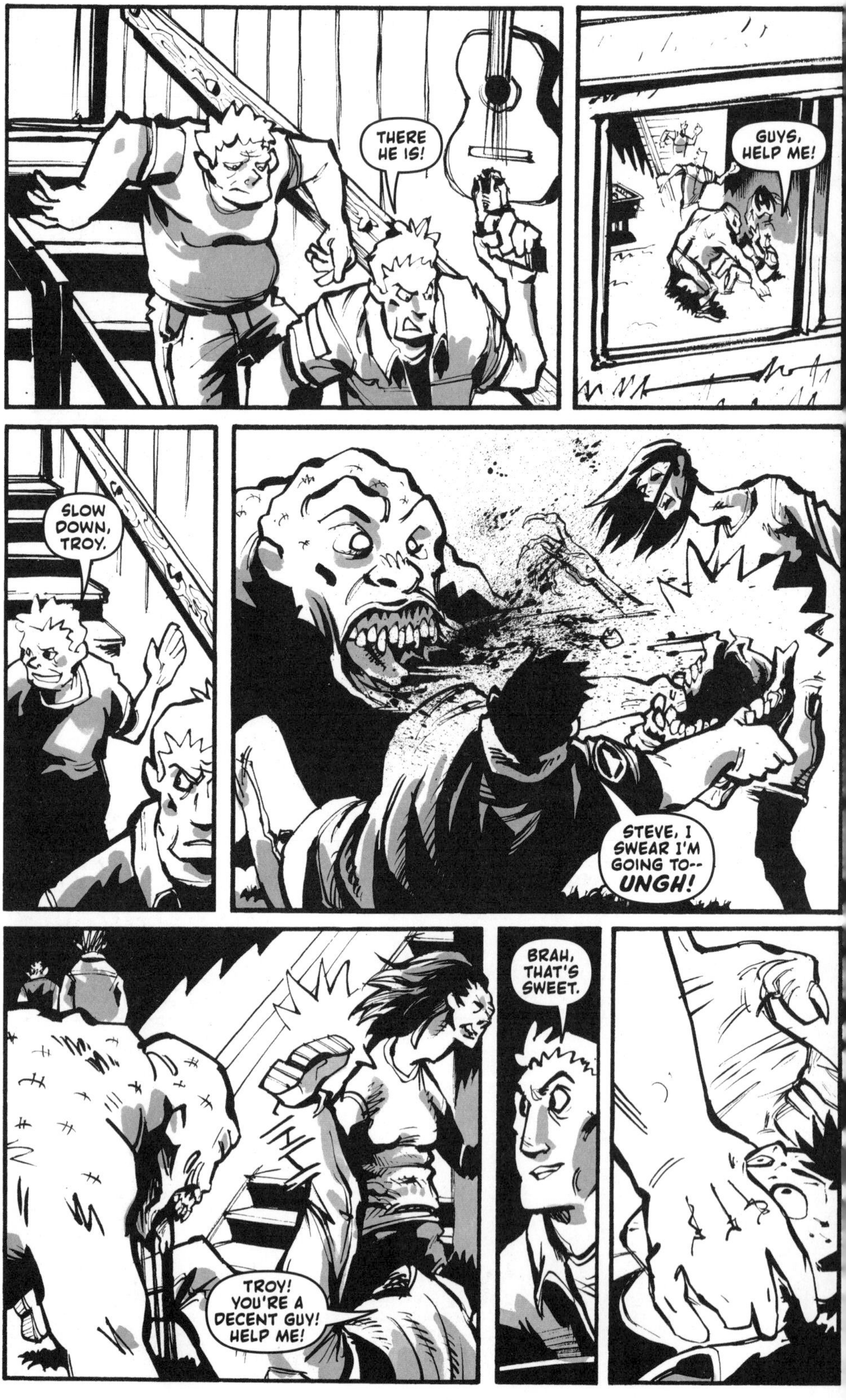
THERE HE IS!
GUYS, HELP ME!
SLOW DOWN, TROY.
STEVE, I SWEAR I'M GOING TO-- UNGH!
TROY! YOU'RE A DECENT GUY! HELP ME!
BRAH, THAT'S SWEET.

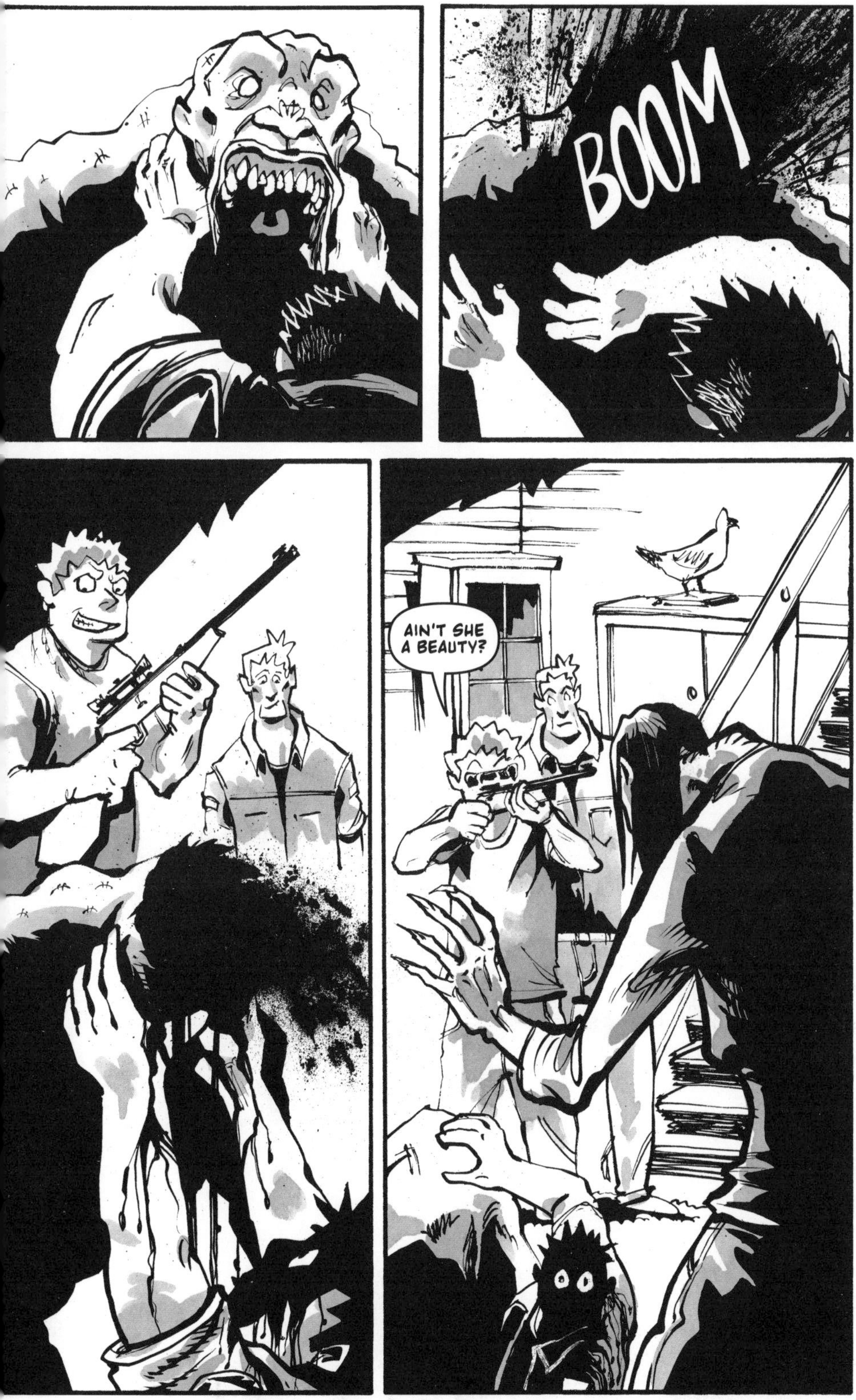
BOOM
AIN'T SHE A BEAUTY?

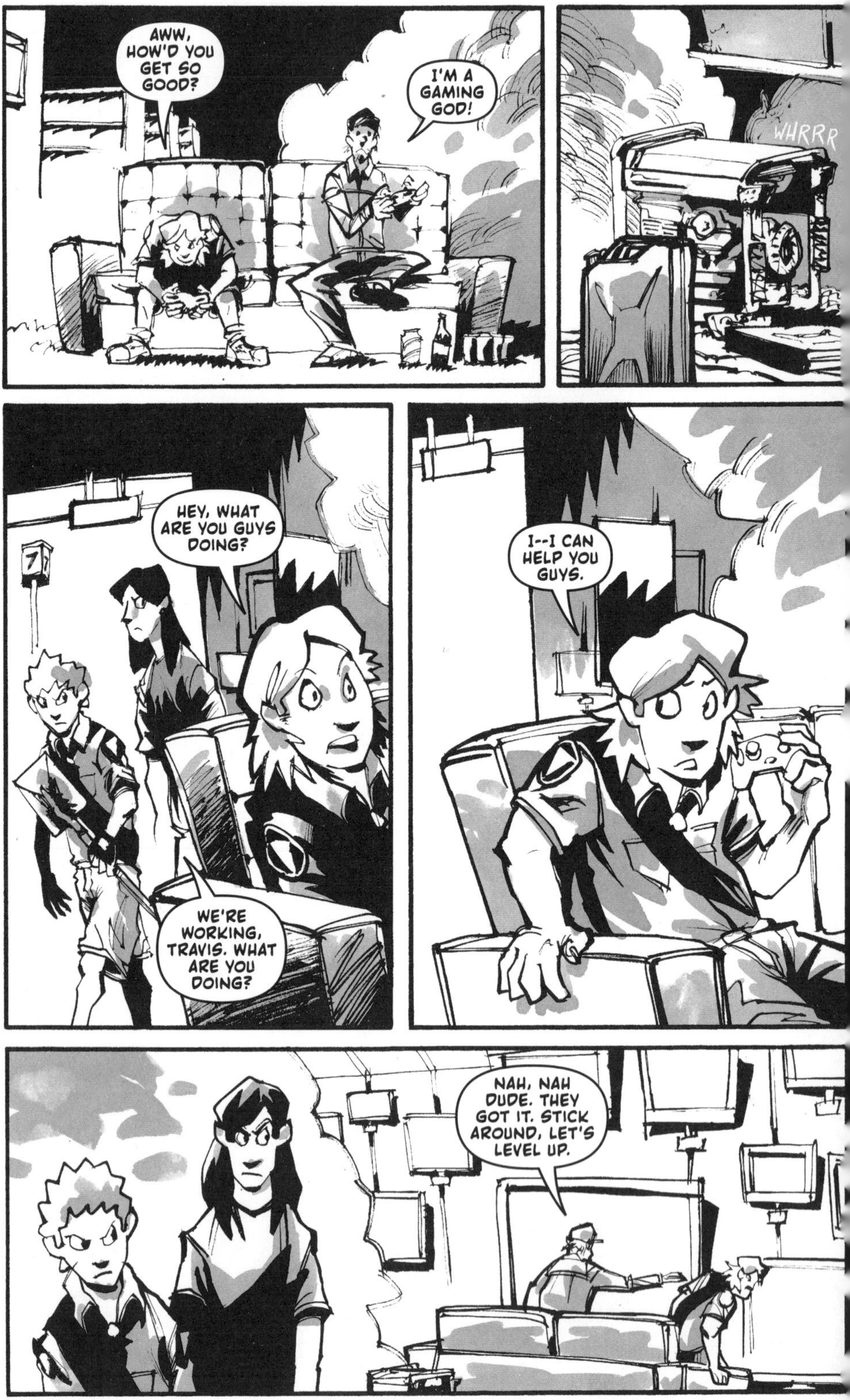
AWW, HOW'D YOU GET SO GOOD?
I'M A GAMING GOD!
WHRRR
HEY, WHAT ARE YOU GUYS DOING?
WE'RE WORKING, TRAVIS. WHAT ARE YOU DOING?
I--I CAN HELP YOU GUYS.
NAH, NAH DUDE. THEY GOT IT. STICK AROUND, LET'S LEVEL UP.

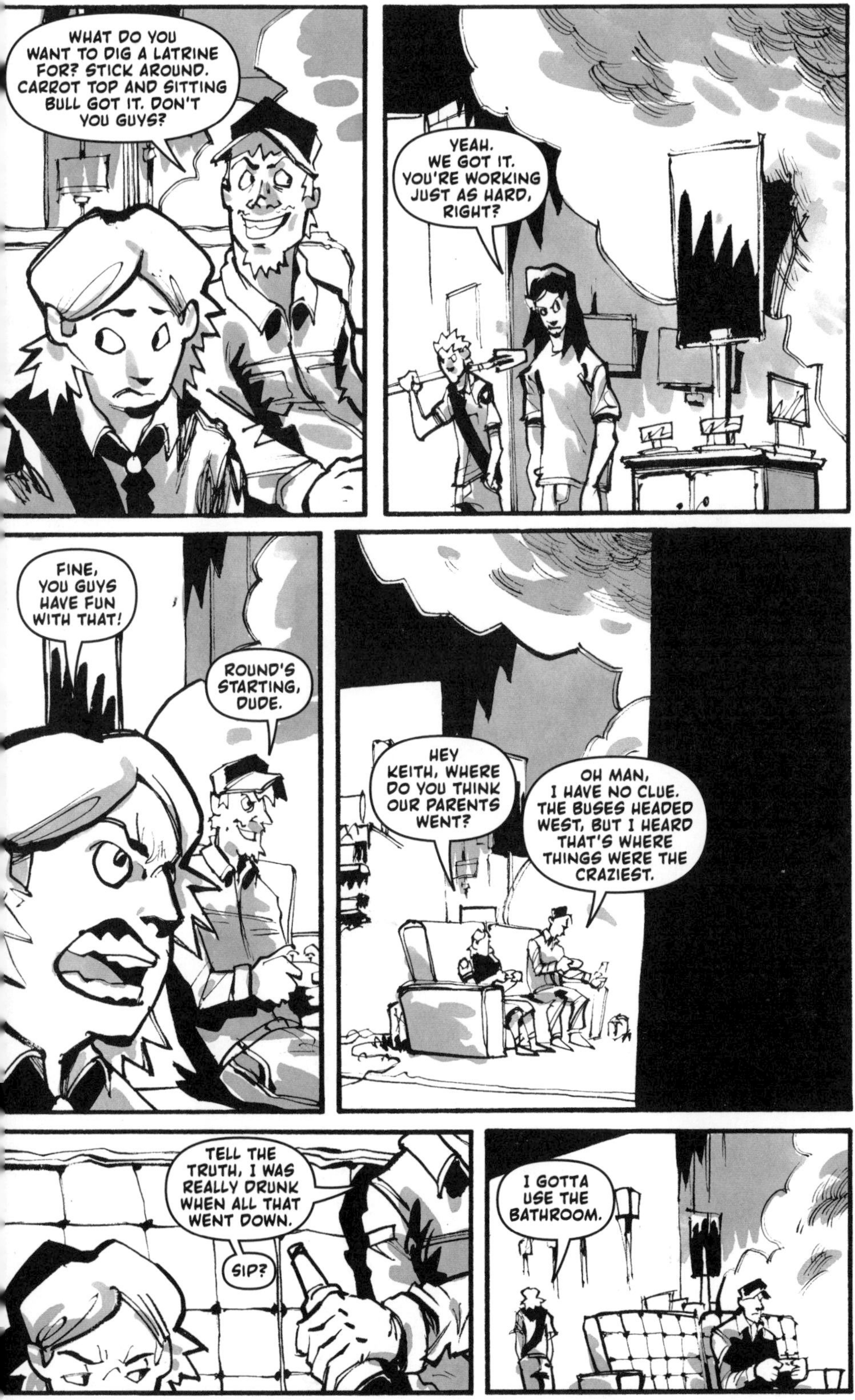
WHAT DO YOU WANT TO DIG A LATRINE FOR? STICK AROUND. CARROT TOP AND SITTING BULL GOT IT. DON'T YOU GUYS?
YEAH. WE GOT IT. YOU'RE WORKING JUST AS HARD, RIGHT?
FINE, YOU GUYS HAVE FUN WITH THAT!
ROUND'S STARTING, DUDE.
HEY KEITH, WHERE DO YOU THINK OUR PARENTS WENT?
OH MAN, I HAVE NO CLUE. THE BUSES HEADED WEST, BUT I HEARD THAT'S WHERE THINGS WERE THE CRAZIEST.
TELL THE TRUTH, I WAS REALLY DRUNK WHEN ALL THAT WENT DOWN.
SIP?
I GOTTA USE THE BATHROOM.

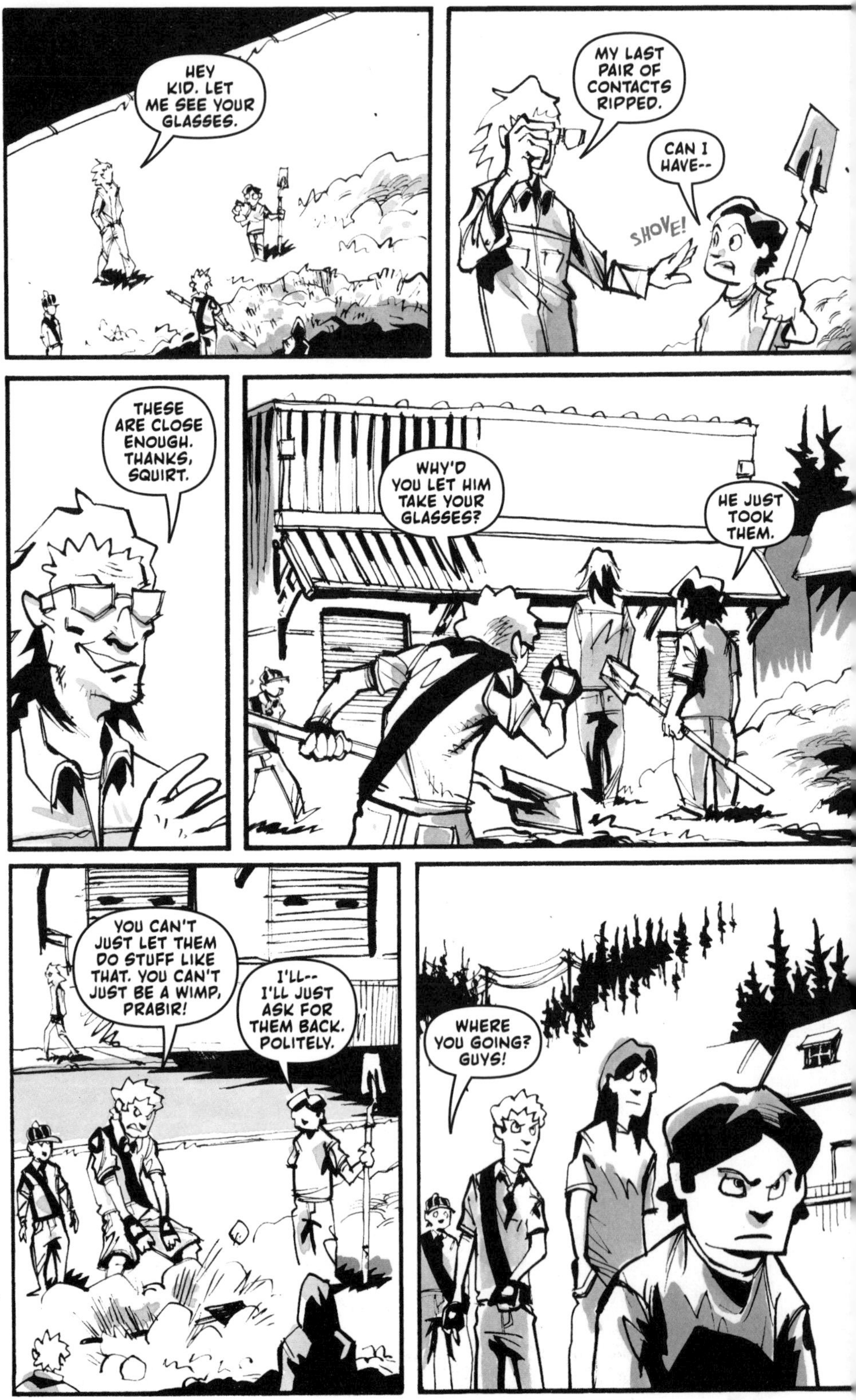
HEY KID. LET ME SEE YOUR GLASSES.
MY LAST PAIR OF CONTACTS RIPPED.
CAN I HAVE--
SHOVE!
THESE ARE CLOSE ENOUGH. THANKS, SQUIRT.
WHY'D YOU LET HIM TAKE YOUR GLASSES?
HE JUST TOOK THEM.
YOU CAN'T JUST LET THEM DO STUFF LIKE THAT. YOU CAN'T JUST BE A WIMP, PRABIR!
I'LL-- I'LL JUST ASK FOR THEM BACK. POLITELY.
WHERE YOU GOING? GUYS!

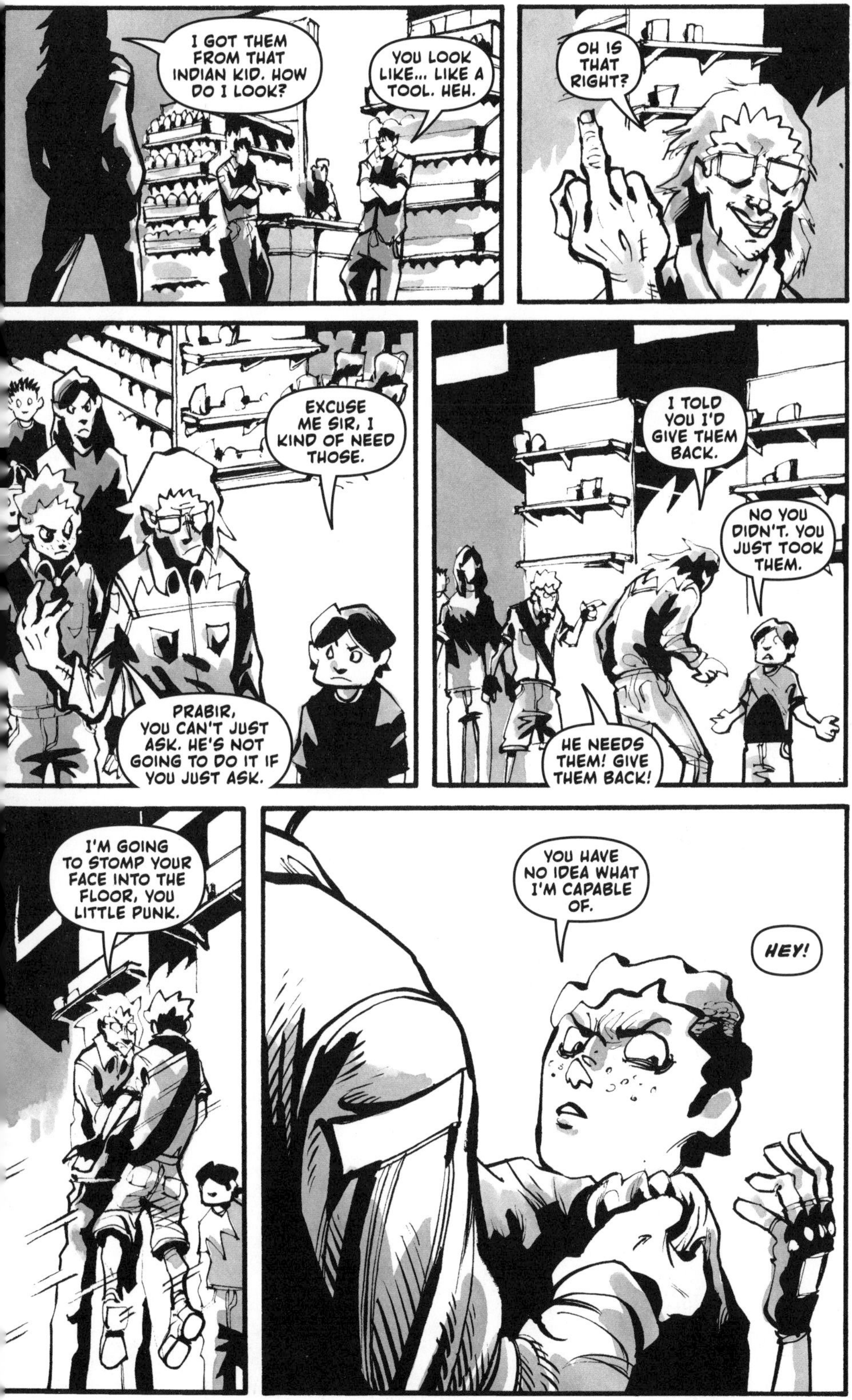
I GOT THEM FROM THAT INDIAN KID. HOW DO I LOOK?
YOU LOOK LIKE... LIKE A TOOL. HEH.
OH IS THAT RIGHT?
EXCUSE ME SIR, I KIND OF NEED THOSE.
PRABIR, YOU CAN'T JUST ASK. HE'S NOT GOING TO DO IT IF YOU JUST ASK.
I TOLD YOU I'D GIVE THEM BACK.
NO YOU DIDN'T. YOU JUST TOOK THEM.
HE NEEDS THEM! GIVE THEM BACK!
I'M GOING TO STOMP YOUR FACE INTO THE FLOOR, YOU LITTLE PUNK.
YOU HAVE NO IDEA WHAT I'M CAPABLE OF.
HEY!

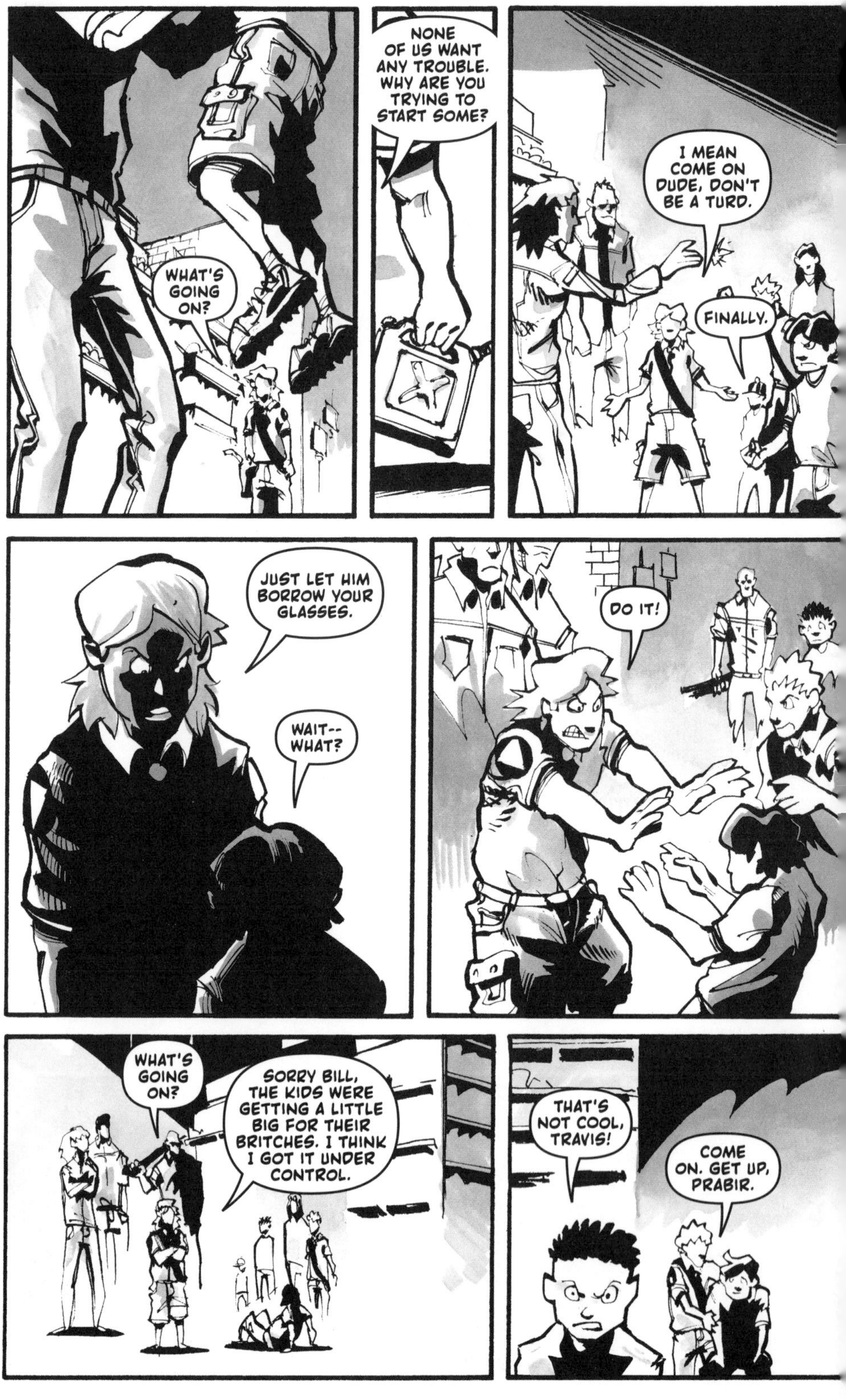
WHAT'S GOING ON?
NONE OF US WANT ANY TROUBLE. WHY ARE YOU TRYING TO START SOME?
I MEAN COME ON DUDE, DON'T BE A TURD.
FINALLY.
JUST LET HIM BORROW YOUR GLASSES.
WAIT-- WHAT?
DO IT!
WHAT'S GOING ON?
SORRY BILL, THE KIDS WERE GETTING A LITTLE BIG FOR THEIR BRITCHES. I THINK I GOT IT UNDER CONTROL.
THAT'S NOT COOL, TRAVIS!
COME ON. GET UP, PRABIR.

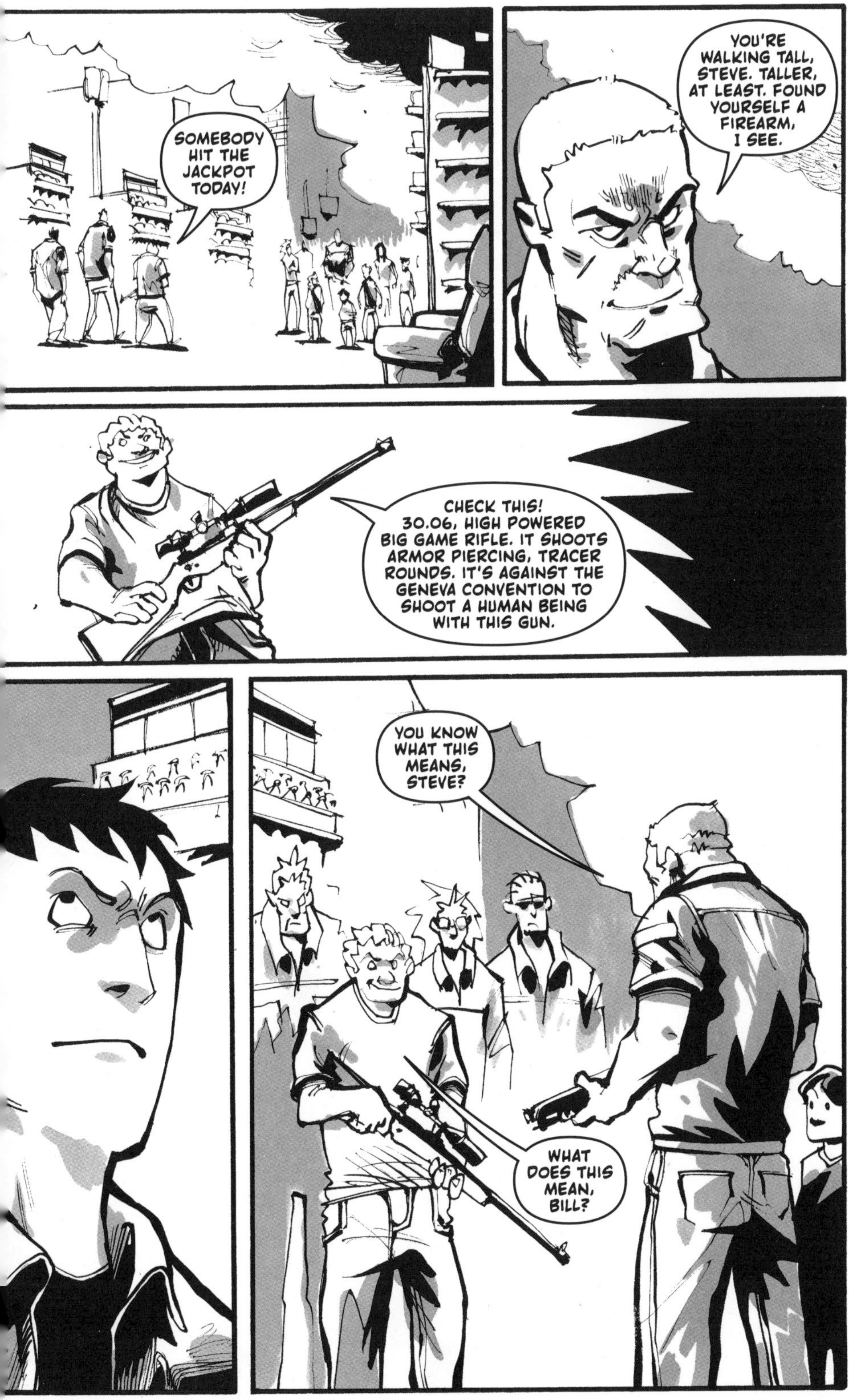
SOMEBODY HIT THE JACKPOT TODAY!
YOU'RE WALKING TALL, STEVE. TALLER, AT LEAST. FOUND YOURSELF A FIREARM, I SEE.
CHECK THIS! 30.06, HIGH POWERED BIG GAME RIFLE. IT SHOOTS ARMOR PIERCING, TRACER ROUNDS. IT'S AGAINST THE GENEVA CONVENTION TO SHOOT A HUMAN BEING WITH THIS GUN.
YOU KNOW WHAT THIS MEANS, STEVE?
WHAT DOES THIS MEAN, BILL?

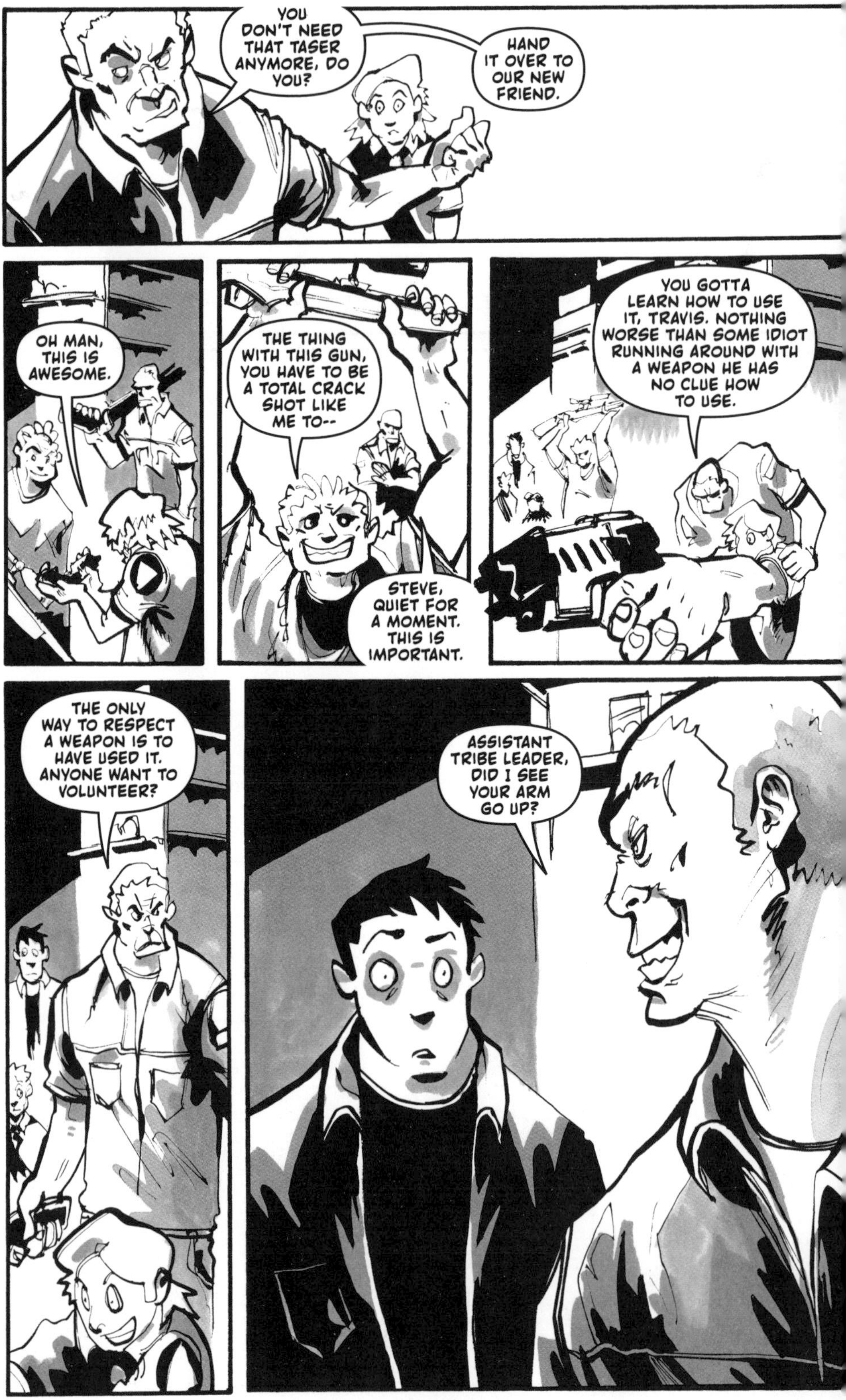
YOU DON'T NEED THAT TASER ANYMORE, DO YOU?
HAND IT OVER TO OUR NEW FRIEND.
OH MAN, THIS IS AWESOME.
THE THING WITH THIS GUN, YOU HAVE TO BE A TOTAL CRACK SHOT LIKE ME TO--
STEVE, QUIET FOR A MOMENT. THIS IS IMPORTANT.
YOU GOTTA LEARN HOW TO USE IT, TRAVIS. NOTHING WORSE THAN SOME IDIOT RUNNING AROUND WITH A WEAPON HE HAS NO CLUE HOW TO USE.
THE ONLY WAY TO RESPECT A WEAPON IS TO HAVE USED IT. ANYONE WANT TO VOLUNTEER?
ASSISTANT TRIBE LEADER, DID I SEE YOUR ARM GO UP?

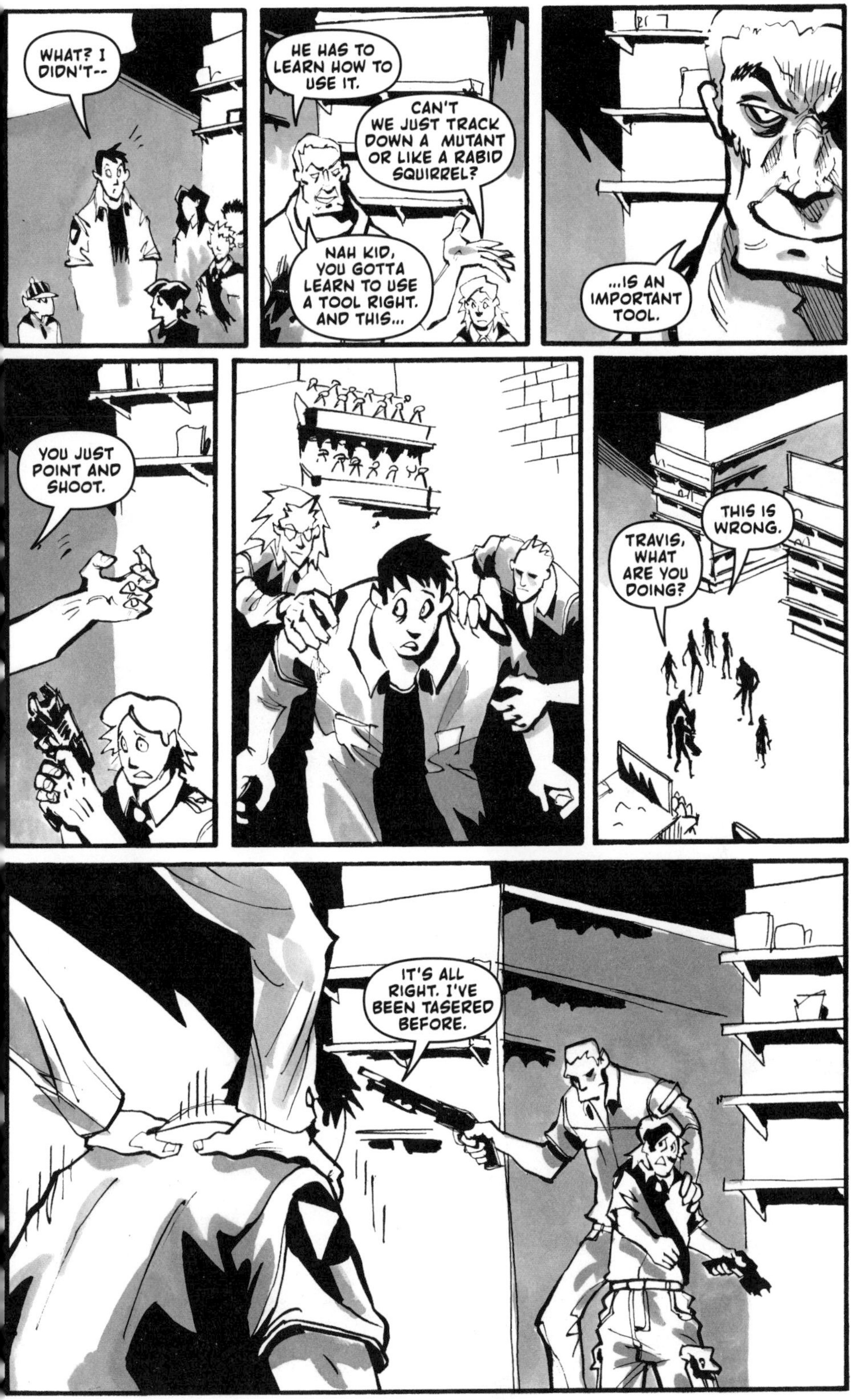
WHAT? I DIDN'T--
HE HAS TO LEARN HOW TO USE IT.
CAN'T WE JUST TRACK DOWN A MUTANT OR LIKE A RABID SQUIRREL?
NAH KID, YOU GOTTA LEARN TO USE A TOOL RIGHT. AND THIS...
...IS AN IMPORTANT TOOL.
YOU JUST POINT AND SHOOT.
TRAVIS, WHAT ARE YOU DOING?
THIS IS WRONG.
IT'S ALL RIGHT. I'VE BEEN TASERED BEFORE.

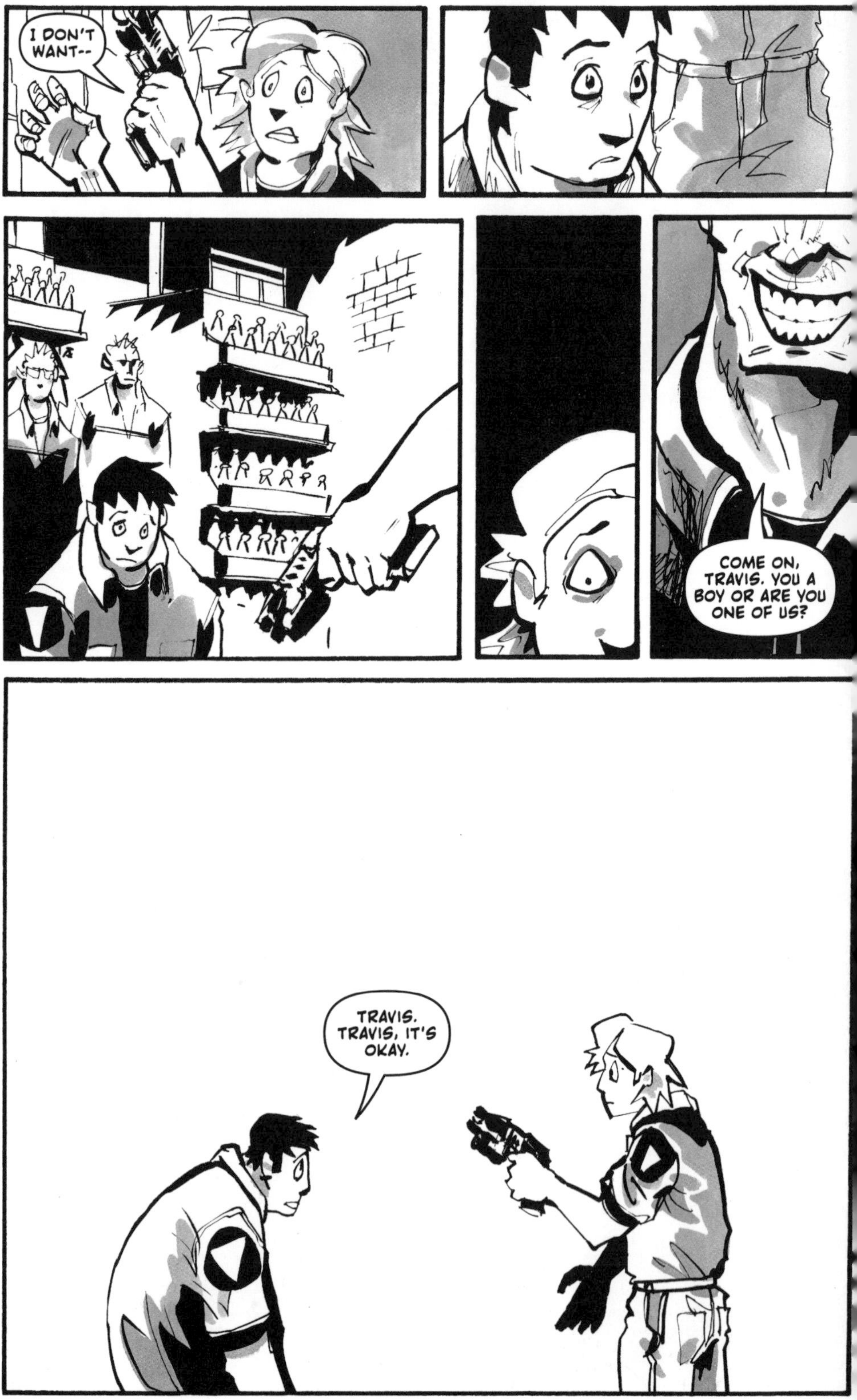
I DON'T WANT--
COME ON, TRAVIS. YOU A BOY OR ARE YOU ONE OF US?
TRAVIS. TRAVIS, IT'S OKAY.

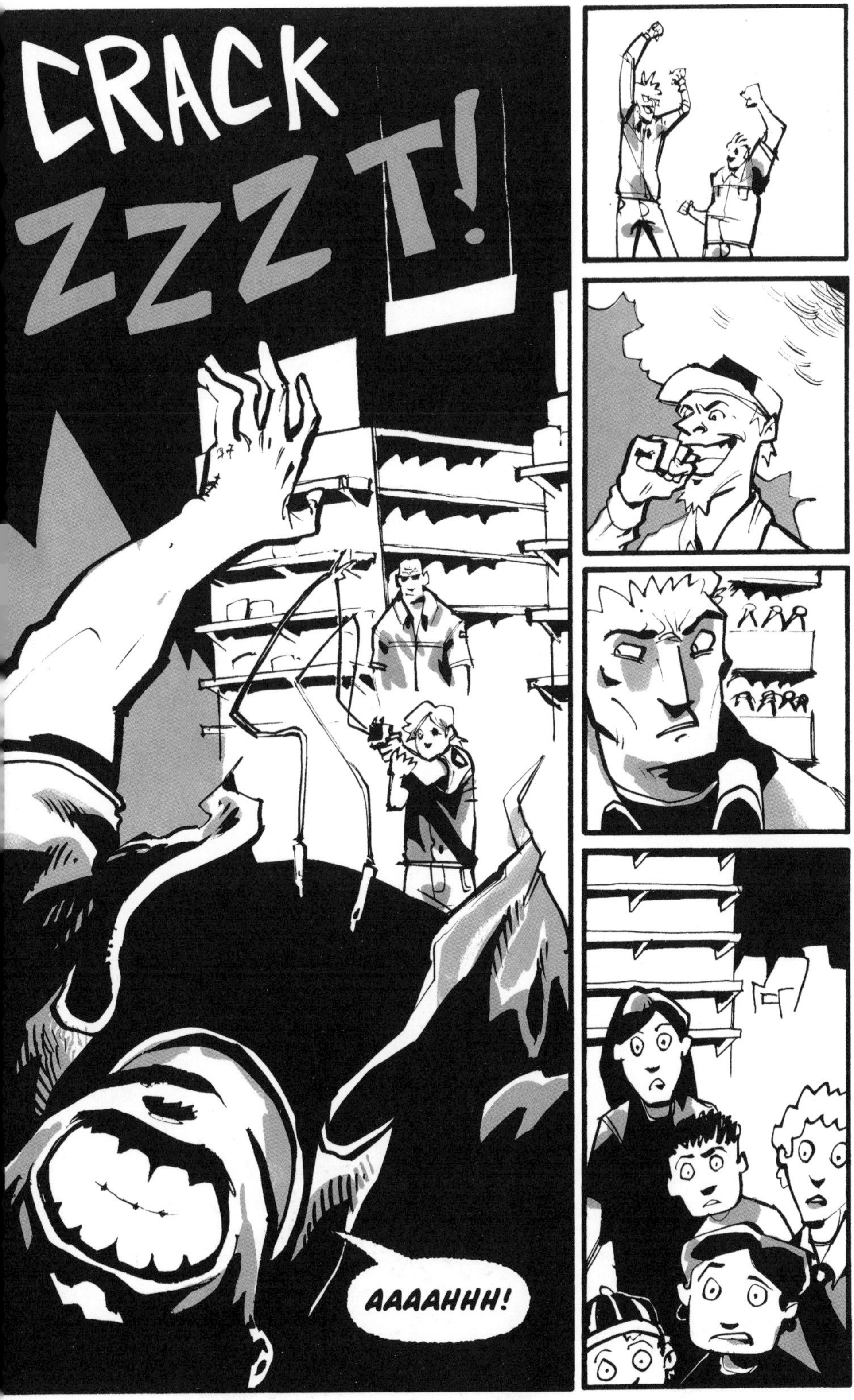
CRACK
ZZZT!
AAAAHHH!

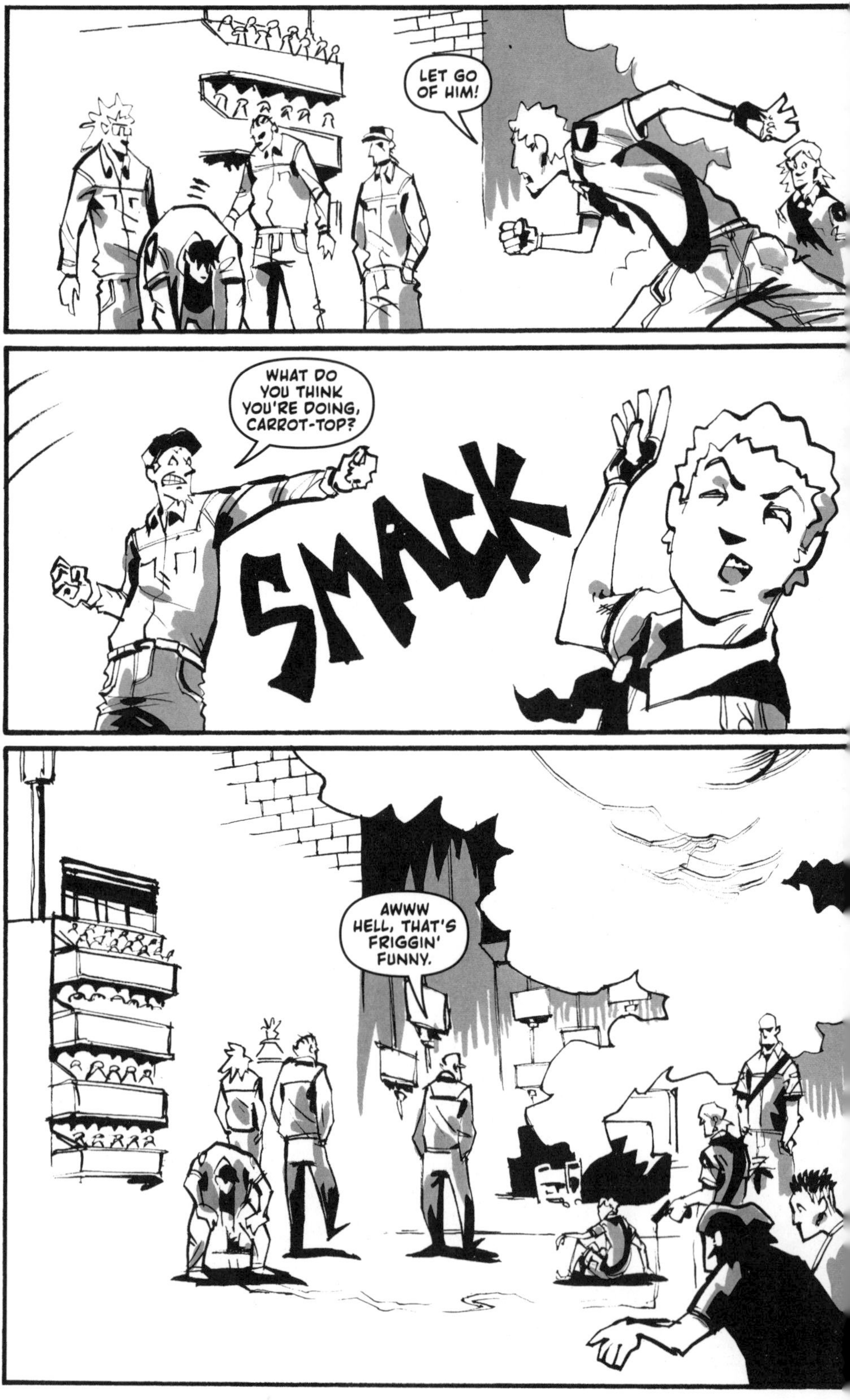
LET GO OF HIM!
WHAT DO YOU THINK YOU'RE DOING, CARROT-TOP?
SMACK
AWWW HELL, THAT'S FRIGGIN' FUNNY.

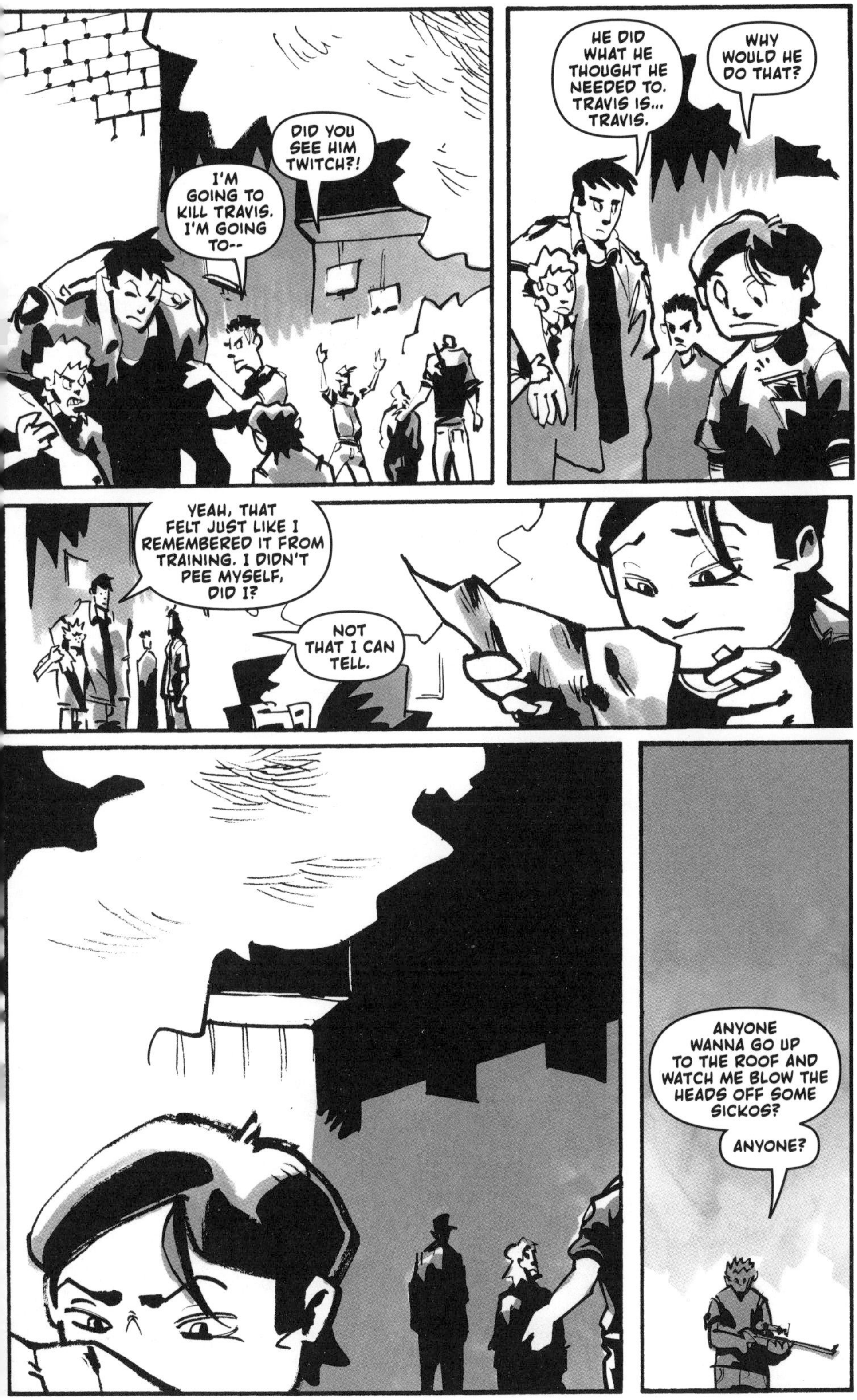
I'M GOING TO KILL TRAVIS. I'M GOING TO--
DID YOU SEE HIM TWITCH?!
HE DID WHAT HE THOUGHT HE NEEDED TO. TRAVIS IS... TRAVIS.
WHY WOULD HE DO THAT?
YEAH, THAT FELT JUST LIKE I REMEMBERED IT FROM TRAINING. I DIDN'T PEE MYSELF, DID I?
NOT THAT I CAN TELL.
ANYONE WANNA GO UP TO THE ROOF AND WATCH ME BLOW THE HEADS OFF SOME SICKOS?
ANYONE?

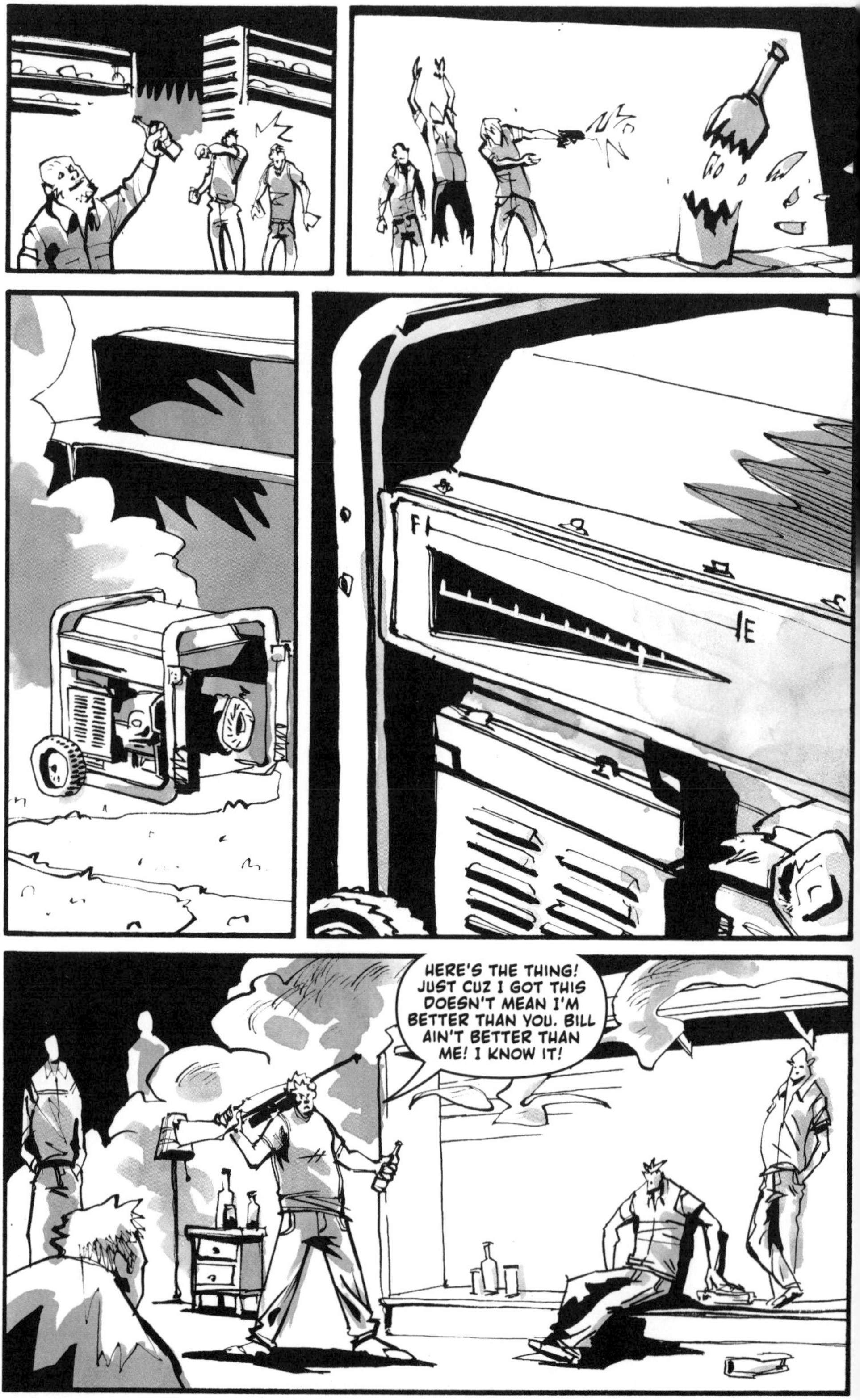
F
E
HERE'S THE THING! JUST CUZ I GOT THIS DOESN'T MEAN I'M BETTER THAN YOU. BILL AIN'T BETTER THAN ME! I KNOW IT!

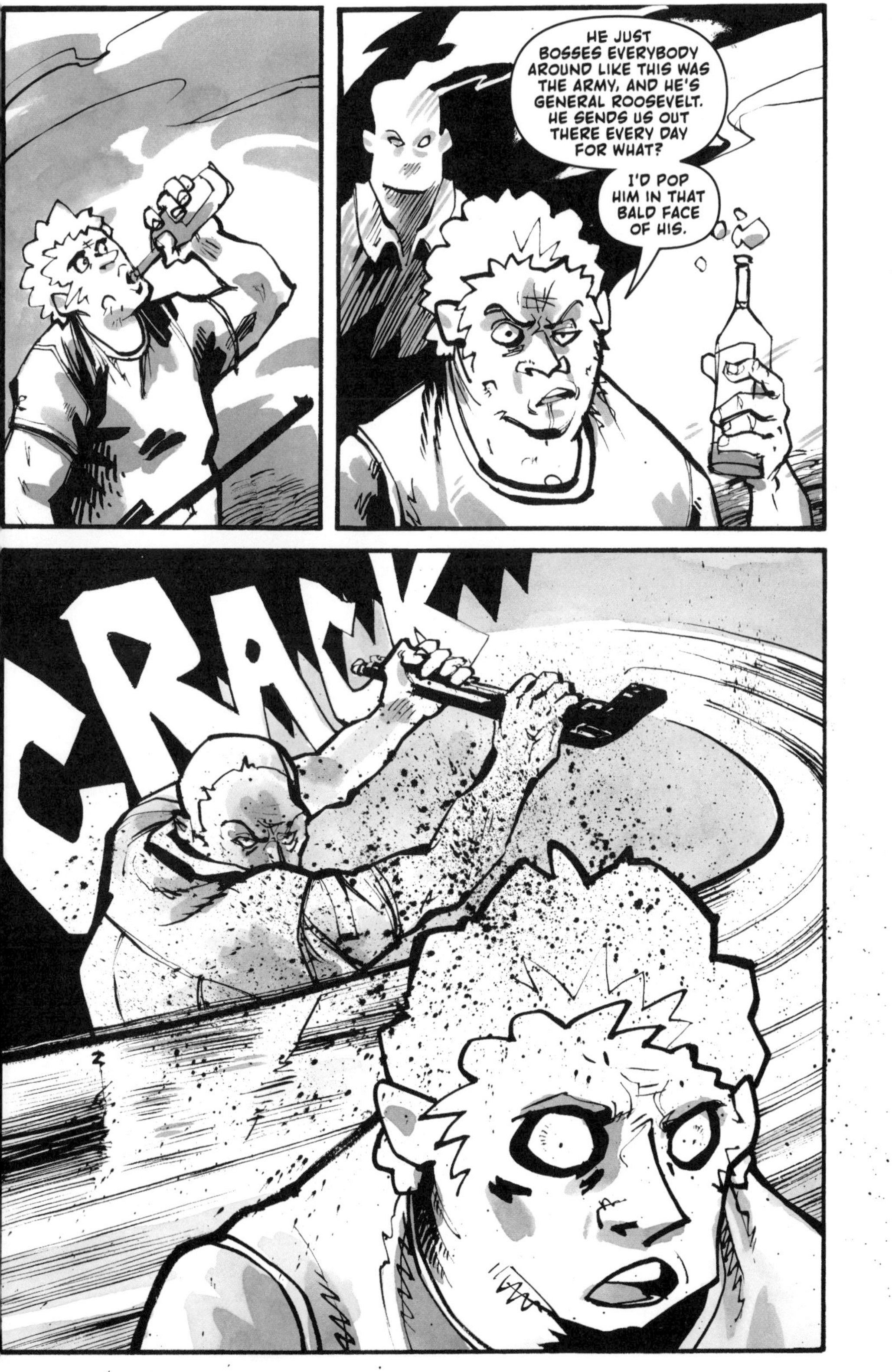
HE JUST BOSSES EVERYBODY AROUND LIKE THIS WAS THE ARMY, AND HE'S GENERAL ROOSEVELT. HE SENDS US OUT THERE EVERY DAY FOR WHAT?
I'D POP HIM IN THAT BALD FACE OF HIS.
CRACK

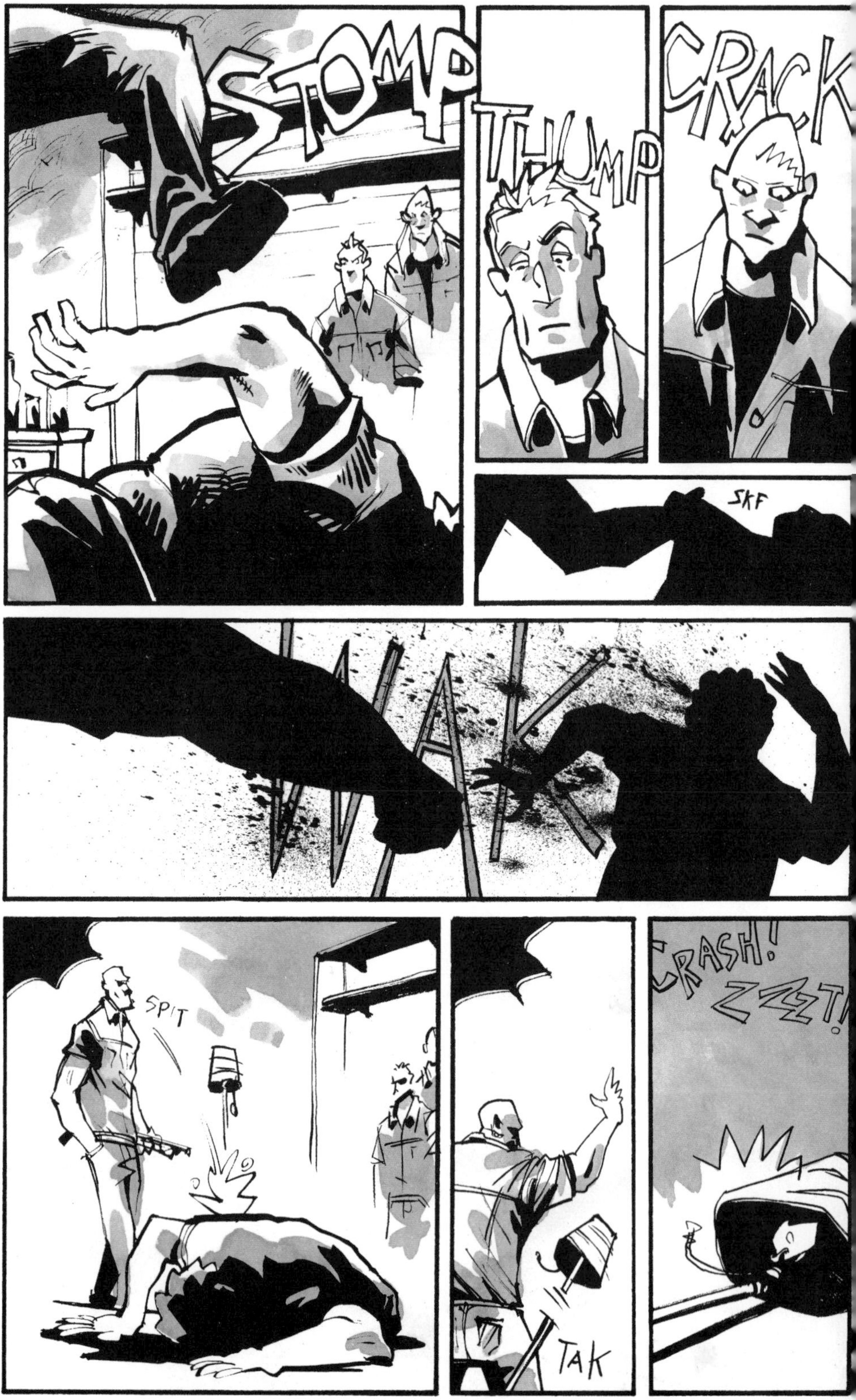

STOMP
THUMP
CRACK
SKF
WAK
SPIT
TAK
CRASH!
ZZZT!

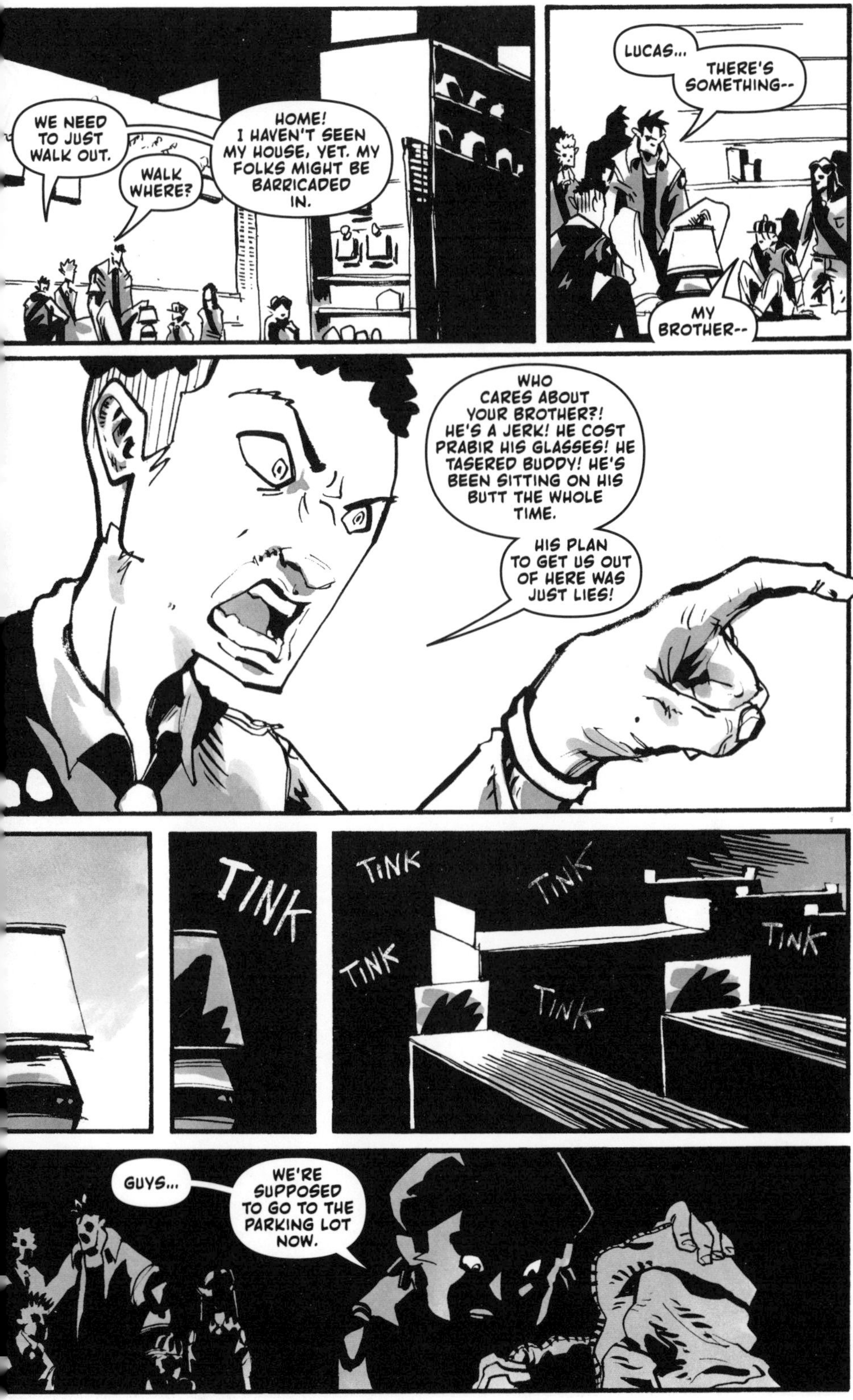
WE NEED TO JUST WALK OUT.
WALK WHERE?
HOME! I HAVEN'T SEEN MY HOUSE, YET. MY FOLKS MIGHT BE BARRICADED IN.
LUCAS...
THERE'S SOMETHING--
MY BROTHER--
WHO CARES ABOUT YOUR BROTHER?! HE'S A JERK! HE COST PRABIR HIS GLASSES! HE TASERED BUDDY! HE'S BEEN SITTING ON HIS BUTT THE WHOLE TIME.
HIS PLAN TO GET US OUT OF HERE WAS JUST LIES!
TINK
TINK
TINK
TINK
TINK
TINK
GUYS...
WE'RE SUPPOSED TO GO TO THE PARKING LOT NOW.

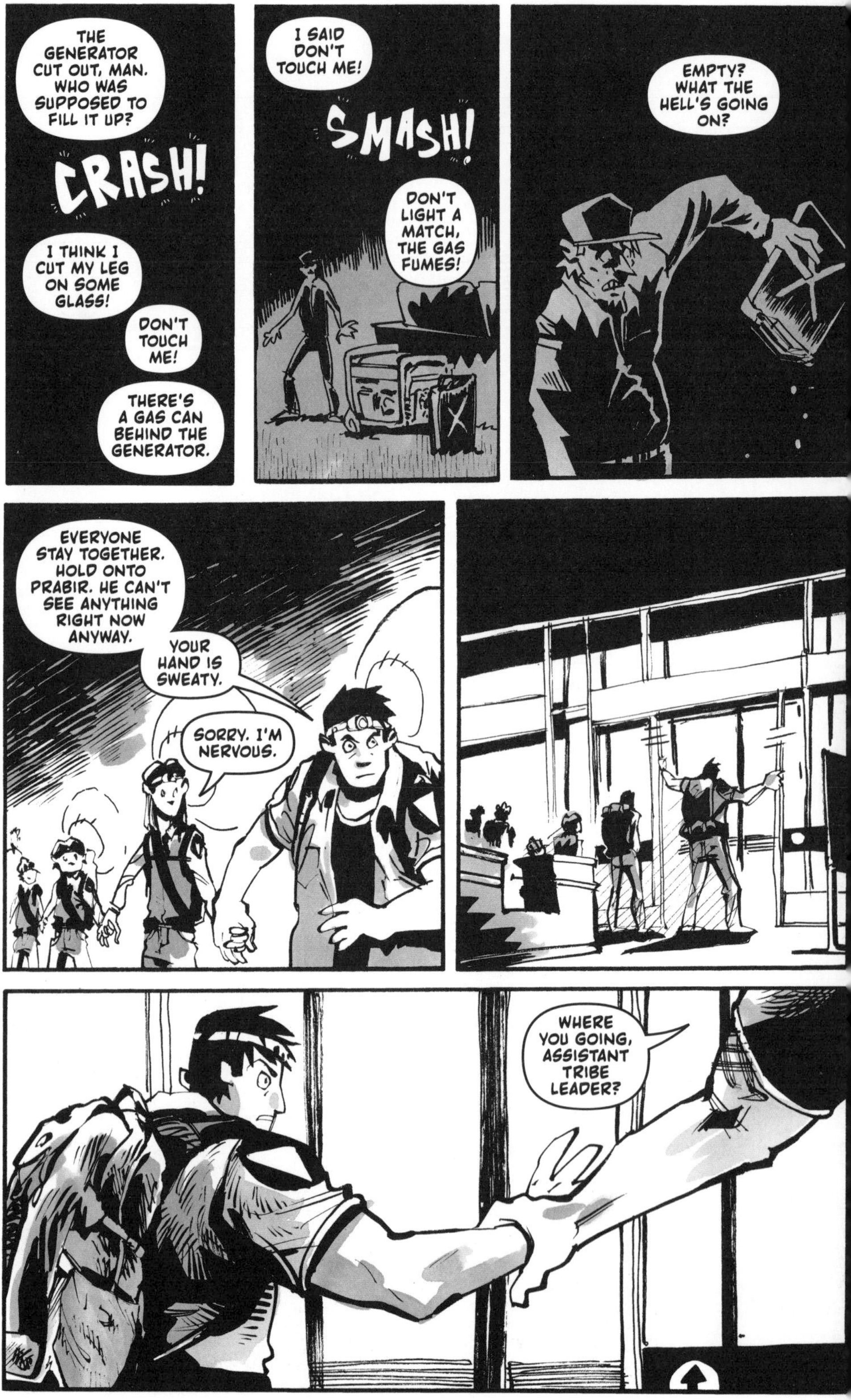
THE GENERATOR CUT OUT, MAN. WHO WAS SUPPOSED TO FILL IT UP?
CRASH!
I THINK I CUT MY LEG ON SOME GLASS!
DON'T TOUCH ME!
THERE'S A GAS CAN BEHIND THE GENERATOR.
I SAID DON'T TOUCH ME!
SMASH!
DON'T LIGHT A MATCH, THE GAS FUMES!
EMPTY? WHAT THE HELL'S GOING ON?
EVERYONE STAY TOGETHER. HOLD ONTO PRABIR. HE CAN'T SEE ANYTHING RIGHT NOW ANYWAY.
YOUR HAND IS SWEATY.
SORRY. I'M NERVOUS.
WHERE YOU GOING, ASSISTANT TRIBE LEADER?

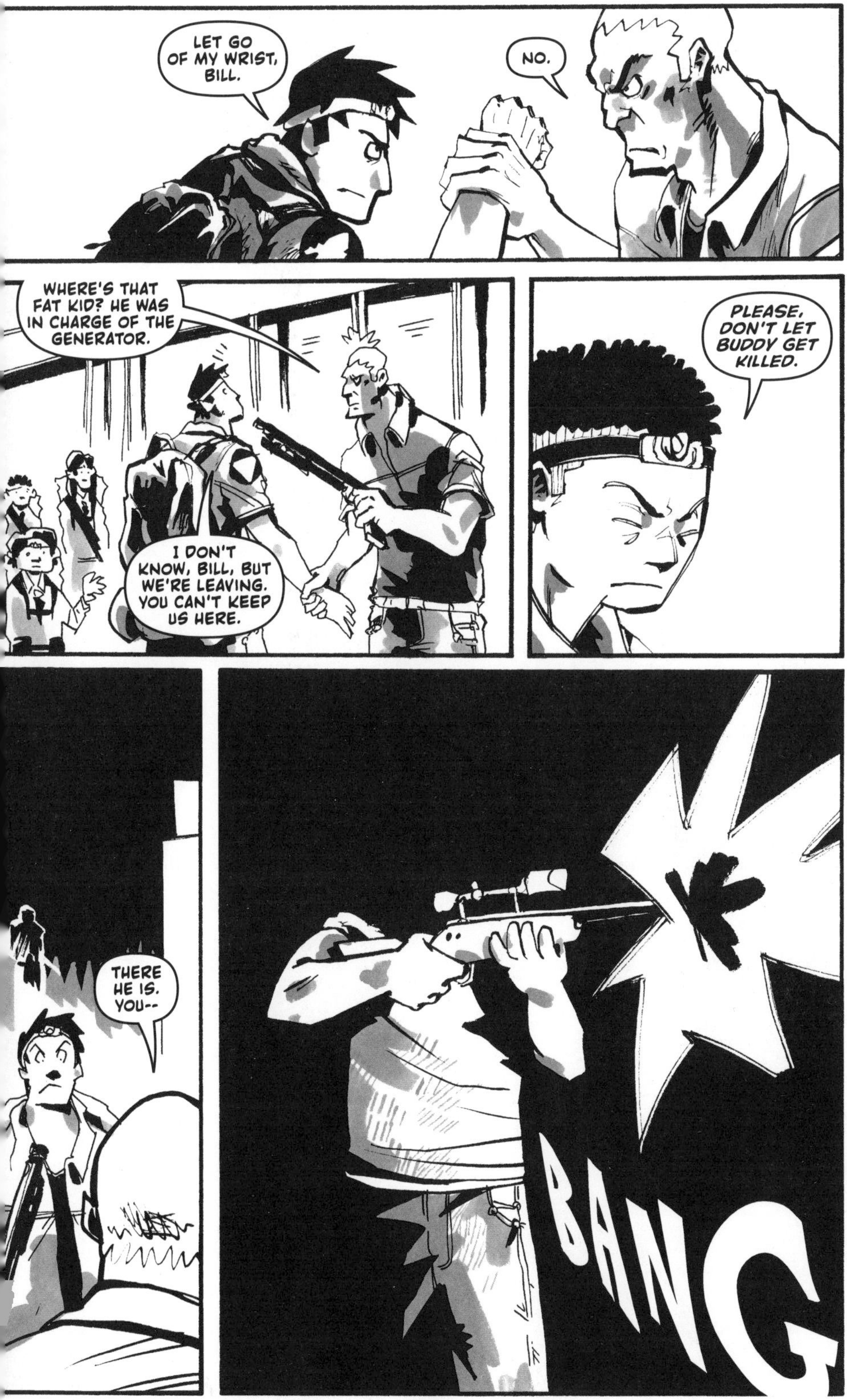
LET GO
OF MY WRIST,
BILL.
NO.
WHERE'S THAT
FAT KID? HE WAS
IN CHARGE OF THE
GENERATOR.
I DON'T
KNOW, BILL, BUT
WE'RE LEAVING.
YOU CAN'T KEEP
US HERE.
PLEASE,
DON'T LET
BUDDY GET
KILLED.
THERE
HE IS.
YOU--
BANG

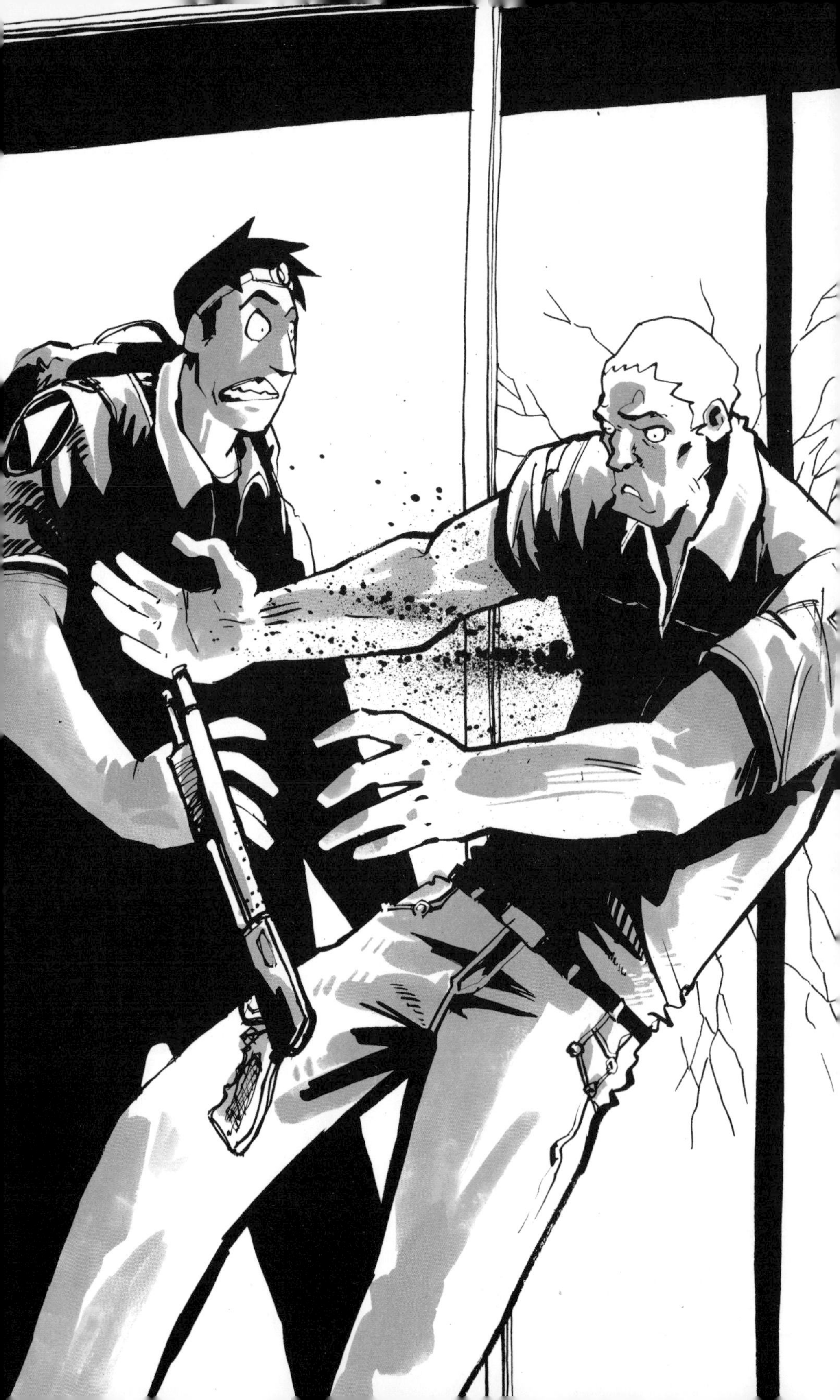

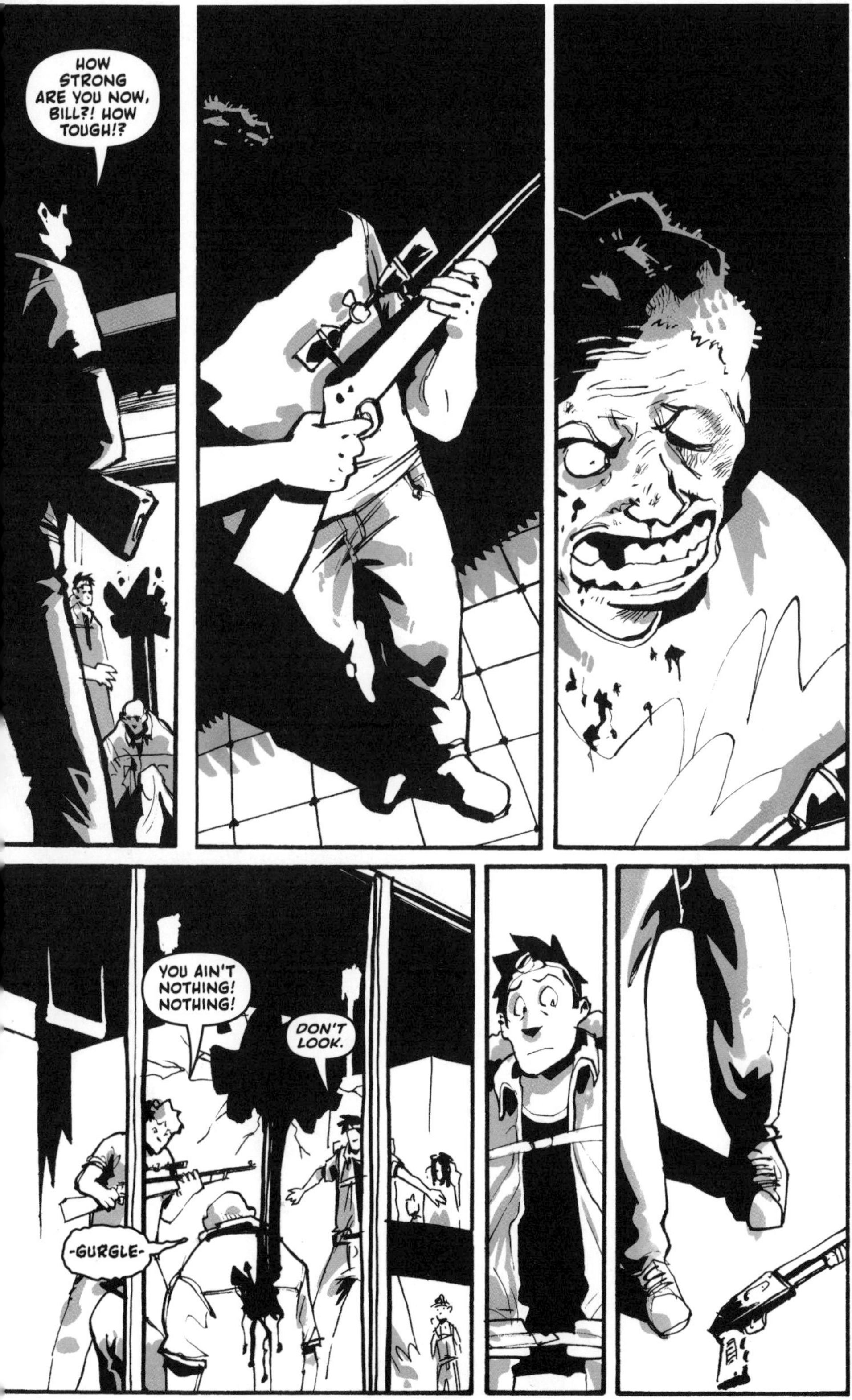
HOW STRONG ARE YOU NOW, BILL?! HOW TOUGH!?
YOU AIN'T NOTHING! NOTHING!
DON'T LOOK.
-GURGLE-

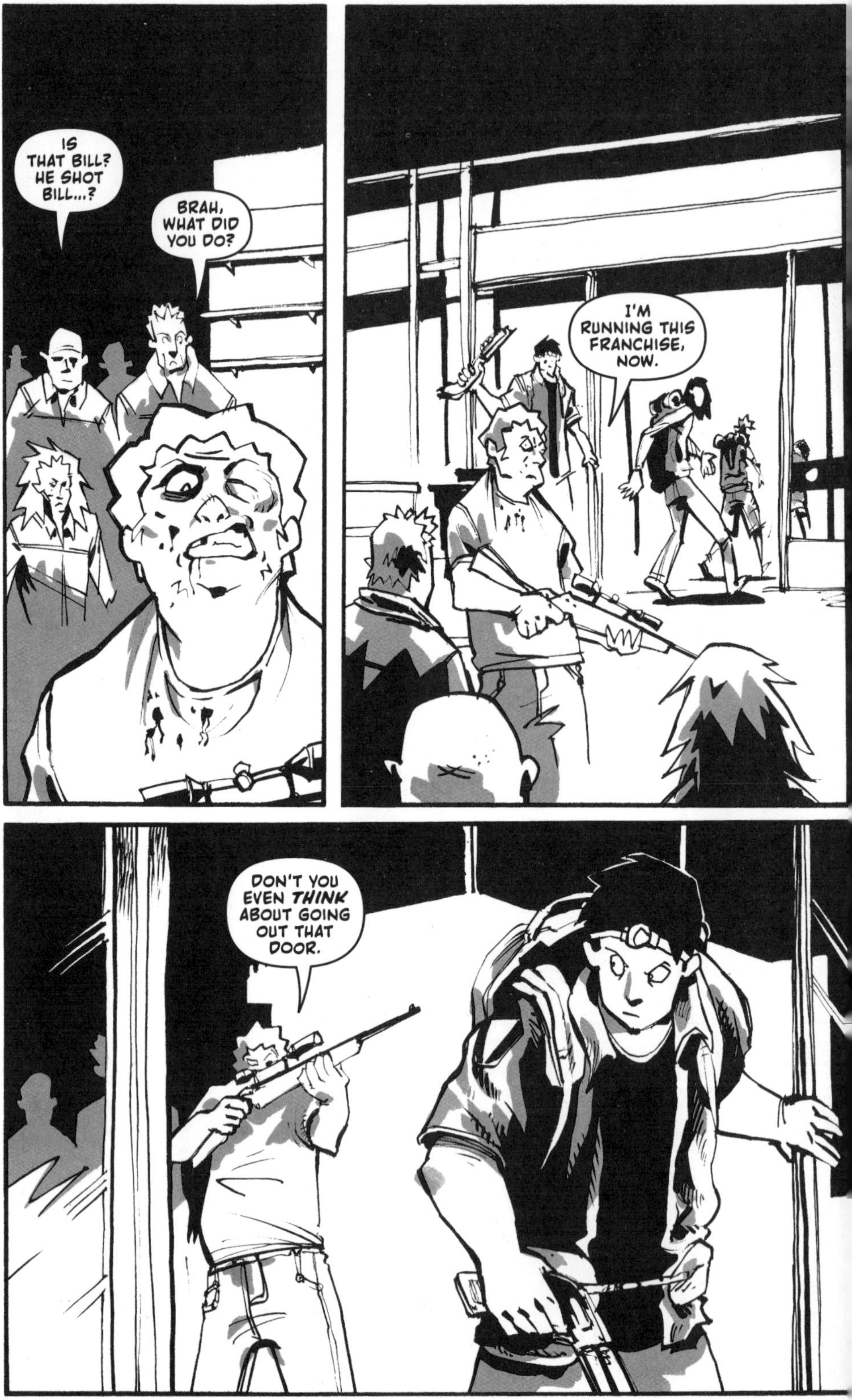

IS THAT BILL? HE SHOT BILL...?
BRAH, WHAT DID YOU DO?
I'M RUNNING THIS FRANCHISE, NOW.
DON'T YOU EVEN *THINK* ABOUT GOING OUT THAT DOOR.

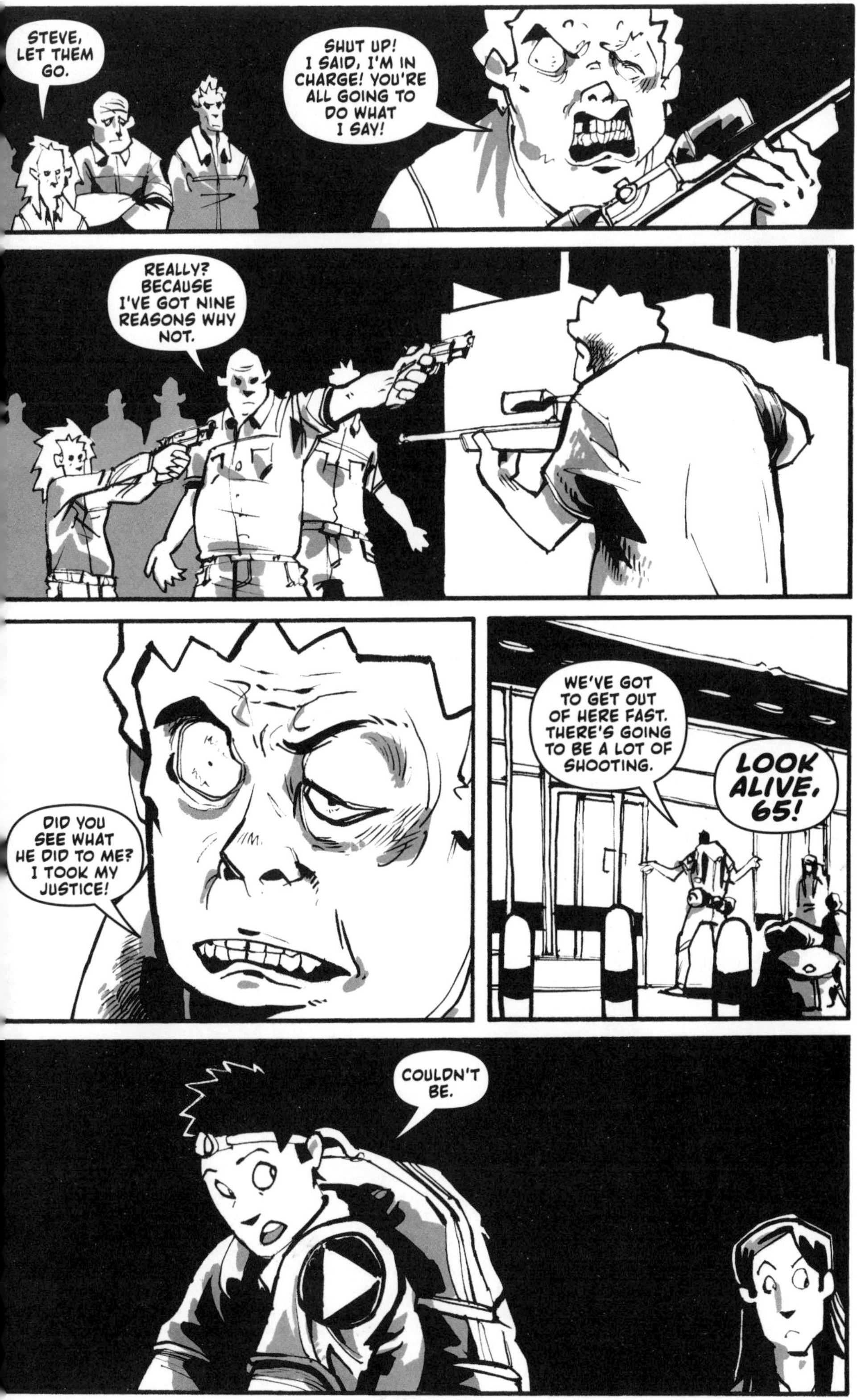

STEVE, LET THEM GO.
SHUT UP! I SAID, I'M IN CHARGE! YOU'RE ALL GOING TO DO WHAT I SAY!
REALLY? BECAUSE I'VE GOT NINE REASONS WHY NOT.
DID YOU SEE WHAT HE DID TO ME? I TOOK MY JUSTICE!
WE'VE GOT TO GET OUT OF HERE FAST. THERE'S GOING TO BE A LOT OF SHOOTING.
LOOK ALIVE, 65!
COULDN'T BE.

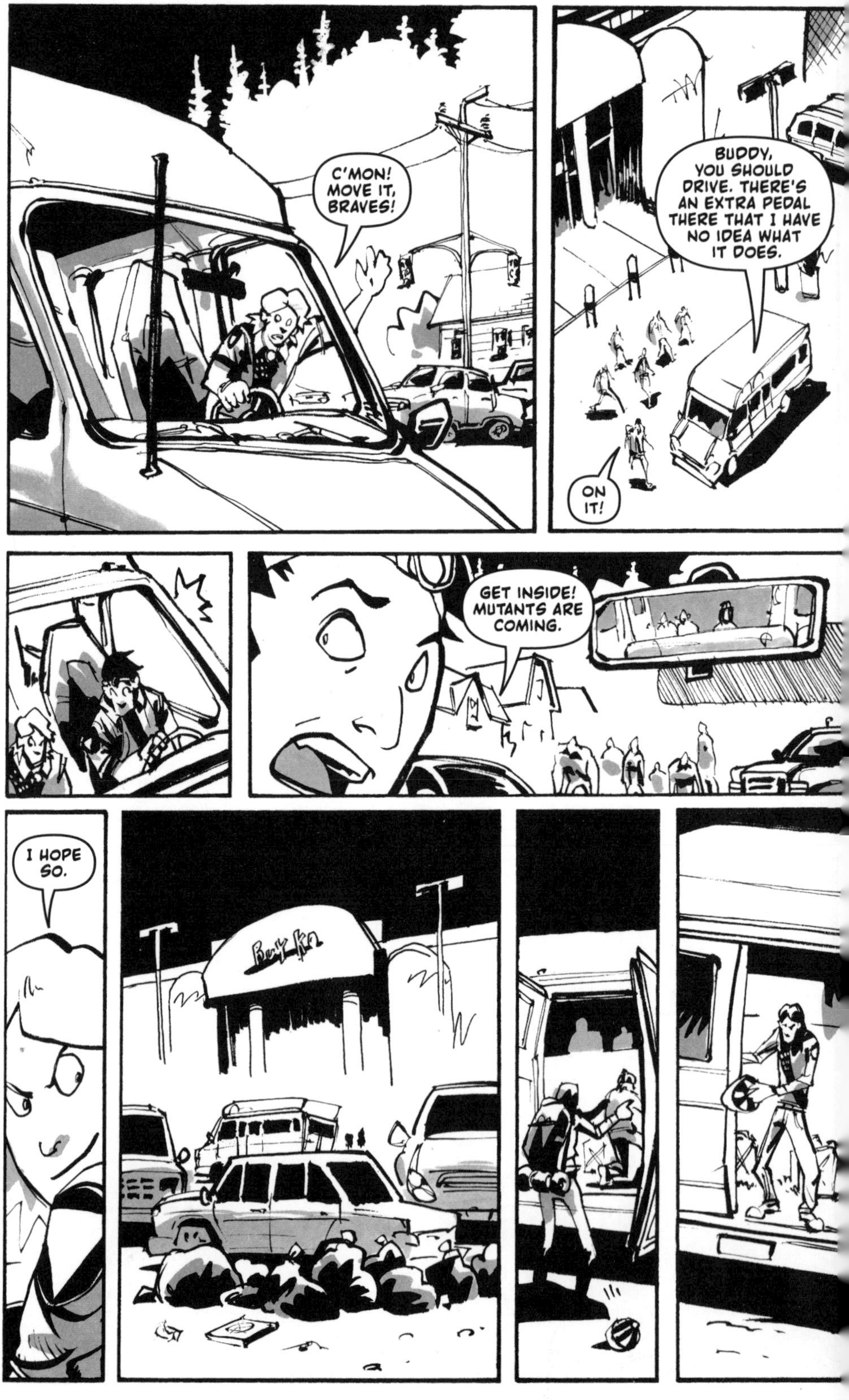
C'MON! MOVE IT, BRAVES!
BUDDY, YOU SHOULD DRIVE. THERE'S AN EXTRA PEDAL THERE THAT I HAVE NO IDEA WHAT IT DOES.
ON IT!
GET INSIDE! MUTANTS ARE COMING.
I HOPE SO.

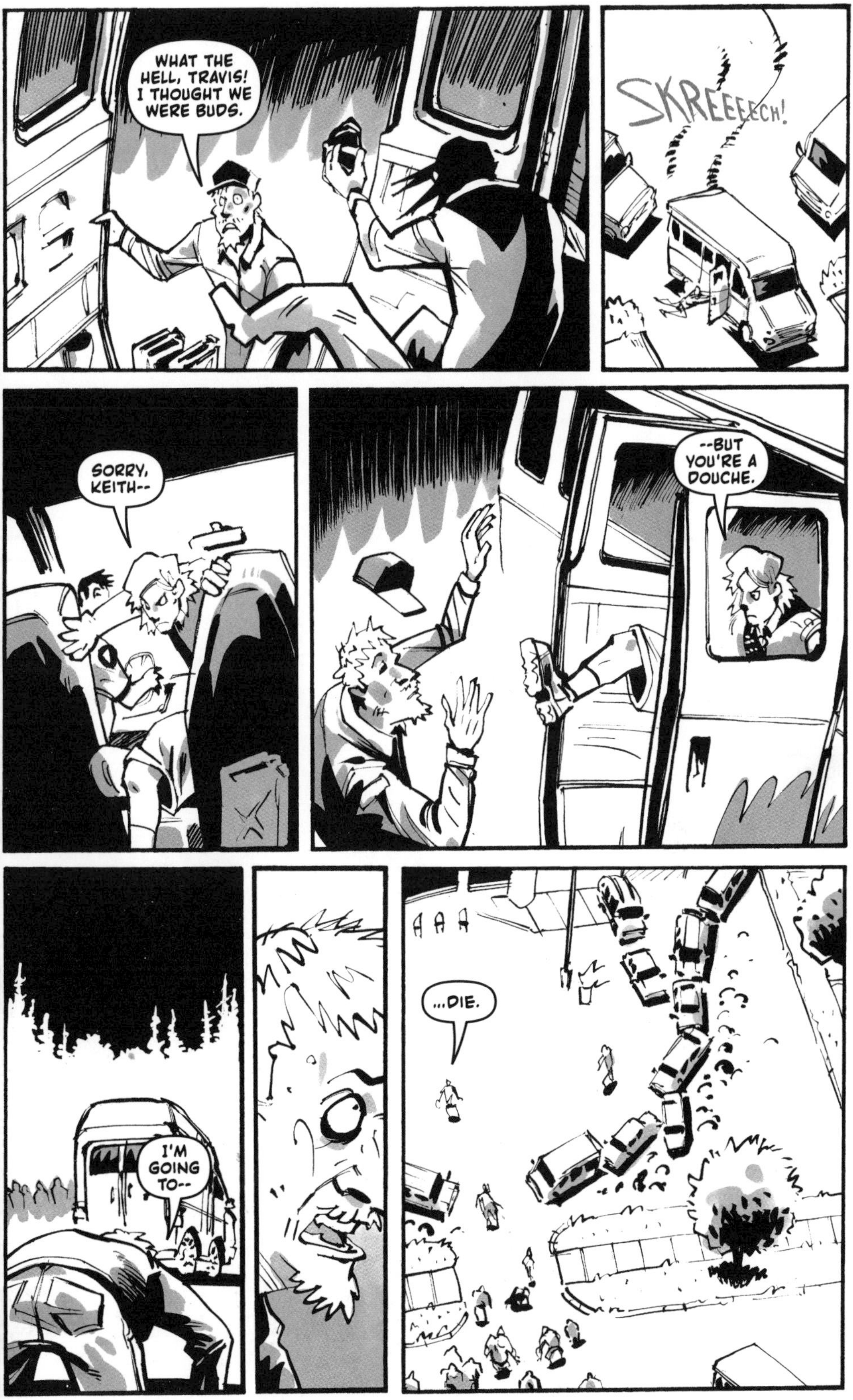
WHAT THE HELL, TRAVIS! I THOUGHT WE WERE BUDS.
SKREEEECH!
SORRY, KEITH--
--BUT YOU'RE A DOUCHE.
I'M GOING TO--
...DIE.

SONGS OF THE JUNIOR BRAVES

by Mr. Benedict Smedberg, Esq.
Founder, Junior Braves
Known to American Indians as "Loyal Oak"

CALL AND RESPONSE SONGS

"Call and Response" songs are a form of interaction between the speaker and the listener, in which every utterance of the speaker elicits an audible response (often in the form of an echo) from the listener. In native cultures throughout the world, call-and-response songs are a revered and important form of group participation.

"THE BRAVE AND HIS BOW"

He sat on a hillside and strung his bow,
 He strung his bow.
He sat on a hillside and strung his bow.
 He strung his bow.

He heard her cry from the river below.
 River below.
He heard her cry from the river below.
 River below

(All together)
He got up and he went down.
 He got up and he went down.
Down in the river she thought she'd drown
 Down in the river she thought she'd drown

The Brave grabbed an arrow and a length of rope.
 A length of rope.
The Brave grabbed an arrow and a length of rope.
 A length of rope.

The girl in the river, he was her only hope.
 Her only hope.
The girl in the river, he was her only hope.
 Her only hope

(All together)
He loosed the arrow and away it flew.
 He loosed the arrow and away it flew.
Stuck in a tree, his aim was true.
 Stuck in a tree, his aim was true.

She grabbed the rope as she floated by.
 She floated by.
She grabbed the rope as she floated by.
 She floated by.

She'd love that Brave 'til the day she die.
 The day she die.
She'd love that Brave 'til the day she die.
 The day she die.

—

wise Chief once told his people, *"The act of singing is a delight to nature, and good to reserve the health of a Brave. It strengthens all parts of the chest, and opens the pipes."*

ne Junior Braves should use the songs in this section on any occasion that they wish to xpress joy and togetherness. On the darkest day, a song can lift the spirit higher than the ings of an eagle.

THERE WAS A BEAR"

ne other day.
The other day.
met a bear.
I met a bear.

ut in the woods.
Out in the woods.
-way out there.
A-way out there.

All together)
he other day I met a bear
ut in the woods a-way out there.

e said to me
He said to me
Why don't you run?
Why don't you run?
see you ain't
I see you ain't
ot any gun
Got any gun.
nd so I ran
And so I ran
way from there
Away from there
ut right behind
But right behind
le was that bear
Was that bear

head of me
Ahead of me
saw a tree
I saw a tree
great big tree
A great big tree
h glory be
Oh glory be

The nearest branch
The nearest branch
Was 10 feet up
Was 10 feet up
I'd have to jump
I'd have to jump
And trust my luck
And trust my luck

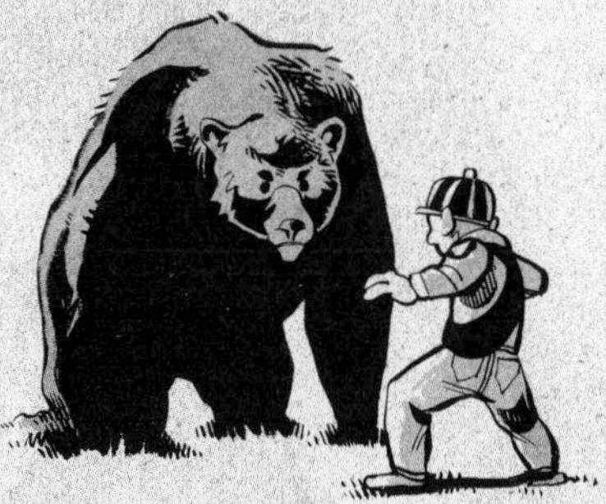

(All together)
The nearest branch was 10 feet up
I'd have to jump and trust my luck

And so I jumped
And so I jumped
Into the air
Into the air
But I missed that branch
I missed that branch
Away up there
Away up there
Now don't you fret
Now don't you fret
Now don't you frown
Now don't you frown

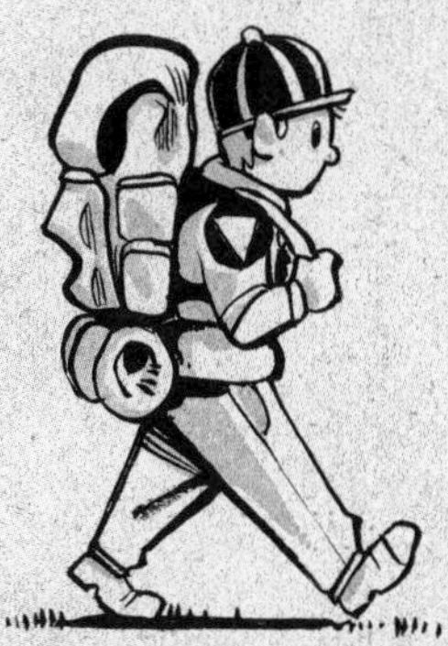

Cause I caught that branch
I caught that branch
On the way back down
On the way back down
That's all there is
All there is
There ain't no more
Ain't no more

Unless I meet
Unless I meet
That bear once more
That bear once more

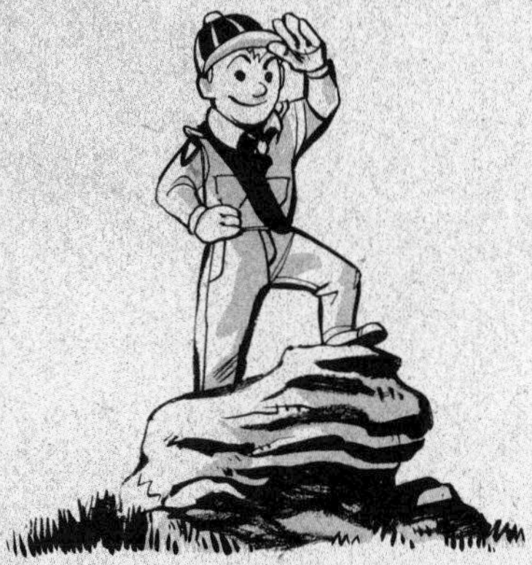

CHAPTER
SIX

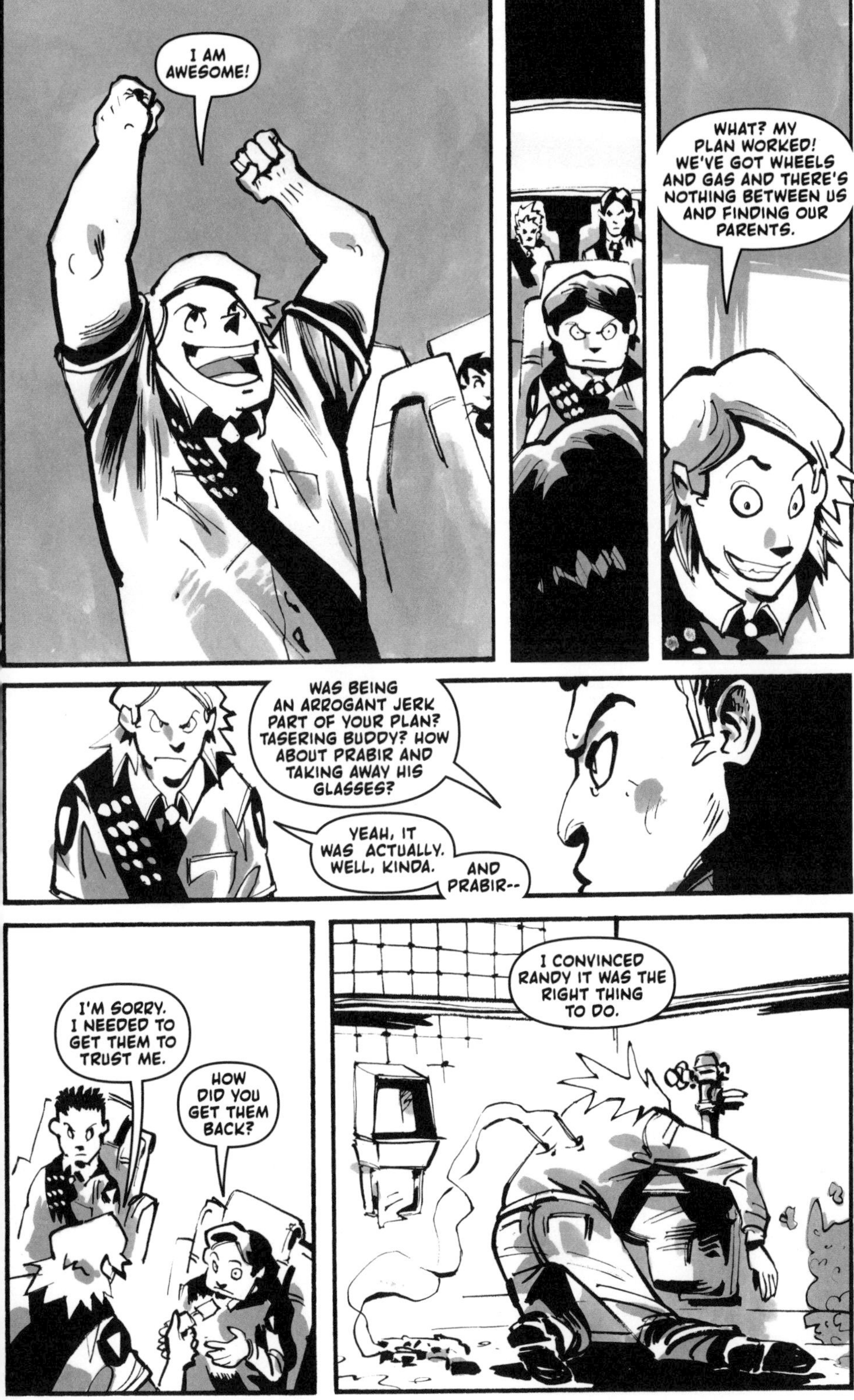
I AM AWESOME!
WHAT? MY PLAN WORKED! WE'VE GOT WHEELS AND GAS AND THERE'S NOTHING BETWEEN US AND FINDING OUR PARENTS.
WAS BEING AN ARROGANT JERK PART OF YOUR PLAN? TASERING BUDDY? HOW ABOUT PRABIR AND TAKING AWAY HIS GLASSES?
YEAH, IT WAS ACTUALLY. WELL, KINDA.
AND PRABIR--
I'M SORRY. I NEEDED TO GET THEM TO TRUST ME.
HOW DID YOU GET THEM BACK?
I CONVINCED RANDY IT WAS THE RIGHT THING TO DO.

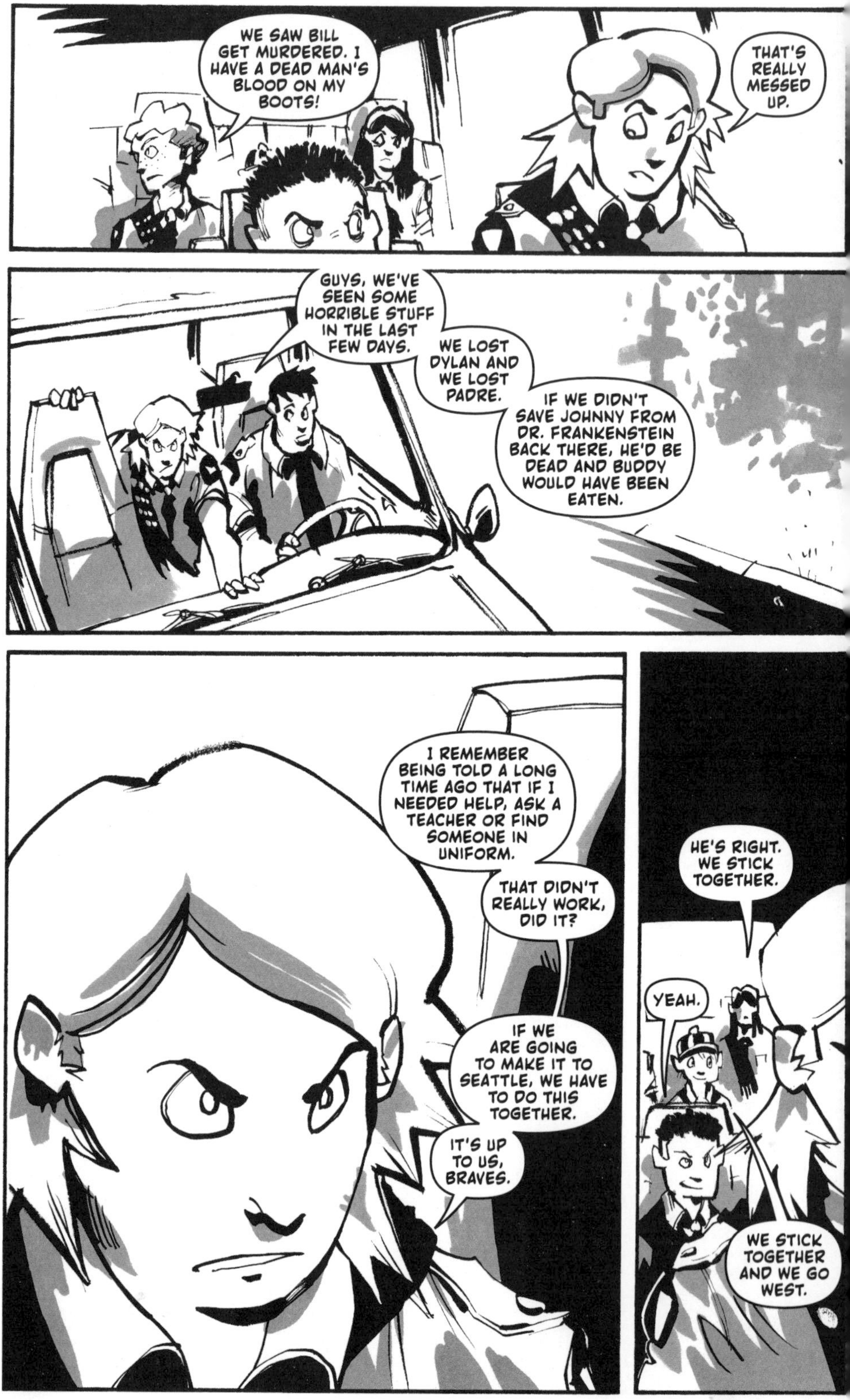
WE SAW BILL GET MURDERED. I HAVE A DEAD MAN'S BLOOD ON MY BOOTS!
THAT'S REALLY MESSED UP.
GUYS, WE'VE SEEN SOME HORRIBLE STUFF IN THE LAST FEW DAYS.
WE LOST DYLAN AND WE LOST PADRE.
IF WE DIDN'T SAVE JOHNNY FROM DR. FRANKENSTEIN BACK THERE, HE'D BE DEAD AND BUDDY WOULD HAVE BEEN EATEN.
I REMEMBER BEING TOLD A LONG TIME AGO THAT IF I NEEDED HELP, ASK A TEACHER OR FIND SOMEONE IN UNIFORM.
THAT DIDN'T REALLY WORK, DID IT?
IF WE ARE GOING TO MAKE IT TO SEATTLE, WE HAVE TO DO THIS TOGETHER.
IT'S UP TO US, BRAVES.
HE'S RIGHT. WE STICK TOGETHER.
YEAH.
WE STICK TOGETHER AND WE GO WEST.

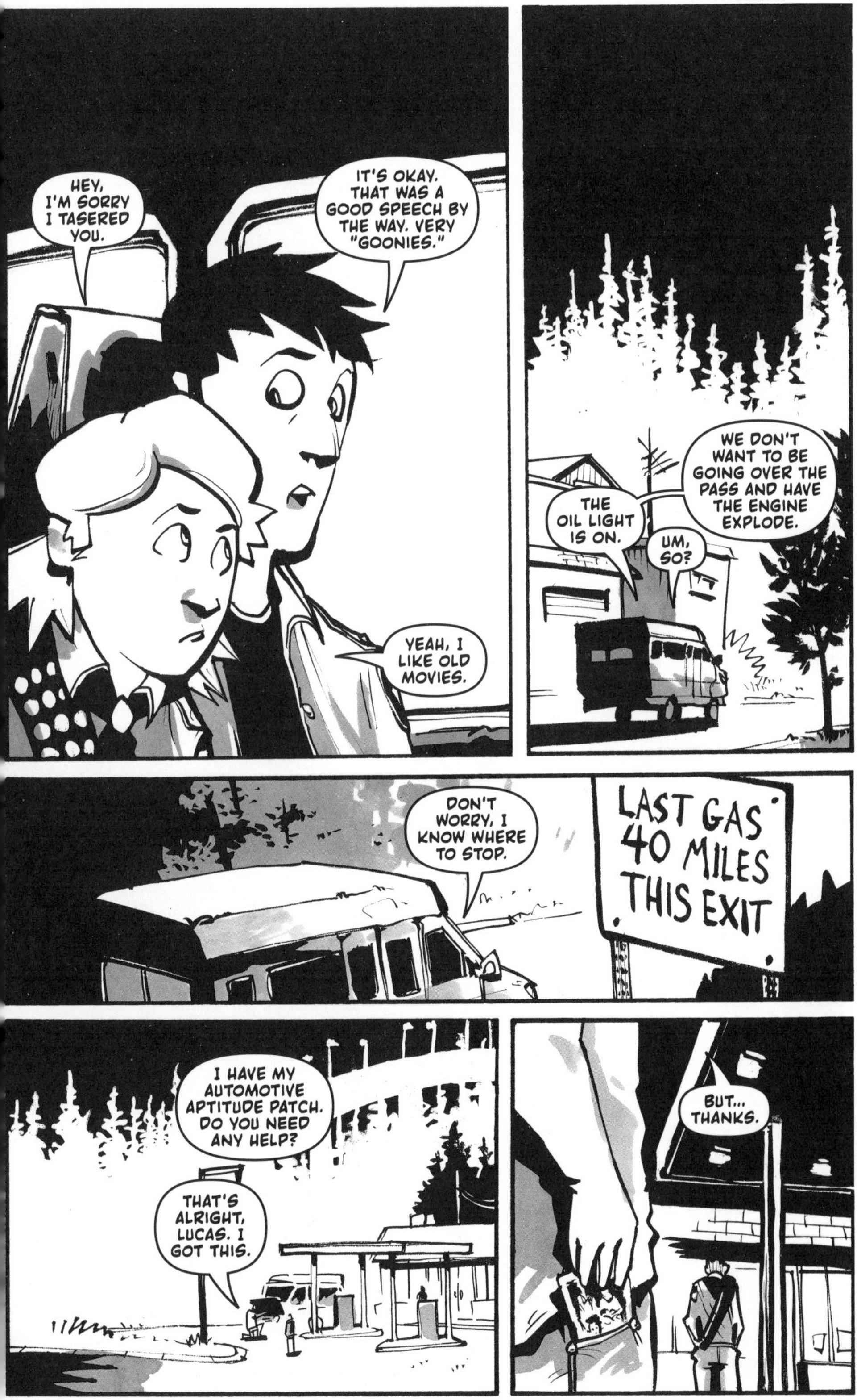
HEY, I'M SORRY I TASERED YOU.
IT'S OKAY. THAT WAS A GOOD SPEECH BY THE WAY. VERY "GOONIES."
YEAH, I LIKE OLD MOVIES.
THE OIL LIGHT IS ON.
UM, SO?
WE DON'T WANT TO BE GOING OVER THE PASS AND HAVE THE ENGINE EXPLODE.
DON'T WORRY, I KNOW WHERE TO STOP.
LAST GAS 40 MILES THIS EXIT
I HAVE MY AUTOMOTIVE APTITUDE PATCH. DO YOU NEED ANY HELP?
THAT'S ALRIGHT, LUCAS. I GOT THIS.
BUT... THANKS.

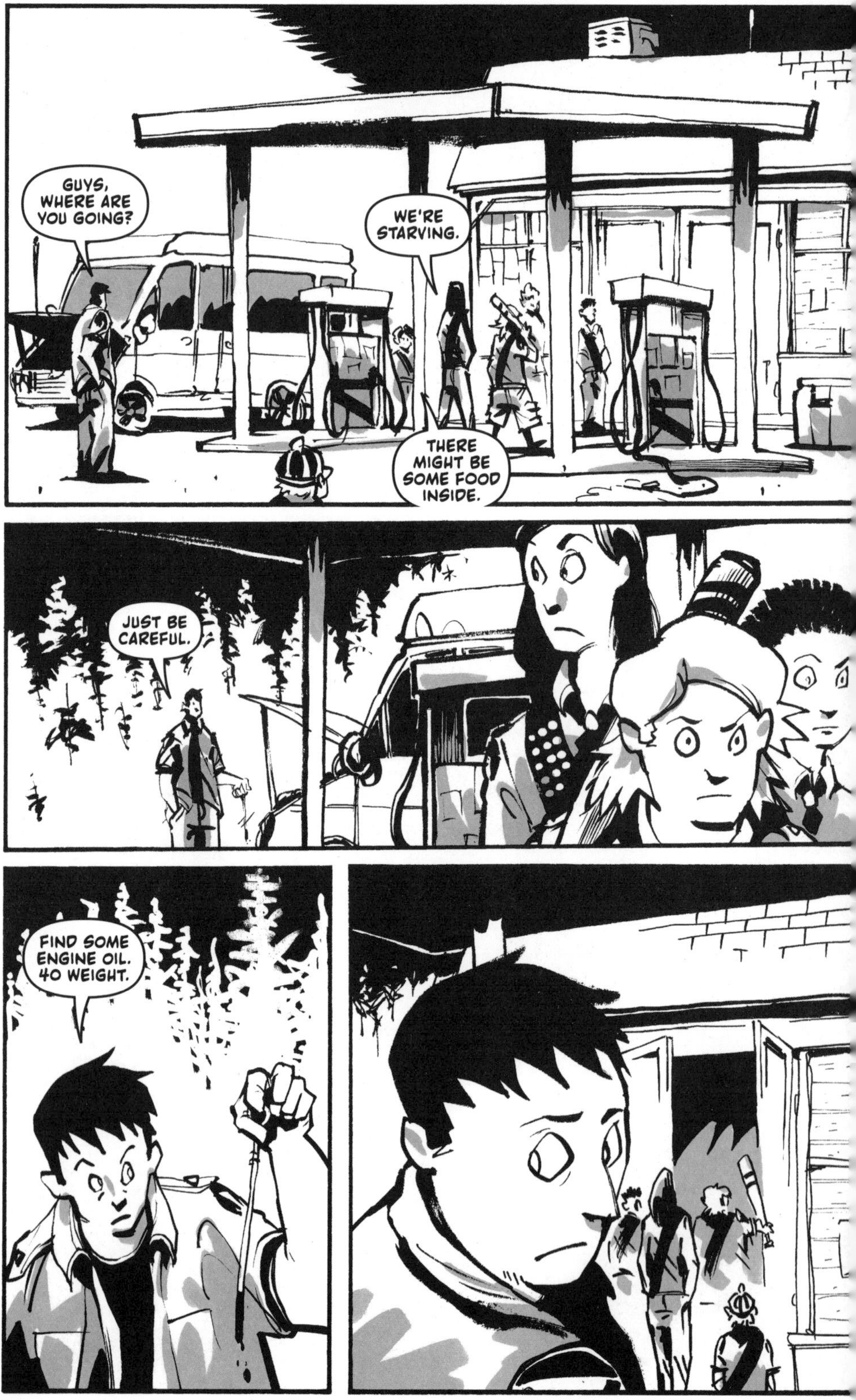
GUYS, WHERE ARE YOU GOING?
WE'RE STARVING.
THERE MIGHT BE SOME FOOD INSIDE.
JUST BE CAREFUL.
FIND SOME ENGINE OIL. 40 WEIGHT.

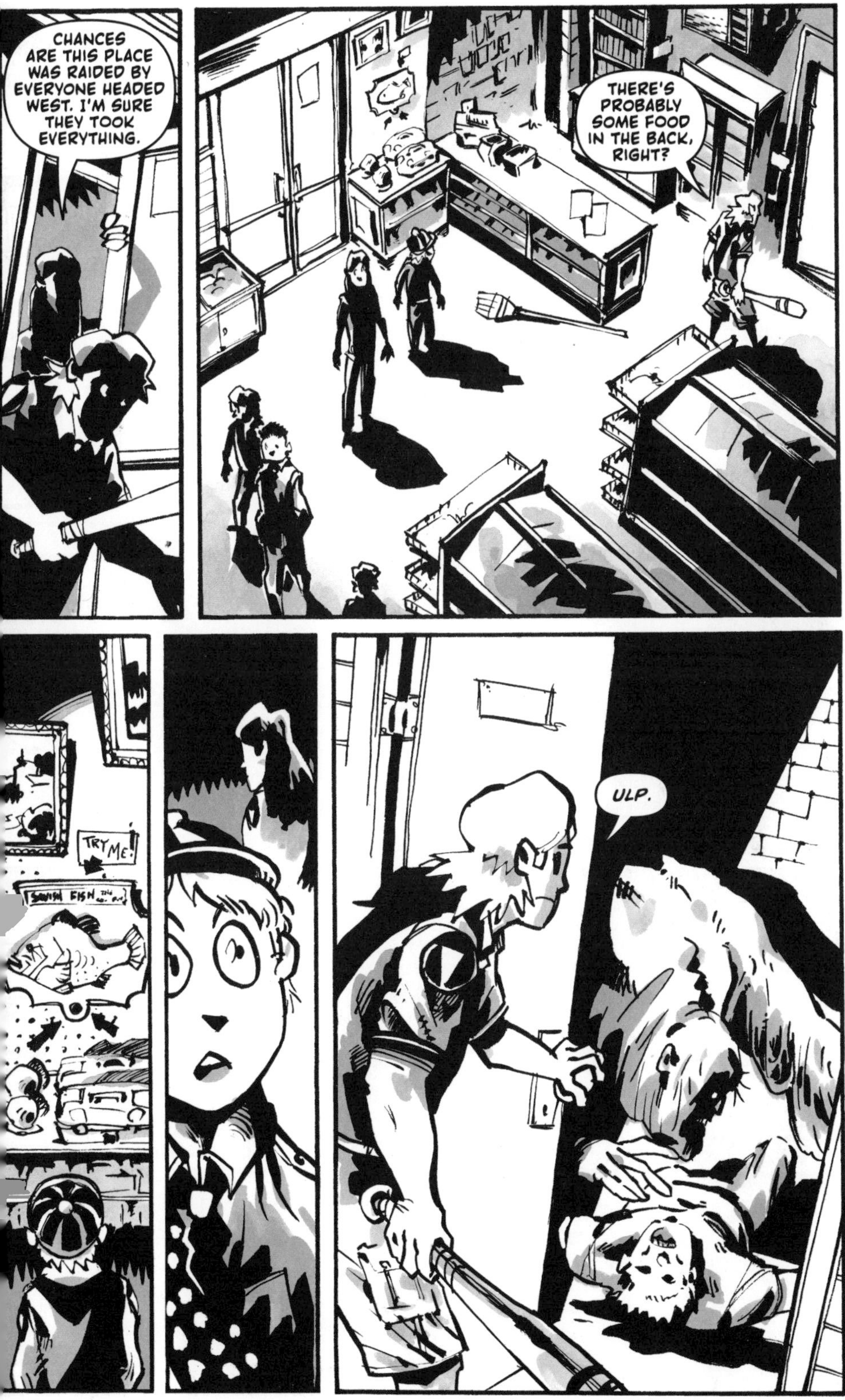
CHANCES ARE THIS PLACE WAS RAIDED BY EVERYONE HEADED WEST. I'M SURE THEY TOOK EVERYTHING.
THERE'S PROBABLY SOME FOOD IN THE BACK, RIGHT?
TRY ME!
ULP.

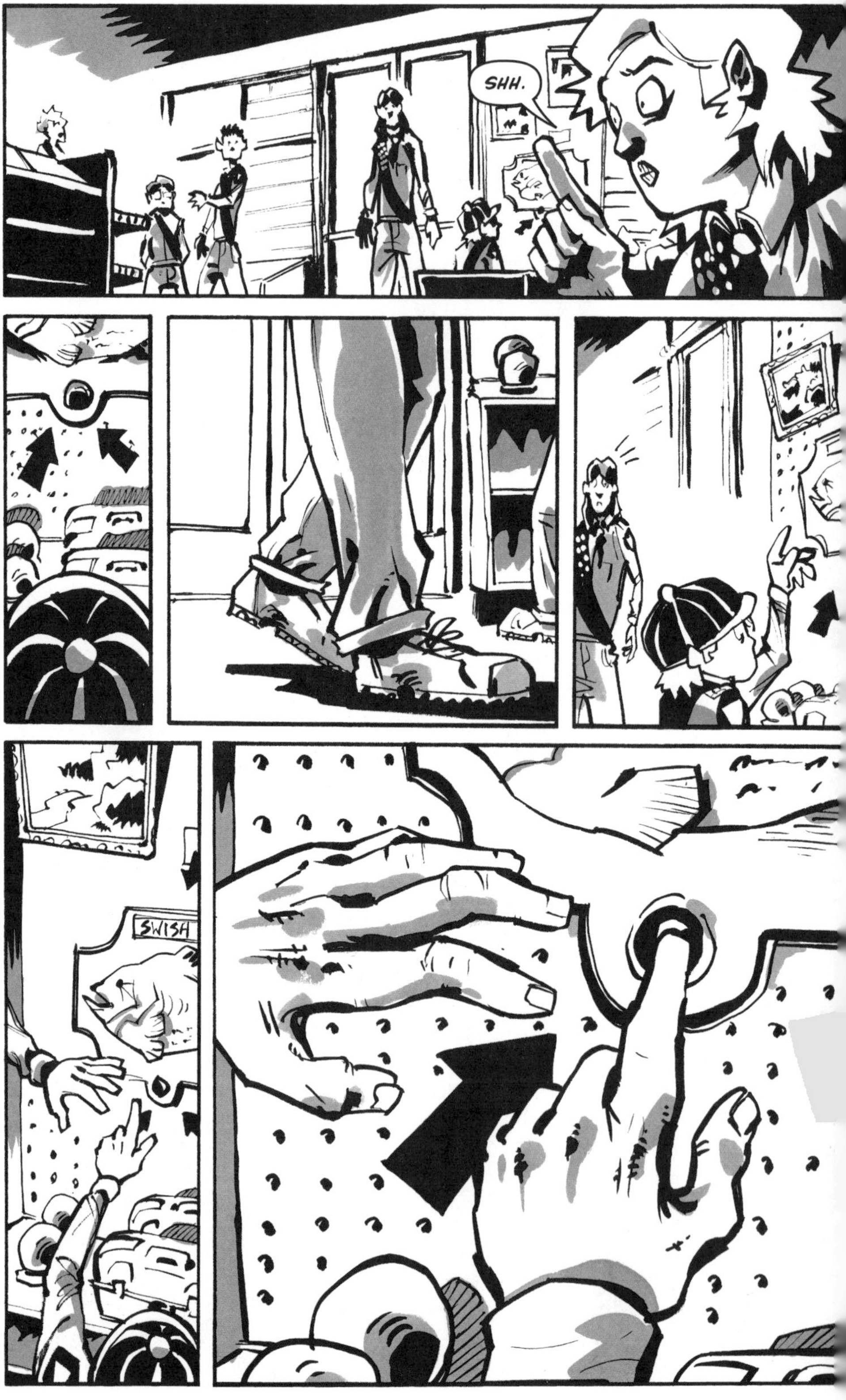
SHH.
SWISH

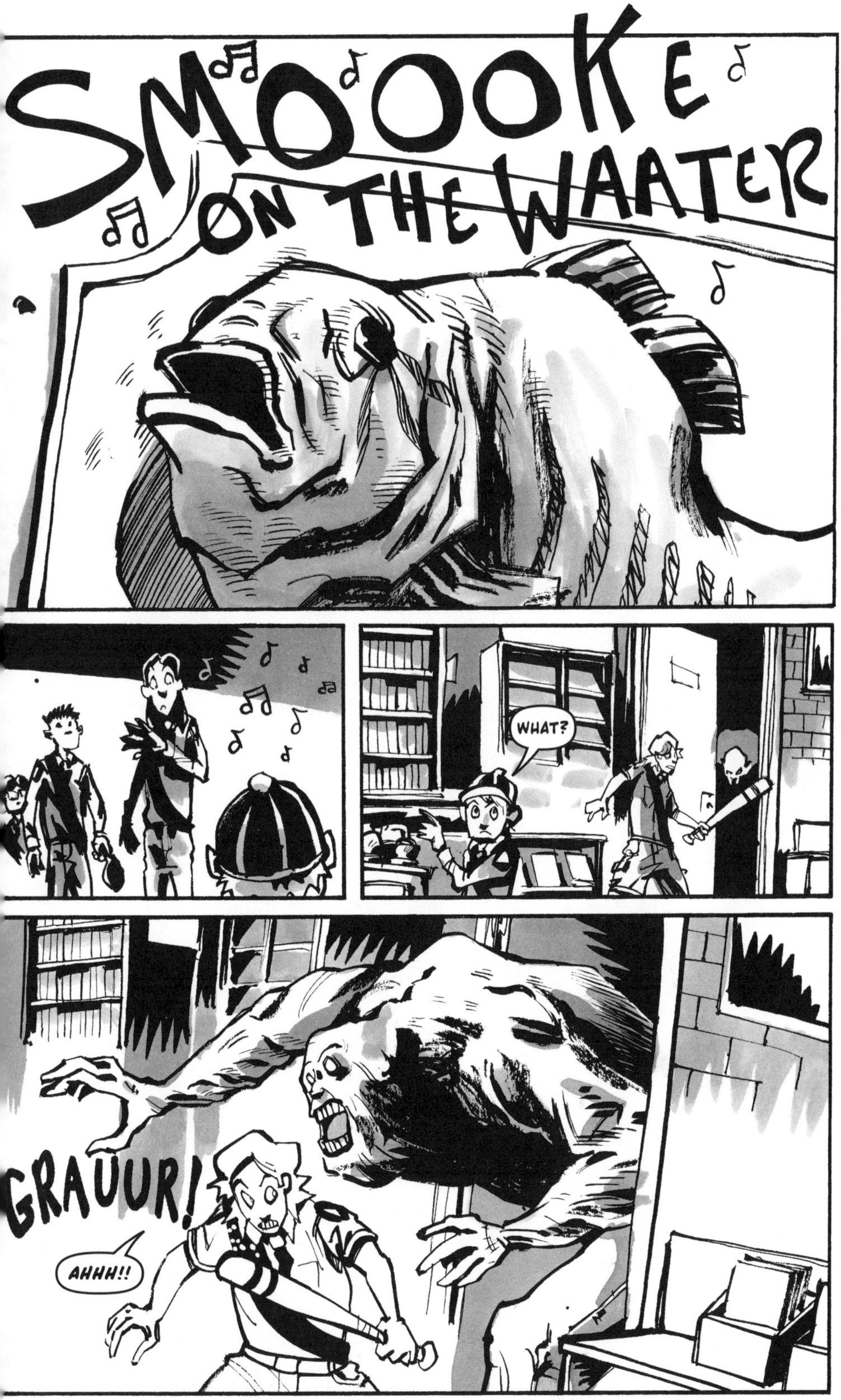
SMOOOKE ON THE WAATER
WHAT?
GRAUUR!
AHHH!!

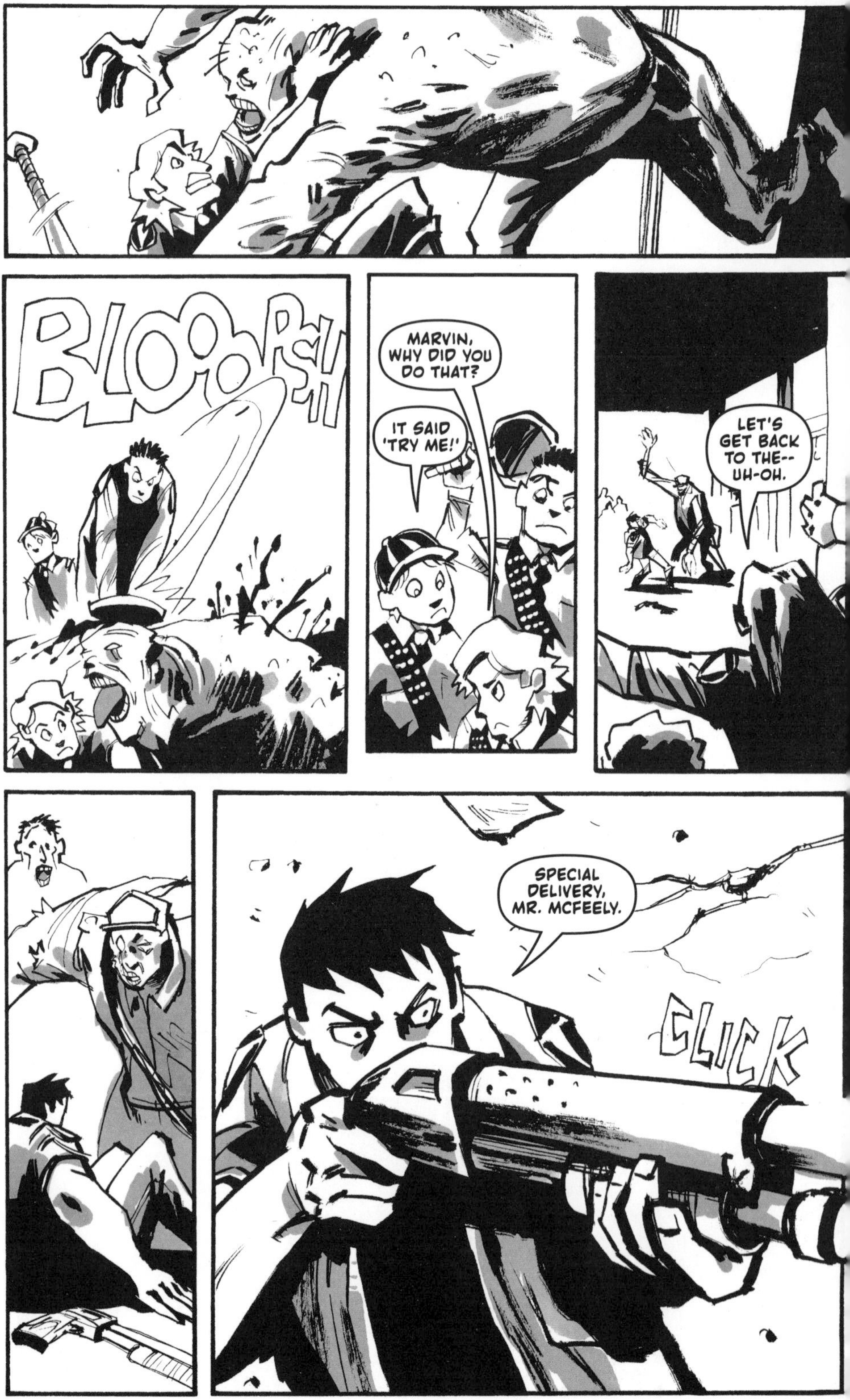
BLOOOPSH
MARVIN, WHY DID YOU DO THAT?
IT SAID 'TRY ME!'
LET'S GET BACK TO THE-- UH-OH.
SPECIAL DELIVERY, MR. MCFEELY.
CLICK

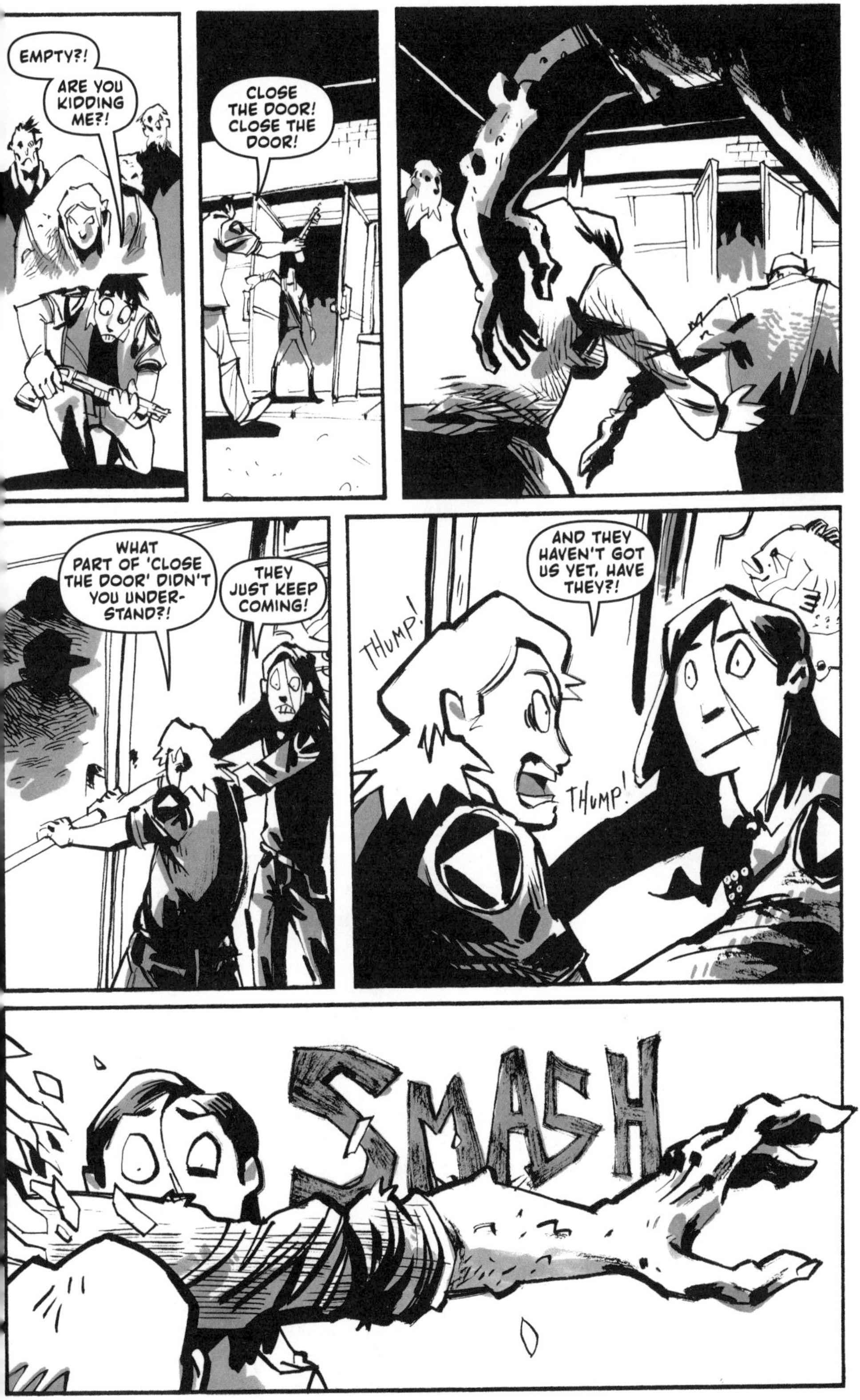

EMPTY?!
ARE YOU KIDDING ME?!
CLOSE THE DOOR! CLOSE THE DOOR!
WHAT PART OF 'CLOSE THE DOOR' DIDN'T YOU UNDER-STAND?!
THEY JUST KEEP COMING!
AND THEY HAVEN'T GOT US YET, HAVE THEY?!
THUMP!
THUMP!
SMASH

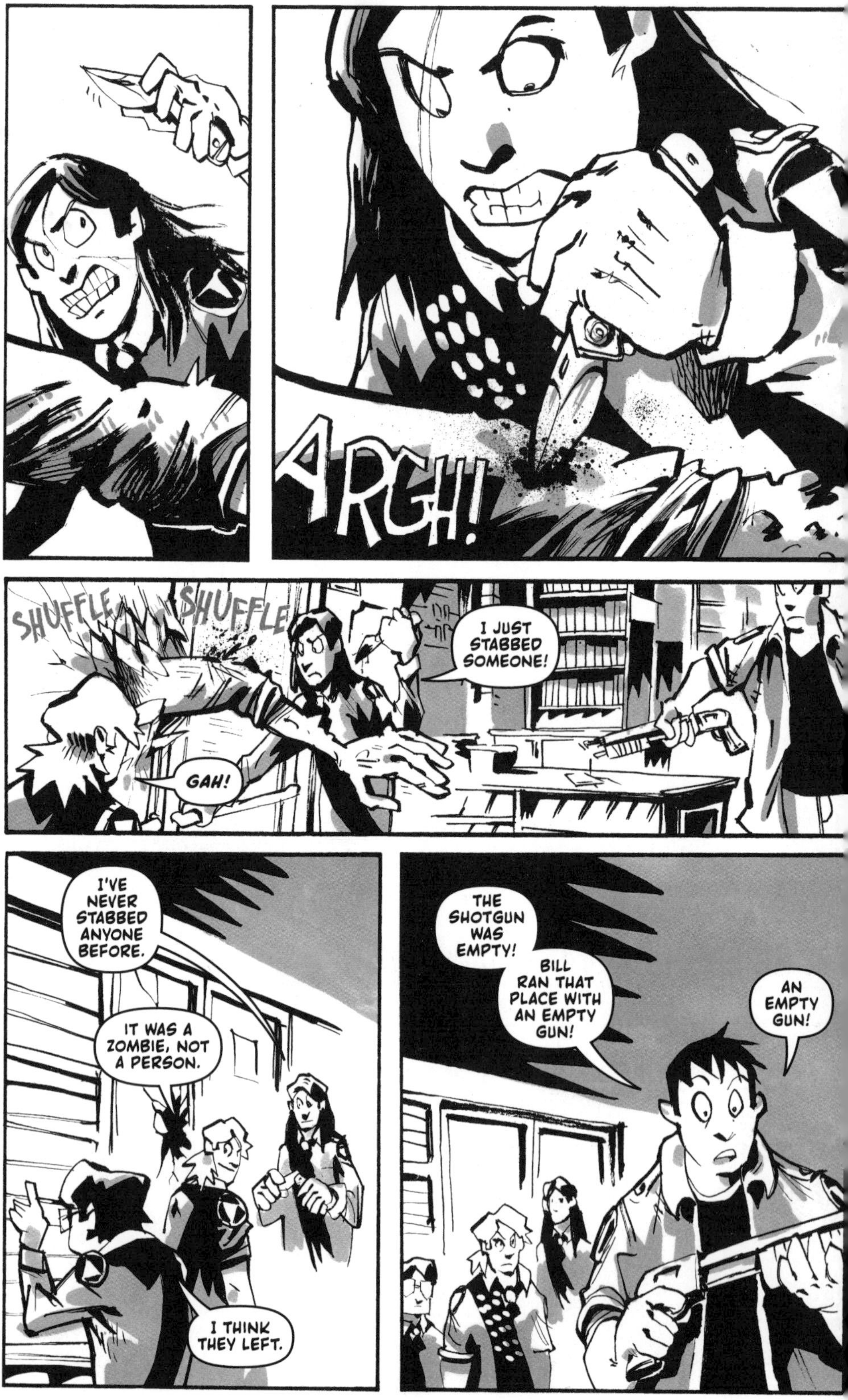
ARGH!
SHUFFLE SHUFFLE
I JUST STABBED SOMEONE!
GAH!
I'VE NEVER STABBED ANYONE BEFORE.
IT WAS A ZOMBIE, NOT A PERSON.
I THINK THEY LEFT.
THE SHOTGUN WAS EMPTY!
BILL RAN THAT PLACE WITH AN EMPTY GUN!
AN EMPTY GUN!

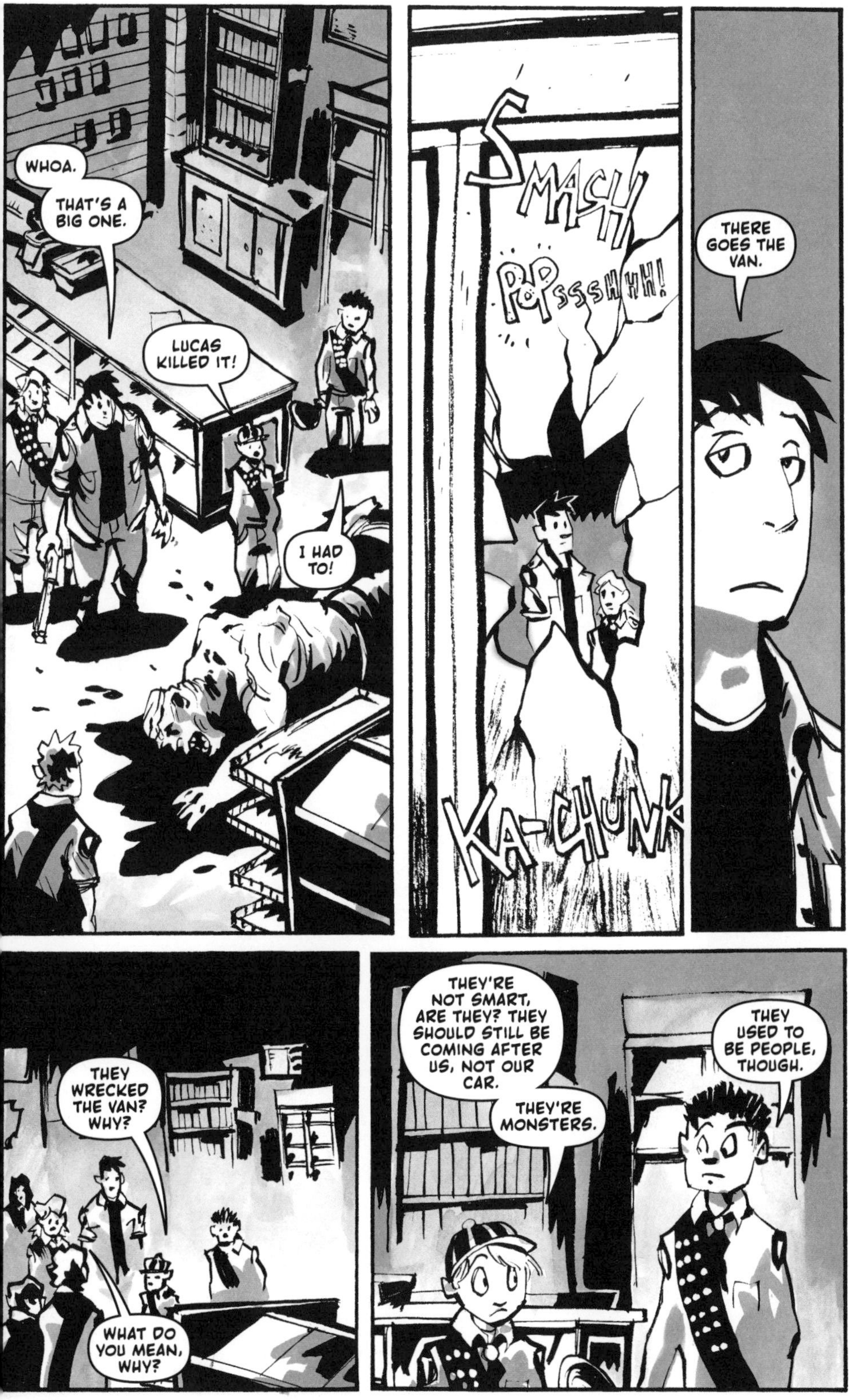
WHOA.
THAT'S A BIG ONE.
LUCAS KILLED IT!
I HAD TO!
SMACH
POPSSSHHH!
KA-CHUNK
THERE GOES THE VAN.
THEY WRECKED THE VAN? WHY?
WHAT DO YOU MEAN, WHY?
THEY'RE NOT SMART, ARE THEY? THEY SHOULD STILL BE COMING AFTER US, NOT OUR CAR.
THEY'RE MONSTERS.
THEY USED TO BE PEOPLE, THOUGH.

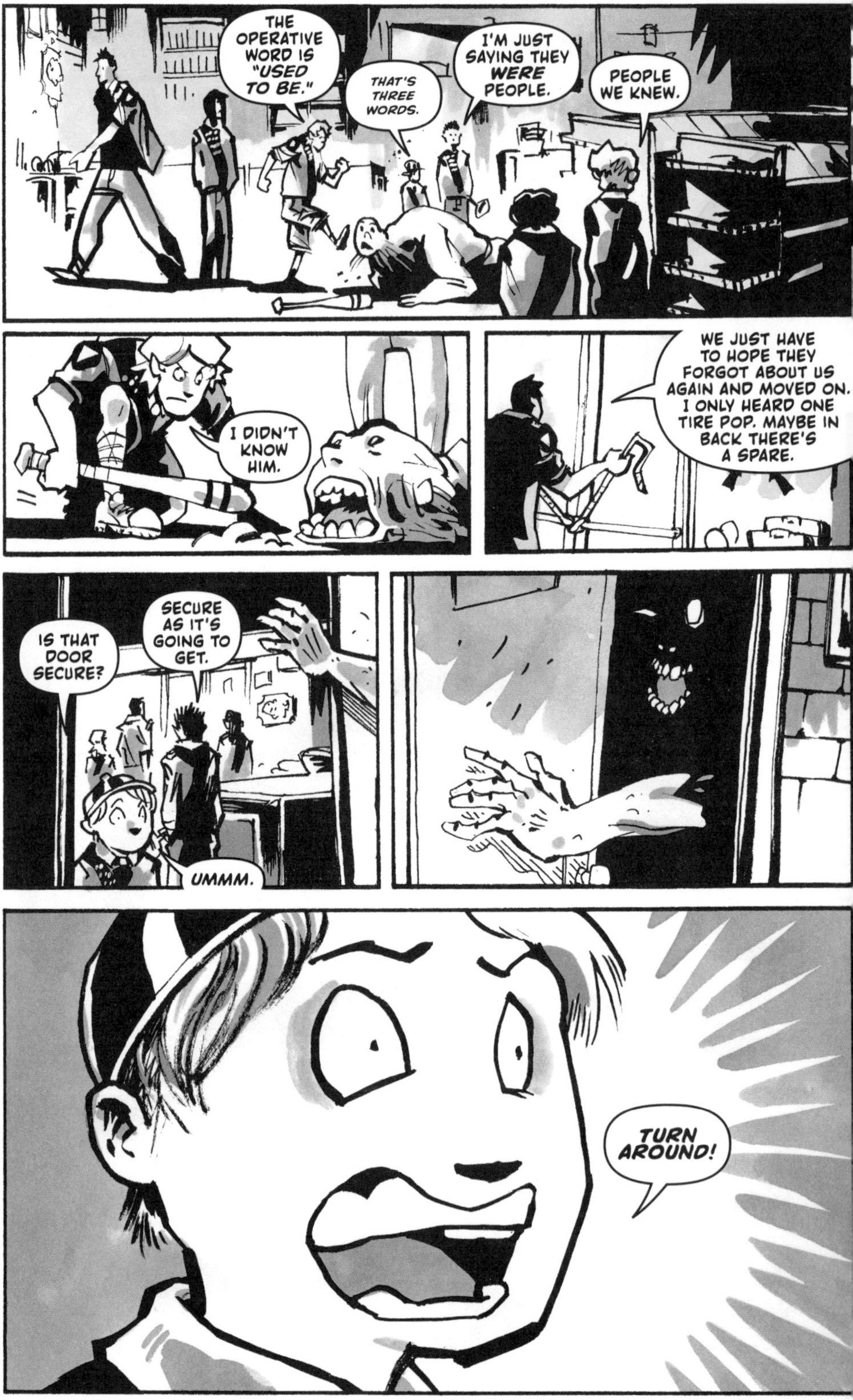
THE OPERATIVE WORD IS "USED TO BE."
THAT'S THREE WORDS.
I'M JUST SAYING THEY WERE PEOPLE.
PEOPLE WE KNEW.
I DIDN'T KNOW HIM.
WE JUST HAVE TO HOPE THEY FORGOT ABOUT US AGAIN AND MOVED ON. I ONLY HEARD ONE TIRE POP. MAYBE IN BACK THERE'S A SPARE.
IS THAT DOOR SECURE?
SECURE AS IT'S GOING TO GET.
UMMM.
TURN AROUND!

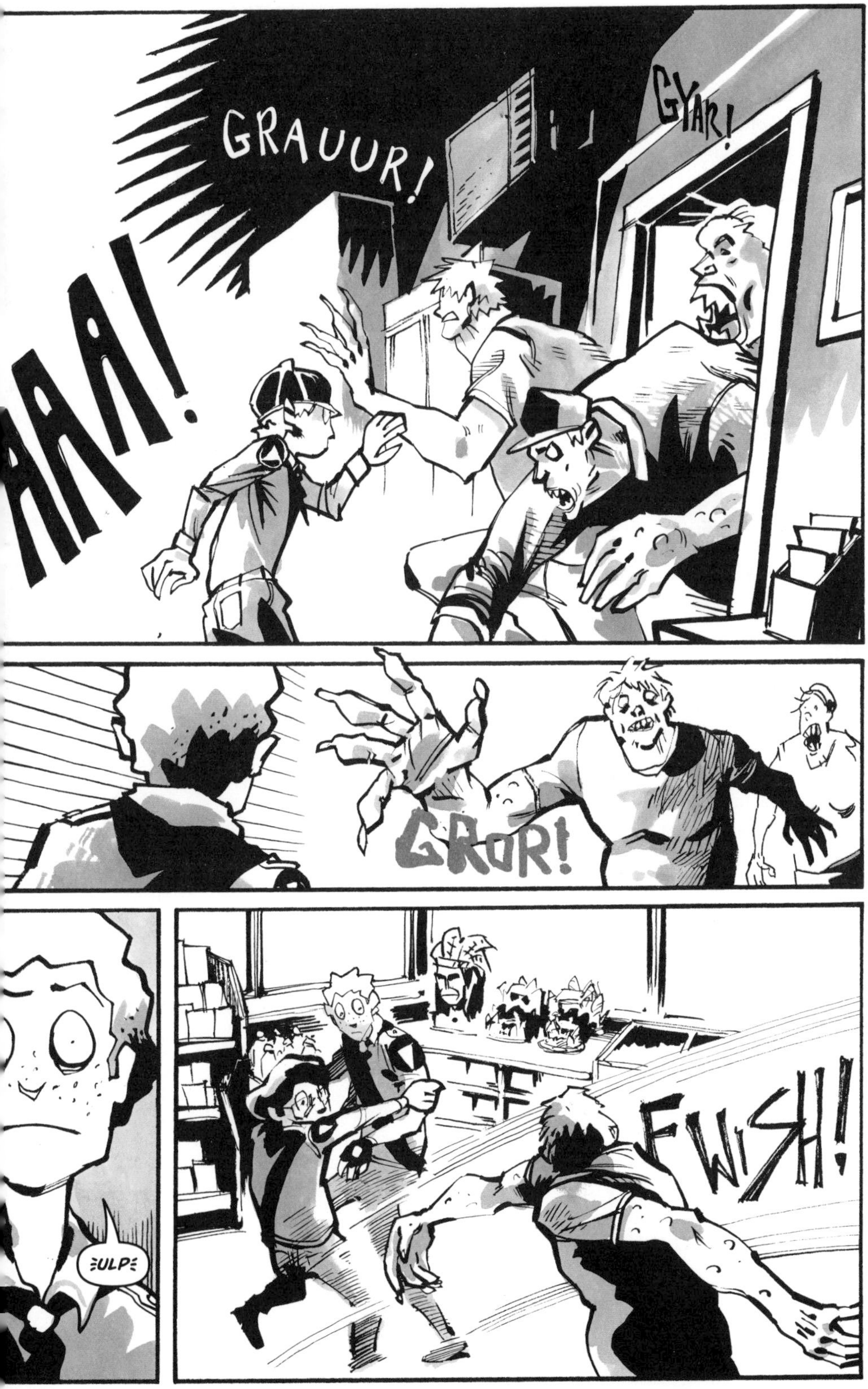
AAA!
GRAUUR!
GYAR!
GROR!
ULP
FWISH!

AHH!
CRUNCH!
GET AWAY FROM US!
CRACK!
MARVIN, YOU'VE GOT TO FIGHT THEM OFF! JOHNNY WATCH--

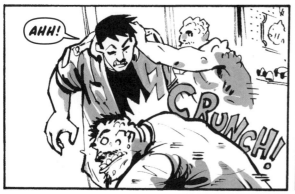

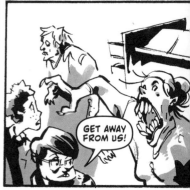

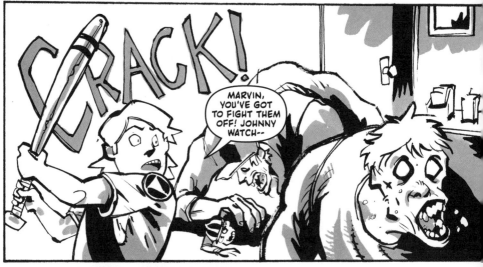

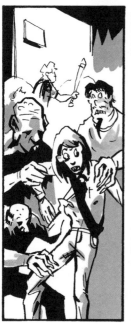

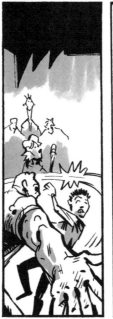

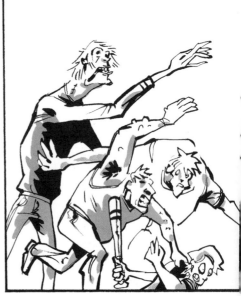

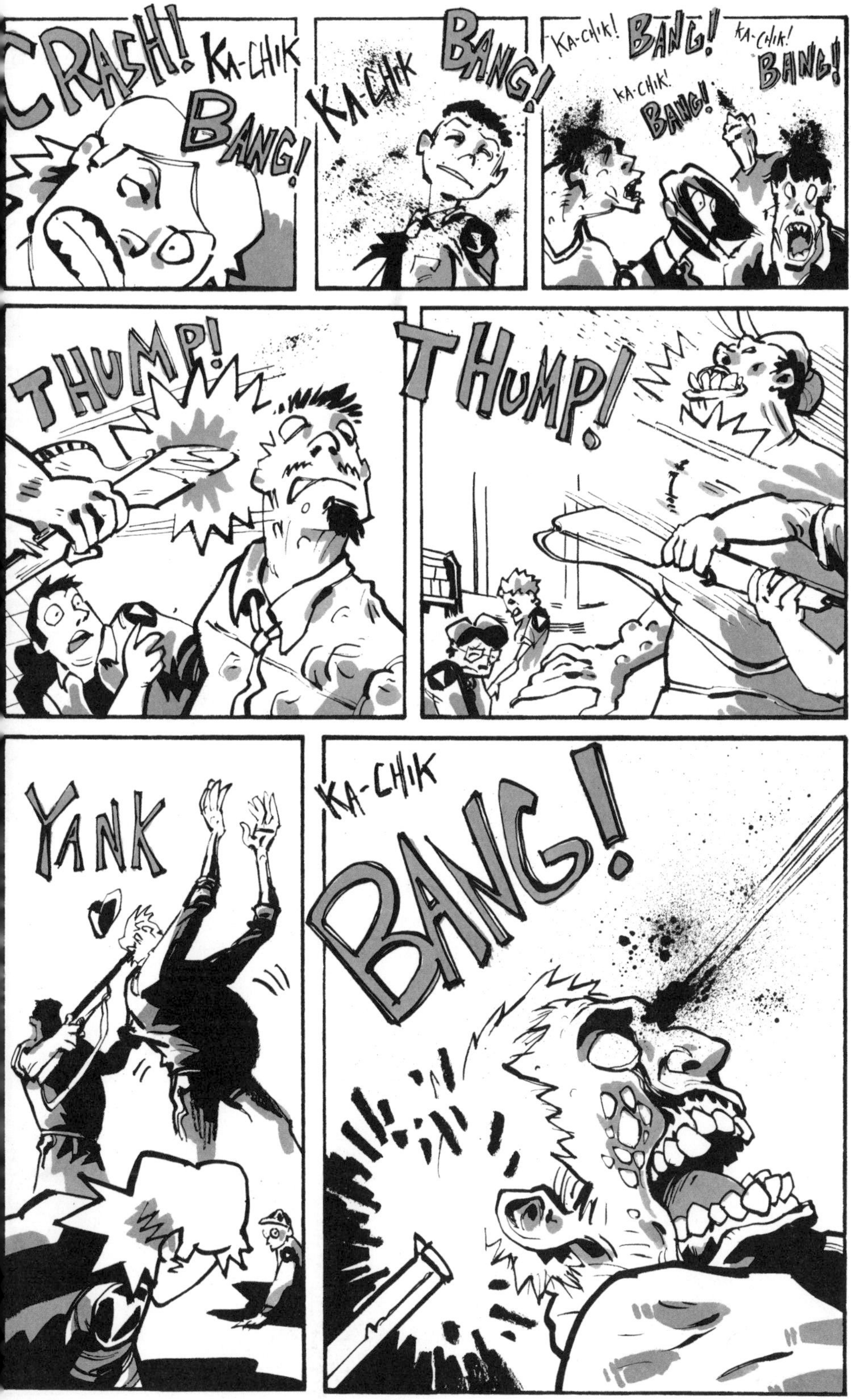
CRASH!
KA-CHIK
BANG!
KA-CHIK
BANG!
KA-CHIK!
BANG!
KA-CHIK!
BANG!
KA-CHIK!
BANG!
THUMP!
THUMP!
YANK
KA-CHIK
BANG!

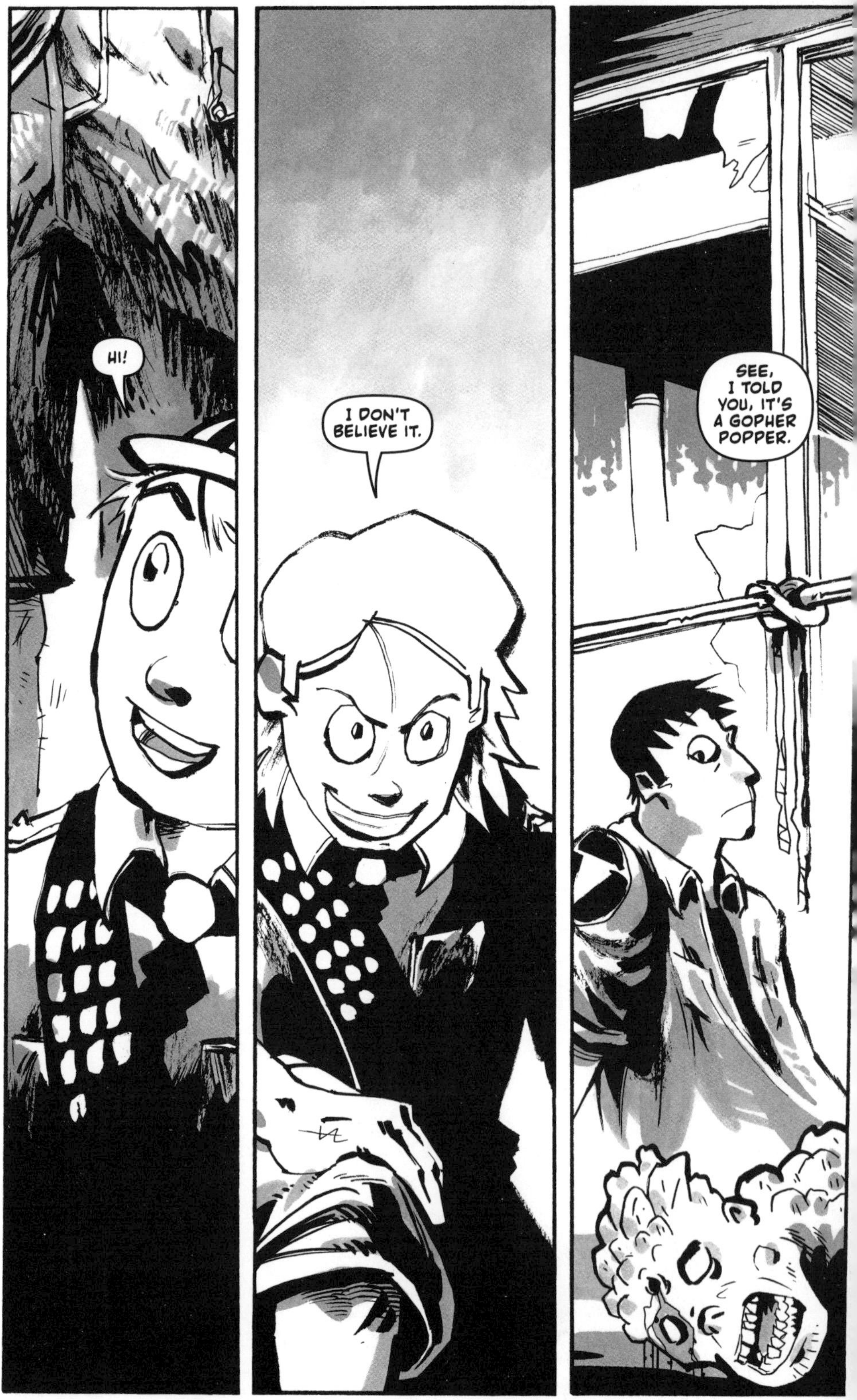
HI!
I DON'T BELIEVE IT.
SEE, I TOLD YOU, IT'S A GOPHER POPPER.

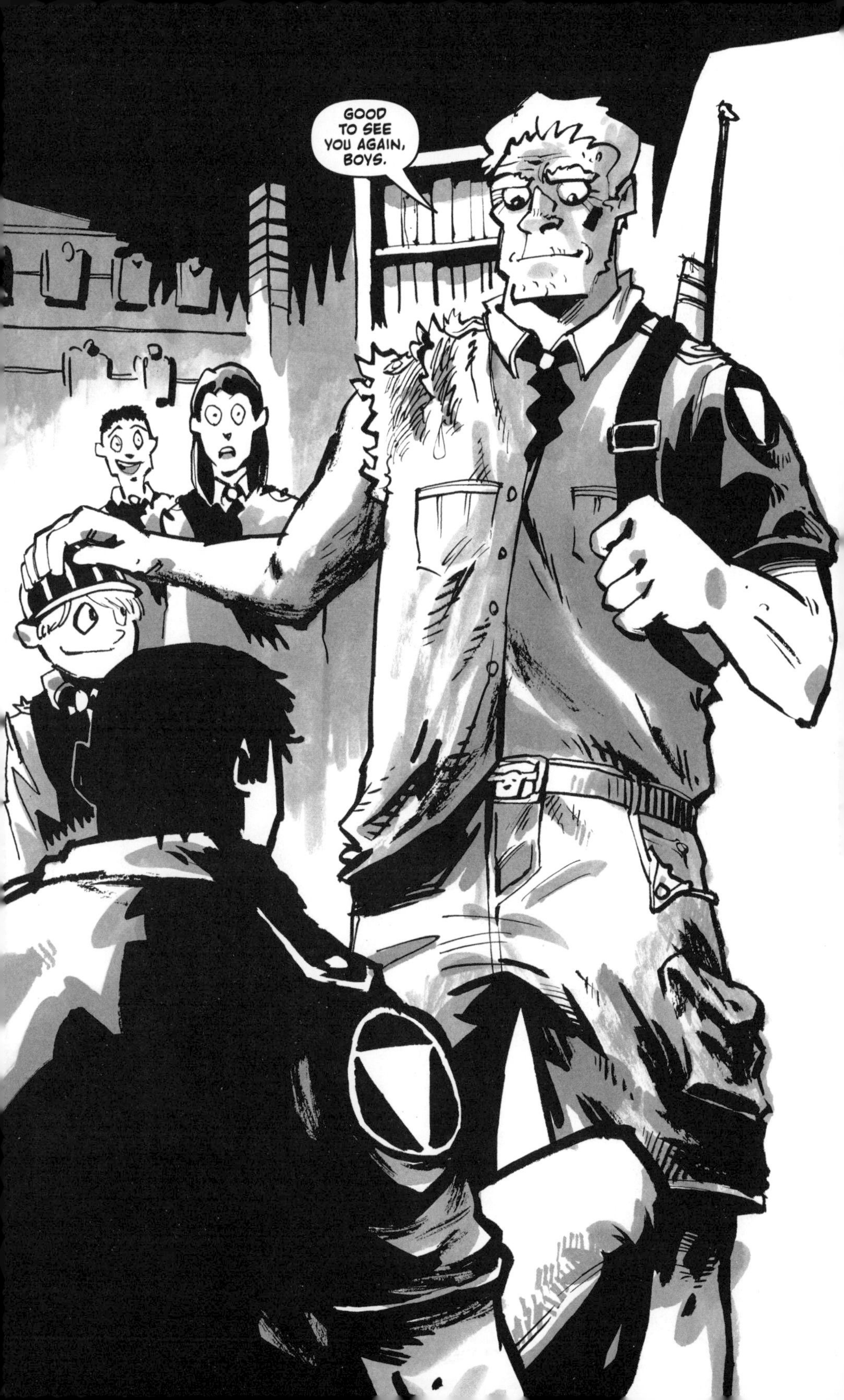
GOOD TO SEE YOU AGAIN, BOYS.

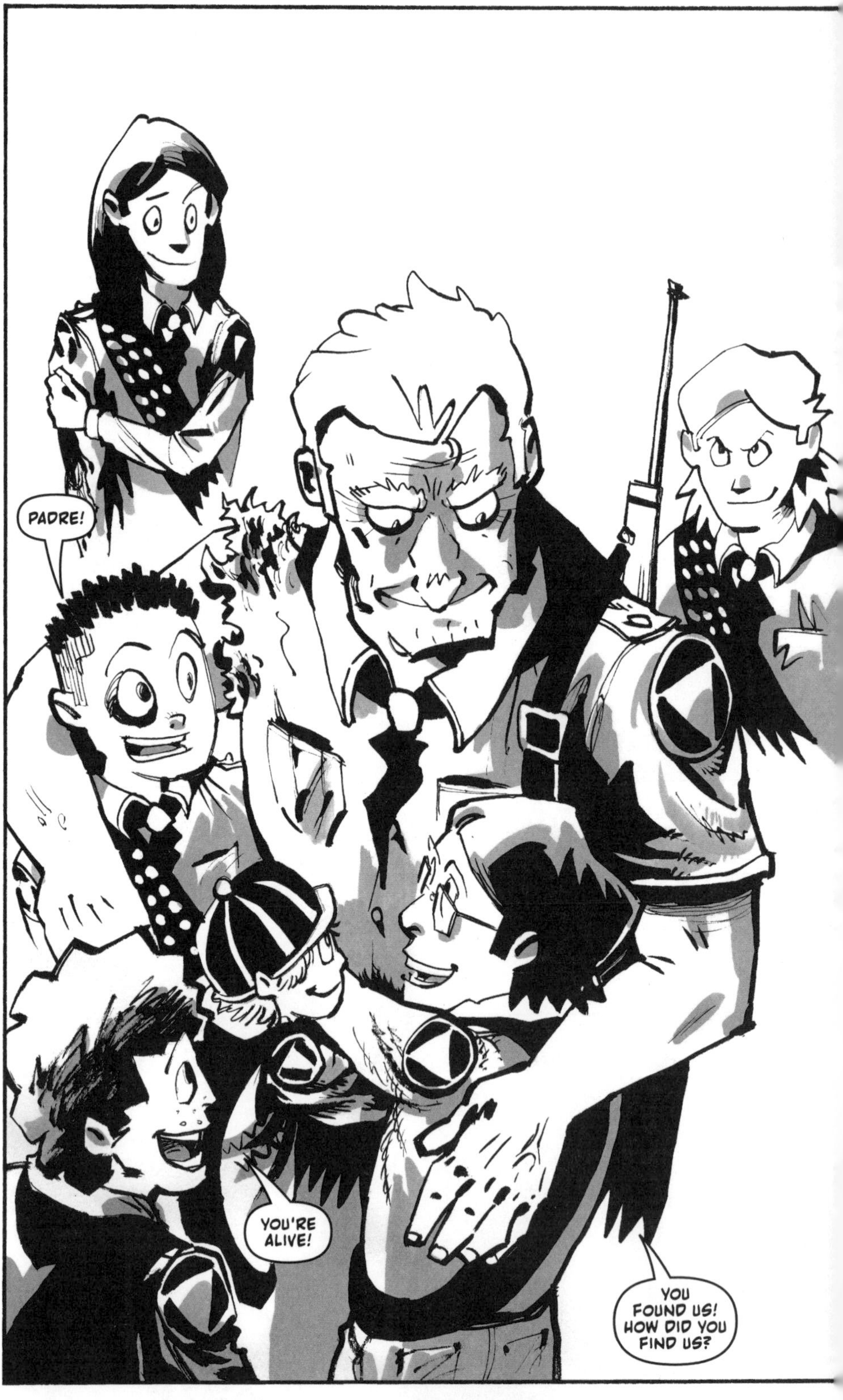
PADRE!
YOU'RE ALIVE!
YOU FOUND US! HOW DID YOU FIND US?

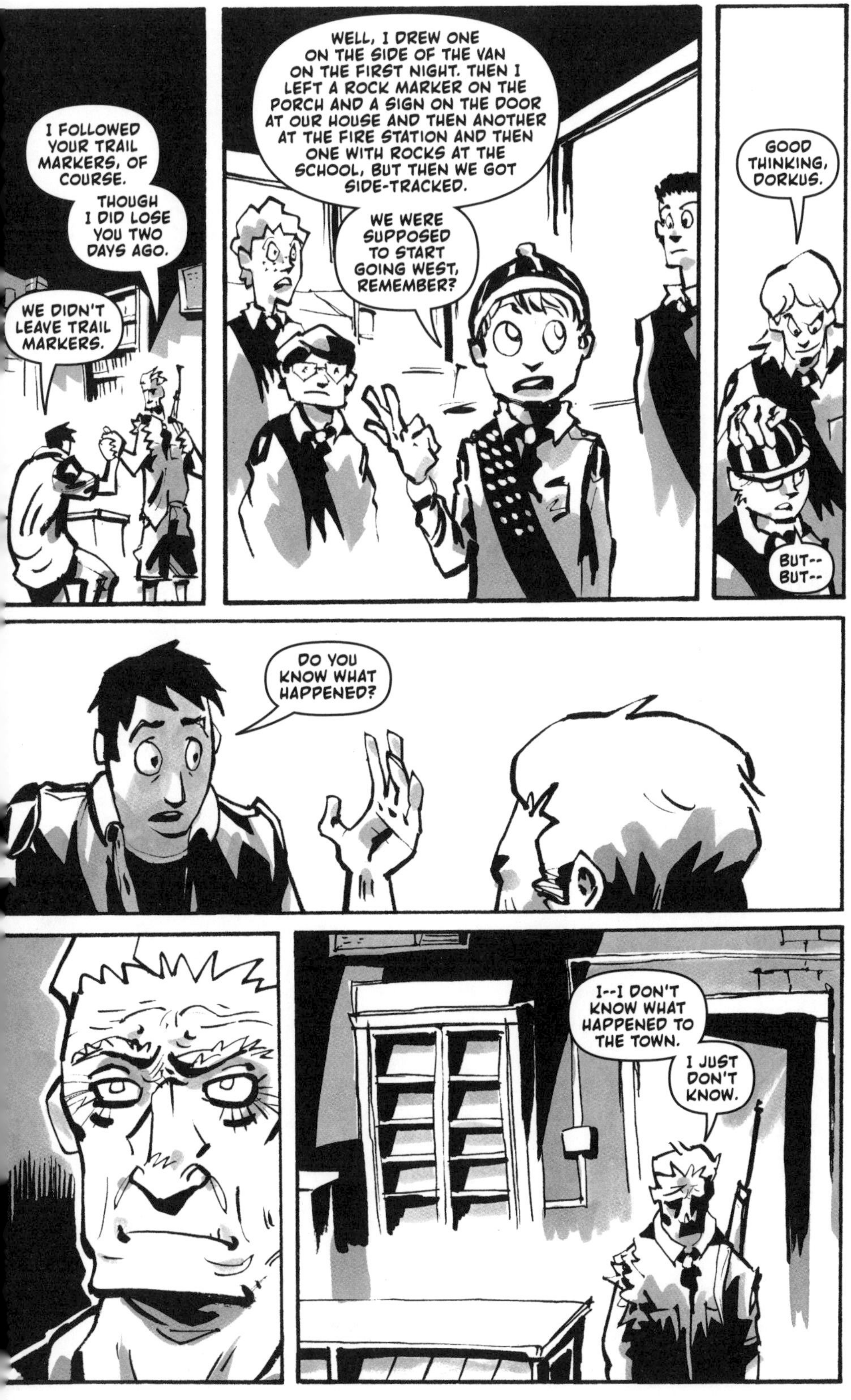
I FOLLOWED YOUR TRAIL MARKERS, OF COURSE.
THOUGH I DID LOSE YOU TWO DAYS AGO.
WE DIDN'T LEAVE TRAIL MARKERS.
WELL, I DREW ONE ON THE SIDE OF THE VAN ON THE FIRST NIGHT. THEN I LEFT A ROCK MARKER ON THE PORCH AND A SIGN ON THE DOOR AT OUR HOUSE AND THEN ANOTHER AT THE FIRE STATION AND THEN ONE WITH ROCKS AT THE SCHOOL, BUT THEN WE GOT SIDE-TRACKED.
WE WERE SUPPOSED TO START GOING WEST, REMEMBER?
GOOD THINKING, DORKUS.
BUT-- BUT--
DO YOU KNOW WHAT HAPPENED?
I--I DON'T KNOW WHAT HAPPENED TO THE TOWN.
I JUST DON'T KNOW.

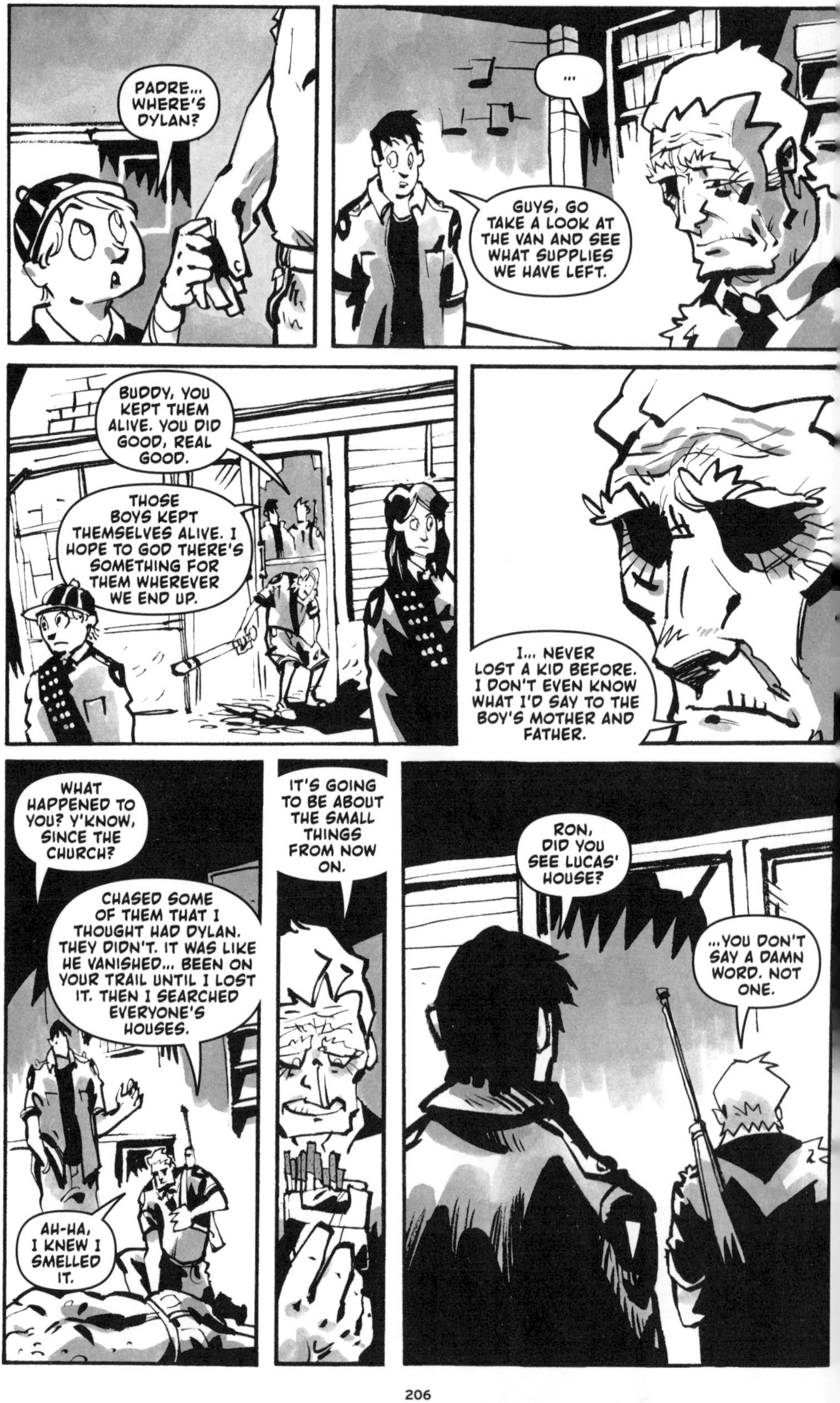
PADRE... WHERE'S DYLAN?
...
GUYS, GO TAKE A LOOK AT THE VAN AND SEE WHAT SUPPLIES WE HAVE LEFT.
BUDDY, YOU KEPT THEM ALIVE. YOU DID GOOD, REAL GOOD.
THOSE BOYS KEPT THEMSELVES ALIVE. I HOPE TO GOD THERE'S SOMETHING FOR THEM WHEREVER WE END UP.
I... NEVER LOST A KID BEFORE. I DON'T EVEN KNOW WHAT I'D SAY TO THE BOY'S MOTHER AND FATHER.
WHAT HAPPENED TO YOU? Y'KNOW, SINCE THE CHURCH?
CHASED SOME OF THEM THAT I THOUGHT HAD DYLAN. THEY DIDN'T. IT WAS LIKE HE VANISHED... BEEN ON YOUR TRAIL UNTIL I LOST IT. THEN I SEARCHED EVERYONE'S HOUSES.
AH-HA, I KNEW I SMELLED IT.
IT'S GOING TO BE ABOUT THE SMALL THINGS FROM NOW ON.
RON, DID YOU SEE LUCAS' HOUSE?
...YOU DON'T SAY A DAMN WORD. NOT ONE.

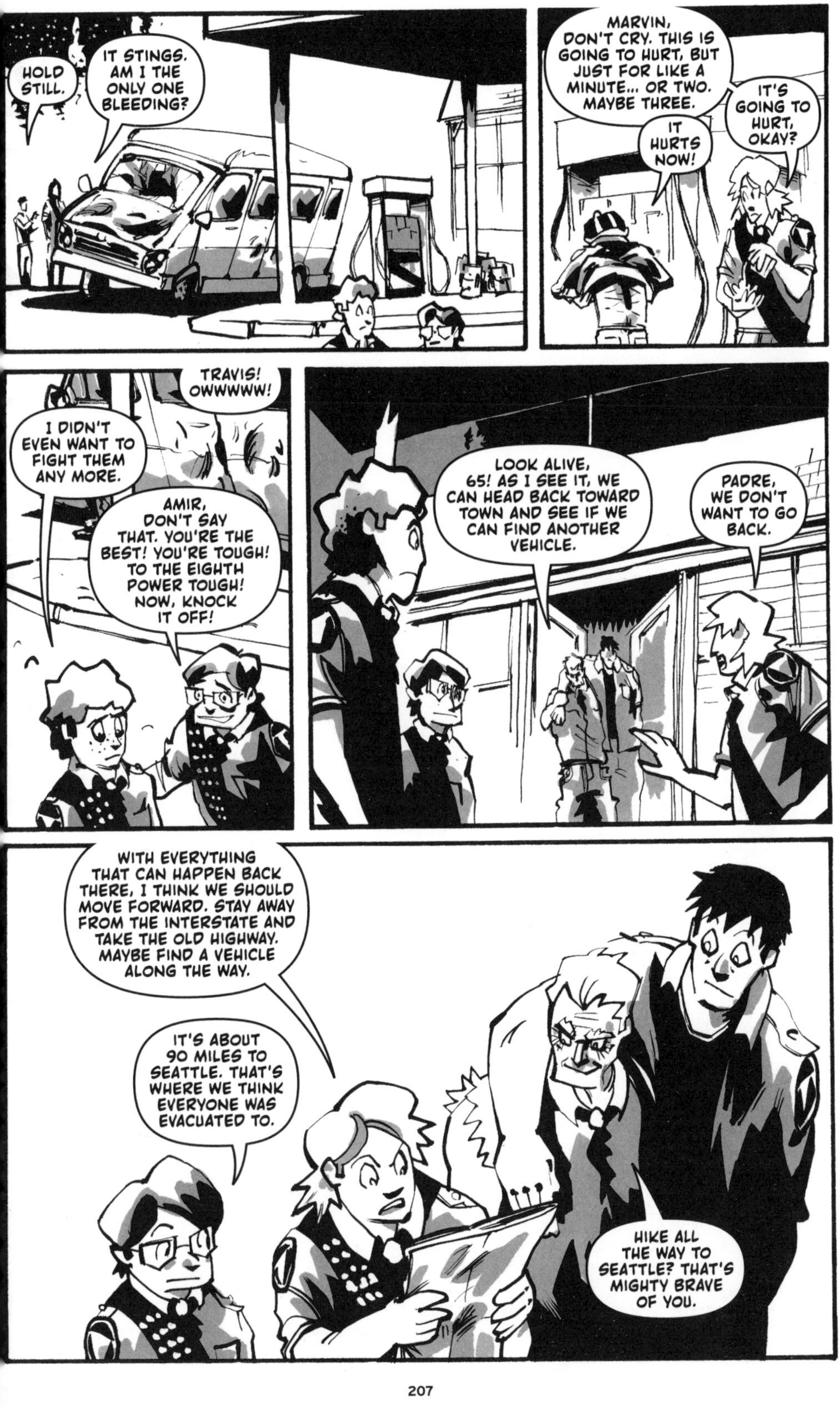
HOLD STILL.
IT STINGS. AM I THE ONLY ONE BLEEDING?
MARVIN, DON'T CRY. THIS IS GOING TO HURT, BUT JUST FOR LIKE A MINUTE... OR TWO. MAYBE THREE.
IT HURTS NOW!
IT'S GOING TO HURT, OKAY?
TRAVIS! OWWWWW!
I DIDN'T EVEN WANT TO FIGHT THEM ANY MORE.
AMIR, DON'T SAY THAT. YOU'RE THE BEST! YOU'RE TOUGH! TO THE EIGHTH POWER TOUGH! NOW, KNOCK IT OFF!
LOOK ALIVE, 65! AS I SEE IT, WE CAN HEAD BACK TOWARD TOWN AND SEE IF WE CAN FIND ANOTHER VEHICLE.
PADRE, WE DON'T WANT TO GO BACK.
WITH EVERYTHING THAT CAN HAPPEN BACK THERE, I THINK WE SHOULD MOVE FORWARD. STAY AWAY FROM THE INTERSTATE AND TAKE THE OLD HIGHWAY. MAYBE FIND A VEHICLE ALONG THE WAY.
IT'S ABOUT 90 MILES TO SEATTLE. THAT'S WHERE WE THINK EVERYONE WAS EVACUATED TO.
HIKE ALL THE WAY TO SEATTLE? THAT'S MIGHTY BRAVE OF YOU.

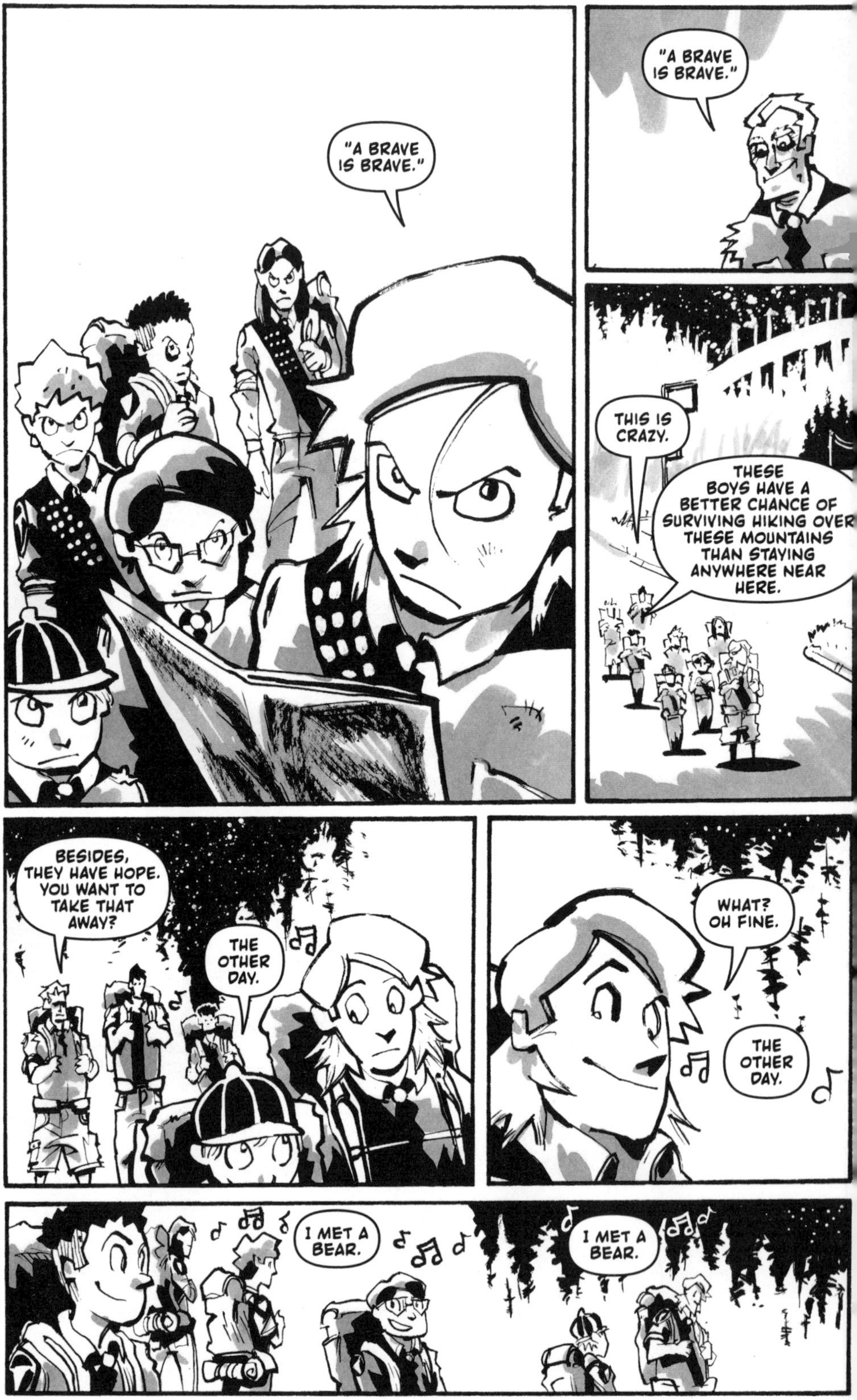
"A BRAVE IS BRAVE."
"A BRAVE IS BRAVE."
THIS IS CRAZY.
THESE BOYS HAVE A BETTER CHANCE OF SURVIVING HIKING OVER THESE MOUNTAINS THAN STAYING ANYWHERE NEAR HERE.
BESIDES, THEY HAVE HOPE. YOU WANT TO TAKE THAT AWAY?
THE OTHER DAY.
WHAT? OH FINE.
THE OTHER DAY.
I MET A BEAR.
I MET A BEAR.

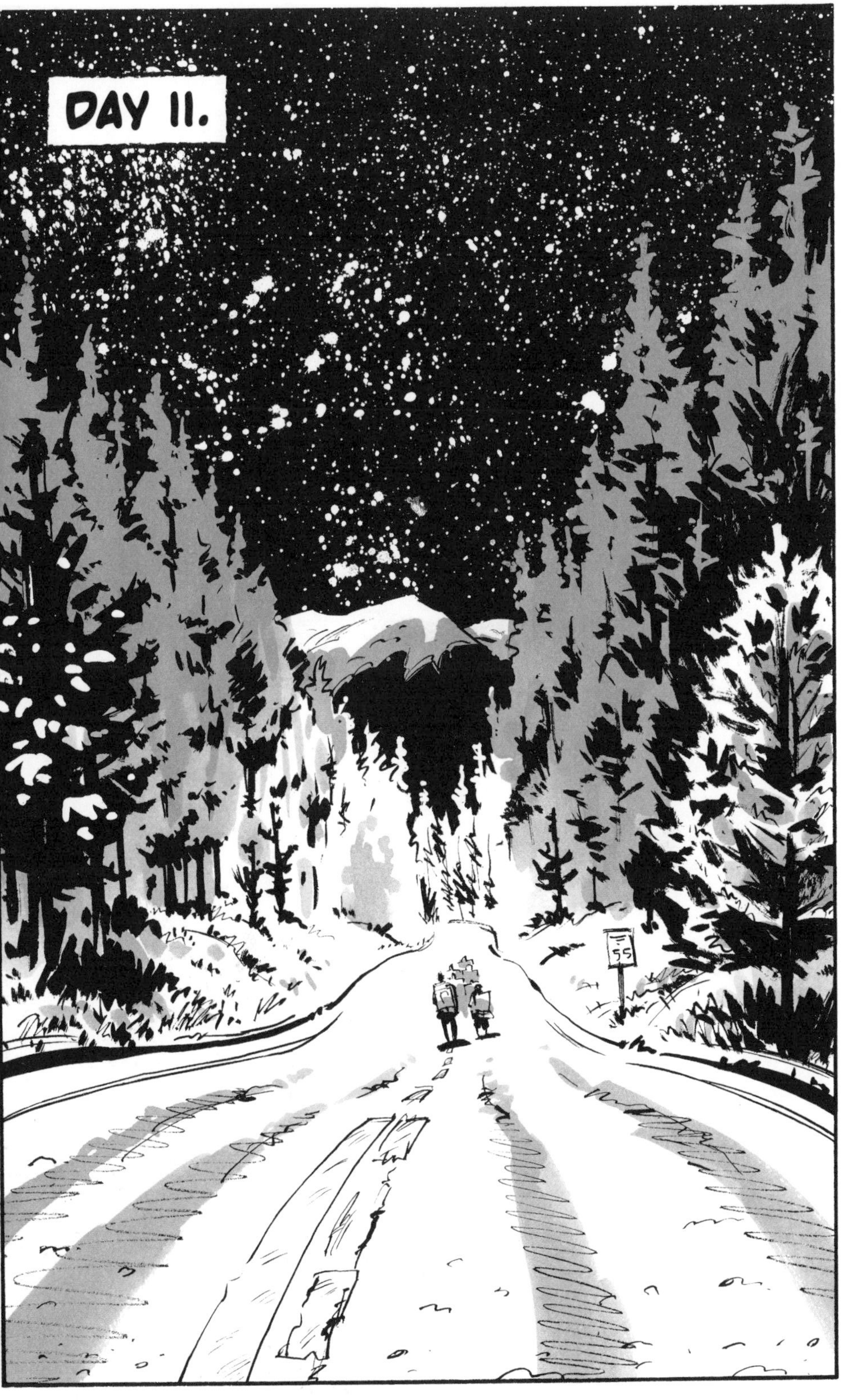
DAY 11.
55

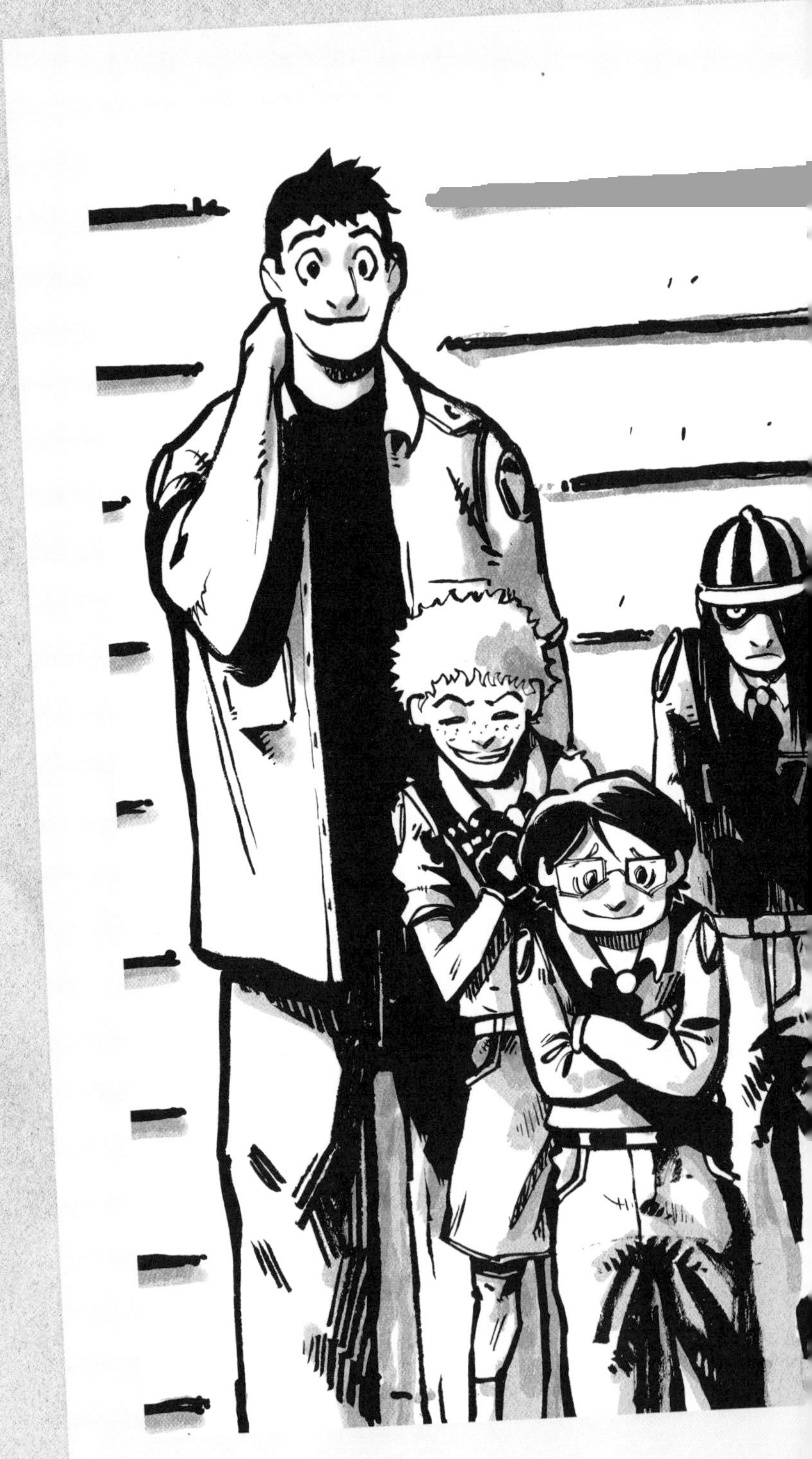

THE

JUNIOR

WILL

BRAVES
RETURN...

ZACH LEHNER graduated from the Savannah College of Art and Design in 2008 with a B.A. in Sequential Art and again with a Masters in 2010. This is his first graphic novel.

He lives in northern Chicago, where he reads a lot of books. You can see more of his work at *zlehner.com* and on Twitter *@zlehner*.

Zach would like to thank his family for their patience and support. Thanks also to Patty Reese, who always said this would happen, and asked to be mentioned when it did.

—

GREGORY K. SMITH grew up in a culturall diverse household. He was smitten with book at an early age when his Assistant Librarian mother brought him to work during summer breaks. Later, his father got him into Boy Scouts, where he achieved Eagle Scout Rank.

Greg gives thanks to his family and friends, without them, this would never have been achieved. Greg also wants to thank his Mom for letting him live in her basement while making comic books as well as his very

MICHAEL TANNER was born in Great Falls, Montana—a thriving metropolis that is actually smaller than the neighborhood of Los Angeles that he currently resides in. He has a B.A. in Theater and Television Production from the Evergreen State College, which is also where he met Greg Smith.

Michael developed a love for comics at a very early age and credits the medium with expanding his vocabulary and imagination. His first published comic work was in the Oni Press anthology *Jam! Tales from the World of Roller Derby*. He feels incredibly lucky to have been given the opportunity to work in a field that he loves.

He would like to dedicate this book to his parents, who have always encouraged his endeavors, no matter how strange.

Follow Mike (and his LA Derby Dolls roller derby Enforcer alter ego) *@mikeisernie*, and check out his reviews of Los Angeles' best, worst, and weirdest diners at *dinerwood.blogspot.com*.

—

nderstanding wife for living with him in his om's basement while making comic books.

ollow Greg on Twitter *@ThatAmazingTwit* or n Tumblr at *thatamazingtwit.tumblr.com*.

—

FOLLOW BOTH MIKE & GREG ON TWITTER @2AMAZINGWRITERS

MORE BOOKS FROM ONI PRESS

SCOTT PILGRIM, VOL. 1:
PRECIOUS LITTLE LIFE
By Bryan Lee O'Malley
192 pages, Hardcover, Color
ISBN: 978-1-62010-000-4

METEOR MEN
By Jeff Parker and Sandy Jarrell
136 pages, Softcover, Color
ISBN: 978-1-62010-151-3

COSTUME QUEST: INVASION
OF THE CANDY SNATCHERS
By Zac Gorman
56 pages, Hardcover, Color
ISBN: 978-1-62010-190-2

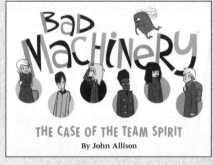

BAD MACHINERY, VOL. 1: THE CASE
OF THE TEAM SPIRIT
By John Allison
136 pages, Softcover, Color
ISBN: 978-1-62010-084-4

BLACK METAL: OMNIBVS
By Rick Spears and Chuck BB
472 pages, Softcover, B&W
ISBN: 978-1-62010-143-8

ORPHAN BLADE
By M. Nicholas Almand
and Jake Myler
192 pages, Softcover, Color
ISBN 978-1-62010-120-9

www.onipress.com

For more information on these and other fine Oni Press comic books and graphic novels visit www.onipress.com.
To find a comic specialty store in your area visit www.comicshops.us.